His Niece

His Niece

"Love always, your tío Richie"

and the silence that followed

Rosie Juarez

Dedication

Disclaimer
The views expressed in this book are those of the author and are intended for educational, inspirational, and ministry purposes. This book is not intended to replace professional legal, medical, psychiatric, financial, or counseling advice.

Publisher: Redeemed Ink Press, El Paso, Tx
Redeemed Ink Press
Ink that tells stories of restoration
Sent to Save. Written in Mercy, Released in Love.
(John 3:17 – John 8:11 – Luke 7:47)
First Edition

Paperback ISBN: 979-8-9953408-1-2

Cover design by: Lucid Dreams Book Designs

Printed in the United States of America

Scripture quotations, if included, are from the Holy Bible Translation noted.

For information, permissions, or special orders, contact:
RedeemedInkPress@outlook.com

Contents

Dedication

His Niece

Dedication

To God,
who never stopped calling me daughter
even when I stopped recognizing myself.
> To my children— this is the proof that love can outlive pain.
>> To Jimmy, my son—my mirror, my heartbreak, my hope.
>> To Marie and Robert, who watched more than they should
>> have and still grew into light.
>> To Izzie Marty and Milo, who gave me a reason to stay.

To the ones who broke me,
thank you for showing me what I would never accept again.
And to the ones who helped rebuild me especially
Eddie—thank you for loving me gently, in all the places when the world
was rough.

And to every woman who has ever whispered,
I can't do this anymore—
this is proof that you can.

To the men in prison who looked me in the eyes and told me,
"You need to write this."
You may not realize it, but you gave me permission to believe that my
pain could become purpose. Thank you for reminding me that even in a
place built for punishment, people can still plant seeds of purpose.

These are only a few out of so many Jeremy Sherrin and his lovely wife,
Alex Hinojos, Homer Urias, Alex Garza, James Snowden, Randy Hunter,
Jeremy Hunter, Brandon Medford, Alan Garcia, Ricardo Mendez, David
Bartley, Joseph Harris, Jake Newton and so many more.

"Let the redeemed tell their story."
—Psalm 107:2 NIV

Acknowledgements

Acknowledgements

This book would not exist without the kindness and support of people who believed in this story.

I am deeply grateful to my dear friends Kyia Whiteman and Cece B. who generously helped edit this manuscript. Your careful reading, honest feedback, and encouragement helped bring clarity and strength to these pages.

I would also like to give special thanks to the designer Cece B. who created the cover of this book and would not allow me to pay her. Your generosity, talent, and belief in this project means more to me than words can express.

To everyone who supported me along this journey, thank you for helping this story find its voice.

Acknowledgements

Introduction

As you read this book, please understand that I do not speak or write on behalf of my family. This book is about me and my relationship with my Tío Richie. My experiences with him, and with other family members, are shared solely from my perspective.

In March of 1996, I asked my Tío Richie if he would be okay with me writing a book. On April 19, 1996, he responded, "It would be okay with me if you wrote a book, but it's real hard to get it published." This was after his apology. He understood what writing this book would entail and granted me permission to move forward. And here I am.

Writing this book was a hard thing. With the power and strength, I draw from God, I was able to complete it.

I am not a counselor, psychologist, therapist, or psychiatrist. I speak only from my lived experience. The sole purpose of this book is to inspire those who find themselves picking up the pieces of what was supposed to be their childhood—and its aftermath. The aftermath of anger, rage, resentment, promiscuity, low self-esteem, and shame, the impulsive risk-taking, the struggle to make sense of what is "normal" and what is not. This book is for those living through domestic and emotional abuse.

I believe true healing, love, and forgiveness can come from only one source: God. Anything less is a cheap imitation.

I hope you enjoy the read. As I learned in recovery rooms, "Take what you need and leave the rest." May these pages light a path toward your own transformation.

November 1989

I came home late one night in November of 1989; my body tired from a long shift at the grocery store where I worked as a cashier. I had just picked up my eight-month-old son from the babysitter's house. He slept against me as I walked into the living room, his small weight familiar and grounding.

My father stood in front of the television, absorbed in the late-night news. I stopped beside him, still holding my son, watching the screen, trying to understand what had captured his attention so completely.

Introduction

Guards were escorting a man out of a building and into a van. His ankles and wrists were shackled. Cameras flashed as he turned toward the reporters and spoke.

"Big deal. Death always went with the territory. See you in Disneyland."

In Spanish, my father said, "Que pinche augite."

I laid my son down and stood there, stunned. Four years, I thought. Four years to convict him. Four years to sentence him. In those same four years, my own life had unfolded in ways I could never have imagined. In 1985, I had been a girl living in Los Angeles. Now I was in El Paso, eighteen years old, a mother to an eight-month-old baby. And the man I had grown up with had just been sentenced to death.

I couldn't stop thinking about what he had said—see you in Disneyland. The words echoed strangely in my mind. Why Disneyland? What did that mean to him?

Then the memory came.

My earliest memory of him was at Disneyland.

I had gone with my grandparents, my brother, and my Tío Richie. A parade wound its way down the street, Disney characters waving as they passed. I was too small to see past the adults gathered around me. I clutched my Tío's hand and tugged at it, trying to rise above the crowd. He lifted me and settled me onto his shoulders, his hands steady on my legs. My small arms wrapped around his neck and chin. My face rested against the soft waves of his hair. I could feel the fine peach fuzz on his skin. I could see the parade now. I could smell the Flex shampoo and conditioner in his hair. My grandfather stood nearby, holding my brother in his arms.

It is strange the things the body remembers.

See you in Disneyland.

The memories I carry of this man are tender—and they are terrible. The man the world would come to know as the Night Stalker was the man I knew as my Tío Richie. The world knows one version of him. I carry another.

These are memories no one has ever heard.

Until now.

Chapter 1

For you created my inmost being you knit me together in my mother's womb. I praise you because I am fearfully and wonderfully made; your works are wonderful; I know that full well. My frame was not hidden from you when I was made in the secret place, when I was woven together in the depths of the earth. Your eyes saw my unformed body; all the days ordained for me were written in your book before one of them came to be.
Psalms 139:13-16 NIV

In 1969, Julian—my father—went to a house party with friends. Like most parties, there was music, beautiful girls, and dancing. My father was young then, charismatic, good-looking, the kind of man who made people feel chosen. That night, he focused his attention on a beautiful girl, easing into conversation, making her laugh, drawing her closer with his warmth. Soon enough, he asked her to dance.

Music and dancing were second nature to him. They were how he moved through the world.

What he didn't know—what no one warned him about—was that she had a boyfriend watching from a distance, cataloging every smile, every step.

Later that night, my father stepped onto the porch to talk with a friend. He didn't hear the boyfriend follow him. He didn't have time to prepare. The attack came suddenly—metal piercing flesh, pain erupting before understanding. My father raised his right arm instinctively, trying to shield himself. "Es cuando me chingo el varso." He fought back, but the blade kept coming—his stomach, his arm. Then the boyfriend ran.

What stays with me is not just the violence, but how ordinary the night had been before it turned. How easily joy became blood.

A friend rushed him to Thomason County Hospital. Surgery followed. Weeks passed in recovery. My father carries the scars still, though he rarely speaks of them. Shame lives where memory should be. Yet that night altered everything. Without it, he never would have walked into the school nurse's office weeks later. Without it, I would not exist.

That's where he first saw my mother.

He wore an arm brace then, rubber bands stretching and snapping as he tried to regain strength in his hand. He was in the tenth grade at

Jefferson High School. My mother, a grade ahead, worked as an assistant in the nurse's office during one class period. One afternoon, he walked in and saw her a five-foot three, green-eyed, brunette, pale Spaniard skinned - Maria Isabel Rodriguez.

The nurse asked my mother to help him, and soon my father found reasons to return during that class period. At the time, my mother had a boyfriend, Luis. He would beat her. Even now, I struggle with how casually that fact lived alongside everything else—as if violence had already been normalized before it ever reached me.

The attraction between my parents was immediate and undeniable.

When Luis found out they were talking, he threatened my father. Unbeknownst to my grandfather, my father took his gun—loaded—and brought it to school. He confronted Luis in the parking lot, aimed the gun at the ground beside him, and fired. The sound must have echoed across the asphalt, across everything they thought they were. My father told him he would not be threatened, would not be scared away, and would talk to whomever he pleased.

Then he walked to his next class.

As an adult, I see this moment differently than I once did. I don't romanticize it. I recognize it as a boy already shaped by violence, responding in the only language he had learned—a language of escalation, of survival, of proving power before power was taken from him again.

Luis reported him to the principal. My father was pulled from class and asked if he had a gun. He denied it—deny, deny, deny.

It didn't matter.

His school days ended there. He was expelled.

By the end of 1970, somewhere between November 23 and December 8, my mother became pregnant with me in the back seat of a car. During that time, rumors followed her—men bringing beer, sneaking it through her window. When my father learned she was pregnant, he assumed the child wasn't his. Distance came easily then.

When I was born, my mother gave me her maiden name—Rosalinda Rodriguez. She chose it without knowing whether my father would claim me. He stayed away until I was six months old. Then, quietly, they found their way back to each other.

Looking back, I understand how fragile that reunion was. Two people bonded not by stability, but by momentum.

By 1971, my parents were living with my grandparents, saving for a place of their own. Their stay stretched longer when my father was arrested again. Time moved strangely then—measured not in months, but in interruptions. By 1972, this rhythm of disruption had already become familiar.

While my father served jail time, my mother gave him an ultimatum: marry me, or I move on. He agreed. She arranged everything herself—the judge, the rings, the courthouse. Officers escorted my father from custody. Vows were exchanged. Rings placed. A kiss shared. My mother went home alone. My father returned to his cell.

June 8, 1972.

Fifty years later, my father and I stood in the El Paso County office asking for a copy of that marriage license. We learned it had never been filed. Somehow, even their marriage existed in a liminal space—real, but undocumented.

By then, I understood something I couldn't as a child: our beginnings were shaped by instability long before I had language for it.

<u>Thoughts</u>

Many times, we question God. We ask Him *why.*

Why did this happen to me? Why did You allow it? Why didn't You stop it?

When my father told me this story, I found myself tracing the invisible thread of everything that came after his stabbing—the rubber bands on his arm brace, the reason he walked into the nurse's office, the moment he met my mother. It was like looking back at a row of falling dominoes and realizing one small moment had set an entire life into motion.

Sometimes we don't understand what is happening while we're still inside it. We can't see the outcome or the ending. We can't see what God might be building from the rubble. We only feel the pain, the confusion, the unfairness of it all. But God sees the future from the beginning. He sees the whole story when we can only see the page we're bleeding on.

When my father finished telling me, I looked at him and said, without thinking, "I'm so glad you were stabbed."

He stared at me like I had lost my mind. Offended, almost shocked, he asked, "Why would you say that?"

And I told him the truth.

Chapter 1

"If that hadn't happened, you wouldn't have gone to the nurse's office. If you hadn't gone to the nurse's office, you wouldn't have met my mom. And if you hadn't met my mom… I wouldn't be here. I wouldn't be sitting with you right now, talking to you."

Then I added, half joking but fully serious, "And I'm the best thing that ever happened to you."

He smiled, the kind of smile that carried both pride and tenderness, and he said, "You're so right."

Of course, life didn't become easy after that. God never promised an easy road. I still faced hard things. I still walked through valleys I wouldn't have chosen. I made mistakes. I made bad decisions. I took questionable routes, and sometimes I learned lessons the hard way.

But even then, I was never abandoned.

God was with me every step of the way—quietly steady, patiently present. He gave me tenacity when I wanted to give up. He gave me resilience when I thought I had nothing left. And even when I stumbled, even when I didn't know how to pray, even when I doubted Him, my life was still being held.

Because my life is no accident.

I was meant to be here.

And long before I ever took my first breath—before my mother knew my name, before my father knew his path, before the pain and the chaos and the turning points—God knew me.

Chapter 2

A friend always loves,
and a brother is born to share trouble.
Proverbs 17:17 GW

There are some people who believe that if you change your surroundings, you can change your life. My grandfather believed that.

My father had a drug problem—one that tangled itself around him like a chain, pulling him into trouble with the law and deeper into the shadows of himself. My grandfather thought the answer was simple: a different environment. A fresh start. A new city where temptation wouldn't know his name.

But life has taught me something harsh and unmovable.

No one can outrun themselves.

You can cross city lines, state borders, and desert highways. You can pack your belongings into boxes, close the door behind you, and swear you'll never return. But as long as you take yourself with you—your wounds, your addictions, your hungers, your secrets—you will find the same problems waiting on the other side.

Especially when you aren't ready to change.

That was the truth my family lived inside of.

And in 1972, my parents stepped onto a path that would shape the rest of my life.

That year, they packed up what little they owned and moved to Los Angeles.

I was still so small then, too young to understand that adults don't always move because they want to—sometimes they move because they are running. Sometimes they move because they believe distance can heal what time hasn't. Sometimes they move because staying feels like dying.

My mother's parents welcomed us into their home in the City of Commerce, in East Los Angeles. But my father insisted it would only be temporary. Just long enough to get on our feet. Just long enough to build something stable.

So for a brief moment, we were together under one roof—my parents, my grandparents, my aunts and uncle, and me—living inside a house filled with voices and cigarette smoke and the kind of tension that hums beneath the surface, even when nobody is speaking.

Chapter 2

It didn't take long for my father to notice what was happening to my mother.

She began drinking more and more with each passing day, as if the bottle was calling her name louder every night.

My maternal grandparents were alcoholics. My aunts and uncle drank too. And when they drank, the atmosphere shifted. It was like the air thickened. Laughter could turn into shouting. A harmless comment could become a fight. There was always a spark waiting for something to catch fire.

That house didn't feel like safety. It felt like something unstable— like a floor that could collapse at any moment.

And then my father discovered something that changed the way he saw my mother's family forever.

He learned that when my mother's sisters were growing up, my grandfather Jose would get his two older daughters drunk so he could sexually abuse them.

That kind of truth doesn't arrive gently. It crashes into a family like a storm, leaving destruction behind even if nobody speaks about it out loud.

My mother had not grown up with her parents. She had been left in El Paso as an infant with her grandparents, Libertad and Inez, and a cousin. This was her first time living with her parents since she was a baby. She was twenty years old—an adult, yes, but still young enough to be vulnerable. Still young enough to be pulled into old darkness.

My mother hadn't endured what her older sisters had endured. But my father feared that she might eventually become one of my grandfather's victims.

Even now, it chills me to write those words. To say them plainly. To place them on the page.

After three months, my father decided we had to leave.

We moved out and found a tiny place off Pico Boulevard, on the west side of Los Angeles.

It wasn't much. But it was ours. A small apartment where the walls held our voices and our footsteps, where the air felt less crowded, where the danger didn't sit at the dinner table with us.

But peace has never been something my family held for long.

My father later told me about one night in that apartment. He and my mother were in bed asleep when they woke up and saw me standing there with rolling paper in my hands, trying to roll a marijuana cigarette like I knew exactly what I was doing.

He called out in Spanish, startled.

"Rosa, ¿qué estás haciendo?"

And I answered with the innocence only a child can carry.

"Nada, Daddy."

Even now, I can almost see it—the small version of myself, tiny hands holding paper, mimicking what she had already seen too many times. A child who had absorbed the world around her like a sponge, learning adult habits before she even understood what they meant.

Not long after that, we moved again.

This time, to Compton—near 71st Street and Florence Avenue.

The streets there had a different energy. Even as a child, I could feel it. The air carried something heavier. Sirens were common. Nights felt sharper. People watched each other differently, as if trust was a luxury nobody could afford.

In the summer of 1973, my Tío Richie came to visit.

I remember him like a bright flash in my childhood—funny, youthful, full of swagger. He was fascinated by the women at the beach, amazed by them, like he'd never seen beauty so bold. My father laughed and handed him binoculars so he could look closer.

Years later, when I told my father I remembered that moment, he stared at me like I'd spoken a miracle.

"You were only two," he said.

But it's funny what a child remembers.

Sometimes you don't remember because you understand. You remember because your spirit does. Because something inside you is paying attention even when you don't have the language for it.

My Tío Richie would sit outside on the steps and smoke a joint. And I would follow him everywhere like a shadow, tagging along like an annoying little sister.

Later, in one of his letters, he mentioned that memory. He wrote it like he thought he was the only one who remembered.

But I remembered.

Not long after that summer, my brother was born.

November 1973.

He weighed five pounds. So tiny my mother would say he could fit in a shoebox.

I remember looking at him and feeling something, I didn't know how to name. A strange mix of wonder and protectiveness. Like the universe had placed something fragile in our home and asked me to guard it.

But when he came home, my parents were still struggling financially. We didn't have much.

So his bassinet was a rectangular laundry basket.

That image stays with me. A baby in a laundry basket. A tiny life already surrounded by survival.

A year later, in the summer of 1974, my grandparents came from El Paso to visit us.

They brought toys.

I still remember my excitement—how my heart lifted when I saw a tub of farm animals, Lincoln Logs, and little green soldiers. Those toys felt like treasure, like proof that someone out there remembered us.

They took my brother, who was still a baby—six or eight months old—and me to Disneyland.

Disneyland is supposed to be magic. And in some ways, it was. But even magic can't erase fear when fear is already planted inside you.

I rode the Snow White ride with my grandmother, and that witch stirring her potion terrified me. Her face appeared out of the darkness like a warning. The music felt eerie, the shadows too thick. I was just a little girl, but my body reacted like it knew evil when it saw it.

The teacups made me vomit.

To this day, I've never ridden them again. Some rides you don't need to repeat. Some memories don't need to be relived.

But the parade…

The parade was everything.

The music, the colors, the characters marching by like they belonged to a different world—one where nothing bad ever happened, one where families were whole and laughter was pure.

We stood in the crowd, packed shoulder to shoulder. I was too small to see past the adults. I remember feeling frustrated, tugging on my Tío Richie's hand, trying to pull myself closer to the magic.

And then he lifted me up and placed me on his shoulders.

He held my legs securely while my little hands wrapped around his neck and chin. My small arms wrapped around his neck and chin. My face rested against the soft waves of his hair. I could feel the fine peach fuzz on his skin. I could smell the Flex shampoo and conditioner in it.

That smell has never left me.

In that moment, I was high above the crowd, safe and weightless. I could finally see the parade.

I could finally see joy.

On our way home, we stood at a bus stop.

Nearby there was a comic bookstore. My Tío Richie saw it and asked my grandparents if he could buy a comic book. My grandfather reached into his wallet, pulled out money, and handed it to him.

I watched my uncle run across the street, a kid himself, excited and carefree.

When he came back, he was smiling wide, flipping through the pages as if he couldn't wait to get lost inside another world.

And for the next several days, he sat on the sofa reading that comic book again and again.

When my grandparents' visit ended, I stood outside while the adults stayed inside talking. I didn't want them to leave. I didn't want the house to go quiet again. I didn't want the comfort of visitors to disappear.

I felt sadness settle into me like something heavy.

My Tío Richie tried to comfort me.

"Don't worry, little girl," he said. "I'll be back soon."

It's strange what children remember.

Sometimes the words people say to you become a promise your heart holds onto for years.

While we lived on 71st Street, my father's heroin addiction deepened.

One day, my mother tried to wake him. He was slumped over on the edge of the bed, wearing a white shirt. His body looked wrong—too still, too heavy, like he had slipped away from the world without telling anyone.

My mother shook him, calling his name.

Nothing.

She began to cry hysterically. The kind of crying that comes from panic, from terror, from the sudden realization that you might be watching someone die.

When he wouldn't respond, she called an ambulance.

The paramedics arrived quickly. Their voices were firm, urgent. They put something in his mouth, trying to pry it open.

Then I was rushed into another room.

I didn't understand the details, but I understood the fear.

The air itself felt like it was trembling.

They took him to the hospital.

And life kept moving the way it always did in our home—like trauma was just another part of the routine.

My mother was friendly, always smiling at strangers. She never met a stranger. Across from us lived an older woman named Ella.

Ella had a piano.

My mother played, and Ella would sit nearby drinking a glass of Thunderbird, listening like my mother was performing in a grand hall instead of a small Compton living room.

I remember sitting on the floor beside the piano, pressing my cheek against its wooden side. The vibrations of the music hummed against my skin, soothing me.

That piano felt like warmth.

Like the closest thing we had to stability.

My mother's favorite pastime was drinking, smoking, and listening to music. We spent a lot of time at Ella's house, and I learned early that adults could smile while they were drowning.

My brother and I spent hours outside playing in the dirt with our toy cars, making tunnels and tracks. Sometimes my mother would wash the windows by spraying them down with water. She hated the cobwebs that gathered around the frames.

She didn't mind us getting dirty. It wasn't a big deal.

It was strange—she cared about cobwebs on windows, but not about the webs forming inside our family.

Walking to the liquor store at night with my mother was normal. It was expected. A routine.

One night, we left the liquor store and saw a man lying on the ground beside the building.

The police were there.

Yellow tape was stretched around the scene like a warning.

Someone had covered the man with a white blanket.

My mother told me he was fine.

"They're just covering him because he's cold," she said. "They're waiting for the doctor."

But I knew better.

Even as a child, I knew what death looked like.

I didn't tell her I knew. I wasn't sure if she believed her own lie or if she was trying to protect me—or maybe trying to protect herself.

I stayed quiet because I didn't want to see her cry.

Soon after, we moved again—from 71st Street to another place on 82nd Street.

A new address. A new attempt at a fresh start.

But my father's addiction followed us like a shadow. And my mother's drinking came with us too.

The scenery changed, but the story didn't.

Because no one can outrun themselves.

Not without surrender.

Not without truth.

Not without change.

Through all of it, one thing remained constant: my brother.

My feelings for him are immeasurable.

We teased each other mercilessly, the way siblings do. We were experts at provoking one another, skilled in the art of getting under each other's skin.

But we were also fiercely loyal.

I could tease him, but nobody else could.

We protected each other in ways children shouldn't have to learn. We learned how to console one another without words, because we didn't always have the safety to speak out loud.

Sometimes a look was enough.

Sometimes silence was the only language we had.

That bond still exists today—unspoken, but unbreakable.

So many things happened to me as a child. Things that shaped me, scarred me, and forced me to grow up too soon.

And my brother… my little brother… he endured his own pain.

He carried his own wounds.

Chapter 2

Yet somehow, that small boy grew into a man who beat cancer despite being abandoned, shamed, neglected, and subjected to physical, verbal, and emotional abuse.

And as hard as our childhood was, I know this:

I don't think I would have survived without him.

Not really.

Because when the world around us was unstable, when the adults in our lives failed us, when danger lived too close and love felt conditional…

my brother was there.

A small heartbeat beside mine.

A witness.

A companion.

A piece of my childhood that wasn't stolen.

And in a life filled with brokenness, he was one of the few things that felt real.

Thoughts

As a child, I didn't understand what I was seeing.

I didn't have words like *addiction*, *abuse*, *predator*, or *trauma*. I only knew feelings—fear in the pit of my stomach, confusion that sat heavy in my chest, and the quiet instinct that something wasn't right, even when adults smiled and told me it was.

I grew up believing chaos was normal.

Moving from place to place felt like breathing. Sirens became background noise. Drinking was just something adults did. And my father's addiction wasn't a shocking tragedy—it was simply part of the landscape of my childhood, as common as cracked sidewalks and dirty windows.

But as I got older, I realized we weren't just moving to survive financially.

We were moving because our lives were unstable.

We were moving because my parents carried storms inside them, and those storms spilled into every room we lived in. It didn't matter if the address changed. The pain always followed. Addiction doesn't care about new beginnings. Trauma doesn't pack itself away neatly in a suitcase.

It rides with you.

And the truth is, so much of what I remember isn't the big moments—it's the small ones. The ones that felt ordinary at the time.

The smell of shampoo in my uncle's hair at Disneyland.

The vibration of piano music against my cheek.

The sight of a white blanket covering a body outside the liquor store.

The sound of my mother's crying when my father wouldn't wake up.

Those memories are like photographs burned into my mind, proof that even as a little girl, I was absorbing more than anyone realized.

As an adult, I now understand what my mother didn't have the strength to admit and what my father didn't know how to fix.

Some families don't raise children.

They raise survivors.

And my brother and I survived in the only way we could—together.

We didn't always have protection. We didn't always have stability. We didn't always have truth spoken out loud. But we had each other. And in a childhood full of danger and disappointment, that bond became our shelter.

It became our lifeline.

People talk about resilience like it's something beautiful.

But resilience is often born from suffering. It is built in homes where children learn too early how to read faces, how to predict moods, how to stay quiet, how to disappear, how to endure.

My brother and I learned those lessons young.

And somehow, despite everything, he grew up to fight cancer and win. Watching him battle for his life made me realize something I had always known but never dared to say:

That boy was never weak.

He was forged.

So was I.

Even now, when I think back on those years, I don't remember a perfect childhood. I remember a childhood filled with broken people trying to survive their own brokenness.

But I also remember the moments when love still managed to exist—small and imperfect, but real.

I remember my brother's tiny body in a laundry basket.

I remember my uncle lifting me onto his shoulders so I could see the parade.

Chapter 2

I remember music in a neighbor's living room, as if God Himself had pressed a small comfort into the middle of our chaos.

And I realize now what I couldn't understand then:

Even when the world around me was unsafe…

God was still there.

He was watching.

He was keeping record.

And He was quietly planting in me the strength to one day tell the truth.

Chapter 3
Treat this Crisis as Practice for the
THE NEXT CRISIS.
— John Parenti

My father was the oldest of five children, and my Tío Richie was the youngest. Because of that, Richie floated in and out of our home for most of my childhood like a storm cloud that never quite drifted away. He didn't just visit—he *arrived*, carrying his moods, his noise, and the unspoken tension that followed him like a shadow.

My father says,

"You three—my kids—grew up with Richie."

And he's right.

Richie wasn't just an uncle. He was a constant presence, a reminder that not everyone fit neatly into the roles families assign. Other relatives in El Paso would kick him out when he tried to live with them. He could be too loud, too defiant, too unpredictable. And Richie and my grandfather? They were like water and oil—forced to share space, but never able to blend.

Even as a child, I sensed Tío Richie wasn't simply "bad" the way the adults implied. He was something else—something harder to name. Looking back, I think Richie was the first person I ever recognized as being trapped inside our family, caught in a web of expectations, discipline, religion, pride, and fear.

He wasn't just fighting my grandfather.

He was fighting the weight of who everyone insisted he was supposed to be.

In 1975, when I was four years old, my father took me with him to El Paso. His family was having a discussion about Richie.

I didn't understand the purpose of the trip, only that something felt wrong. The adults didn't speak the way they normally did. Their voices stayed low, secretive. Conversations stopped when I entered a room. The air felt heavy with cigarette smoke and tension, like the house itself was holding its breath.

I remember the scrape of a chair against the floor. The smell of coffee. My grandmother's rosary beads slipping through her fingers. And my father's hand on my shoulder—steady, protective—warning me without words to stay quiet.

That meeting wasn't about love.

It was about control.

Richie had become too much for my grandparents. My grandfather couldn't tame him. Richie talked back, and in that house, talking back wasn't just disrespect—it was rebellion.

My grandfather believed discipline meant obedience.

Richie believed survival meant resistance.

When my grandfather tried to physically discipline him, Richie fought back. He had taken karate classes to defend himself from bullies, and my grandfather never imagined he would become the one on the receiving end.

My dad said Richie would sometimes sleep outside at night just to avoid the fights inside the house.

That image still stays with me—a teenage boy choosing the darkness outside over the darkness inside.

The family tried to control Richie, but what they really feared was what Richie revealed about them.

As I write this now, I understand Richie more than I ever expected to. I understand what it feels like to live under constant pressure, always bracing for the next accusation.

What else did I do wrong?

What else will they decide makes me unworthy?

That was how I often felt around my grandmother. I can't even fully explain why. It wasn't always what she said—it was what I felt in her presence. Like love was conditional, and I didn't know the rules.

My father suggested Richie join the military. Richie was willing, maybe even hopeful. But my grandmother wouldn't allow it. She couldn't bear the thought of her youngest leaving.

Later, she regretted it.

Regret always arrives after the damage is done.

I remember that trip because it was my first time on a plane. I remember the hum of the engines, the strange weightlessness in my stomach, and my father's voice sounding calm even though I could feel the tension underneath him.

It was also the first time I met my half-brother, Tony.

Tony was born when my father was nineteen, to another woman. I didn't understand what a half-brother was. I only knew there was a boy connected to me, and that connection felt important—like finding a missing piece of a puzzle I didn't know existed.

So many people in our family recognize the photograph taken that day—Richie standing with his siblings in the backyard.

Tío Robert on the left. My dad with a beard his hands on my Tía Ruth's shoulders. Then Richie. Then my favorite, loving Tío Joseph.

My grandmother took that picture behind the house they grew up in at **321 Ledo Street**. That house no longer exists. Years later, flooding destroyed much of that area, washing away streets and foundations as if the earth itself was trying to erase the past.

But in my mind, that house still stands—small, crowded, full of separate rooms that held separate lives. A home where everyone loved each other, but no one really knew how to live together.

That day, Tío Robert lifted me up and called me his beautiful butterfly. I remember laughing as the world spun.

But my father snapped, **"¡Cuidado!"**

My uncle set me down immediately.

Even joy in our family came with a warning.

I remember the kitchen too. My grandmother poured me a glass of Coke and served me chicken egg noodle soup that my aunt's husband had made. To this day, I remember that soup—the smell, the warmth, the way it tasted like comfort. It felt like safety poured into a bowl.

Years later, I asked about it again and again, but no one remembered it. No one remembered eating it.

But I did.

I sat at the table with Tony. My cousin Gloria she was still a baby in a high chair. I remember the clink of spoons and the murmur of adult voices, the way sunlight filtered into that kitchen like it belonged there.

That house is tangled up in my dreams. When I think of 321 Ledo Street, I don't just think of walls and furniture. I think of secrets. I think of tension. I think of prayers whispered behind closed doors.

My mother later told me Tío Richie claimed he met the devil in that house, in his bedroom.

I was too young to understand what that meant, but the way she said it left a mark on me—as if Richie had seen something he couldn't unsee.

Chapter 3

Richie's bedroom was always dark. Not dim—dark, as if he wanted to shut the world out. He loved the band KISS. I remember staring at the album covers and thinking they looked like terrifying clowns.

I wasn't allowed to stay in his room long. He would shoo me out and close the door. But even then, I sensed something complicated in him— like he could be kind in private, but angry in public. Like he wanted love, but didn't trust it enough to reach for it.

He kept his albums stacked in a milk crate on his dresser, a record player beside them. He liked his music loud. He had drumsticks too, tapping them against furniture like the beat of a restless heart.

My grandmother hated that music. She didn't understand Richie's noise or his hunger for escape.

My grandmother believed in God.

Richie believed in leaving.

My grandmother spent her days reading her Bible and praying the rosary. My grandfather, when he wasn't home, was often in Ciudad Juárez at the bars, dressed in cowboy boots, a guayabera shirt, and a hat— carrying himself like he owned the world, even though he couldn't control his own house.

Religion in that home felt heavy. Not comforting. It was rules. Guilt. Endurance.

And Richie, I think, felt suffocated by it.

Before we left El Paso, my grandmother gave me a rag doll and my father's old Green Hornet lunchbox.

I held them against my chest like treasure, not realizing she wasn't just giving me toys—she was giving me a piece of my father's childhood, a piece of the family story.

And as we drove away from that house on Ledo Street, I carried it home without understanding what else I was carrying too.

A family pattern.

A silence passed down like inheritance.

Years later, I would realize my family wasn't good at family meetings. They could see there was a problem, but they didn't know how to solve it. They didn't know how to talk and listen without judgment. They loved Richie, but love in our family often came tangled with control.

Back then, mental health wasn't something people spoke about. Men weren't allowed to show weakness. They were taught not to cry, not to feel, not to break. So they stuffed everything down.

And when the pain became too heavy, it spilled out in anger, addiction, and destruction.

And now, looking back, I see something else.

I see how my body was trained long before my mind ever understood.

Silence meant safety.

Closed doors meant protection.

Darkness felt private, not dangerous.

Watching Tío Richie disappear behind his door taught me how to make myself smaller, quieter, less visible. By the time harm entered my life directly, my body already knew what to do.

Stay still.

Stay alert.

Don't make it worse.

That is why, when it happened, nothing in me screamed.

Nothing ran.

I did not yet have language for violation—only for survival.

My body recognized the familiar rules:

Don't draw attention.

Don't resist.

Don't tell.

The danger did not announce itself.

It arrived already inside the boundaries I had been taught to keep.

And so I stayed.

Because in that family, I learned early:

Sometimes you survive not by escaping—

but by disappearing.

Thoughts

There are things I understand now that I couldn't see then.

As a child, I believed the adults were in control—that meeting meant something was being fixed, that someone knew how to make things right.

But they didn't.

Chapter 3

They were building walls the only way they knew how—out of fear, pride, and survival. They called it discipline. They called it faith. They called it family. But beneath it all was silence.

Richie wasn't the problem.

He was the signal.

He was the one who refused to stay quiet inside a system that depended on it. And for that, he was labeled too much. But "too much" is often just truth no one wants to face.

What happened to him didn't end with him.

It echoed—

in the way love was given and withheld,

in the way fear moved without a name,

in the way silence became both protection and prison.

That house on Ledo Street may be gone, but what was built inside it remains. It shaped how we survived, how we stayed quiet, how we endured.

For a long time, I thought survival meant disappearing.

Now I understand—survival was never meant to be the final form.

The walls that protected me also confined me.

The silence that kept me safe also kept me unseen.

And healing—real healing—has required something my family did not know how to do:

To name what happened.

To feel what was buried.

To tell the truth, even when it breaks the shape of the story we were given.

I carry my family with me—every version of them.

The ones who loved imperfectly.

The ones who caused harm.

The ones who didn't know how to stop it.

And the ones, like Richie, who tried to fight their way out.

But I am not only what I inherited.

Some walls are built to keep people in.

Others are built to keep pain out.

I am learning the difference.

And, slowly—I am learning how to take them down.

Chapter 4

**Any fool can make a baby,
But only a real man can
Raise his children
— Boyz n the Hood**

1975

We moved into a small duplex tucked behind a house on 82nd Street, between South Central and Hooper Avenue. It sat hidden from the street, as if it had been placed there to disappear—out of sight, out of reach, out of the way. I didn't know it then, but that little duplex would become one of my first classrooms. Not the kind with crayons and storybooks, but the kind that teaches a child what fear feels like before she ever learns the word for it.

I started pre-kinder while we lived there. I was still small enough to believe that adults could keep the world from hurting you. Small enough to think danger only existed in fairy tales, and that if something bad happened, someone would surely stop it.

My mother became close friends with our neighbor, Juanita. She was older, soft-spoken, the kind of woman who moved slowly, as if she had learned not to waste energy on anything that didn't matter. She cared for her grandson, Geraldo, who was about my age.

Geraldo and I spent hours outside playing tag and hide-and-seek, darting behind fences and trash cans, weaving through the narrow space between houses. We ran until our lungs burned and our legs felt rubbery, until our laughter echoed against the alley walls. Sometimes Juanita would sit outside and watch us, her hands folded in her lap, her eyes following us with a kind of tired tenderness. Her porch always smelled faintly of coffee and cleaning powder. She felt safe in a way I didn't yet understand.

My mother loved her company. Looking back now, I think she loved what Juanita represented—calm, steadiness, a woman who didn't live in chaos. A woman who didn't slam doors or raise her voice. Juanita made our world feel softer.

Then one afternoon, Geraldo came pounding on our door.

His fists hit the wood again and again, fast and frantic, like he was trying to break through the fear itself. When my mother opened it, he was crying so hard he could barely speak.

"My grandma," he choked out. "She fell… she won't wake up!"

My mother ran without hesitation. She didn't stop to grab shoes, didn't stop to think. She just ran. I followed behind her, my little feet struggling to keep up, the air suddenly thick and strange. I remember the way Geraldo's voice sounded—high and cracked, like a child's voice should never sound.

Juanita was on the floor.

My mother knelt beside her and tried to help, her hands moving quickly, her voice urgent. She called 911 and stayed there until the ambulance arrived. But Juanita didn't open her eyes. She didn't speak. She didn't move.

She had suffered a heart attack.

She died there, in her own home, while the world outside kept spinning like nothing had happened.

My mother took it hard. For days afterward, I would find her crying—quietly, like she was ashamed of her sadness. Sometimes she cried at the kitchen table, her head bowed. Sometimes she cried in the bedroom, her back turned. I didn't know how to comfort her. I didn't understand death yet, but I understood what it meant when someone disappeared.

Juanita's absence left a hollow space in the air, like a missing piece of the neighborhood itself.

Not long after Juanita died, everything seemed to grow darker.

South Central Los Angeles was tightening like a fist. Unemployment, poverty, street crime—things people talked about like weather, as if it was unavoidable. This was during the height of the gang war between the Crips and the Bloods. At night, helicopters hovered overhead, their searchlights sweeping across rooftops, scanning the streets as if they were hunting for someone. Gunshots cracked through the dark. Police sirens screamed down the roads. Those sounds became so common they stopped startling us. They folded themselves into the night and became part of what we breathed.

Even as a child, I could feel it.

The neighborhood didn't sleep.

One night, while my father was incarcerated, my Tío Richie stayed with us for the summer. He was only fifteen years old—still a boy, but already forced into a man's position. He slept on the living room sofa, like a guard posted at the edge of our world.

That evening my mother was drunk.

I remember her voice being too loud. Her movements unsteady. The air in the room felt off, like the walls were leaning in.

And then it happened.

A group of men tried to break into our home through the front door.

At first, it was a hard knock, aggressive and demanding. Then the door shook. The frame rattled. The metal knob jerked violently, twisting back and forth. The whole door groaned as something heavy slammed into it. My mother screamed.

I froze where I stood. My brother and I didn't know where to go. We didn't know if we should hide, run, or cry. We were too small to make sense of it. I remember the coldness in my stomach, the way my heartbeat felt like it was in my throat.

Tío Richie bolted up from the sofa and rushed to the door.

He pressed his whole body against it, bracing it with his shoulder, his hands spread wide, his feet planted hard against the floor. He fought like a child trying to hold back a storm. I remember the strain in his face, the tightness in his jaw, the way his arms trembled.

The men on the other side shoved and slammed, trying to force their way in.

The door bowed inward.

For a moment, it felt like the entire world was going to split open.

But Tío Richie didn't move. He held it.

And eventually, the men gave up.

Their footsteps faded. Their voices disappeared into the night. And the silence that followed was worse than the noise, because it was full of what might have happened if the door had opened.

I was very young, but the fear stayed.

My memories of that house are thin and uneven—either because we lived there so briefly, or because my mind buried parts of it to survive. Childhood has a strange way of saving you. It keeps what you can handle and hides what you cannot.

Years later, I asked my father why we moved from the duplex on 82nd Street.

He didn't hesitate.

"They tried to break in twice," he told me. "Your mom was drunk one of those times. Good thing your Tío Richie was sleeping on the living room sofa."

There was another attempted break-in when my father was home.

Again, they came through the front door. Again, it was loud and violent. The same shaking, the same rattling, the same force slamming into the wood as if the men outside believed they could take whatever they wanted.

Tío Richie was asleep on the sofa.

He woke up fast and called out to my father. Together they pressed their weight against the door, shoulders and arms straining against the force on the other side.

At one point, Tío Richie shouted, "Bring me the gun!"

Whether there was a gun or not didn't matter.

The men ran.

Even now, I can still hear it—that moment when his voice became a weapon. A bluff, maybe. A desperate lie. But it worked. Sometimes survival is nothing more than saying the right words at the right time.

I was about four years old.

During that time, I attended pre-kinder. My mother made me egg burritos for breakfast and walked me to school. I can still see her holding my hand, her grip tight, her eyes always scanning the street. When we arrived, she gave me a quarter for milk.

I always wanted chocolate milk.

But I never asked.

I never asked for more than what I was given.

Even then, I could sense that my mother carried too much already. I learned early that love sometimes meant being quiet. That survival meant not needing too much. That wanting was dangerous.

That was also when my night terrors began.

I would wake inside my dreams, still asleep, trapped somewhere between worlds. I'd kick off the blankets, drenched in sweat, yelling and thrashing like I was fighting someone no one else could see. My eyes would be open, but I wasn't there. No one could wake me. They had to wait it out, helpless, watching my small body battle invisible enemies.

My mother took me to doctors. Wires were placed on my head. Tests were run. My little body became a mystery on a clipboard, a puzzle no one could solve.

No one could explain it.

My father tried everything he could think of. He played the radio at night so I could fall asleep listening to it. He used a light sheet instead of a heavy blanket. He wondered if lighter dinners would help, or if I shouldn't sleep right after eating.

He searched for answers the way a desperate man searches for mercy.

And when nothing worked, he went down on his knees.

Every night, he prayed the Our Father over me.

It became routine. Sacred. He had me recite it with him, my small voice following his, syllable by syllable, like a rope we could hold onto in the dark.

Looking back now, I think he feared something darker—something he couldn't name, something he couldn't fight with his fists.

Even so, what I remember most is his care.

No matter what was happening in his life, no matter how broken or burdened he might have been, he always checked on us before bed to make sure we were covered. As if a blanket could protect us from everything outside the door.

I am fifty years old now. My father lives with me.

And if I fall asleep on the sofa, he still brings me a blanket.

Eventually, we moved to Watts. We lived in a one-bedroom apartment on 52nd Street, between Avalon and McKinley. I enrolled at 49th Street Elementary. Our duplex sat at 613 East 52nd Street—the unit farthest from the gate. My father believed it was safer that way, like distance might create protection.

Most of the neighbors were Hispanic, and they watched out for one another. People kept an eye on the children. They shared warnings, gossip, and sometimes food. In a neighborhood like that, community wasn't a luxury—it was a kind of survival.

Our landlord, José, treated my mother like a daughter. The rent was two hundred and fifty dollars.

When I think back, I know this much: Tío Richie was more than an uncle. He was like an older brother. He was still a kid himself, but he stood between danger and the people he loved as if that was simply his role in the world.

I was too small to protect myself.

I thank God he was there for my mother, my brother, and me. Sometimes I wonder if I would be here at all if he hadn't been.

My parents lived with a disease—a disability. That did not make them less loving. They loved their little family, and we felt it, even when the world outside our door was ugly. Even when the air was full of sirens and shadows.

But by the time we left that house, my body already understood things my mind did not yet have language for.

Fear no longer came from one place.

It came from everywhere.

From doors.

From voices.

From footsteps.

It lived in my muscles, in the way I learned to stay still, in the way I learned not to ask for more than what was offered.

The night terrors were not just dreams.

They were my body speaking before I knew how.

The adults searched for answers outside of me—doctors, prayers, routines—but no one asked what I might already be carrying.

And I did not know how to tell them.

Some dangers announced themselves loudly—sirens, shouting, hands pressing against doors.

Others arrived quietly.

Without warning.

Without witnesses.

I would not understand the difference until much later.

Thoughts

Looking back now, I realize my childhood didn't begin with innocence—it began with vigilance.

I was only four, but my body already knew what my mind could not explain: that safety could disappear in an instant, that a locked door was not always a barrier, and that the night carried its own kind of hunger. The break-ins, the sirens, the helicopters overhead—those weren't just sounds. They were lessons. They taught me to listen harder, to stay quiet, to need less.

Even my night terrors made sense later. They weren't random. They were my small body releasing fear the only way it knew how—through sweat, through screaming, through invisible battles fought in the dark.

And yet, inside all that chaos, there was love.

There was my father praying over me, night after night. My mother taking me to doctors. There was Tío Richie, still a boy himself, holding the door shut with his whole body like he could keep the world out by force alone.

Some children are rocked to sleep by lullabies.

I was rocked to sleep by survival.

And somehow, I made it through.

Chapter 5

**A mother is not defined by the
number of children you can see,
but by the love she holds in her heart.
— Franchesca Cox**

In 1976, my father was twenty-six and my mother was twenty-three. My tío Richie was sixteen and back in El Paso. We had just settled into our new home in Watts, at 613 East 52nd Street.

I was attending 49th Street Elementary, still learning how to read—not just books, but people, faces, body language, silence, moods, danger, and love. The invisible weather inside a room. I was learning how to recognize danger before it spoke its name, and how to tell when love was about to change its mind.

Around that time, my father had a friend named **Chacho**. I never knew his real name—only the nickname that drifted through our home like cigarette smoke. He was married to a woman named **Maria Luz**, though everyone called her **Luz**. They had a baby girl named **Elissa**, or at least that's what we called her. I never knew if that was her birth name or something we gave her because it felt easier to love a baby when you could name her.

Chacho and Luz were heroin addicts.

No one explained that to me directly. I only knew they moved differently than other adults. Their eyes were either too wide or half asleep. Their voices could be sharp one moment and hollow the next. Sometimes they laughed too loud, too suddenly, like the sound was coming from somewhere behind them. Their clothes smelled like sweat and smoke and something sour I didn't yet have a word for. Their lives looked messy, like a bed that had never been made.

But they were part of our orbit. In neighborhoods like ours, people didn't always get chosen into your life. Sometimes they were simply there—woven into your family by proximity, by poverty, by the strange loyalty that grows between people who are all just trying to survive.

By the time Jimmy Carter was elected president, my father and my maternal grandparents were no longer speaking. When we visited my grandparents in East Los Angeles, my dad would drop us off in the morning and return for us in the evening, like he was delivering something fragile that didn't belong to him.

That house in East L.A. felt safer than ours. It smelled like beans simmering on the stove and furniture polish. My grandmother kept everything neat, like order itself could keep bad things away.

One afternoon, while we were there, my father called.

That alone was unusual.

My grandmother answered.

"Hello," she said, her voice clipped, suspicious. Then she handed the phone to my mother with one word.

"Toma."

She wouldn't speak to my father herself.

My mother took the receiver, and I watched her face tighten. Her eyes narrowed the way they did when she didn't trust what she was about to hear.

Then I heard her ask, "Is she yours?"

The room went still.

Even at five, I understood that question meant something dangerous. Something that could split a family in half.

There was a pause. The kind of pause that fills up a room and makes the air feel heavy.

Then my mother said, "Okay. That's fine. We'll help."

Someone had called Child Protective Services on Chacho and Luz. They were looking for the baby.

My father wanted to hide her within our family, but first he needed my mother's consent. My mother—who knew my father sometimes had a wandering eye—needed reassurance before she agreed to bring another woman's baby into our home.

The baby wasn't his.

He said no.

And for reasons I didn't understand, my mother believed him.

I was five years old. My brother was three. We were too small to know what was being arranged, but we were old enough to feel the shift in the adults—the invisible tremor that meant something serious was about to happen.

My mother agreed.

Chapter 5

That afternoon, while we were still at my grandparents' house, my mother walked down the street and around the corner. I remember watching her leave, her sandals slapping against the sidewalk. I remember thinking she looked like she was walking into a secret.

When she returned, she was carrying a diaper bag and a baby pressed against her chest.

The baby's head rested under my mother's chin, like she belonged there. Like she had always belonged there.

And the moment I saw her, something inside me softened.

We were instantly taken.

Elissa was about five months old—small and luminous, with cheeks like ripe peaches and dimples that appeared when she smiled. She had just enough hair to make us argue over who would brush those curls. I wanted her to look like me. I wanted her to be mine in whatever way a child could claim another child.

"What's her name?" we asked.

My mother looked down at her as if she were reading a blessing.

"We'll call her Elissa," she said. "She's your sister."

And just like that, she was.

My mother fell in love with that baby in a way that felt urgent and complete, like her heart had been waiting for someone to pour itself into. My father did too. I often found them sitting together on the bed, Elissa balanced between them, her little hands gripping their fingers. The room would be quiet except for their laughter—soft laughter, the kind that didn't happen often in our house.

Elissa brought something new into our home.

A gentleness.

A tenderness.

A brief illusion of safety.

I remember the smell of baby powder on her skin, the way it cut through the usual odor of beer and cigarettes. I remember her tiny socks, always slipping off. I remember the sound of her breathing at night, a soft rhythm that made me believe for a moment that nothing bad could happen as long as she was there.

For a while, things felt peaceful.

At first, both Luz and Chacho came by to see her. They stood awkwardly in the doorway, their faces too thin, their eyes darting around the room. Luz would reach for the baby and then pull back, as if she didn't trust herself to hold her. Chacho would smile too hard, like he was trying to convince us all he was still a father.

Later, only Chacho came.

He would leave money behind—crumpled bills placed on the kitchen table like an offering. Each visit he stayed a little less. He looked like someone fading from his own life.

Eventually, we learned Luz had been arrested, and later checked herself into rehab.

We visited her there, Elissa in tow.

Luz would come out to the car with a cigarette burning between her fingers, her hair pulled back, her face tired. She would kiss Elissa's cheeks again and again, breathing her in as if she needed the smell of her baby to stay alive. She held her as long as she could before handing her back to my mother.

By then, Elissa was calling my parents **Mom** and **Daddy**.

Luz didn't like it. I could see it in the way her jaw tightened, the way her eyes flashed with something wounded and furious. But she swallowed it. She said nothing.

Weeks turned into months.

Luz completed the program and began piecing her life back together. She found a way to stand up straighter. Her voice steadied. She started talking about work, about a new apartment, about being clean. She spoke as if she could rebuild herself brick by brick.

And when she finally decided it was time for Elissa to come live with her again, the baby didn't recognize her.

Elissa clung to my mother. She cried when Luz reached for her. She turned her face away as if Luz were a stranger.

My mother tried to reason with her.

"Come by more," she told Luz. "Let her get used to you. Give her time."

But Luz didn't want time.

She wanted her child.

One day, she came and took Elissa.

I remember the way Elissa screamed. It wasn't just crying—it was panic, raw and desperate. Her little arms reached for my mother as Luz carried her away.

Chapter 5

My mother stood there empty-handed, watching them walk down the sidewalk.

She didn't cry—not then.

Her mouth tightened. Her shoulders went stiff. Her eyes went blank, like something inside her had shut off.

There was nothing she could do.

Elissa wasn't her child in the eyes of the world. She couldn't call the police. She couldn't claim what she had lost. She couldn't demand the return of something she had loved into belonging.

She grieved the way she always did.

Quietly.

And with a bottle.

Not long after, my father was gone again, spending another brief stay in Los Angeles County Jail. His disappearances were so common they began to feel like weather—storms that came and went without warning.

Luz still needed a babysitter sometimes. And my mother, despite everything, was always available. Maybe because Elissa was the closest thing to joy she had ever been allowed to hold.

One Friday night, Elissa was dropped off.

The next day was cold and rainy. The kind of rain that soaked through shoes and made the whole neighborhood smell like wet dirt and exhaust. It fell steadily through the night, tapping at the windows like impatient fingers.

Elissa wasn't picked up as planned.

It was nearly ten o'clock Saturday night when Luz finally arrived.

She was high.

I could tell before she even spoke. Her movements were too loose, her eyes glassy, her voice too sweet. She swayed slightly in the doorway like she couldn't find her balance in the world.

My mother was drunk.

Her words slurred. Her laugh came too quickly.

Her anger was already awake, pacing inside her.

Luz reached for Elissa.

My mother stepped back.

"It's cold," my mother said. "It's raining. The baby is asleep."

Luz insisted.

My mother refused.

"Come in," my mother said. "Stay."

They argued. Then they fought—hands, bodies, voices colliding over the same child they both loved. Two women tugging at the same truth: *this baby mattered*, and neither of them trusted the other to keep her safe.

I stood frozen, holding my brother's hand. I remember the way my stomach hurt, the way my throat tightened. I remember thinking, *if they break something, they might break her.*

Eventually they wore each other down.

They sat on the floor drinking together until night gave way to morning. Luz's laughter became sloppy. My mother's voice softened. And somehow, like magic or madness, the fight dissolved into companionship.

Luz and Elissa stayed.

The next day, they cooked. They played music. They played cards. They danced in the living room as if the night before had never happened. As if violence could be erased simply by pretending it didn't exist.

I watched, confused, trying to understand how two women could fight like enemies and then move like friends. How love could turn violent and then soften again. How chaos could sit at the table like family.

Around that same time, my brother began having trouble urinating.

He would stand at the toilet crying, saying he needed to pee, but nothing would come out. His little body trembled with frustration and fear. And when it finally did, he screamed.

His urine was dark yellow, streaked with blood.

I stood beside him, rubbing his back, whispering comfort the way children do—helpless, desperate, trying to fix what they cannot fix.

But nothing helped.

I remember his face twisted with pain. I remember how his tears looked too big for his small cheeks. I remember feeling panic rise in me like fire.

My mother eventually took him to the doctor.

By then, my father was out of jail again, as if nothing had happened.

As if disappearing and returning were just normal parts of being a father.

My brother needed surgery.

He had to stay in the hospital for three days.

My mother stayed with him the entire time.

And I—five years old—was left behind.

Chapter 5

I remember sitting in the hospital parking lot with my father, the air smelling like wet asphalt and exhaust. The sky was gray and low, and everything looked tired. My father smoked a cigarette, tapping the ash onto the ground. He didn't talk much.

I sat quietly, feeling small and invisible, like an extra child nobody had ordered.

My mother came out, desperate for a cigarette. She smoked fast, like she was trying to swallow her fear. She kissed me goodbye and went back inside.

And I missed her so much it felt like something was tearing loose inside my chest.

Even though I was with my dad—even though my mother was an alcoholic—I loved her fiercely.

All I wanted was to be with her.

It didn't matter that she drank. It didn't matter that she yelled sometimes. She was still my mother. She was still the center of my world.

My mother and Luz shared something essential: they loved their children, each in her own deeply dysfunctional way. And I believe love—even crooked love, even broken love—can still give a child something to hold onto.

My mother believed she was a better mother to Elissa than Luz was.

And maybe, in some ways, she was.

That little girl was lucky.

She had two women who loved her and wanted what they believed was best for her. Two women who would fight, drink, and bleed for her in their own ways. Two women who were both trying—imperfectly, painfully—to do what they thought a mother was supposed to do.

I've often wondered what became of Elissa.

I never knew her real name.

I never knew her actual birthdate.

All I knew was that she existed, that she lived inside our home for a while, and that she left a mark on us as deep as if she had been born into our blood.

Chacho, Luz, and Elissa remained part of our lives for another three years, but even then, their presence always felt temporary—like something borrowed that could be taken back without warning.

I hated seeing my brother in pain. Even now, the memory brings tears to my eyes. I was only five, but I felt I had failed him, as if loving him should have been enough to protect him.

Years later, when I had children of my own, I circumcised all four of my boys—because I never wanted them to suffer the way my brother did. I never wanted to stand helpless beside a child I loved and watch pain take over his body.

Only later did I understand what Elissa was preparing me for.

She was my first lesson in loving someone without permission.

Without protection.

Without any guarantee that love would be enough to keep them.

I learned, before I had words for it, that attachment could arrive suddenly and disappear just as fast—and that grief did not always announce itself with ceremony. Sometimes it simply walked out the door in someone else's arms.

Watching my mother lose Elissa taught me that love and power are not the same thing.

You can give everything and still have no claim.

You can do your best and still be left empty-handed.

My mother never spoke about that loss, but I watched how it settled into her. I watched how it joined the other unspoken griefs she carried in her body. How it hardened inside her like a stone she refused to name.

For me, Elissa became a rehearsal.

A quiet training in impermanence.

In how to hold on while knowing you might have to let go.

In how early a child can learn that love is not always safe, and that leaving is sometimes unavoidable.

I didn't know then that this pattern would repeat—that people would come into my life needing care, needing shelter, needing love, and that I would open myself to them anyway, even when it cost me.

I only knew that once, a baby slept in our home.

She smelled like powder and warmth.

She called my parents Mom and Daddy.

She laughed in our living room.

And then she was gone.

Chapter 5

After she left, the house felt different. Quieter, but not peaceful. The crib disappeared. The diaper bag was no longer hanging by the door. Her little socks, always slipping off, were gone too.

And my mother—my mother sat at the kitchen table with a drink in her hand, staring into nothing.

Not crying.

Not speaking.

Just sitting there, as if part of her had been taken and she had no language for what was missing.

That was the first time I understood something I wouldn't have words for until years later:

Some losses don't make a sound when they happen.

Sometimes grief doesn't scream.

Sometimes it simply becomes the air you breathe.

And something in me learned to miss what I loved—

even before it was gone.

<u>Thoughts</u>

Now, I understand that Elissa was never just a baby who passed through our home—she was a warning and a prophecy. She was my first experience of loving someone deeply and still being powerless to keep them. I watched my mother pour herself into a child she didn't legally belong to, and I saw how quickly love could be erased by circumstance, addiction, and the simple fact of biology. Elissa taught me that families like mine were built on temporary miracles—borrowed children, borrowed peace, borrowed hope—and that everything beautiful came with an expiration date. Even now, I can still feel the shape of her absence, as if my heart learned early to make room for loss. And maybe that is why, as an adult, I loved the way I did: fiercely, urgently, as if holding on tighter could prevent the inevitable.

Chapter 6

**Thank [God] in EVERYTHING
[no matter what the circumstances may be,
be thankful and give thanks],
for this is the will of God for you [who are] in Christ Jesus
[the Revealer and Mediator of that will].
1 Thessalonians 5:18 AMPC**

1977

The call came in the middle of the night—the kind of call that didn't belong to ordinary life. The kind that meant something had happened. Something violent. Something irreversible.

My Aunt Carmen was my mother's second-oldest sister. My mother was the youngest of twelve, the baby of a family that carried too many stories and too much pain. Like many in the family, my aunt drank. Her first husband— like so many men in the Rodriguez family—alcohol rarely stayed only alcohol. It became a fuse. It became rage. It became hands that couldn't stop themselves.

That night, the emergency room called.

We had to go pick up my aunt.

My mother didn't drive often—not because she didn't know how, but because her anxiety climbed into her throat the moment she got behind the wheel. Her breathing would tighten. Her grip would lock. She only drove late at night, when the streets were empty, or in extreme emergencies.

This night qualified as both.

My father was once again paying a visit to the Los Angeles County Jail. So my mom loaded my brother and me into the car. Elissa wasn't with us.

It was the middle of the night. The city felt hollow, like the world had stopped turning for everyone but us. My mother drove slowly, her knuckles white against the steering wheel. Even then, I watched her face, watched the tension in her jaw, and wondered what a person would do for a sibling.

How far love could stretch.

How far it could bend.

Chapter 6

And how often it broke anyway.

At the hospital, my mom told the nurse at the front desk she was there to pick up her sister. When the double doors opened, another nurse leaned in and spoke softly, her voice careful. She suggested it would be better if my brother and I stayed in the waiting room.

The desk nurse kept an eye on us while my mom disappeared into the back.

A few minutes later, Aunt Carmen emerged in a wheelchair, a nurse pushing her while my mother walked beside them.

I stepped forward to kiss her cheek, the way I had been taught. Family meant greetings, even when you didn't want to. Family meant you showed love even when you felt fear.

The smell hit me before I reached her.

Blood and alcohol—sharp and sour, heavy like a wet blanket. It clung to her skin as if it had soaked all the way into her bones. I have forgotten many things from childhood, but I have never forgotten that smell.

She and her husband had been in a drag-out fight. And she lost.

He beat her badly. Badly enough that neighbors called the police. Badly enough that the emergency room became the only place left to go. It felt like no one was surprised, not even the adults. Like this was just another chapter in a family book that always ended the same way.

We took her to my grandparents' house, waking them in the middle of the night. Lights flicked on. Doors opened. Voices rose and fell in tired concern. And there, heartbreak and bruises were soothed the only way that household knew how—with a cold Coors beer.

Even as a child, I could feel it: the way pain was never truly healed, only dulled. Covered. Buried under the familiar rituals of survival.

The next day, we went to her apartment and packed her belongings. She gave my mom her refrigerator and stove, both nearly new. The stove was almond-colored, leaning toward yellow, typical of the era. But what made it special was the little window in the oven door, and the small button that turned on the light inside.

The refrigerator matched.

My mom was thrilled.

It wasn't just an appliance. It was proof that something could be replaced. Proof that something could be given without being taken. Proof that our life could hold something clean, something new, something hopeful.

She baked us a chocolate cake, and my brother and I sat on the kitchen floor watching it rise through that oven window as if it were magic.

We stared like it was a television show meant only for us.

A cake rising.

A light glowing. Something sweet happening in our house.

For a moment, it felt like the world could be soft.

Not long after that night at the hospital, my mother, my brother, and I traveled from Los Angeles to El Paso to visit my paternal grandparents.

We rode El Paso–Los Angeles Limousines—back when they were actual limousines—and sat all the way in the back. The trip took sixteen hours. At some point during the night, I woke up. My mother and brother were asleep; their bodies folded into exhaustion. I pressed my face to the window and stared out into the dark.

And there it was.

The sky.

Vast and breathtaking, filled with more stars than I had ever seen in my almost six-year life. They glittered like scattered diamonds, bright against velvet black. I stayed awake for a long time, afraid that if I blinked too long, they might disappear.

I still remember how beautiful they were.

Even then, even at five, I think I was looking for proof that something bigger existed beyond our chaos. Something untouched. Something safe.

The next morning, we arrived in El Paso and were greeted by my grandparents. We stayed with them at 321 Ledo Street.

My grandmother had fresh tortillas waiting—hot and fragrant, butter melting so fast it dripped down my hand and arm. She handed me a glass of Coke like it was a treasure.

Food tasted different in my grandparents' house.

It tasted like comfort.

It tasted like being taken care of.

After we ate, my mom unpacked and settled into the room where we would sleep.

Chapter 6

My grandmother gave my brother and me a bath. She washed him quickly, took him to my mom to get dressed, then returned for me.

I lay in the almond-green bathtub, half asleep in the shallow water. It was deeply relaxing, like my body was letting go of something it didn't even know it had been holding.

She washed me gently, wrapped me in a towel, and walked me down the hallway.

And that's when I saw my Tío Richie sitting on the sofa, watching television.

Later that afternoon, my grandmother had errands to run. My brother was napping, and my mom wanted to take a shower. She asked Tío Richie if he wouldn't mind watching me.

"Not at all," he said. "Come over here, little girl.

What do you want to watch?"

I shrugged.

He flipped through the channels and landed on Sesame Street.

My mom checked on me once more before heading into the bathroom.

Tío Richie sat on the sofa. I lay on my stomach on the carpet, my hands tucked under my chin, watching the television. It was one of those huge floor models, the kind so big it doubled as furniture.

I wore shorts and a backless blouse tied at the neck and lower back—the kind everyone wore then.

At first, everything felt normal. Then I felt him sit down beside me. Close.

Close enough that the air shifted.

Close enough that I noticed the space between us disappear.

Then his fingertips moved slowly across my back.

At first, I didn't understand. Touch from adults was common— hugs, pats, closeness. I turned my head and smiled at him, then looked back at the television.

But a moment later, everything changed.

He flipped me onto my back and pulled at my shorts.

I told him to stop.

My voice sounded small, like it belonged to someone else. I grabbed my waistband and tugged, trying to keep my clothes where they belonged.

I don't remember what he said. I only remember the sound of the shower turning off.

The water stopped.

The bathroom door creaked.

He froze.

Then he stood up quickly and moved back to the sofa like nothing had happened.

My shorts were halfway down my thighs.

My hands shook as I pulled them up as fast as I could.

When my mom came out of the bathroom, I went straight to her and followed her into the bedroom.

I didn't say anything.

I didn't know how.

The shower had saved me.

Looking back now, I understand why I stayed silent. Silence wasn't a choice—it was a skill I was already learning. My body recognized danger before my mind had words for it.

What stayed with me wasn't only fear, but confusion—the sudden understanding that safety could disappear quietly, even in ordinary rooms. I didn't yet know what boundaries were, but I knew when one had been crossed.

And I knew, instinctively, that surviving sometimes meant saying nothing at all.

After that afternoon, life in my grandparents' house went on as if nothing had happened.

No one noticed a change in me, and I didn't offer one.

Children are good at folding themselves back into routine.

I stayed close to my mother. I watched where people sat. I paid attention to doors. I didn't know I was doing it—I only knew it felt necessary.

We visited family—Tio Joseph and Sophia, later Tío Robert. There was food and laughter and drinking, sometimes too much of it. My grandmother's disapproval of my mother's drinking lingered quietly in the background like a shadow no one mentioned.

My little cousin Rudy was there, only two years old, blond-haired and bright. My brother and I played with him. In moments like that, the tightness in my chest loosened.

Years later, Rudy would become one of my closest friends.

We also visited my mother's cousins, Raul and Francisca. My mom took my brother and me to Sears to have our pictures taken.

My dad was missing.

That photograph became the only semi-family portrait we ever had.

One morning, Tío Richie had to report to the El Paso Juvenile Probation Center. My mom offered to go with him because he needed an adult present. We waited in the car—a small Volkswagen Beetle.

I didn't understand why he had to report. I had overheard something about an incident at the Holiday Inn where he worked, but I was just a child, collecting fragments of adult conversations the way children do.

Looking back, I realize something I couldn't have known then:

The adults in my family carried secrets the way other families carried groceries—everyday burdens, heavy in their arms, never set down.

That August, my grandmother threw me a birthday party for my sixth birthday. I had never had one before.

There were other children, a piñata, and gifts. I was the center of attention. It made me shy, but I loved it too. For once, I wasn't invisible.

My grandmother did many kind things for me when I was young. I don't know what changed as I grew older, but I always felt out of place with her—like I was never quite good enough, like my presence came with a quiet measurement I could never meet.

Eventually, it was time to leave.

We took the Amtrak train back to Los Angeles. My mom fell asleep stretched across two seats. My brother and I sat nearby, but when she fell deeper asleep, we slipped away and explored the train like it was a new world.

When she woke up, she dragged us back to our seats—only to find them taken. Furious, she scolded us through clenched teeth and pinched us hard under our arms.

My mother could pinch.

Even now, I can remember the sting, the sharp punishment hidden in a place no one could see. It wasn't just pain. It was humiliation. It was a reminder that even joy had consequences.

When we arrived home, we took a taxi. My mom unlocked the back door, and we walked inside.

The house felt wrong immediately. The air was different. Too empty. Too quiet.

The stove was gone.

So was the refrigerator.

My mom took a few steps into the kitchen and stopped. Then she sat down on the floor, her back against the cabinet, and covered her face with her hands.

She cried quietly at first.

Then harder.

Not loud, not dramatic—just broken. Like something inside her had finally given up.

I stood there, unsure what to do. I knew something important had been taken—not just the stove with the little oven window, not just the refrigerator—but the feeling that something new meant something better.

That small bright flicker of hope.

I sat down beside her.

I didn't speak.

I wrapped my arms around her.

My brother joined us.

We sat there on the kitchen floor for a long time; three bodies huddled together in the aftermath of another loss we couldn't afford.

And in my mind, I saw it again—the oven light glowing behind that little window. The cake rising like a promise. Something sweet becoming real. And now it was gone. Just like that.

The Return of the Storm. My father's addiction had returned again, this time with a vengeance.

Thoughts

I've learned that uncertainty is common for adults who grew up in dysfunctional homes. As a child, I was conditioned to express only emotions that were acceptable. If I showed the wrong feeling—especially when my mom was drunk—it could lead to anger.

And it could lead to beatings.

Over time, I learned to swallow my feelings before they ever reached my mouth. I learned to disappear in plain sight.

That trip stayed with me for many reasons. Even then, I searched for the good.

Chapter 6

The Bible says to give thanks in every circumstance. I didn't realize it at the time, but gratitude became a survival skill for me. If I could find something good—something beautiful, something small to hold onto—then maybe I could make it through what came next.

When I look back now, I remember both the bad and the good.

I got toys, including a tiny Tupperware pitcher with matching tumblers. I loved it. I played with it like it was a real life I could pour myself into—one where things were clean, measured, and safe. With addiction, the entire family suffers.

I'm not a counselor or therapist—I speak only from experience. Families make excuses. They bargain with hope. They are manipulated by promises and apologies. They tell themselves this time will be different.

My mom did that too.

She wanted to believe each time would be different.

She was an addict as well.

And without realizing it, she contributed to both my father's addiction and her own—two storms circling the same house, pulling everyone inside into the same undertow.

And still, even in the middle of it, I was learning how to survive.

How to stay quiet.

How to watch closely.

How to find stars in the dark.

How to sit on a kitchen floor beside my mother's grief and hold on, as if holding her could hold the whole world together.

Chapter 7

Sister

When the sun shine, we shine together
Told you I'll be here forever
Said I'll always be your friend
Took an oath, I'ma stick it out to the end
Now that it's raining more than ever
Know that we'll still have each other
You can stand under my umbrella
Umbrella by Rihanna (feat. JAY-Z)

In late 1977, my mom realized she was pregnant with my baby sister, Marci. Even though she knew she was expecting, she continued to smoke and drink, as if the baby inside her was something she could ignore—something that could simply wait.

I was in first grade, six years old. My brother was four and had just started Head Start. We were still so small, still supposed to be living in a world made of cartoons, bedtime stories, and scraped knees.

But that wasn't our world.

Those next few years were hard. I won't pretend they weren't.

My mother's addiction to alcohol escalated, and my father was in and out of jail. Luz and Chacho still came around, and Elissa was still being left behind like an afterthought—like she belonged to our home more than to them. The adults moved in and out of our lives like the wind, careless and unpredictable, while the children stayed rooted in place, waiting to see what would come next.

Our apartment was often thick with cigarette smoke and the sour smell of beer. The kind of smell that clung to curtains and furniture, that seeped into clothes and hair. It was the smell of my childhood, even if I didn't understand that yet.

Mom would keep us up late, even on school nights, drinking and playing cards—twenty-one, gin rummy, simple poker. We used clothespins as money. The table would be crowded with hands and laughter, the shuffle of cards, the clink of bottles. The air felt loud.

I would quietly send my brother to bed, guiding him down the hallway like I was the parent, like I was the one responsible for making sure he slept. Then I would return and sit with her, staying awake long past the hour a child should have been dreaming.

We watched *The Gong Show* and *The Twilight Zone*. Some nights it was *Alfred Hitchcock Presents*. The television flickered across the room, casting shadows that danced on the walls. I remember the eerie theme songs, the canned laughter, the dramatic pauses, and the way my mother's face would change as the night went on.

When she drank too much, she became someone else.

She lost her warmth. She lost her patience. Her voice turned sharp, and her eyes turned distant, like she wasn't really seeing me at all. Sometimes she became verbally abusive. Sometimes she became physical. And I learned early that love could disappear in an instant, replaced by something unpredictable and dangerous.

Even at six years old, I worried constantly.

I worried about my mom. I worried about the baby she was carrying. I worried about my little brother. I worried about what might happen while I slept. I worried about what might happen if I didn't stay awake.

I was six—almost seven—but I felt much older. I didn't feel like a child most of the time. My role wasn't to be a daughter. My role was to be a caretaker. I didn't have the language for it then, but I was learning fear. I was learning hypervigilance. I was learning how to read the air in a room before I even stepped into it.

People would make comments to my mom about how responsible I was.

"What a good little girl," they would say. "She's so helpful."

And I would smile, because it felt good to be praised. It felt good to be seen. But inside, I lived with a tight knot of anxiety that never fully loosened.

Because every day I wondered: *What mood will she be in today?*

What mess would I find when I got home from school?

I remember walking home each afternoon with my stomach twisting, my heart beating too fast for a child. The closer I got to our duplex apartment, the more nervous I became. I would pray quietly that things would be fine, that she would be sober, that the apartment would be calm.

But I never knew until I opened the door.

The one thing I could count on was that I never knew what I would find.

When my mother was sober—especially when my father was locked up in county jail—she could be loving and warm. She could be everything I wanted a mother to be: caring, funny, interested, involved. In those moments she would brush my hair, laugh at my jokes, ask about my day. She would feel like home.

And I knew she loved me. I could feel it.

But when she wasn't sober, I lived in constant worry.

Sometimes she would pass out so deeply we couldn't wake her. It was terrifying. The apartment would go quiet in a way that didn't feel peaceful—it felt wrong. I remember standing over her small body on the couch or on the floor, my brother nearby, both of us holding our breath.

I would get a mirror and hold it under her nose to see if it fogged.

If it fogged, she was breathing.

If she was breathing, she was alive.

And if she was alive, then maybe everything could still be okay.

It sounds insane now, but at six years old, that mirror became my security blanket. I learned to measure safety by breath.

When my mom was drunk, she would come at me. Her eyes would narrow, her voice slurred, and her anger would find me like I was the reason her life hurt. Then, the next day, my mother would forget all the pain she caused the night before.

"I'm sorry," she would say. "I won't do it again."

"I'll do better."

"I promise."

And then the next night came, and the promises vanished like smoke. It confused me. It felt strange, because I always believed she meant them. I would lie in bed thinking,

Why doesn't she do what she promised? Why can't she stop?

When my father was home, the fights were worse.

They would explode into arguments that filled the apartment, bouncing off the walls like gunshots. Their voices rose and crashed into each other, and I would stand there frozen, feeling my heart pound, my stomach turning.

It was terrifying.

I would often get between them, trying to keep the peace, trying to stop the yelling before it turned into something more. I was a child playing referee between two adults who didn't know how to love each other without destroying everything around them.

I often felt desperate.

When my father was home, even with his addiction, I still preferred him. At least my father stayed the same. My mom changed into someone unrecognizable. She carried irritability like a coat she couldn't take off. She seemed exhausted, bitter, as if the whole world rested on her shoulders and she resented everyone for it.

And slowly, without anyone ever saying it out loud, I began taking over the role of a mother.

I took care of my younger siblings. I cleaned. I cooked. I tried, even when I didn't know what I was doing. I helped my mom clean herself up. I helped her off the floor after she fell. I helped her to bed when she couldn't walk straight.

No one told me to do these things. I just did them because no one else would.

It was confusing and uncomfortable. There was no place for me to hide. No place to escape. The apartment was small, and the chaos filled every corner. There was no door I could shut to keep it out.

This was my life from the time I was six until I was almost fourteen.

As my mother's due date got closer, my father was finally home. He tried to make up for his absence by spending extra time with us. Sometimes he would take us to the park, where the world felt almost normal.

At that age, the park was simple—slides and swings. The metal chains would squeak as we swung higher and higher, and for a moment I could pretend I was just a kid. I could pretend I belonged to a family like everyone else.

Sometimes he took us to a park with a lake full of ducks. He would buy an old discounted loaf of bread, the kind already turning stale, and sit under a tree. My brother and I would tear off pieces and toss them into the water.

The ducks didn't care if the bread was moldy. They came anyway, gliding across the surface like they owned the lake. Their feathers shone in the sunlight, and their calmness made me feel calm too.

Those were rare moments of peace.

Then the day came for my baby sister to be born.

On a Saturday in the middle of July 1978, my mom woke up with contractions. My father and mother started timing them. I watched everything, standing near the bedroom door, too nervous to play, too worried to leave.

My father held my mother's hand as she tried to lie still in bed. Sweat covered her forehead. Her face tightened with pain. I watched my dad grab a washcloth, wet it, and press it gently against her forehead.

Instead of comforting her, it irritated her.

She swatted it away, frustrated, restless.

Finally, she sat up, and my dad rubbed her lower back. Then she stood and began pacing. A strong contraction hit, and she leaned against the bedroom doorway, bracing herself as if the doorframe was the only thing keeping her upright. She breathed through it in sharp, strained breaths.

My dad stood behind her, rubbing her back, whispering things I couldn't hear.

I kept asking him, "Is Mommy okay?"

He smiled at me and said,

"Yes, of course she's okay. Now go play with your brother."

But I didn't go.

I stayed where I was, peering through the crack of the door, keeping my eyes on my mother. My father was so attentive to her. He looked like the kind of husband who would never leave, the kind of man who would protect his family.

Moments like that made me believe in his love for her.

They made me believe we might be okay.

But it was short-lived.

It was the middle of the month, the day my mom collected welfare and food stamps.

When she finally said it was time to go to the hospital, my father made her cash the check and food stamps first.

I remember standing there, watching her grimace in pain while waiting in line. Her hand pressed against her belly, her breathing tight, her face pale. I didn't understand it. I didn't understand why money mattered more than getting her to the hospital.

Even then, something in me recognized it as wrong.

After she collected the money, he drove her to Los Angeles County Hospital. When we arrived, he dropped her off at the main entrance.

My mother walked into the hospital alone.

We drove away.

That image stayed with me—the way she disappeared into those big hospital doors without anyone beside her. A woman in labor should not have to walk alone.

Everything that happened while she was in the hospital is mostly a blur. I remember Luz, Chacho, and Elissa coming to stay with us. Luz gave my brother and me baths in cold water. The kind of cold that made my teeth chatter. My skin prickled and my body trembled.

Afterward she dressed us and sent us outside to play.

I remember standing outside in front of our apartment, my hair still damp, my arms wrapped around myself. I missed my mom.

I missed the version of her that felt safe.

I missed the idea of her.

I was so cold.

Eventually my mom came home with Marci.

I was happy she was back, but by then I had caught a cold. It started with a runny nose and sneezing, then turned into a cough. It dragged on for weeks, like my body couldn't fight it off.

One Sunday afternoon—I'm not sure what time—my parents were hungover from the night before. They were trying to nap, so my dad sent us outside to play even though I didn't feel well.

I stood on the sidewalk near the huge tree in front of our home, feeling lightheaded. I looked up at the branches, watching the leaves rustle. And then the world shifted.

The ground began to shake.

At first, I didn't understand what was happening. The tree seemed to sway, and the air felt strange. Then my dad ran out the door, yelling for me and my brother. His face was panicked, but focused.

He scooped us both up and held us tight until the earthquake passed.

I remember the strength of his arms, the way he clutched us as if he could hold the world still.

When it stopped, he set us down. He dropped to one knee and checked us over, his hands moving quickly over our arms and shoulders.

"Are you okay?" he asked.

We nodded yes.

He hugged us again, hard and tight, then brought us inside.

My mom and baby sister in her arms were standing in the kitchen doorway, braced against the frame, her face pale.

After that, my cold got worse.

I ended up in bed coughing, running fevers. My chest hurt when I breathed. My mom tried to nurse me back to health. She spoon-fed me chicken noodle soup with crackers and gave me 7-Up in small sips. She tucked the blankets around me and checked my forehead.

For a moment, she looked like a mother again.

But then one day my lips turned blue—purple—and I refused to eat.

I felt heavy, like my body was made of wet sand. My fever stayed above 101.

Early one morning, they rushed me to the emergency room.

The doctors said I had pneumonia.

I was hospitalized for five days.

They placed me in an oxygen tent. The plastic smelled sharp and sterile. The hospital smelled like disinfectant and fear. The machines hummed, and the air felt cold against my skin.

My mom stayed with me until I was settled. She adjusted the blankets, spoke softly, then told me she had to leave to tend to my brother and baby sister.

Then she left.

And I was alone.

The next day, both my parents came for about thirty minutes. They brought me a box of crayons and a coloring book. They smiled and asked if I was okay. I tried to smile back. I tried to be good. I tried to be the easy child.

Then they left again.

Not through the front door.

Through the back.

I remember watching them through the hallway window. I could see them go down the stairs and walk across the parking lot. I watched until they were too far away to make out their faces.

That night, and the next, and the next, I climbed out of the oxygen tent. I slipped off the bed and walked to the window.

Every night, I searched for them.

Chapter 7

I kept thinking, *Maybe now. Maybe this time.*

But they didn't come.

I stayed in that hospital for all five days alone, with only one visit—the crayons, the coloring book, and the sight of my parents walking away.

The oxygen tent kept my lungs alive.

But the loneliness did something else.

It taught me, even at six years old, what it felt like to be left behind.

<u>Thoughts</u>

Even now, I can still picture that little girl holding a mirror under her mother's nose, checking for breath, checking for life. A child should never have to do that. A child should never have to wonder if her mother will wake up.

And the hospital… the oxygen tent… the window.

For years, I told myself it didn't matter. I convinced myself it was normal. I learned to swallow disappointment so easily that it became second nature. But deep down, something shifted in me during those five days. Something cracked. I learned that love could be temporary, that comfort could disappear, and that if I wanted to feel safe, I would have to create safety for myself.

That lesson followed me into adulthood. It showed up in the way I overprepared for everything, the way I stayed alert even in peaceful moments, the way I carried the weight of other people's needs as if they were my responsibility. It shaped the kind of woman I became—the kind of mother I swore I would be.

But it also gave me something else: compassion. Not the soft kind, but the hard-earned kind. The kind forged in chaos. The kind that sees people clearly and still chooses to love.

And sometimes, when I think about that little girl standing at the hospital window night after night, I wish I could go back and wrap my arms around her. I wish I could tell her what no one told her then:

You are not invisible.

You are not forgotten.

You are not responsible for the brokenness of the adults around you.

And most of all—

You deserved to be held.

Chapter 8

**In life we all go through trials and tribulations.
So now tell me, will you pass or will you make a mess?
— Jonathan Anthony Burkett**

In late 1978, my Tío Richie decided he no longer wanted to live under my grandfather's rule. He was eighteen—an adult. I was in second grade.

He packed his belongings into a blue, boxy suitcase and boarded a bus to Los Angeles. When he came to live with us, I noticed first how handsome he was, how grown. We all went with my dad to the terminal to pick him up. Afterward, they took us to a park. The adults sat at a picnic table talking while we played. That was when my dad told us Tío Richie would be staying with us.

I felt hopeful. I believed he would help—help keep the peace between my parents, help my mother when my dad went back to county jail. I imagined him as a steady presence in a house that rarely felt steady.

That belief didn't last.

Tio Richie spent his days stretched across the furniture, smoking marijuana. He wasn't a protector or a helper. He was an older brother who barked orders and sent us running errands. We fought with him often, poking at him on purpose because his temper was quick. When he snapped, we laughed. It felt like control.

My dad worked for Goodwill then, collecting donations. He always stopped home before heading to the warehouse. My mom would climb into the back of the truck and pull out what we needed—clothes, toys, furniture. Most of what we owned came from Goodwill. I didn't know any other way to live.

We lived in a one-bedroom house. That bedroom belonged to my brother and me. Tío Richie was supposed to sleep in my bed until they found one for him. I was told to sleep with my brother.

One night, my dad brought us walkie-talkies. We lay under the covers whispering into them, the static popping and fading. My brother on one side of the bed, me on the other. The lights were off. We were giddy with the small thrill of being awake when we weren't supposed to be.

Tio Richie was trying to sleep.

Chapter 8

Eventually, he lost his patience. He told me to come sleep in his bed and sent my brother back to his own.

As I drifted toward sleep, he took my hand and placed it on his penis. My body went rigid. I didn't understand what was happening, only that something had shifted, something had gone wrong. I pretended to be asleep. He wrapped his hand over mine and moved my fingers until he finished.

I stayed silent.

That silence became practice.

It happened again. And again. Weeks passed. Maybe months.

The next day, I acted as if nothing had occurred. I avoided him when I could. One afternoon, he was lying in my bed and called me over. I hesitated, then obeyed. He took my hand—the same hand—and studied my palm as if it held meaning. Then he placed a dollar in it.

"Go to the store," he said. "Get me an apple juice and a candy bar. Bring back the change."

The store was steps away, in front of our duplex. I walked slowly, lingering inside. The apple juice came in a glass bottle shaped like an apple. The candy bars were locked behind glass; you had to ask the cashier which one you wanted. When I returned, I handed him his things. He said thank you.

I skipped away.

Running errands for him became routine.

As the abuse escalated, he pulled down my shorts and underwear. He forced my legs apart and used his mouth on me. When he was finished, he dressed me again, pulled the blankets up, and turned me onto my side. I clutched the covers, my body buzzing with a shame I had no language for.

I felt betrayed by my own body—by the way it responded to the touch of his mouth.

That response is natural. It is even beautiful when it comes from choice, from safety, from adulthood. But as a child, it confused me. It made me feel complicit in something I did not choose.

Even now, when that shame tries to return, I remind myself: my body's response was not consent. I was a child. He was an adult. No matter what, it was not my fault.

Near Christmas, Tío Richie left for a short trip to San Francisco. One night while he was gone, my brother and I were locked in our bedroom, as we often were. They had installed a hook, and eye latch to our bedroom. My parents were fighting again. We heard shouting, objects crashing, the sound of my father hitting my mother.

Then everything went quiet.

I slid a paper through the door and the door frame crack unlocking the door. I slipped into the living room—used more like a dining room. My dad was asleep. I turned on the light and saw an unwrapped doll. That was the night I learned there was no Santa Claus.

Beside it lay my mother.

She was naked on the floor, blood matted in her hair and smeared across her face. Welts covered her back where my father had used his belt. She whispered for me to turn off the light, then called me to her. The air smelled of blood and alcohol.

I helped her into the bathroom. I was nearly eight years old. I filled the sink with warm water and cleaned her face and body, rinsing the cloth again and again. I wish this were the only time I did that.

It wasn't.

After nights like that, my parents would go out for caldo de res. They left us waiting in the car while they ate. I didn't question it then. Waiting was normal.

What wasn't normal was the weight I carried.

When my parents fought, I believed it was my fault. If I cleaned more, cooked earlier, behaved better—maybe it wouldn't happen. That belief settled into my body. Even now, raised voices make my stomach tighten. When my own children laugh too loudly, my first instinct is to shout—an echo of fear I have learned to quiet.

For years, I blamed myself for not telling anyone about the abuse. I blamed the walkie-talkies. I never touched another pair. When my son asked for some years later, my answer was immediate and absolute: no.

Now I know the truth.

Nothing I did caused what happened to me. My Tío Richie was an adult. I was a child. The responsibility belongs to him alone.

As an adult, I understand that healing does not come from erasing the past, but from acknowledging it. My history does not define me, but it does testify to my ability to survive.

I carry it— and I move forward.

<u>Thoughts</u>

As a child, I did not know the word *trauma*. I knew only the language of quiet. I learned how to disappear inside my own body, how to listen more than speak, how to sense danger before it arrived. Silence became my shelter. Stillness became my prayer.

I believed, in the way children believe, that harm must have a reason. That if something terrible happened, then something in me must have invited it. This was how I tried to make sense of a world that did not protect me—by turning the blame inward and calling it understanding.

My body learned lessons long before my mind could name them. It learned how to brace, how to endure, how to respond without consent. It learned to obey in order to survive. I mistook these responses for weakness, not yet knowing they were the wisdom of a child reaching for safety in a place where none was offered.

There was no sanctuary in my home, only vigilance. Love came tangled with fear. God felt distant then—not absent, but silent, like a witness waiting for the moment I would be able to look back and see that I had not been alone.

Now I understand that what carried me through was not failure, but grace. A quiet, persistent grace that lived in my breath, in my endurance, in the small, unseen choices to keep going. I survived not because I was spared, but because something holy within me refused to let me break.

Healing has not come as forgetting. It has come as remembering differently. As reclaiming my body not as evidence of shame, but as proof of survival. As trusting that God did not create me to be harmed, but to endure—and eventually, to be restored.

The child I was did not have words, but she had faith in motion. She kept walking forward, even when the path disappeared. I honor her now. I bless her. And I carry her with me—not as a wound, but as a testament.

Chapter 9

**I've been through the desert on a horse with no name
It felt good to be out of the rain
In the desert you can't remember your name
'Cause there ain't no one for to give you no pain
La la la la...
A Horse With No Name by America**

The summer I turned eight, my brother and I learned how to escape. Not by running away, not by disobeying, but the only way children like us could—quietly, obediently, with suitcases packed and bus tickets handed to strangers.

It was 1979. I was between second and third grade. My brother was six. At the beginning of every summer, we climbed aboard the El Paso–Los Angeles limousine bus and traveled to Texas until the season ended. My parents gave us pocket money and told us to sit near the front so the driver could keep an eye on us. The bus made two stops—one for dinner, one for breakfast—and then the road became a long ribbon of darkness.

I should have been excited. Instead, I felt sick with worry.

I hated leaving my mother. Not because I didn't love El Paso—I did—but because leaving my mother felt like leaving someone behind in a burning house. I worried about my baby sister, still in diapers, still learning to walk. I pictured her wobbling around the house, falling, reaching for things she shouldn't touch.

And I worried about who would take care of my mother.

Tío Richie was no help.

If anything, he was another storm waiting to break.

Even at seven, almost eight years old, anxiety lived in my body like it belonged there. I didn't have words like *addiction* or *dysfunction* yet, but I understood fear. I understood chaos. I understood what it meant to always be listening, always watching, always preparing for what might happen next.

When we arrived in El Paso early the next morning, my grandparents were waiting for us. Behind them stood the house at **321 Ledo**, a place I spent so many summers in that it still appears in my dreams.

That house held a different kind of life.

It smelled like warm tortillas and laundry soap. It sounded like the radio playing Spanish in the kitchen and my grandfather's booming laugh echoing down the hallway. There was food. There was routine. There was a sense that children could be children.

My cousins were there too—Gloria, Rudy, and Ruby. Five of us together every summer, gathered like the season demanded it.

And then there was my Tía Ruth.

Almost every summer followed the same rhythm: five cousins placed under her care. She registered us for camps at the YWCA, UTEP, or the recreation center. After camp she picked us up and took us back to my grandmother's house for lunch. Then we were off to the swimming pool until five in the afternoon, sunburned and laughing, our hair stiff with chlorine.

Sometimes Tía Ruth took us to museums. Sometimes she took us to festivals. And sometimes she took us out into the desert to visit a friend's home, where the night sky felt endless and the stars looked like they had been scattered by God's own hands.

El Paso gave me space to breathe.

And it wasn't just the desert—it was her.

My aunt Ruth was the kind of woman who could look at a child's anger and not be afraid. She wasn't a pushover. She had a temper—she was a Ramirez—but she had also learned restraint. She could discipline us, love us, and protect us all at once.

If we made her mad, we heard about it.

But if we were in trouble, she came.

Even if she was still angry.

My fondest childhood memories include her because she was the only one who could reach me when I was seeing red. My parents didn't know how to calm me down. My aunt did.

There's a song that always takes me back to those summers. One line speaks about a man walking into the desert to escape the rain.

That was me.

Los Angeles was my rain. The rain was yelling, slammed doors, and chaos that seeped into every corner of our home. The rain was my name being called constantly—*do this, go there, take care of her, hurry up.*

But in El Paso, something strange happened.

No one called my name.

Not with demands. Not with fear. Not with responsibility.

In El Paso, I didn't have to be the third parent. I didn't have to carry adult worries inside a child's body. I could simply exist. I could be a kid.

And I don't think my aunt ever realized what she was giving me. She probably thought she was just helping, just doing what family does. But she was giving me something priceless: a break from the storm.

Even so, I never fully relaxed. I still thought about my baby sister. I wondered who was watching her. I worried about my mother drinking, falling, getting hurt, being left alone in the aftermath of another fight.

It was too much for a child to hold.

I never worried about my father the way I worried about my mother. My father always seemed untouchable, like stone. But my mother felt fragile, like glass.

When summer ended and we returned to Los Angeles, my brother and I always came back heavier. In El Paso, my grandmother fed us constantly. There was abundance. At home, food was scarce. My mother didn't cook much—TV dinners, pot pies, quick meals that tasted like exhaustion. When she did cook, it was delicious: tacos, fish soup, meatball soup.

That was the contradiction of my childhood: I wanted to stay in El Paso forever, but I also wanted to go home as soon as possible.

Because my mother needed me.

And I hated that she needed me.

And I loved her too much not to return.

My brother and I never spoke about what home was really like. We were taught early: *what happens at home stays at home.* My father warned us that if Child Protective Services ever got involved, we would be taken away, separated into different foster homes, never see each other again.

So we lied. Everyone lied. My mother covered my father's addiction. We covered my mother's drinking. We told my father she was "taking a nap" when she was passed out on the couch. My father lied about why he nodded off while standing.

The lies became automatic. Denial became the air we breathed.

And I didn't feel guilty lying to my grandparents, aunts, and uncles. I didn't tell them what it was like living with an alcoholic, a heroin addict, and a pothead. I dressed up our lives in pretty words because it was safer than the truth.

Chapter 9

How would I have known my life was abnormal when it was the only life I knew?

This was my normal.

Even if it was abusive.

Even if it was twisted.

Even if it was evil.

It took me years to see my childhood from the outside, to understand what should have happened instead of what did. Still, even then, there was a quiet voice inside me whispering:

It's not right for mom to be drunk all the time.

It's not right for dad to be nodding off.

But I wanted stability. I wanted structure. I wanted a family like the ones on television. And that desire turned into a prison because I believed I could fix everything if I just tried harder.

If I cleaned more, maybe my father wouldn't rage.

If I behaved perfectly, maybe my mother wouldn't drink.

I became a prisoner to hope.

Slowly I realized the truth: it was never enough. I would never be enough. And no child should ever have to learn that lesson.

My grandmother was strict and judgmental, especially toward my mother. My grandfather was the opposite—warm, loud, easy to laugh. Their marriage confused me, especially knowing my grandmother endured his cheating in silence. Even now, I don't understand how she carried that kind of pain without breaking.

Maybe it was weakness.

Maybe it was strength.

Maybe it was love.

I will never know.

But I do know this: my Tía Ruth gave me something sacred. She gave me laughter. She gave me safety. She gave me childhood memories that still feel like sunlight.

I always knew my parents loved us. Addiction distorted everything, but it did not erase love. Their love was broken, but it was still love.

And I believe love is the one thing the devil cannot imitate.

When I think of those summers—of the desert sky, the swimming pool, the smell of tortillas—I think of the little girl I was.

A child who carried too much.

A child who needed a break from the rain.
Every summer, the desert gave me silence.
And in that silence, I remembered I was still a child.

Thoughts

As an adult, I can finally name what I couldn't understand as a child: El Paso wasn't just a summer trip—it was refuge. It was the only place where my nervous system could unclench, where my shoulders could drop, where I could stop scanning the room for danger. I didn't realize then that Tía Ruth wasn't simply entertaining five cousins—she was quietly rescuing one little girl from drowning in responsibility. She gave me laughter when my home gave me fear, and in doing so, she gave me proof that another kind of life was possible. Even now, when I think of the desert sky, I don't just remember summer. I remember survival.

Chapter 10

The Cadillac
She's not just four wheels and an engine, she's home
— Anonymous

When we went back to El Paso, my uncle had a new car.

Not just any car—*his* dream car. A friend of my dad's who worked at Goodwill had helped Tío Richie buy it at an auction: a **1979 Cadillac Fleetwood**, navy blue and shining like something too beautiful to belong to our family. The kind of car that looked like it should be parked in front of a fancy restaurant, not sitting outside a crowded house full of kids and tension.

Richie loved that Cadillac like it was alive.

He washed it, waxed it, polished it until the paint gleamed like deep water. He stood back and admired it, proud and smiling, like he had finally earned something that couldn't be taken away.

But that was Richie—restless, unpredictable, full of contradictions. He could have the car of his dreams sitting right outside and still decide to leave it at home, jump on the bus, and wander the city like he was chasing something invisible. Adventure always pulled harder than comfort. Trouble always called his name louder than peace.

One afternoon, somewhere near downtown, Richie stepped off the bus with music pounding in his head, his mind moving faster than his feet. He stopped at a gas station to buy candy and a drink.

And then he saw it.

A man pulled up, stepped out, and left the car running with the keys still in the ignition. Back then, people didn't lock everything down the way they do now. They didn't stand there gripping their wallets and watching their backs. They still believed the world could be trusted.

Richie watched the man walk into the store.

And then Richie jumped into the car and took off.

Just like that.

He hit the first freeway and disappeared into the city, the stolen car swallowing him up like it had been waiting for him all along. When he came home, his whole body was buzzing. His eyes were bright, his grin too wide, adrenaline still rushing through him like electricity.

He didn't look guilty.

He looked alive.

My father went outside with him to see the car, and that's when they noticed one of the tires was low. They decided to change it.

At first, it was only drizzling, a soft mist hanging in the air. But within minutes the rain grew heavier, tapping against the metal, soaking the pavement, turning the sky gray.

My brother and I watched from the window.

They placed the jack under the bumper. They loosened the lug nuts before lifting the car. They worked with the steady rhythm of men who believed they were in control.

Finally, the car lifted off the ground, the front end suspended.

My father went to grab the spare tire from the trunk.

And that's when everything changed.

He found a bag.

Inside were **South African Krugerrand coins**, about eight of them. They didn't look like much to me—just gold circles. But my dad's face told me they were something dangerous. Something that could split a house wide open.

When he told Richie what he'd found, it was like throwing a match into gasoline.

Then their voices started rising.

They were arguing—sharp words cutting through the rain.

My father wanted to keep three of the coins.

Richie refused to give him even one.

Their argument ignited instantly. Their bodies squared off, face-to-face, close enough to breathe the same air, close enough to turn words into violence. We could see it through the window—two grown men, pride and anger swelling in their chests.

Tío Richie's fists clenched.

He grabbed the L-shaped bar from the jack, the tire iron held tight in his hand. His knuckles went pale. His jaw locked.

For a moment I truly thought he was going to hit my father.

My stomach tightened. My heart raced.

But Richie didn't swing.

Instead, he started jumping up and down in rage, stomping the wet ground like the earth itself had betrayed him. He looked like a man possessed, a man so angry he couldn't hold himself still.

We called for my mother.

She pulled us away from the window with urgency, her hand firm on our shoulders, her voice low and sharp. "Go watch television."

But I didn't want cartoons.

I wanted to know if my father was going to be hurt.

In our house, danger and tenderness lived side by side. They shared the same rooms. They breathed the same air. They sat at the same dinner table.

That day, Richie kept all the coins.

He sold them for three hundred dollars each.

My father always claimed they were worth fifteen hundred apiece back then. But it wasn't really about the money. It was about what always lay underneath everything in our family: resentment, pride, and the fear that if you didn't grab what you could, you'd be left with nothing.

THE GENTLE THINGS HE TAUGHT ME

Around that time, I had begun showering and washing my hair on my own. That was when Tío Richie taught me how to comb it.

It's strange, the memories that stay.

Not the loud ones. Not the dramatic ones. But the small ones—quiet moments that don't match the rest of the chaos.

My hair was the same texture as his: thick, stubborn, the kind of hair that refused to behave. My mom's hair was straight and dark. My dad's was wavy, but he didn't grow it long the way Richie did. Richie was the one who took his time. Richie was the one who seemed to understand it.

"When you get out of the shower," he told me,

"Brush it once. Just once, to get the tangles out."

He spoke slowly, like he was giving me instructions for survival.

"Then don't brush it anymore," he said. "Let it dry on its own. Just run your fingers through it. Once it dries, don't touch it with a brush or it'll frizz and puff out."

He looked me in the eyes and emphasized it like it mattered.

"Just let it be."

To this day, I do my hair exactly the way he taught me.

And sometimes, when I'm standing in front of a mirror, fingers combing through damp strands, I think about how someone like Richie—reckless, angry, unpredictable—could still offer me something gentle.

How he could teach me a small kind of care when so much around us was rough. In our family, tenderness didn't come wrapped in safety.

It came in fragments.

THE MOTORCYCLE

When I was about nine, Tío Richie came home with a motorcycle. He was excited, grinning ear to ear, his whole face lit up like a child on Christmas morning. I didn't ask where it came from. I didn't need to. Some things in our family were understood without being said. My father sent him to Church's Fried Chicken to buy a family pack. Richie asked me to go with him.

My brother wanted to go too, but Richie shook his head.

"No. Only one."

So I climbed on behind him.

The engine roared alive beneath us, vibrating through my bones. Richie told me to hold on tight. I wrapped my arms around him and felt the heat of his back through his shirt. The air rushed past us as we took off, fast enough to make my eyes water.

My brother decided to follow us on his bike.

It was yellow and green with a banana seat. We called it **Sweet Pea**.

He pedaled hard, determined, stubborn, refusing to be left behind.

But he couldn't keep up.

We sped ahead, the motorcycle swallowing the distance, and soon my brother disappeared behind us.

We bought the fried chicken and rode back home.

And when we arrived, my brother wasn't there.

The yard was too quiet.

My stomach dropped like I had swallowed a stone.

Fear flooded my chest so fast it made me dizzy. I looked at Richie, and anger exploded out of me like fire. I started hitting him, punching him with my small fists, screaming because he lost my brother.

And Richie started laughing.

My parents started laughing too.

Like my terror was funny.

Like my love for my brother was something childish.

But in our house, love didn't feel childish. Love felt urgent. Love felt like something you had to protect with your whole body.

Then my brother came into the yard on Sweet Pea, riding slowly, safe and steady, like nothing had happened.

Relief hit me so hard I burst into tears.

I ran to him and threw my arms around him, sobbing against his shoulder like I had been holding my breath the entire time he was gone. My whole body shook with it. And in that moment, I understood something that would follow me through life:

In our family, the people you loved could vanish in an instant.

And you never knew if they would come back.

WHEN THE ADULTS FELL APART, I BECAME ONE

In our family, kids learned early who to become when the adults fell apart.

When my dad was in jail, Tío Richie would disappear. He'd stay away for days, drive around, sleep in his car, sometimes take off to San Francisco or back to El Paso like he was running from something that lived inside him.

And as strange as it sounds, I was relieved when he left.

When my father was gone, my mother needed me.

Not in the way a mother should need her child.

She needed me to fill the space my father left behind.

I became the one who watched the clock. The one who listened for danger. The one who made sure my younger brother and sister ate. The one who made sure they got changed and got to bed.

I was still a child, but I carried responsibility like it was my job to keep everyone alive.

On most school nights, I stayed up with my mother while she drank. I sat with her long past the hour children should be asleep, keeping her company, watching her mood change with every drink.

Sometimes I stayed awake until 12:30.

Sometimes until 2:00 a.m.

Then I'd wake up the next morning and get myself and my brother ready for school, as if the night before hadn't happened. As if we weren't living two lives at once.

We walked to 49th Street School, only two blocks away.

Those two blocks felt like a border between worlds.

At school, we were expected to be normal.

At home, we were expected to survive.

My mom taught us how to play poker. We used clothespins as currency. We laughed and played cards while the smell of alcohol lingered in the room, thick as fog.

And sometimes those nights felt almost warm.

Almost like a family.

But that's the cruelest part of it.

In our house, tenderness and danger lived side by side.

Sometimes in the very same hour.

THE SCARY NIGHTS

There were scary times with my mother.

When she was drunk, something small could set her off—something as simple as spilled milk. Her eyes would sharpen, her body would stiffen, and suddenly she was no longer my mom. She would lunge at us.

She would slap us, hit us, pull our hair, drag us across the floor. She beat my brother and me more times than I can count. There was no warning. No logic. No way to stop it once it started.

And then there were the enemas.

Even now, that memory makes my skin crawl.

Sometimes she would get it in her head that we needed one. We would see the red bag and the white hose with the clamp, and fear would crawl up our throats.

There was no telling her no.

She would fill the sink with warm water and a bar of soap until the water turned cloudy and soapy. She would fill the red bag, attach the hose, and come after us.

She would put Vaseline on the tube and insert it into our bodies.

Then she would release the clamp.

Water would rush into our colon, and we would cry and squirm and beg. She would make us hold it until she decided we could sit on the toilet. Then she'd do it again.

Three or four times.

She wouldn't stop until she was satisfied.

We weren't children in those moments.

We were trapped.

Chapter 10

THE FRONT STEPS

Other times she'd throw us out at night—nine or ten o'clock—
because we made a mess and she wanted to clean the house.
The music would be blaring inside, loud enough to shake the walls.
We would be the only kids outside, sitting on the front steps, waiting
in the dark.
Sometimes we stayed out there for two hours.
Sometimes longer.
Time moves differently when you're cold and scared and hungry.
It stretches like it wants to punish you.
My mom would lean out the window and yell that if we did a better
job cleaning up after ourselves, she wouldn't have to put us outside so she
could clean.
It didn't matter if it was hot or freezing.
When she yelled, "Get out!" she meant it.
So we sat on the cold steps, cuddling each other for warmth, our
bodies pressed together like puppies, waiting to be allowed back into our
own home.
When she finally let us in, the house always smelled like Pine-Sol.
Clean.
Sharp.
Almost cruel in its brightness.
That smell still lives in my memory.
It smelled like punishment.

THE FREEZER

One night, after she had cleaned out the refrigerator and freezer, I
opened the freezer door and saw frost forming inside. It looked like
shaved ice—white and sparkling.
I was a kid.
I wanted to taste it.
I leaned in and stuck out my tongue.
The second my tongue touched the frost, it froze fast and stuck.
Instantly, I panicked.
I tried to yell, but I couldn't.
My brother came running and pulled me, but it only made it worse.
I started crying, terrified. My tongue felt trapped in ice.

My brother ran to get my mom, who was outside hanging clothes on the line. When she came inside, the first thing she did was yank me too.

Still stuck.

Finally, she grabbed a cup of hot water and poured it into the freezer until the ice loosened.

My tongue finally came free.

But a tiny piece of it stayed behind on the freezer wall.

After that, my mom would laugh and say,

"Do you want some ice from the freezer?"

Like it was funny.

Like it didn't hurt.

Like I wasn't still tender inside.

THE GOOD MEMORIES THAT STILL GLOW

And yet… I have good memories of my mother too.

That's the part people struggle to understand.

They want pain to be pure evil. They want the story to make sense.

They want villains and heroes.

But real life isn't clean.

In our house, danger and tenderness lived side by side.

My mother drank too much, yes. But she also tried—

sometimes with everything she had.

She often took us to the library. She checked out stacks of books and read to us for hours. Those were the moments I saw her softness. Those were the moments she felt like the mother I longed for.

She loved puzzles too. The more pieces, the better. She'd sit at the table for hours, focused and calm, fitting them together like she was building order in a life that refused to stay steady. When she finished, she'd glue them to cardboard and hang them on the wall like trophies.

We played cards.

We watched sitcoms.

Sometimes we laughed.

And for a little while, it almost felt like we were safe.

Chapter 10

THE BIRTHDAY PARTY

One of the saddest memories I carry is the year I asked for a birthday party.

I wanted to invite school friends over. I wanted to feel normal, even if only for one day. My mom wrote out invitations and gave them to me to hand out at school. I passed them out like they were golden tickets, like I was certain my friends would come.

Some of them said they didn't have a ride.

When I told my mom, she said she would pick them up.

That was a big deal.

My mom didn't drive much because her anxiety would take over. She would grip the steering wheel too tight, her eyes wide, her breathing shallow. Driving wasn't easy for her.

But she was willing to do it for me.

On the day of my party, she baked my cake. She decorated it. She bought special plates and cups. She hung balloons and streamers. She put effort into everything, like she was trying to build a version of motherhood she had never been taught.

She was even sober.

That alone felt like a miracle.

Before the party began, we went to pick up one friend who needed a ride. My mom drove slowly, carefully, as if she was afraid the car might break apart beneath her. We arrived at the house and I got out, excited, hopeful, nervous.

I knocked.

No answer.

I knocked again.

Nothing.

I kept knocking until my mom leaned over, rolled down the passenger window, and said gently, "No one's home, mija. Come on."

Then she said, "I'm so sorry."

We drove back home.

She turned on music and we waited for guests to arrive.

We waited.

And waited.

But no one ever came.

The house stayed full of decorations and empty of laughter. The balloons hung there like a cruel joke. The cake sat untouched like it didn't know what to do with itself.

And I remember my mom trying to smile through it, trying to pretend it didn't break her heart too. That day, she tried so hard to be a normal mom. And the world didn't meet her halfway.

Even now, that memory makes my chest ache—not only because no one showed up, but because I saw her effort. I saw her hope. I saw her trying to give me something she didn't know how to give consistently.

In a house like ours, those moments mattered.

They were rare.

They glowed.

WHAT WE LEARNED

We learned how to take care of ourselves.

We learned how to feed ourselves, clothe ourselves, and protect one another. We learned how to read moods, how to anticipate danger, how to disappear when necessary.

We learned too early what adults were supposed to do.

I won't deny it.

It was terrible.

It was bad.

It shaped me in ways I didn't understand until I was grown.

The things that happened in my life—things God did not prevent— hurt me emotionally, physically, and mentally. I wish they hadn't happened, but they did. And they left marks I carried into adulthood.

For years, I tried to pretend I was fine.

But I wasn't.

I made bad decisions and blamed my childhood. I blamed my parents. I blamed my past like it was a sentence I could never escape. I carried anger like a weapon and bitterness like armor.

It took me thirty years to finally surrender it.

Thirty years to understand that survival is not the same as healing.

And that God was not asking me to pretend it didn't happen—He was asking me to bring it to Him.

I hold tightly to Genesis 49:22–26 KJV, the image of Joseph as a vine, climbing over a wall.

A wall meant to confine him.

A wall meant to stop him.

But the vine grows anyway.

It reaches over what tried to hold it back. It stretches toward light.

It produces fruit.

That is what God has done with my life.

He took a childhood filled with fear and made something grow from it. Not because the pain was good—but because He is.

In our house, danger and tenderness lived side by side.

But so did God's mercy.

Quiet.

Patient.

Waiting.

He never forced Himself into my story.

He never kicked down the door of my heart.

He stood like a gentleman at the threshold until I was ready.

And when I finally opened the door, He began the work of turning survival into purpose.

If He could do that for me, He can do it for anyone.

Even you.

Thoughts

When I look back now, I can see that Tío Richie and my mother were both carrying storms they never learned how to calm. Richie moved through life like fire—reckless, bright, and destructive, but still capable of tenderness in the smallest, strangest ways. My mother, too, could be cruel in her drinking, yet she also tried—sometimes clumsily, sometimes beautifully—to give us moments that felt like love. As a child, I only understood fear and confusion. As an adult, I understand something harder: they were wounded people raising wounded children. That doesn't excuse what happened, but it explains the shape of it. And somehow, in the middle of all that chaos, God still left me with fragments worth holding onto—small mercies, small lessons, and the strength to build a different kind of home.

Chapter 11

It's never as bad as it seems.
You're stronger than you think you are.
Trust me.
— Superman

1979

When I returned from El Paso, Richie was still living with us. I began third grade, and the molestation continued. With nowhere to turn, I quietly carried on the charade—pretending to be asleep at night and pretending nothing had happened during the day.

My father was on-again, off-again with heroin and constantly in and out of jail. My mother was still struggling with alcohol. I truly had no one to report it to. I also had no real personal connection with any of my teachers at school—no adult who felt safe enough to confide in.

My mom bought my Tío Richie a twin bed so he could sleep in what had been the living room. It was set up in a corner. I felt relieved that he would no longer be sleeping in our bedroom and that I could finally have my bed back. But now he found excuses to get up at night and come into our room anyway.

One night, it was late, and I was awake watching television while everyone else slept. He came into the room wearing only a towel and sat beside me. He said, "I'm having a pain here. Do you think you can rub it?"

"Yes, Tío," I replied. "Where?"

"The pain is moving further up my leg," he said. "Can you rub higher?"

I pulled my hand away and shook my head no. I felt apprehensive and didn't know what to do. He continued to insist. When I refused, he finally walked out of the room and left me alone.

I was terrified. Every other time he touched me, I pretended to be asleep. This time felt different. This time, I felt like he wanted me awake—aware, participating.

Another time, my parents left my brother and me at home with Tío Richie to babysit us, taking my sister with them. I was angry that they did that. My brother and I sprawled on our parents' bed to watch television, lying on our stomachs with our chins in our hands at the foot of the bed. I was wearing a strapless tube-top dress.

Tío Richie came in and sat at the head of the bed. As I watched the television, I felt his hands gently caress my buttocks. It frightened me. My body went tense.

What do I do? I asked myself. If I stay, he will continue.

I got up and went into the bathroom to think. When I returned, he was still sitting at the head of the bed, waiting. I chose to sit on the floor between the bed and the television instead.

That seemed to upset him. He stood up, turned off the TV, and ordered us outside.

"But we're watching TV," we protested.

"I don't care," he snapped. "Go outside."

He locked the screen door behind us, turned on his music, and began smoking pot in our bedroom, the music blaring. I walked around to the back of the house—the side facing the alley. I told my brother to wait by the back door and that I would let him in.

I climbed through the kitchen window, which my mom always left cracked open. I stood on the sink, listening to see if he heard me. When it was quiet, I unlocked the back door and let my brother inside. Then I grabbed a large kitchen knife.

I crept into the bedroom with the knife drawn and charged at him. He ran out of the house. We locked the front door and rushed to check every window, making sure they were all secured.

He sat on the front steps until my parents came home. When we saw them arrive, we unlocked the door. He walked in with them. To our amazement, he never told on us.

My father didn't learn what I had done until December 1985, when Richie was incarcerated at the Los Angeles County Jail. During a visit, Richie laughed about the incident, making light of it. That was how my dad found out I had chased him with a knife.

Years later, when I wrote to Richie and told him I remembered pretending to be asleep while he molested me, he apologized—but then deflected, reminding me that I had once chased him with a "huge psycho kitchen knife."

As many memories as I have of my Tío Richie molesting me, I also have many good memories of him.

One time, he brought home Yoplait yogurt. I had never had yogurt before. It was boysenberry. He handed me the cup and said, "Try this. It's good—you'll like it."

I peeled back the lid, looked at the white yogurt, smelled it, and took a bite. "Yuck! This is nasty, Tío!"

He burst out laughing. "No, it's not. You have to stir it. Here, give it to me."

He stirred the fruit into the yogurt until it turned purple and handed it back. I took another spoonful. It was delicious. He was right—I liked it.

Back then, the fruit sat at the bottom of the container.

Tío Richie wasn't odd or outwardly off in any way. That's why my feelings about him are so conflicted. He was friendly and talkative, inquisitive, with a contagious laugh. I have a nephew who laughs just like him, and every time I hear it, I'm reminded of Richie in a good way.

Richie didn't work. He stayed home in our bedroom, smoking pot, watching TV, and listening to music. He constantly sent my brother and me to the store for apple juice, Pepsi, and candy bars. We complained to my dad, and eventually he told us to charge Richie every time.

At first, Richie wasn't happy, but he gave in. He gave us a quarter each time, and we were finally able to get something for ourselves. Eventually, going to the store for him was no longer an issue.

Cindy, who was about thirteen, moved in next door with her brother, Chino. Like most of our neighbors, they were Hispanic. Cindy was at that in-between age—not quite a child, not yet a young woman. She was much taller than I was, fair-skinned, with dark blonde hair, already developing.

One afternoon, while Richie was cleaning out his Cadillac, I went next door and asked Cindy if she could come out to play. She and her brother joined us, and we played tag, then freeze tag, until she was called in for dinner.

My brother wandered over to Richie's car, where the doors were open and the music blared—hard rock. He loved AC/DC, KISS, Pink Floyd, and Led Zeppelin.

When I went to get my brother, Richie stopped me and asked me questions about Cindy—too many. It made me uncomfortable.

His car was always filled with trash: fast-food wrappers, candy wrappers, empty soda bottles, and apple juice bottles. He had a serious sweet tooth. Mixed in with the trash were Playboy and Hustler magazines.

As a child, flipping through those pages leaves an impression. That's where I found my brother—sitting in the back seat, door open, staring at a topless woman in one of the magazines.

Richie also read crime and detective magazines like True Crime, Official Detective, and Master Detective. Those were the ones that fascinated me. Looking back, I realize he had replaced comic books with those magazines. I grabbed one from the floorboard and slid into the back seat beside my brother. We sat there for hours while Richie worked on the engine.

As it got dark, he shooed us away, took the magazines, sent us inside, then jumped in his car and drove off.

We spent a lot of time following him around, asking questions. Sometimes he explained patiently; other times he ran us off like any older sibling annoyed by tag-along kids.

In many ways, we saw him more as a big brother than an uncle. We laughed with him, fought with him, yelled at him like siblings. I loved him like a brother. I never truly hated him.

Genuine love is the greatest healer of all.

During this time, a small Pentecostal church met in a storefront across from our duplex. They went door to door inviting people, and my mom sent my brother and me.

There at that little store front church, I met a man who loved me more than I could imagine and who was always there when I called on Him. He comforted me when I was scared—emotionally and physically. Words cannot explain the comfort He gave me.

As the years passed, I often thought about my cousins on my father's side. They may have spoken to Richie on the phone, written letters, or even visited him in prison. But I lived with him. I knew him in ways they never did. I knew his favorites, how to push his buttons, how he combed his hair. I knew things no child should know.

His arrest in 1985 shattered our family. Our life had never been ideal, but we had been together. The separation felt like abandonment.

The media surrounding the case was relentless. They followed us, snapping pictures without consent. We were forced to leave Los Angeles and live with relatives we only saw during summers—always feeling like outsiders, surrounded by people yet deeply lonely.

We missed our parents. Despite their addictions, my father was always affectionate, and my mother was too when she was sober. Even after a few drinks, she made it a point to hug us, tickle us, wrestle.

Thoughts

Looking back now, I understand that the girl I was did not live inside choice. She lived inside endurance.

Her world had already taught her that speaking did not lead to safety. Silence, on the other hand, could sometimes pass unnoticed. So she learned to disappear without leaving. At night, she performed sleep like a shield—still, compliant, breath shallow enough to convince herself she wasn't there. During the day, she learned the other half of survival: how to move through sunlight as if nothing had happened in the dark.

She did not yet have the language for what was being done to her, only the sensations—the tightening of her body, the way fear arrived before thought. She knew instinctively that if she stayed still, if she asked for nothing, she might remain intact. Being asleep allowed her to pretend the harm belonged to dreams. Being awake shattered that illusion. Awake meant choice, and choice felt like blame.

When fear could no longer fold inward, it sharpened. The knife in my hand was not rage—it was clarity. It was the moment my body chose *fight* after too many nights of *freeze*. I did not want to hurt him. I wanted him gone. I wanted the room back. I wanted myself back.

What confused me most was not the harm, but the kindness that lived beside it. The laughter. The yogurt stirred until it turned purple. The ordinary moments that felt almost safe. A child cannot hold contradiction without swallowing some of it whole. So I learned to love and fear the same person, to trust and retreat in the same breath. That confusion followed me for years, long after the house changed.

I watched people closely then—not out of curiosity, but necessity. I memorized patterns, moods, the way voices shifted before danger arrived. Knowing became a form of control. If I could anticipate the world, maybe it couldn't surprise me.

When comfort finally came, it came quietly, without demands. Faith was not doctrine to me; it was presence. It was the first place where love did not ask me to disappear in exchange for belonging. When I called out, something answered. And for a girl who had learned that no one was listening, that was everything.

I did not know then that what I was doing was surviving. I only knew how to make myself smaller, quieter, easier to overlook. I believed that if I needed less, I could last longer.

Now, from this distance, I can name her bravery. She did not break. She adapted. She learned how to live inside contradiction and carried herself forward anyway.

She endured.
And one day, she learned how to return.

Chapter 12

That is not a drug, it's a leaf.
— Arnold Schwarzenegger

My dad was serving time in the Los Angeles County Jail, and visiting him was simply part of childhood. Weekends meant long lines outside, metal benches, vending machines, and waiting for our name to be called over the intercom. My mom stood for hours. Once inside, we waited again.

My brother, sister, and I played with the other kids whose families were there for the same reason. Tag. Freeze tag. Kickball if someone had a ball. We spent whole weekends there. Jail didn't feel strange — it felt familiar.

That familiarity followed us into adulthood. In 2019, at forty-five, my brother made a trip to Los Angeles. One of the places he wanted to visit was the jail. He and my dad walked the grounds together while my brother shared childhood memories, like they were remembering a park.

Tío Richie had been gone for several days. One early morning, after a trip to San Francisco, we heard the front door open and voices in the house. I woke to the sound of excited talking and recognized his voice. Not knowing why he was so happy, I drifted back to sleep.

Later, in what was supposed to be our dining room, the table meant for six held a mound hidden beneath black trash bags. I stared at it, trying to figure out what was underneath. Tío Richie came in drinking apple juice, walked over, and pulled the plastic back.

Fresh marijuana stalks.

We learned to strip leaves from stems, make piles, and fill bags. We did it for days. Our fingers stayed sticky with green residue, the smell clinging no matter how much we washed. It felt less like crime and more like a chore — something between homework and housework.

Soon there were scales and baggies. Leaves dried in the oven. That was when I learned about nickel bags and dime bags. Before that, joints and roaches in ashtrays beside cigarette butts were just part of the house. My brother and I never wanted to smoke. It was so ordinary it didn't feel interesting.

With the money, my dad bought a huge wood-grain floor console color television. When Superman came on, my brother and I sat on the floor in front of it, stunned by the colors. We'd had TVs before, but only black and white. We'd seen color sets in neighbors' homes. Now we had one. It felt like luxury.

At school, a group of girls began following my brother and me on our walk home, taunting us. We tried ignoring them. One afternoon, they ran up and hit my brother hard between the shoulder blades.

He cried.

Something hot rushed through me. I dropped my backpack. She was taller, but that didn't matter — I hit her with everything I had. She tried to run, but I grabbed her braids and yanked her down. She scrambled up and I kicked her in the face. My heart pounded so loud I could hear it in my ears.

"Get up!" I yelled. She didn't.

When I turned, my brother had run home with my backpack. I walked the rest of the way shaking, the fight still buzzing in my hands. My mom met me in the alley, checked me over, and hugged me. My dad later gave us a speech about sticking together. My brother never lived it down.

The house stayed the same. Marijuana being sold. My dad using heroin. My mom drinking heavily. Knock-out fights. Noise, then silence, then pretending everything was normal.

And underneath it, something else continued — something I didn't have words for yet. I only knew certain footsteps in the hallway made my body go still. I learned how to stare at the wall with my eyes closed and leave my thoughts somewhere else. In the morning, I still had to eat cereal, get dressed, and go to school like every other kid.

Life, as I knew it, went on.

My mom began using heroin too. My parents locked themselves in the bathroom for long stretches. My brother and I used to peer through the keyhole until they plugged it with tissue. By then, we understood more than children should.

She started nodding off, losing weight. Twice she overdosed. My dad mixed salt water in a syringe and injected her, then lifted her like a rag doll and walked her around until she woke. No one explained. We didn't ask.

One Saturday morning, my dad woke early for Dunkin' Donuts. I woke too. He set me on the counter while he made instant coffee in a plastic glass — we didn't use cups. He always let me sip from his.

"Want donuts?" he asked.

I nodded. Off we went.

Next door was a poultry shop full of chicks and ducklings. I stared through the window. He saw.

"Want to go look?"

Inside, the chirping filled the air.

I picked up a duckling, soft and warm. "Can I have one?"

He said yes.

I named him Daffy. He followed me everywhere, even to the corner store, waiting outside like a dog. That duck felt like pure happiness, living right alongside everything else. Even on hard days, he would waddle after me like I was his whole world.

At school, during recess, the cafeteria window sold peanut butter cookies. The smell drifted across the yard, warm and sweet. Kids lined up with coins in hand. I watched, wanting one so badly it almost hurt. Friends sometimes offered me a piece. I always said no. I knew money was tight. I never asked my parents.

One afternoon, my parents told me to wait after school on the bench behind the baseball cage. I watched the other kids leave, one by one. The yard grew quiet. Then the rain started.

At first I thought they'd be there any minute. I stayed on the bench as the rain soaked my clothes, my hair dripping into my eyes. The sky darkened. The playground emptied completely. I was cold, hungry, and trying not to cry, telling myself they were just late.

I knew how to wait. I knew how to be quiet. Those were things I was already good at.

When they finally arrived, it was nearly dark.

At home, they handed me a pair of Big Bird slippers like a prize. My dad kept hugging me, saying he was sorry. I nodded, but something inside me had gone still in a way I recognized.

Thoughts

Looking back, I can see how ordinary the extraordinary became. Jail felt like a weekend routine, drug work felt like chores, and chaos felt like family life. I learned early that being useful earned belonging, that silence kept the peace, and that waiting without asking made me less of a burden. I mistook survival skills for personality traits — toughness for strength, watchfulness for maturity, endurance for patience. I didn't yet have words for what was happening in the shadows, only the instinct to leave my body and return by morning, dressed for school like nothing had touched me. Love, as I understood it then, looked like crisis and apology, gifts instead of change, closeness mixed with fear. It would take years to untangle those lessons, to realize that what I called normal was adaptation, and what I called love was often survival. But the child I was did exactly what she needed to do: she stayed, she watched, she endured, and she found small, bright things — a color television, the smell of cookies, a duckling at her heels — to remind her the world held more than what was happening inside.

Chapter 13

Everything will be okay in the end.
If it's not okay, it's not the end.
— John Lennon

As we got older, my dad began taking us places—museums, parks, zoos. He wanted us to see more than the boundaries of our neighborhood, to believe there was a wider world waiting for us beyond the streets we walked every day. He didn't always know how to give us stability, but he knew how to give us effort. And sometimes, effort was the only kind of love our family could afford.

One weekend, he promised to take us to the Los Angeles Zoo.

When Saturday arrived, he woke up with a severe toothache. Bad teeth ran in his family. Cavities followed many of us like an inheritance—myself included. No matter how faithfully I brushed or flossed, I still seemed destined for the dentist's chair.

My dad hated the dentist. He avoided it for as long as he could, enduring pain the way he endured many things—quietly, stubbornly, privately.

Still, he kept his promise.

The zoo was loud and sunbaked, filled with the smell of popcorn, animal musk, and warm pavement. Children shrieked with laughter, parents called out names, and somewhere nearby a lion's roar rolled through the air like thunder. My brother and I ran ahead, dazzled by everything—striped bodies behind fences, birds with bright feathers, monkeys that moved like mischief.

But every so often my father disappeared from view.

I would spot him a few yards away, standing off to the side with his hand pressed against his jaw, pacing near the edges of the crowds as if motion might dull the ache. His face tightened with pain, but he kept his posture steady, as if refusing to let the world see him falter.

I asked my mom what was wrong with him, and that was when she told me about his tooth.

As a child, I noticed his absence more than his sacrifice. I noticed what I wanted—what I didn't have—what I thought should have been easier.

As an adult, I recognize something else entirely.

Love expressed through endurance. Love that shows up even while hurting. For my father, love wasn't softness. It was follow-through.

Another day, he took us to Travel Town Railroad. We climbed through old trains, touched rusted metal, and pressed our hands against the cool steel as if it could still remember where it had been. The air smelled like dirt and oil, like sun on iron. I imagined those engines cutting through deserts and mountains, carrying strangers into new lives.

My dad talked the way he always did—explaining, teaching, wanting us to know more than he had known. He tried to be the kind of father he wished he'd had, present in ways he himself had once gone without. He didn't have much money, but he had stories. He had attention. He had the determination to give us something beyond survival.

One weekend, we drove to San Diego. We arrived late on a Friday night and slept in the back of the station wagon. The vinyl seats stuck to our skin. The night air was damp, thick with the smell of ocean salt and gasoline. I remember the hum of distant traffic and the way the car rocked slightly when someone shifted in their sleep.

I didn't mind. There was something comforting about being packed together like that—my brother's breathing beside me, my parents' voices fading as they drifted into sleep. Even then, I understood that this was how we traveled: not with comfort, but with intention.

The next morning, they took my brother and me to the San Diego Zoo. It felt endless—larger than the Los Angeles Zoo, alive with sound and movement. The air buzzed with chatter, the screech of birds, the steady shuffle of feet on gravel paths. Everything seemed brighter there, bigger than anything I'd ever seen.

At the entrance, my dad handed me money for two tickets and told us to stay together, to take care of each other.

He said he would come back when the zoo closed.

I must have been nine or ten. My brother was younger. We spent the day wandering freely, animal to animal, wonder carrying us forward. We stood close to the glass of exhibits, stared up at giraffes, watched elephants sway their massive bodies as if they were rocking babies to sleep.

It felt like freedom.

And then, somewhere along the way, we lost each other.

One distraction, one unmeasured step, and suddenly I was alone.

Panic didn't arrive loudly. It crept in, quiet and cold, tightening my chest. The crowd became a moving wall. Every face looked unfamiliar. My hands began to sweat. My throat tightened until swallowing felt difficult. I walked faster, then faster still, searching for the familiar shape of my brother's body, his shirt, his hair—anything.

I called his name, but my voice felt small against the noise.

We spent hours searching for one another before finally finding each other again.

When we did, we didn't cry. We didn't collapse into relief the way you might expect children to. We just stood there, breathing hard, eyes wide, as if both of us understood without saying it: we had disappeared too easily.

We never told our parents.

At the time, it felt like independence. Looking back, I see how thin the line was between trust and vulnerability. That afternoon planted something in me—a self-reliance born too early, paired with a silence that learned to keep fear to itself.

When our parents picked us up, they took us to a park. Above us, the sky was filled with kites—brilliant colors lifting against a crystal-blue expanse. The wind snapped their tails like flags. The strings hummed. Some were enormous, needing two people to guide them, pulling hard against the air as if they were alive.

My brother and I lay back in the grass and watched.

The kites reminded me of a rainforest I had once seen in a book—birds soaring freely overhead. We had never seen so many at once. So many shapes, so much color, so much movement against the open sky. It felt like the world was putting on a show just for us.

We stayed until night fell before beginning the long drive home.

Even now, when I see kites stretched across an open sky, my body remembers that moment—beauty arriving after fear, rest after vigilance. I did not yet know how to name gratitude, but I knew what it felt like to be held again by safety.

Our parents tried to give us experiences. Not because they had everything figured out, but because they didn't want our lives to shrink into the same limits they had been born into. They didn't always know how to give us stability, but they kept trying to give us something else:

memory, wonder, a sense that life could be larger than the block you lived on.

There was a park with a shallow public pool, only two or three feet deep. Often, my parents dropped my brother and me off there, and we swam until nearly closing time, watching for one of them to appear at the fence and call us home.

It was routine—until my dad discovered an indoor pool.

This pool was different. Vast. It ranged from three feet to twelve feet deep and had two diving boards. I didn't understand that yet. I believed all pools were like the shallow one we already knew. Feeling crowded in the shallow end, I decided to move to a quieter space.

I stepped into deeper water.

I didn't realize how far down it went until the bottom disappeared beneath my feet.

I jumped in anyway.

And then I was drowning.

The water was colder than I expected. It swallowed me whole. Chlorine burned my eyes and scraped my throat. I tried to breathe and sucked in water instead. It filled my mouth and nose, sharp and chemical, like my body had been tricked into drinking poison. My arms flailed wildly, slapping the surface, but I couldn't find balance. I couldn't find air.

The pool was crowded. People laughed and splashed. No one noticed.

My body panicked before my mind could. The world turned into noise and bubbles and the desperate pounding of my heart.

A girl wading nearby felt me grab her. She recognized what was happening and held onto me, guiding me back toward the shallow end. Her hands were steady, strong in a way mine were not. She saved me before I even understood I was being saved.

Before I could fully process what had happened, my father was already there.

He had jumped the fence.

I still see it in my mind like a scene frozen in time—his body cutting through space, his face sharp with fear, his hands reaching for me without hesitation. He was at the pool's edge, ready to dive in, pulling me out the moment he reached me. His grip was tight, almost painful, like he was trying to make sure I stayed in the world.

The lifeguards yelled at him. He yelled back, furious, cursing, accusing them of failing to watch.

His voice echoed off the walls of the indoor pool, loud and raw, the sound of a man who had almost lost something he didn't know how to live without.

We gathered our things and left.

As a child, that memory was terror—water, noise, helplessness.

As an adult, it is about rescue.

It is about a father who did not hesitate. About how quickly danger can arrive, and how fiercely love responds when it does. Long before I had language for faith, my body learned what deliverance felt like.

We spent many evenings at the park, mostly with my dad. He preferred going at night—less heat, fewer people. The air cooled and softened after sunset, and the streetlights made the basketball court glow like a small stage. He taught us how to throw and catch a football, how to play baseball. He bought us mitts and showed us how to stand, how to swing, how to aim.

We played basketball—two on two: my mom and me against my dad and my brother. We played around the world, laughing, competing, arguing over shots that didn't count, sweating through our shirts.

Sometimes we stayed so late we didn't get home until after midnight.

It may not have been ideal. We were often tired. But we were together. My parents didn't always protect routines, but they protected connection. They gave us presence instead of perfection, effort instead of ease.

Still working for Goodwill, my dad brought home tennis rackets and tried to teach us to play, though we didn't care much for tennis. What we loved was wall handball—fast and loud, the smack of the ball against concrete echoing like a heartbeat.

As far back as I can remember, we helped my dad check the oil in the car. He handed us old newspaper, showed us how to wipe the dipstick clean, how to measure what the engine needed. The smell of motor oil clung to our fingers. He talked while he worked—about life, about choices, about education.

He told us not to be like him.

Not in bitterness, but in hope.

"Monkey see, monkey do," he said. "Don't be like that."

I didn't realize then that these lessons were also confessions. Teaching us how to care for a car was his way of admitting he hadn't always known how to care for himself. When he warned us not to follow others, he was naming the roads he had already walked.

When my dad came home from jail, he read the Bible and made us read passages too. He loved the book of Revelation, though it frightened me. Faith in our home came in fragments—scripture after incarceration, church walks on Sunday mornings, warnings delivered with sincerity rather than certainty.

What stayed with me wasn't doctrine, but intention: the belief that our lives were meant for something better.

One Monday night, I stayed up late watching television with my mom when breaking news interrupted the program.

John Lennon had been shot.

The words flashed across the screen, and my mother's hand flew to her mouth. Her eyes filled instantly. Then she began to cry—quietly at first, then with a trembling sadness that made her shoulders shake.

She loved the Beatles. She sang their songs while she cleaned. She played their music often, filling our home with melodies that sounded like something brighter than our real life.

I didn't understand why she was crying for someone she didn't know.

"He has a wife and a son," she said, her voice cracking. "They'll miss him. He won't be there to watch his son grow up."

That night, my mother taught me compassion. She showed me grief does not require proximity—only recognition. She taught me that love extends beyond personal loss.

I didn't understand then.

I do now.

My parents were imperfect, struggling, and often overwhelmed. They were not storybook parents. They had addictions. They made mistakes. But threaded through everything was effort—real, human effort. Even in their brokenness, they were reaching for something better, stretching toward it, trying to build a bridge out of what little they had.

They didn't always know how to give us stability.

But they gave us moments.

They gave us parks and zoos and long nights under streetlights. They gave us laughter and danger and rescue. They gave us lessons spoken like warnings, and tenderness that showed up in unexpected places. They gave us love the only way they knew how—through trying, through showing up, through refusing to let our world stay small.

Now, with my own children, I keep what was life-giving and release the rest. I read with them. I build puzzles. I show up. In their own way, my parents were planting seeds—instilling values, teaching us how to live, even when they were still learning themselves.

And some of those seeds grew.

I understand today that love in our home rarely announced itself. It moved quietly through ordinary days—through promises kept even when bodies were tired or in pain, through late nights that stretched past bedtime, through hands that reached for us before we could even ask.

My parents did not always know the right words, and sometimes they did not know the right way. But they showed up anyway, trusting that something larger than themselves was at work.

Faith did not live loudly in our house. It lingered in fragments—in gestures, in the unspoken hope that what was offered in sincerity might be enough.

As a child, I absorbed these moments without understanding them, storing them somewhere deep in my body. As an adult, I recognize them as grace—unpolished, imperfect, but persistent.

What was planted then did not bloom quickly or evenly. But it endured. My father wanted us to see a wider world—and somehow, even with all his brokenness, he gave it to us.

Thoughts

As an adult, I understand my parents weren't trying to give us a perfect childhood—they were trying to give us a larger one. They didn't always know how to create stability, but they offered what they could: effort, presence, and moments that stretched beyond the limits of our neighborhood. My father's love often came disguised as endurance, my mother's as tenderness that reached even strangers. And somehow, through their imperfections, they still managed to plant something lasting in me—the belief that love is not always gentle, but it is meant to show up.

Chapter 14

Your scars tell beautiful stories
— Billy Chapata

One afternoon, my dad dropped my mom and my sister off at my grandparents' house. He had tickets to an amateur boxing match, something he'd been looking forward to, and some of his friends were meeting us beforehand. Before the fight, we stopped at their place near downtown Los Angeles—a narrow, three-story building that felt enormous to me.

There was a fire escape outside the building. My dad told my brother and me to wait there while he ran inside. None of us noticed that the ladder had been left open.

I was ten years old. I didn't know what fire escapes were for or how easily a body could slip through space. I only knew music and movement and the pleasure of being loud without consequence. My brother and I stood there together, and I sang and danced to the newest McDonald's commercial—the one everyone knew in 1981. I remember feeling happy. Loose. Unwatched.

Then the floor disappeared.

At first, my mind couldn't make sense of what my body was doing. I wasn't standing anymore. I wasn't dancing. I was falling. My brother reached for me, his small hands grabbing air, and I remember his face more than anything else—wide-eyed, terrified, helpless.

What followed doesn't live in language easily.

I knew I was falling, but I was also somewhere else. I saw my brother run to the door and bang on it with everything he had. I saw my dad burst out and race down the stairs, jumping the railing in two steps. It was as if I were floating above the scene, watching it unfold without sound, without weight.

Then I was back.

Back in my body. Back in pain. Back in my father's arms.

That's when I started to cry.

Blood ran down my face—from my nose, my mouth, my chin. My dad kept asking if I was okay, his hands shaking as he checked me over. My ankle and leg were already swelling. My chin burned. My mouth tasted like metal. One of my front teeth was broken.

I didn't understand then that my nose had been badly broken. That knowledge would come decades later, folded quietly into memory.

My dad looked scared. He said maybe we shouldn't go to the fight. Something inside me panicked at the idea of plans changing, of things breaking further. My brother and I begged him. I told him I was fine. I needed him to believe me. I needed the day to keep going.

He stopped at a convenience store. Bought a beer. Bought Tylenol. He told me to take a sip to calm myself and handed me two pills. He thought about calling my mom. I begged him not to.

"Daddy, I'm okay," I said. "Please."

He agreed, but only if I promised to tell him if I felt bad in any way.

"I promise," I said quickly. I always promised.

The boxing match was loud and bright and full of noise. We ate candy and junk food and drank soda. I laughed. I felt proud that I had survived something without stopping the world.

Later that night, we picked up my mom and sister. When my dad told my mom what had happened, she insisted we go to the emergency room. Even through the haze of alcohol, she could hear the danger in his voice.

The doctor examined me and said, "You are a fortunate young lady."

It's nothing short of a miracle I'm here. I didn't know then how close I'd come to something else. I only knew that I was hurt, and that somehow, I had landed back in the arms that knew me.

Not long after that, my dad was arrested again. This time it was serious. He was facing years. Life reorganized itself quietly around his absence.

Tío Richie stopped staying with us regularly. My mom began attending a business trade school, learning how to work the new computers—the kind that used punch cards. She rode the bus every day. Her drinking hadn't disappeared, but it had softened around the edges.

We found a rhythm without my dad.

I was finishing fifth grade. My brother, third. My sister was only three, in Head Start. We walked to school. We walked home. We learned how to be small and steady.

Weekends were spent at the county jail. Before or after visits, my mom often took us to the movies. That was her refuge. Sitting in the dark, watching other lives unfold on a screen. She bought us crayons and markers and coloring books. She taped our drawings to the walls, as if she needed proof that something good was still growing.

In June of 1982, she took us to see *E.T.* She loved it so much we saw it three times. Popcorn, soda, churros for my brother. When my dad was gone, she leaned toward us more, as if trying to close a distance she hadn't known was there.

At the bus stop, there was a Chinese restaurant. She loved Chicken Chow Mein and often bought enough for all of us. We ate from white cartons, steam rising between us, waiting for the bus to carry us home.

Eventually, my mom listened to her parents. In the fall of 1982, we packed what we could and gave the rest away. Our next place would be smaller. We were learning, again, how to leave.

I was eleven. My brother nearly nine. My sister four. My mom twenty-nine. My dad thirty-two.

We moved to East Los Angeles, next door to my maternal grandparents. Up to this point I had only lived in predominately black neighborhoods. It was a different neighborhood, a different soundscape, a different kind of belonging. We moved without my dad—and without knowing when or how he would return.

When my aunt Carmen came to visit with her new family, she looked genuinely happy. I remember noticing it, quietly, and wishing my mom looked like that. My mom was so thin from the heroin use, her body bearing the marks of what she'd survived. She wasn't using anymore, but she was still drinking. Still pushing forward. Still trying.

Then, unexpectedly, my dad came home.

My paternal grandparents had hired a lawyer. He was released sooner than anyone expected. Both sets of grandparents gathered the day he returned. The tension between them filled the room, heavy and unspoken. His parents took the yellow station wagon in exchange for the lawyer's fees.

My dad didn't love living next door to my mom's parents, but he stayed.

Thoughts

Sometimes I think about that fire escape—how quickly the ground vanished, how easily I slipped through space. How I learned, without words, that things can fall apart in an instant and still keep going.

I think about my mother during those years—how she held everything together even when she didn't feel held herself.

And I wonder who I became because of it.

I don't remember the sound of my body hitting the ground. What I remember is the feeling of leaving myself—and how easy it was.

That moment taught me something before I had words for it: if things move too fast, I can float. I can watch instead of feel. I can survive by stepping just outside my body and returning later, when it's safer.

For a long time, I mistook that ability for strength.

I learned how to promise quickly. How to say I was fine when I wasn't. How to keep the day moving so no one had to stop for me. I learned how to hold still inside chaos, how to make myself small enough to fit whatever space was left.

When my father left and then came back, when our lives rearranged themselves and pretended nothing had changed, I followed the pattern I already knew. I adjusted. I adapted. I didn't ask for more than what was offered.

Only now can I see how much my body remembered—how it braced even when my mind moved on, how it carried the fall long after the bruises faded.

I was a child who fell through a gap and landed in her father's arms.

I became an adult who spent years learning how to land inside herself.

Chapter 15

Sticks and stones may break my bones
But names shall never hurt me.

When we moved to East Los Angeles, my brother and I started school at Ford Boulevard Elementary. I was in sixth grade; he was in fourth. The school year had already begun, so the moment we walked into our classrooms, we were marked—the new kids. Being new is always hard. Friendships had already taken root, desks already claimed. There was no empty space waiting for us.

My brother and I walked to school together at first. Not long after, he got a small job through the school office as a flag monitor. He made friends easily. He always had. That year, in fourth grade, his love for the flag took hold—something steady and honorable he could belong to. Years later, he would carry that same pride into the Navy. Even then, he walked with purpose.

Soon he began leaving earlier than I did, stepping ahead into his own independence.

I stayed behind and slowly found my way. I became friends with the girl who lived next door—Patty. She was in my grade but in a different classroom. We walked to school together, met up at recess, and before long, she felt like mine. After school, a small group of us walked home together, several of us living along Brannick Street. For the first time since the move, I felt something loosen in my chest.

But not everything softened.

My grandmother lived next door, and my cousin Simon—twenty years old when I was eleven—came by often to do yard work for her. Simon never called me by my name. He called me *Ugly*. He said it like a joke, like something affectionate. He said it every time he saw me. Over three years, the word settled into me, quiet and permanent, shaping how I would see myself long after he stopped saying it.

One afternoon, walking home from school, a girl began teasing my brother. She mocked him for being bald. We'd had lice, and one of my parents' solutions had been to cut hair—my brother's and my sister's. Mine survived only because I fought for it. Diana.

At first, we ignored her. I told my brother to walk closer to me, just in case. Our route took us south from the school to Olympic Boulevard, then west to Eastern Avenue, across the overpass that stretched above the freeway. Cars roared beneath us. It was there that she grabbed my brother's baseball cap.

I yelled for her to give it back. She laughed, tossed it into the air, taunting us. *Come get it.*

I handed my backpack to my brother.

"You wait here," I told him. "Don't move."

I walked toward her and demanded the cap. She put it on her head and turned away. When I reached for her shoulder, she pulled back. I grabbed her blouse. It tore. She swung at me. The first punch missed. The second landed hard against my cheek. Then another to my stomach, knocking the breath from me.

Fear rushed in fast and hot. I saw her torn blouse, her hand still gripping the cap. Something in me shifted—not rage, not thought—just instinct. I rushed her. She fell. Her head hit the concrete.

I climbed on top of her and struck her face. Blood bloomed from her nose and lip.

The sight of it startled me back into myself. I jumped up, grabbed the cap, and walked back to my brother and sister. "Let's go home," I said. Behind us, her friends helped her to her feet. No one followed.

We didn't speak of it.

Later that afternoon, my grandmother leaned out her kitchen window and called for my mother. That wasn't unusual. But this time, it carried weight. Diana's grandmother had called to complain about the torn blouse.

When my mother called for me, I walked into my grandmother's house with shaking hands. I told them everything. To my surprise, they believed me. My grandmother called Diana's grandmother back and let loose a string of curses that filled the room. She refused to buy a new blouse and offered instead to sew the torn one.

My grandmother was a gifted seamstress. She could recreate a dress from a photograph alone. She made me beautiful things—dresses I picked from magazines, tailored just for me. Once, she made me a red pantsuit with white polka dots. I wore it proudly to school picture day—and never again. The teasing was relentless. I never told my mother. I learned early how to swallow pride.

After my grandmother repaired the blouse, Diana never bothered my brother or my friends again.

Most afternoons, we rushed home to clean before my mom returned from school. Some days my brother helped. Some days we argued. I spent many afternoons with Patty. She loved playing Barbies. I felt awkward, unsure of the rules, but I played anyway. Friendship felt worth the discomfort.

Patty was the youngest of four. Her older brother Gustavo was a year older than me and already at Robert Louis Stevenson Middle School. He dressed like a cholo—plaid shirts, Dickies, confidence. He was my first crush, though I didn't yet have a name for the feeling.

When parent-teacher conferences came around, I hoped my mother would forget.

She didn't.

She arrived intoxicated. I noticed the crooked seam of her pants, the way her clothes didn't quite align. She spoke with my siblings' teachers first, then mine. I wanted to disappear. But on the walk home, as the alcohol softened, she told us how proud she was of our grades. The real her surfaced—the one who loved us.

The next day at school, I overheard teachers whispering about her. About the smell of alcohol. About her clothes. They looked at me. I stared at my desk and waited for recess.

That year, I became friends with Monica, a girl no one else liked. She had bad breath and was bullied for it. I recognized something familiar in her isolation. We ate lunch together. I defended her when others wouldn't.

At home, the tension thickened.

One night, my mother—drunk and furious—stood my brother and me in front of her. She hurt me in ways I didn't yet have language for. I cried. She hit me. When my father came home, she lied. He believed her.

At school not long after, a former student visited our classroom and guided us through a meditation. We lay on the floor, eyes closed, following a path through a forest toward light. I was hungry for anything unseen—ghosts, astrology, signs. Soon, strange things seemed to happen in our apartment: shadows in the hallway, lights flickering. My grandmother said a boy had once died there. Whether it was true or not, the story fit the feeling of that place.

Looking back now, I see it clearly: I was born a fighter. I fought for my brother. I fought for my friends. Fighting for myself was harder. I didn't yet know what I deserved.

My grandmother did. She stood up for me. She stitched care into fabric. Late at night, I would watch her sew, the hum of the machine steady, the light warm on her hands. Thread pulled tight. Seams aligned.

She always made things that fit.

<u>Thoughts</u>

It took me years to understand that some wounds don't bruise. They don't swell or bleed. They settle quietly into the body and learn how to wait.

As a child, I didn't have language for what was happening to me. I only knew what it felt like—to flinch at certain tones, to scan faces for danger, to brace myself before speaking. I learned early that words could be weapons, and that love and harm sometimes came from the same mouth. When you are small, you don't question that contradiction. You adapt to it.

I was called names often enough that they began to sound like facts. Ugly. Useless. Only good for one thing. I didn't argue with those words. I absorbed them. Children do. We don't yet know how to separate who we are from what we are told we are.

What no one explains is how verbal cruelty teaches silence. It trains a child to guard their inner life, to hide what matters, to offer only what feels safe. I learned not to share joy too loudly, not to admit fear, not to ask for too much. I learned how to be useful, agreeable, strong. I did not learn how to be protected.

I fought when others were threatened. That came easily. Defending myself felt foreign, even wrong. Somewhere along the way, I learned that my pain was inconvenient, that my needs created trouble. So I became good at enduring. I became skilled at minimizing. I became practiced at surviving.

Looking back now, I can see how deeply those early lessons shaped me. The vigilance. The self-doubt. The voice inside my head that replayed old insults long after the speakers were gone. I carried those echoes into classrooms, friendships, marriages, and motherhood. Sometimes I mistook that voice for truth.

But time does something important—it gives us distance. And distance allows us to name what once felt unspeakable.

I can now see my mother as both loving and deeply ill. I can honor my grandmother's protection without pretending it erased the harm. I can hold compassion and grief in the same breath. None of this excuses what happened. But it explains how it continued.

Healing did not come all at once. It arrived slowly, through recognition. Through learning that the way someone treats you is not a measure of your worth. Through understanding that a child should never have to earn safety. Through realizing that resilience, while admirable, is not the same as wholeness.

What I know now is this: words shape us. They wire themselves into memory, posture, breath. But words can also be reclaimed. Rewritten. Spoken back with intention.

The child I was survived because she learned how to endure. The woman I am heals by learning how to listen—to herself.

And that, finally, feels like a different kind of strength.

Chapter 16

Jesus answered, "It is written:
'Man shall not live on bread alone, but on every
word that comes from the mouth of God.'
Matthew 4:4 NIV

1983-1984

In early 1983, my Tía Ruth came to Los Angeles looking for my Tío Richie, who had drifted so far from the family that even his name felt fragile when spoken aloud. She tried to convince him to return with her to El Paso, to come home where my grandparents still believed love could outpace addiction.

While she was there, I asked her if I could go with her.

I didn't say *why*. Children rarely do. I just said I wanted to live with her, as if wanting were enough to explain itself. She told me that if I kept my grades up, she would consider it. From that day on, every report card became a kind of prayer. I mailed them to her like proof of worthiness—evidence that I could be good enough to be taken somewhere else.

But my Tío Richie didn't go back with her. And neither did I.

Later that year, my Uncle Robert came looking for him too. He stayed only a few days and left the same way—empty-handed. It wasn't until much later that my mother told me the truth: Richie was addicted to cocaine, and the family was trying to bring him home so my grandparents could help him. Rehab, or at least the hope of it.

That year, hunger began to shape the days.

My mother had stopped going to school after a car accident left her injured. I remember my Grandpa Jose rubbing her lower back, his hands moving slowly, reverently, as if pain might loosen if treated gently enough. Lawyers were hired. Lawsuits were filed. On paper, help was coming.

In our kitchen, the cupboards were bare.

We had welfare and food stamps, but still—no milk, no bread, no sugar, no beans, no potatoes. Hunger wasn't dramatic; it was quiet and persistent, like something that learned our schedule. Sometimes my mother sent me next door to ask for sugar or money. I hated it. I stood at the door rehearsing my lines, my face burning with a shame I didn't yet have words for.

Even though my mother's parents lived right next door, my father would not allow her to tell them how bad things were. Pride was another thing we learned to live on.

In food lines, we were given powdered milk, eggs, peanut butter, and blocks of government cheese. The peanut butter was so thick it bent spoons. The powdered milk tasted like compromise. My father tried to convince us it was real—poured carefully into a gallon jug, sealed with hope—but we always knew.

You drink powdered milk when you have no choice.

The cheese, though—that cheese was gold. Thick slices eaten plain, standing at our kitchen counter. Even now, I remember it as abundance.

Hunger taught us discernment. It taught us what was worth savoring.

One day I stayed home from school, and a social worker knocked on the door. Someone had reported that my sister looked malnourished. I told the woman my parents weren't home. She asked to come in and wait. I said no. I told her everyone on my father's side was thin. I showed her the liquid vitamins my sister took.

When she asked to wash her hands, I believed her.

Shame has a way of disguising itself as politeness.

The house wasn't clean enough. Soon, Child Protective Services was involved. I felt responsible in the way children do—entirely, irrationally. My father told me it wasn't my fault, that from now on we had to stick together so no one would take us away.

Fear, too, became something we swallowed.

My father worked through Manpower—lining up early, hoping to be chosen. One day he wasn't. He came home carrying disappointment like an extra limb. We asked to go to the park. On the way, he drove past warehouses, scanning groups of men shooting dice, looking for my Tío Richie.

When he found him, the humiliation was quick and public. A twenty-dollar bill tossed to the ground. Laughter. A turned back. A raised finger. My father said nothing when he returned to the car. He just drove us to the park and watched us play, as if joy might still be salvaged in small doses.

Later, he bought groceries—milk, bread, bologna, beans, potatoes. My mother was grateful in the way people are when survival briefly loosens its grip.

Our car—a 1965 Plymouth Belvedere—was held together with wire hangers and stubbornness. The bumper sagged. The doors flew open. The trunk was tied shut. My father parked it a block away, as if even the street didn't need to see how close we were to falling apart.

I was ashamed of that car. I ducked down when he dropped me off at school. I thought shame belonged to me.

I didn't yet know it belonged to circumstance.

When the car was stolen, something in my father cracked. He threw his Bible into the trash and said he was done believing. My mother pulled it back out and said she wasn't.

Faith, in our house, was not gentle. It was argued over.

Wrestled with. Thrown away and retrieved.

When my father found the car again—stuffed with stolen food from a restaurant—the police told him to keep it. Steaks. Rice. Cheese. Chiles. Tortillas. Milk. Eggs.

We ate like grace had finally found our address.

Looking back now, I see how hunger, faith, and shame braided themselves through our lives. Hunger taught us endurance. Shame taught us silence. Faith—imperfect and frayed—taught us how to keep going even when belief felt like a luxury.

My parents were in the same rowboat, facing storms with one paddle, going in circles. But somehow, we didn't drown.

We learned what to swallow.

And what, despite everything, to keep.

Thoughts

I carried those years with me longer than I realized. Hunger taught me to measure worth in portions—to believe that having enough meant *being* enough, and that scarcity was a personal failure instead of a circumstance. Even now, I feel safest when the pantry is full, when food is not just nourishment but proof that I am no longer one missed paycheck away from vanishing.

Faith became complicated. I learned it first as endurance, not comfort—a muscle you flex when there is nothing else to hold onto. I believed in God the way my mother did: fiercely, imperfectly, sometimes desperately. I also learned how easily belief can fracture under shame, how quickly gratitude can turn into guilt when survival feels undeserved.

Chapter 16

And shame—shame lingered the longest. It taught me to make myself small, to duck down, to swallow need without complaint. It convinced me that wanting more meant being ungrateful, that asking for help risked being exposed.

Only as an adult did I understand this: there was nothing wrong with wanting to be fed, to be safe, to be seen. Worth was never something I had to earn with good grades, clean kitchens, or quiet endurance.

I was already worthy.

I just didn't know it yet.

Chapter 17

Yes, Mother. I can see you are flawed.
You have not hidden it. That is your greatest gift to me.
— Alice Walker

Even after God had revealed Himself to my parents—after the miracles, the narrow escapes—they were still not ready to turn their lives around. Faith brushed past them, but addiction held tighter. My parents were using heroin, again.

One afternoon, they were high—floating somewhere far above the ground. I had been outside playing with my friend Ruth when I felt the familiar urgency and told her I needed to use the bathroom.

"I'll be right back," I said.

"Well, hurry up," she called after me.

I ran inside. My dad was in the front room, hunched over the radio, turning the dial back and forth as if clarity might suddenly come through static.

"What's the hurry?" he asked.

"Nothing, Dad. I just need the bathroom."

I ran down the hallway and pushed the door open—and that is when the world split open.

My mother was sitting on the toilet. Her skin was pale, almost gray. Her lips held a bluish tint, like breath had already begun to leave her. I nudged her.

"Mom… wake up."

She didn't move.

I yelled for my dad. He rushed in and lifted her like a rag doll, shaking her, calling her name, begging her to wake up. She didn't respond.

My body flooded with adrenaline. I ran to the kitchen, grabbed a glass, poured warm water, added salt—because, I had learned from father that this helps because it had done so before. My dad laid her on the bed and prepared a syringe with salt water. He injected her. Tried to make her walk. Pounded on her chest. Nothing worked.

Then he turned to me and said, "Go next door. Call 911."

I ran to my grandparents' house and told my grandmother what was happening. As I dialed, my hands shook. I explained to the operator that my mother wasn't breathing.

My grandmother was furious—not afraid, not worried. Furious. She cursed my father and said, in Spanish,

"Ojalá que tu mamá muera para que tu padre se vaya a la cárcel por asesinato."

I hope your mother dies so your father goes to prison for murder.

Something in me snapped.

"I hope you die—old and alone," I yelled back,

slamming the screen door so hard I hoped it would break.

I ran home. My dad was still trying CPR when the EMTs arrived. They took over. Chest compressions. One shock—no response. A second shock—and suddenly, her heart began to beat again. She woke up.

They wanted to take her to the hospital. My father refused. They asked her questions. She answered just enough. Paperwork was signed. Equipment packed away. And just like that, they left.

Our nerves were shredded. Emotions ricocheted through the room with nowhere to land. My dad, seeing how shaken we were, gave us a sip of his beer to "calm us down."

We never spoke about what happened that day, this was not the first time she had almost died. This was the first time we had to call 911 to revive her.

My parents said my mother had a weak heart.

My brother and I knew better.

This was just our normal.

Family in El Paso never knew what we lived through.

Eventually, things returned to their version of "normal."

In December of 1983, my father was incarcerated again.

Whenever my mother went to the liquor store at night, I went with her. Outside, a group of boys always loitered. As we approached, they mocked her unsteady walk. One boy—Chepe—usually led the taunts. He had long hair, like many of the rockers back then.

The store was owned by Koreans. I never understood how they kept selling her liquor when she could barely stand, but they did. They always did.

One night, I'd had enough.

As we exited the store, Chepe stood closest to the door. Before he could react, I grabbed a fistful of his hair from behind and yanked him down onto the concrete. His friends froze in shock.

I climbed on top of him and started punching. Rage poured out of me—years of swallowed anger finally finding a body to land on. My mother tried to pull me off him, tugging at my arm. I shook her off and kept hitting until I saw blood.

Then fear hit me.

I jumped off him and looked for my mom. She stood off to the side, stunned.

"Let's go," I said.

I turned back to the boys and screamed,

"Make fun of her again, assholes!"

They never did.

That winter, my father was being held closer to East Los Angeles, with weekday visitations. We were on winter break. My brother stayed with a friend to play Atari. My little sister stayed with the friend's sister.

I went with my mom, as I always did.

After visiting my dad, we sat at a bus stop when a car pulled over and offered us a ride. My mom smiled and said yes. She told me to get in the back seat.

Then I recognized him.

"Tío!" I said.

"Hi, sweety," he replied.

It was Tío Richie.

He drove us to a parking lot. My mom told him about my dad and asked if he could take her to the grocery store. He agreed.

When we arrived, she got out and told me to wait in the car. My Tío told me to move to the front seat. As we drove, he took my hand and caressed it.

"You're so beautiful," he said. "You've grown so much."

My stomach tightened.

He touched my leg.

Told me if I ever needed anything, he'd be there for me.

When my mom finished shopping, he drove us home and helped unload groceries. Later, my brother showed him a picture of Jesus with the verse *"I am the way, the truth, and the life."* Tío Richie said he didn't believe in that sort of thing.

That night, my mom invited him to stay over.

"You can sleep in Rosa's bed," she said. "She'll sleep with me."

I climbed into her bed, telling myself he wouldn't bother me this time. I was wrong. As they watched television, she sat at the corner of the bed and my Tío Richie joined her on the other corner.

As I drifted toward sleep, I felt his arm slide under the blankets. I froze. I pretended to be asleep. My mother was drunk. I knew if I spoke, I would be the one punished.

When she got up to use the restroom, he leaned over me and kissed me—slow, wet, deliberate.

When she returned, he acted like nothing had happened.

I pretended to have a nightmare and kicked him.

He pulled away. My mom told him I was just dreaming.

That night—**December 23, 1983**—

was the last time he ever touched me.

Three months and eighteen days later, on **April 10, 1984**,

he murdered nine-year-old Mei "Linda" Leung in the basement.

From age six to twelve, for six years and four months, he abused me.

I am not a therapist. I can only speak from experience.

That abuse reshaped my understanding of safety, trust, and self-worth. It seeded shame where innocence once lived. It taught me to freeze, to disappear, to survive by silence. I grew hypervigilant, anxious, angry, sorrowful. I learned to expect betrayal before kindness arrived.

Even now, I still have nightmares. In them, he is alive, chasing me because I have spoken out.

Trauma does not stay in the past. It lives in the body, in memory, in breath. The mind tries to protect itself—sometimes by forgetting, sometimes by remembering too vividly.

These responses were never weaknesses. They were survival. And I am still here.

<u>Thoughts</u>

Looking back now, I understand that what stayed with me most was not the violence itself, but the silence that followed it. The way catastrophe could pass through our home and leave no language behind. We learned how to survive by not naming things, by smoothing over the unspeakable until it disappeared into routine. Love, danger, faith, and betrayal lived side by side, indistinguishable in the dark.

As a child, I believed endurance was the same as strength. I believed staying quiet was a kind of loyalty. I did not yet know that my body was keeping a record my mouth was not allowed to speak, or that fear could settle into the bones and call itself normal. I grew up learning how to listen for footsteps, how to read moods like weather, how to protect others while neglecting myself.

As an adult, I see how early I learned to stand watch over the world instead of living inside it. How often I confused hypervigilance for love, vigilance for safety. I carried the responsibility long after the danger had passed, as if laying it down might invite the past to return. I mistook survival for identity.

What I know now is this: silence kept me alive, but it also kept me small. Naming the truth does not erase what happened, but it loosens its grip. Speaking is not betrayal—it is release. And in telling this story, I am no longer the child bracing in the dark. I am the witness. I am the one who lived.

Chapter 18

What's Love Got to Do with It?
— Tina Turner 1984

As the city prepared for the 1984 Summer Olympics and Tina Turner climbed the charts with *"What's Love Got to Do With It,"* my body was learning two languages at once.

One was fear. The other was awakening.

May of 1984—right before we left for El Paso—was the first time those two languages collided.

The neighbor upstairs had a son named Guillermo, though everyone called him Memo. He was a rocker, with shoulder-length wavy hair and an ease about him that made him seem older than he was. He was in ninth grade, moving back and forth between his mom and his dad, who lived upstairs from us. By then, Patty and her family had moved away to Bakersfield, and the neighborhood felt altered, as if something familiar had quietly slipped out of place.

It was the summer before I began eighth grade. My parents were still struggling with their demons, but we kids were growing older and spending most of our afternoons outside with friends. Evenings belonged to us—playing tag and hide-and-seek with the neighborhood kids. By then, there were twelve of us, running wild through the dusk.

Late spring, right before summer, was my favorite time of the year. In the evenings as the sun would begin to set, music drifting from somewhere nearby, and we'd lean against parked cars, laughing and talking. Those hours mattered because whatever lived inside the house stayed out of sight. I hurried home after school to get things in order before my dad arrived. If there was something I could cook, I did. We never sat down together to eat. Everyone served themselves and plopped down in front of the television, plates balanced in one hand, forks in the other, drinks placed on the floor beside us. No TV trays. Just habit and hunger.

When we were outside, my dad would flick the porch light on and off—a signal that it was time to come inside, or that he wanted to speak to us.

Some nights, after everyone else had gone in, Memo and I lingered. We talked about the future—whether there would be flying cars, what it might feel like to be grown and on our own. Would we still know each other? Would we remember these nights? We argued about pop versus rock music, about which mattered more, as if we were debating something harmless and not rehearsing how to dream.

One night, in the middle of laughter, everything went quiet.

Memo lifted my chin and kissed me—slow, deliberate, lingering. And just like that, my body betrayed me. The familiarity of it tightened my chest, shortened my breath. The moment collapsed inward, folding over itself.

It reminded me of the kiss my Tío Richie had once given me.

When Memo pulled away, I ran inside.

I didn't yet understand that my body had learned fear before it learned joy—that it couldn't tell the difference between affection and harm. All it knew was that closeness had once meant danger, and danger had learned how to disguise itself as tenderness.

I avoided Memo for days. When he finally stopped me as I was bringing laundry in from the clothesline, his voice carried confusion, not menace.

"Why are you avoiding me?"

"I'm not," I lied.

"If I did something wrong the other night, I'm sorry," he said.

"I thought you liked me too."

Inside, I was screaming *I do.*

But fear had already taught me silence.

A few nights later, Memo joined us again outside. Everything returned to how it had been—jokes, laughter, tag, hide-and-seek. Still, something in me stayed alert, watching my own reactions, unsure whether my body would betray me again.

At the end of the night, my brother and sister ran inside. Memo called me over to the stairs as he headed home.

"I miss you," he said. "I miss our talks."

"Really?" I asked. "Me too."

"Do you like me?"

I couldn't say it, so I nodded.

This time, he held my face gently, as if asking permission. Our lips met softly, opening just enough to meet each other halfway.

And my body answered.

Not with panic.

Not with fear.

But with electricity.

A rush moved through me—warm, alive, unmistakable. This kiss didn't steal my breath; it gave it back. It didn't collapse me inward; it expanded me outward. For the first time, my body recognized the difference between being taken and being chosen.

That was my first real kiss.

A welcome kiss doesn't confuse the body—it awakens it. It imprints itself not as a wound, but as a memory worth keeping.

I left for El Paso the following week. Part of me didn't want to go because of Memo—but El Paso was also my escape.

When my brother and I arrived, my Tía Ruth discovered we had lice. She was furious. Angry that we hadn't told her. Angry that my mom hadn't taken care of it. Angry that we'd brought it into her home. Shame burned through me as I stood there, head bowed, my body already practiced at shrinking.

And then she sat down.

She placed my head in her lap.

No rush.

No punishment.

No harm.

For hours, she combed through my hair—slowly, patiently, section by section. Her fingers were firm but careful. She didn't yank. She didn't sigh. She didn't leave when it grew tedious. Each pass of the comb felt deliberate, as if she were saying without words: *You are worth the time this takes.*

That kind of touch does something different to a body.

It doesn't electrify.

It steadies.

Between her legs, my head heavy in her lap, I felt something loosen that I hadn't known was clenched. This was touch without danger. Contact without consequence. Care that stayed.

She did the same for my brother, day after day, until there was nothing left to remove.

She didn't know what else needed tending. She didn't know how much of me had learned to flinch. But her hands were already teaching my body what safety felt like—slow, repetitive, patient. The opposite of harm.

When I returned to Los Angeles, I tried to do the same for my six-year-old sister. Without the proper shampoo and comb, I failed. In the end, my parents shaved her head. The worst part wasn't the haircut—it was that she had to go to school like that, carrying the evidence of what adults couldn't fix.

I see it now: the kiss and the comb were speaking to the same wound.

One awakened my body to pleasure without fear.

The other taught it endurance without pain.

Harm rushes.

Care takes its time.

Violation leaves you frozen.

Care lets you soften.

Years later, I would learn about serotonin and dopamine, about the chemistry of connection. But back then, all I knew was this: my body remembered the difference. It knew fear when it felt it. And it knew—finally—what it meant to feel safe.

As poor as we were, as broken as our home was, we were never placed in foster care. And I know without doubt that if that had ever happened, my Tía Ruth would have been on a plane to Los Angeles without hesitation. She would never have allowed us to be lost.

Because she already hadn't.

She crossed the invisible border between neglect and care every time she sat down and combed our hair. She crossed it every time she chose patience over convenience. She crossed it without knowing that she was teaching a damaged body how to trust touch again.

When I think of my first kiss now, I don't remember just the electricity. I remember the quiet afterward—the way my body knew it had not been harmed.

And when I think of my Tía Ruth, I don't remember her anger.

I remember her hands.

Both moments told me the same thing, in different languages:

Not all touch is danger.

Not all closeness takes something from you.

Some hands are here to give.

<u>Thoughts</u>

It took me years to understand that my body was not betraying me back then—it was protecting me. It remembered what my mouth could not say, what my mind was not yet ready to name. Fear and joy lived side by side, and my body learned to tell them apart long before I did.

I have faith—real faith—in God. Not the kind that arrives with certainty or answers, but the kind that reveals itself slowly, through patience and care. I believe now that God does not always come as rescue. Sometimes He comes as repetition. As endurance. As hands that return again and again to the same small task until something wounded can finally rest.

Sometimes God comes as a kiss that asks instead of takes.

Sometimes as a woman sitting with a child's head in her lap, combing through what has been neglected without turning away.

What saved me was not one moment, but many—

small mercies layered over time.

Touch that did not harm.

Presence that did not leave.

Love that did not demand payment.

My faith lives there—in the quiet evidence that God can be felt in the body before He is understood by the mind, and that even in chaos, He finds ways to reach us through human hands.

I did not know it then, but I was being taught how to trust again.

Slowly. Gently. One careful touch at a time.

Chapter 19

She works hard for the money
So hard for it, honey
She works hard for the money
So you better treat her right
She Works Hard for the Money by Donna Summers 1983

At the end of summer 1984, when I returned from El Paso, my mother had found a job as a receptionist at a warehouse within walking distance of our home. She managed the invoices—paper moving in and out like a controlled current—and for the first time in a long while, there was a faint suggestion of steadiness. Around that same time, I was accepted into a magnet school. I felt proud, though pride arrived tangled with anxiety. When I told my dad, he said it was a great opportunity, and I held onto his words as if they might anchor me.

The school sat in a wealthy neighborhood and offered things my old school never had—photography, art, clubs, and a sense of possibility I'd never quite felt before. It was like stepping into another version of life, one where doors opened easily and people assumed the future would meet them halfway. In photography class, we were required to buy a 35mm camera and film. At the time, it sounded like a simple detail. Later, I would understand it as the quiet hinge on which everything turned.

The school was diverse, but I still felt out of place, as if I'd arrived without knowing the unspoken rules. Eventually, I found a group of Hispanic girls who had been there the year before. They welcomed me without interrogation. They introduced me to bagels and cream cheese—something I'd never tasted before. Most days, I brought my own lunch, when there was food at home. Other days, I didn't eat at all, unsure whether the school even offered free lunch. One day, when I had nothing, one of the girls split her bagel in half and handed it to me. I took it quietly. Hunger has a way of teaching you how heavy kindness can feel. I never forgot that moment.

Getting to school was an ordeal. The bus stop was half a mile away, at Dennison Street and Downey Road, and the ride itself took nearly an hour each way. I left home before sunrise and returned at dusk. I hated being so far away. Distance felt dangerous. Every day, the same questions followed me onto the bus and back again: Was Mom drinking? Were my brother and sister safe? Who would protect them if she lost control again?

The dread of opening our front door at the end of the day was almost unbearable. *Unpredictable* doesn't begin to describe what waited on the other side. Like many children raised by alcoholics, I had developed a reflexive sense of hyper-responsibility—a belief that it was my job to hold everything together. I felt accountable for things I could not possibly control, especially with a father who loved us deeply but wasn't home often enough to stop the chaos.

During the first week at the magnet school, each teacher went over classroom rules and supply lists. Rules were fine. Supplies were not. When the photography teacher announced we'd need a 35mm camera, my stomach dropped. I knew better than to ask. I knew my family couldn't afford it. I never told my parents.

Instead, one morning while my dad and I sat in his car waiting at the bus stop, he asked how I liked the new school. I lied. I told him I didn't like it—that the teachers favored the kids who had money. He didn't argue or push back. He simply said that if I didn't feel comfortable, I could go back to my old school.

And that was that.

I returned to Robert Louis Stevenson Junior High the following week. They didn't offer photography, but they offered something the magnet school never could: closeness. I was near home. I signed up for home economics—half sewing, half cooking—and I loved it. When my grandma heard I was taking sewing, she was thrilled. She bought all my supplies. I made a denim duffel bag and hot plate holders, proud of each careful stitch, proud of something I could finish and hold in my hands.

My last class of the day was English, taught by a woman who had no classroom management skills. The students ran all over her. She quit a quarter into the school year. What followed was a parade of substitutes, each more disengaged than the last. Eventually, I decided the class was a waste of time. I started ditching. I'd walk home, clean the house, and start dinner. That routine went on for nearly three weeks until my grandma casually mentioned to my mom that I'd been getting home early.

My mom was furious. I was forced back into class.

By then, we had a new English teacher—Mr. Rivera. With him, English came alive again. We read *The Red Badge of Courage*, and later *The*

War of the Worlds. Stories about fear, survival, and unseen danger resonated in ways I couldn't yet explain. I just knew I wanted to keep reading.

Before Christmas break, Mr. Rivera invited me to go to Disneyland. I hadn't been since I was almost three years old. My dad agreed, but only if my brother could come too. Mr. Rivera didn't hesitate—of course, he said.

The morning, he picked us up, he brought along one of his former students, now in tenth grade. My dad had given us money for my brother's ticket and spending money, but Mr. Rivera paid for everything, insisting, so we used the cash for meals instead. Throughout the day, I noticed how easily he and the former student moved together—how they shared glances and private jokes, how their familiarity felt unguarded. They didn't behave like teacher and student. They behaved like something else.

Even then, I knew how to watch without asking questions. Years of living inside other people's instability had taught me when to stay quiet. Still, something in me tightened, alert. I didn't have language for what I sensed, only a small warning I'd learned not to ignore. I've carried questions about that day ever since—questions that never needed answers to leave their mark.

Around that same time, I met a boy while walking home from school. We were headed in the same direction and began talking. He shared the gospel of Jesus Christ with me as we walked, his words steady and sure. Right there on the sidewalk, he led me in the prayer of salvation. Once again, I received the Lord Jesus Christ as my Savior.

Thoughts

Looking back now, I see how deeply my parents' alcoholism and drug abuse shaped me—how responsibility was pressed into me early, how silence became both shield and habit. Growing up, there were unspoken rules that governed our lives, rules many children from similar homes would recognize.

Don't talk about your family.

Keep your feelings to yourself.

Share as little as possible—openness is dangerous.

Nothing you do is ever good enough, yet everything is somehow your fault.

Put others first. Always.

Do as I say, not as I do.

Never have fun—joy is reckless.

Avoid conflict at all costs.

These rules helped me survive my childhood. But they followed me into adulthood, where they no longer protected me. Instead, they shaped my relationships, teaching me to disappear, to endure, to mistake silence for strength.

It wasn't until I became brutally honest with myself—until I dared to look directly at the past—that I began to challenge them. The work was slow and uncomfortable. I learned to share my feelings in small ways, to speak before fear could silence me. I opened up to a Christian friend, joined a small Bible study, and practiced saying the things I'd spent years swallowing.

Little by little, I realized I wasn't alone. And in learning to listen—to others and to myself—I began to find my voice.

I see how faith kept finding me in fragments—in classrooms and sidewalks, in borrowed kindness and half a bagel, in books that spoke of fear and courage before I knew those words belonged to me. I didn't yet understand God as refuge or rest. I understood Him as something I could cling to while standing still, something solid when everything else felt unsteady.

I believed because believing felt safer than silence. I prayed because prayer asked nothing of me except honesty, and honesty—when whispered—felt possible. Faith didn't remove the chaos of my childhood, but it gave me moments of breath inside it. It gave me a sense that I was seen, even when I was invisible to myself.

I didn't know then that God would later ask me to unlearn as much as I learned—to loosen my grip on fear, to speak instead of endure, to trust joy without bracing for punishment. I only knew that on those days, walking home with the weight of too much responsibility on my shoulders, I was not entirely alone.

And for that season of my life, that was enough.

Chapter 20

If time travel were possible, you still wouldn't be able to change the past - it's already happened!
— Sean M. Carroll

By the summer of 1985, Back to the Future was in theaters, and most people were daydreaming about time travel for fun. My family, though, would soon be wishing we could go back in time for real.

Like every year, school let out and a couple of days later my brother and I boarded the familiar bus to Grandma and Grandpa's in El Paso. I'd been making that trip since I was eight, and it always felt like the beginning of freedom. As always, they were waiting for us at the station, smiling and waving as if nothing in the world could ever go wrong.

But this summer was supposed to be special. My grandmother's brother Ignacio had a daughter, Sonya, who would be turning fifteen at the end of August. My second cousin was having her quinceañera, and I—along with my cousin Gloria—had been chosen as her damas. The thought of being part of something so important made me feel grown and excited all at once. Each week we practiced the waltz, trying desperately to stay in sync.

Our days followed the comforting rhythm we'd known for years: summer camp in the mornings, Grandma's house in the afternoons, and the swimming pool whenever the El Paso heat became too much. By the end of the day, four or five of us squeezed into my Tía Ruth's old Pinto, heading back to the house on Ledo Street—the same house where my father and his siblings grew up. It wasn't fancy, but to us it felt like the center of everything.

Summer came with its usual surprises, too. At the pool, Gloria and I met two boys—Carlos and his little brother Andres. Carlos was sixteen, and to my thirteen-going-on-fourteen self, he was a full-blown McDreamy. Gloria was only ten, but she giggled and blushed just like I did.

Suddenly, we were eager to get to the pool every day. I wasn't just looking for a kiss; I was chasing some new feeling, something like electricity in my stomach. Carlos smiled at me like he knew.

But not everyone at the pool was friendly. One girl, whose name I never learned, started taunting us. I'd never done well with being taunted. One day, after too much pushing, something inside me snapped.

"You got something?" I said, stepping toward her.

I didn't wait for an answer. My fist landed on her cheek before I even felt my arm move. She grabbed my hair, pulling me down hard, but I didn't panic. I wasn't tender-headed—my mother had made sure of that—and I used it. I took her down, climbed on top, and swung until the lifeguard dragged me off.

We were kicked out of the pool, of course. My knees burned from the cement, but otherwise I was fine. What mattered most was that grandma and Tía Ruth never found out.

Later that evening, Carlos and Andres came by Grandma's house. My grandparents sat on the porch as always, and when the boys asked if they could talk to us, Grandpa yelled inside:

"¡Rosa, Gloria! ¡Hay unos pelados que las están buscando!"

We wanted the ground to swallow us whole. But we went outside, laughing nervously, and sat with the boys until Grandpa called us in. My grandparents thought it was a happy, peaceful summer. They had no idea how quickly everything was about to break.

In July, a story entered our lives—one we didn't fully understand at first.

Tía Ruth had cable, and every night she tuned into KTLA Channel 5 from California. The station was following a terrifying man breaking into homes, stealing, raping, and murdering. A different world. A different state. A different problem.

Or so we thought.

Meanwhile, our summer marched on with quinceañera fittings in Ciudad Juárez, dance practice, camp, and more pool days. I turned fourteen in August, and Tía Ruth celebrated me with a cake and a pair of sandals I adored.

One weekend, we went to a friend's quinceañera. The ballroom was huge, full of teenagers dancing under glimmering lights. Gloria and I danced together while Tía watched wearily from the side. When she said she was too tired to stay, we left early, not knowing that in less than a week, our innocence would be gone.

Back at home in Los Angeles, the news grew louder. The reports became more urgent. One evening, KTLA flashed a sketch of the suspect on screen. A chill moved through my Tía.

"Rosie, come here," Tía Ruth called.

"Mande, Tía?"

"Mija… does that sketch look like anyone you know?"

I laughed it off. "No, Tía."

She stared harder at the screen. "Take a good look."

I did. And I still shook my head.

"No, Tía. It doesn't look like anyone."

She hesitated. "I think it looks a little like your Tío Richie."

Something inside me tightened—but I pushed it down.

"No… I don't think so, Tía."

I didn't want to think so.

Then, on Thursday evening, the news reported that investigators had found a fingerprint.

And everything we thought we knew about our summer—about our family—began to unravel.

Thoughts

That summer began gently, wrapped in the kind of joy that feels ordinary only in hindsight. I spent my days with my cousins, my Tía, and my grandparents—floating through pool afternoons, quiet crushes, quinceañera preparations, and small rebellions that felt safe because we were together. Beneath it all, though, a terrifying news story began to hum in the background: a serial predator operating in California. None of us could have imagined how closely that story would come to our own lives.

When a sketch of the suspect was released, my Tía recognized something familiar in it—a resemblance to her baby brother. I saw it too, though I didn't want to. I loved him, and I clung desperately to the normalcy of that summer, as if denial could keep us safe. But soon investigators announced they had a fingerprint, and with it came the quiet certainty that our world was about to fracture. The chaos we thought belonged only to home, to Los Angeles, had found me in El Paso.

That summer changed the way I understand my own emotions. The possibility that someone I loved could be tied to something so violent unsettled me in ways I did not yet have language for. Fear became a quiet companion, not loud or immediate, but always present, shaping my thoughts and softening moments that should have felt carefree. I noticed how quickly my mind learned to avoid what it was not ready to face.

Loving him while suspecting him forced me to live in contradiction. I wanted to protect my family, but I also wanted to protect the version of the world where we were still safe. That tension followed me inward, turning into guilt and confusion. I questioned my instincts and learned how fragile trust can be—how easily it bends under fear.

Looking back, I see how that summer lingered in my body and memory. It made me more cautious, more aware of silence, more sensitive to what goes unsaid. I lost something then—an ease, an innocence—but I gained a deeper understanding of love's complexity. What remains with me now is the knowledge that trauma does not always arrive as a single moment; sometimes it unfolds slowly, teaching you who you are as it changes you.

Chapter 21

Wait a minute, Doc.
Are you telling me you built
a time machine… out of a DeLorean?
— Marty McFly in Back to the Future 1985

Friday August 30, 1985

Summer camp had ended, and we spent the whole day at the swimming pool. Just six days earlier, I had turned fourteen. When the pool closed, we walked to my grandma's house, as we had always done. We ate dinner, and the boys decided to spend the night at Joseph's and Sofia's house. Gloria and I went home with my Tía Ruth to the old house on Ledo Street.

Tía Ruth was watching television in our bedroom, so Gloria and I were talking, listening to the radio, and flipping through the latest Seventeen magazine in my Tía's bedroom. Then Tía Ruth walked in, crying and covering her face, saying, "It's him, it's him." I couldn't tell if she was laughing or crying. I tried to remove her hands from her face so I could understand what she was trying to tell us.

Finally, she said, "Richie—he's the Night Stalker.

That was his fingerprint. It's him."

I was in shock and didn't know what to say. I told her, "We need to go tell Grandma." We didn't have a landline, so we got into the car with Tía Ruth. We stopped at a convenience store, where she bought a can of beer to calm her nerves. This was the first and only time I ever saw my Tía Ruth drink.

We drove to my grandma's house. It was way past midnight, and the house was quiet—all the lights were off. They were asleep. My Tía went into their bedroom to wake them up. Later, I learned that my parents had already called my grandparents to notify them of the news, but they weren't believed. My parents were told they were high on drugs and that it couldn't be true.

My dad later told me that was when they decided to drive around my Tío Richie's usual hangouts to see if they could spot him, but they were unsuccessful. They returned home, hoping he would show up at our house in East Los Angeles.

Chapter 21

At my grandma's house, my Tío Joseph and Tía Sofia arrived with my brother and my cousins Rudy and Ruby. My brother came into the bedroom where I was lying on the floor, trying to fall asleep. He said,

"Hey, did you hear about Tío Richie? Do you think it's true?"

"I don't know," I replied. "Maybe."

He lay next to me for a while. All the adults—my grandma, grandpa, Tío Joseph, Tía Ruth, and Tía Sofia—were in the kitchen, quietly crying, praying, and waiting by the phone. My grandpa began drinking, which he never did.

Saturday, August 31

We woke up to people talking and noise coming from the front yard. Gloria and I peered out the window to see what all the commotion was about. On the sidewalk and in the street were crowds of people and cameras. We later learned they were reporters, broadcasting breaking news from the front of my grandma's house.

Soon my Tío Robert, his wife, and their daughter Shelby arrived. The only ones missing were my parents. I walked into the kitchen looking for something to eat. Seeing the onslaught of reporters and camera flashes as my Tío Robert and his family tried to make their way into the house was nerve-racking. We had never experienced anything like that before.

My cousin Gloria asked me, "What are you looking for?"

"Something to munch on. I'm nervous," I answered.

I wanted to turn on the television, but my grandma wouldn't allow it. We had no idea what was really happening. Later that day, they piled all of us kids into Tía Ruth's Pinto, and we drove to the Ledo Street house. We were followed by either reporters or detectives—we didn't know which.

It was Labor Day weekend in 1985, and the family decided it would be best to get all the kids out of the city. A high school friend of Tía Ruth offered to take us camping, so we had to pack quickly. This family friend lived down the street at Ledo Street and Durazno.

All the kids sat in the back of the truck, waiting to leave—my brother, three of my cousins, and four other children who belonged to my aunt's friend. Before we left, Tía Ruth came to say goodbye. She stopped and asked all of us, "They're accusing Richie of some really bad things. I need to ask you—has Richie ever touched any of you?"

I looked down and wondered if I should say something. She told us, "You can tell me." I looked up at everyone sitting in the truck. One by one, they all said no. I just nodded no too.

Would they even believe me? Was I the only one he had molested? What would the other kids think of me? The shame and embarrassment I would feel if I said, "Yes, me"—there was no way I could put myself through that. I kept the secret for two more years.

Before we left on the camping trip, we learned that Tío Richie had been captured. He was heading to our home in East Los Angeles when he was arrested just a couple of blocks away—exactly one and a half miles from our house. He was a twenty-eight-minute walk from where my parents were waiting. The street where he was arrested was across from the middle school I attended, Robert Louis Stevenson.

There was so much media publicity that my father decided it would be better for my brother and me to remain in El Paso longer. The quinceañera was canceled. My parents eventually drove to El Paso with my little sister to tell us we wouldn't be returning to Los Angeles. What was supposed to be a short stay ended up lasting two years.

I went to live with my Tío Joseph and Tía Sofia. My parents stayed in Los Angeles to serve as guides for family members traveling there for my uncle's legal proceedings. They kept my little sister with them. My brother went to live with my grandparents.

There was a massive media frenzy. My family was harassed by reporters, and many lies were printed. One story claimed that Tío Richie had mailed my Tía Ruth a pair of eyes taken from a victim. That was not true. He had mailed her jewelry and asked her to hold onto it for him. Tía Ruth suspected it might be stolen, but she didn't ask and had no concrete knowledge of where it came from.

Detectives eventually obtained a search warrant and collected all the jewelry. It turned out that some of it did belong to victims.

<u>Thoughts</u>

I didn't know the word trauma then. I only knew that something had been taken from me long before I had words for it, and that whatever it was had followed me into that August night. The hardest part wasn't just what he did. It was that he was family. Someone who belonged at our tables, in our living rooms, in the ordinary noise of our lives. After that, safety became confusing. Love and danger lived too close together. I learned early that the people who were supposed to protect you could also be the ones you needed protection from.

When my aunt asked us if he had ever touched any of us, time slowed. I remember staring at my hands, at the floor, anywhere but at her face. I knew the truth, but the truth felt too heavy to lift. I was a child, surrounded by other children, and the weight of what I carried felt unbearable. Everyone else said no. I nodded along with them, my silence sealing itself inside me. In that moment, I learned how to disappear while still being present.

I didn't stay silent because I didn't want justice. I stayed silent because I was afraid. Afraid of not being believed. Afraid of being different. Afraid of what would happen to my family if I spoke. Afraid of the shame I already felt, even though it was never mine to carry. I didn't have language for any of that then. I only knew that saying nothing felt safer than saying everything.

After that night, the world became loud and unstable. Adults cried behind closed doors. Prayers were whispered. Phones were watched. Reporters stood outside my grandmother's house, cameras flashing, turning our private pain into public spectacle. I learned what it felt like to be exposed without being seen, known without being understood.

Home stopped being a place. We were moved, separated, rearranged. Parents in one city, children in another. Suitcases packed quickly, questions left unanswered. I learned not to get too comfortable, not to expect things to stay the same. I learned how to adapt, how to go quiet, how to survive.

What stayed with me most was the feeling of carrying something unspeakable while the adults around me searched for answers. They prayed and waited by the phone, not knowing that part of the truth was lying on the floor in the next room, pretending to sleep. I felt guilty for what I knew and ashamed for what I couldn't say. I mistook survival for weakness and silence for failure.

Years later, I would understand that my body and mind were doing exactly what they needed to do to get me through. The fear, the distance, the numbness—they weren't flaws. They were armor. They were the way a child protects herself when the world becomes unsafe.

This is what trauma looked like in my life: not one moment, but many. Not just violence, but secrecy. Not just fear, but loyalty. Not just loss, but dislocation. It lived in my nervous system, in my relationships, in the way I learned to brace myself even in calm moments.

I am still learning how to put down that armor. Still learning that telling the truth—now, in my own time—does not destroy families or break me open beyond repair. It brings breath back into places that have been holding it for decades.

This is not a story about weakness. It is a story about survival.

Chapter 22

Behold, I am doing a new thing:
Now it springs forth, do you not perceive it?
I will make a way in the wilderness and
Rivers in the desert.
Isaiah 43:19 ESV

I started ninth grade in September 1985. By then, I was living with my Tío Joseph and Tía Sofia and their two children, Rudy and Ruby. It felt like being dropped into a new world. I felt out of place—like a stranger. My Tía Sofia tried her best to win me over, but all I wanted was to go home. The calm of my Tío and Tía was both comforting and suffocating. They were stable, disciplined, loving—but I couldn't appreciate it. I had grown used to chaos. I wanted my parents, and I wanted the world I had lost. I didn't realize that their calm, their care, was a gift I couldn't yet recognize.

My Tía Ruth went with me to register for school. She encouraged me to take ROTC. I had no idea what it was, but wanting to please her, I agreed. My Tía Sofia ran the household. She was strict, but nothing out of the ordinary looking back. Both she and my Tío worked full-time jobs.

I shared a bedroom with my cousin Ruby. My Tía Sofia bought me a twin-size bed and gave me a chest of drawers where I kept my clothes—mostly summer clothes—because I was supposed to return home to Los Angeles. At the time, I was an angry, lying, rebellious know-it-all teenager. In my eyes, my Tía Sofia was a goody-two-shoes.

I wanted to stay with my Tía Ruth and didn't understand why we couldn't remain at the Ledo house. Later, I learned the house would soon be sold, likely to help pay for my Tío Richie's legal fees.

I tried my best to settle into my new normal. My relocation from Los Angeles to El Paso included a new school and a new education system. In Los Angeles, ninth grade was part of junior high; in El Paso, it was part of high school. School was much harder than I was used to. I struggled immensely. I didn't know how to study, and during my first semester I failed four out of six classes. Academically, I was drowning—gasping for air. My Tía Sofia kept close tabs on our grades, yet I still couldn't get it right.

Socially, however, school was much better. In Los Angeles, I had faced a lot of rejection and bullying. When I started school in El Paso, I expected the same treatment based on my past experiences. Instead, I found that boys actually found me attractive, and many girls were friendly. Students were more accepting of Mexican culture than those I had encountered in Los Angeles.

Sharing a bedroom wasn't new to me. My cousin Ruby and I generally got along—except when it was time to clean. She was seven years old, and I tried to explain that if we worked together, we'd finish faster. But her priorities revolved around play, not chores. Wanting our room clean, I came up with a new strategy: anything she left out, I threw onto her bed. My Tía Sofia didn't allow anything under the bed, so I was constantly pulling toys and clothes from beneath it. Instead of getting angry, I'd pile everything on Ruby's bed. By bedtime, she had to put everything away before she could sleep.

Years later, Ruby called me laughing. She had seen a girl on TikTok recommending the exact same cleaning strategy—and suddenly remembered that I used to do that to her. Even in my mischief, I had left a mark.

One afternoon, while waiting for my Tío Joseph to come home from work, I didn't have a key to the house. My cousins had been picked up by my grandmother, so I was left alone outside. My Tío Joseph's van was parked under the carport and was unlocked. I climbed inside and, out of boredom, began searching around. Under a seat, I found a magazine with something wrapped in newspaper. Carefully unwrapping it, I discovered my Tío Joseph's stash of marijuana.

I knew he smoked occasionally—I had seen him do so with his siblings at Lincoln Park near my grandmother's old house on Ledo Street. My Tía Sofia didn't approve, so he kept it to a minimum. Still, I had found his secret stash.

After school, we were required to call my Tía Sofia at work to let her know we were home. Then we'd have a snack—mine was always a bologna sandwich. I loved opening a refrigerator full of food and knowing I could have whatever I wanted. Afterward, chores awaited us. I vacuumed the living room daily and washed breakfast and dinner dishes. On Tuesdays and Thursdays, I dusted furniture and mopped the kitchen and hallway floors.

This was before caller ID. When I called her each day, she'd tell me what needed prepping for dinner—cutting onions and tomatoes, shredding cheese, roasting chiles. Everything had to be ready by the time she walked in the door. Every night, I helped her cook. Often, she'd share life lessons with me. At the time, I didn't care to learn any of them. I missed my parents terribly. All I wanted was to go home.

As I grew older, her words of wisdom echoed loudly in my mind. Back then, I thought I knew everything. Eventually, I realized I knew nothing.

The first few months were hard. I was trying to fit into a new family dynamic with relatives I barely knew. Before moving in, my contact with them had been limited. My Tío Joseph had always been my favorite uncle—he was always laughing, always trying to make people laugh. Some days he came home in a bad mood and went straight to his room. Most days, though, he joked around, making us laugh with his "smell my finger" jokes.

Being alone with him for a couple of hours after school was my favorite part of the day. When my Tía Sofia came home, he'd say, "Okay, okay—stop. Your Tía is home," and suddenly he became serious Tío Joseph.

Tío Joseph, working every day, meticulous, disciplined, never letting his prosthetic leg stop him. My Tío Joseph worked at Fort Bliss in the housing department and always dressed sharply in button-down shirts and slacks. He woke early, made breakfast, and insisted it was the most important meal of the day. On weekends, he gardened endlessly— planting tomatoes, jalapeños, grapes, and fruit trees.

Tía Sofia, elegant and capable, running the household with grace and patience, making sure we were fed, ready, and loved. Sundays were for Mass, family lunch, and preparation for the week—a rhythm that made the world feel safe, even if I didn't know it yet. After Mass, we had lunch, my Tía Sofia napped, and then prepared for the week ahead. She worked in an office and always dressed professionally, business casual with heels. She was petite but powerful in personality—a wonderful wife and mother. My dream has always been to be half the woman she is.

I had mixed feelings about staying with her. Those feelings were unfounded. She tried her best to make me feel comfortable. She often let my brother come over on weekends, and sometimes my cousin Gloria joined us.

My brother understood me—the good, the bad, and the ugly. Even when we argued, I knew I was loved and accepted by him. One weekend, after everyone else had fallen asleep, we stayed up talking. That's when I remembered the stash. I told him about it and suggested we try some. He hesitated, worried my Tío would find out.

I laughed and said, "What's he going to say—

'Rosa, did you take my weed?' He can't.

He'd get in trouble with Tía Sofia."

He agreed. We quietly snuck outside, went to the van, unwrapped the stash, took a handful, and carefully put everything back exactly as we found it. We had no rolling papers, so we tore a blank page from the back of a Bible. We rolled it like pros and smoked. It was both our first time. We laughed uncontrollably, covering our mouths so we wouldn't wake anyone, and opened the window to let the smell out.

We never told a soul—until now. Sorry, Tío.

Sometimes you just need a good laugh.

Despite spending time with my brother, I still missed my parents and my home, chaotic as it was. Being told we couldn't return to Los Angeles made me feel abandoned, unwanted, and unlovable. No one seemed to care how we felt. This deeply affected my self-esteem.

Years later, while studying psychology, I learned that the basic need to feel wanted and worthy of love is crucial. When unmet, it can lead to needy behavior, emotional numbness, promiscuity, and drug use—all of which applied to me. I constantly sought approval and even had suicidal thoughts. I exhibited behaviors my Tío and Tía were not prepared for when they took me in.

In my later teens, I became angry and sad, often feeling I wasn't good enough. I craved love and attention and accepted it from anyone—especially boys—no matter how insignificant. Before I knew it, I was "in love" again and again. My Tío Joseph called me "Prima Donna." He thought I was vain, proud, moody, and difficult. Today we'd call that a drama queen or diva. Sadly, that description fit me at the time—and I would eventually add even more negative traits to my persona.

Living with them was very different from what I was used to. It was calm. There was no yelling, no throwing things, no violence, no heavy drinking or drugs. They both worked hard and modeled a strong work ethic I still admire.

They taught me there was a better way to live. I couldn't see it then, but over time, I came to long for the stability and calm they embodied. Throughout it all, the fate of my Tío Richie loomed over the family—especially my grandparents—like a dark cloud.

<u>Thoughts</u>

I felt abandoned, unwanted, like I didn't matter. It made me angry, moody, and desperate for attention—any kind of attention, even from strangers or boys who barely noticed me. I lied, I rebelled, I acted out. Looking back, I realize I was trying to fill a hole no one could see.

I found ways to reclaim control—or at least the illusion of it. I experimented, I took risks, I laughed in the dark with my brother as we smoked Tío Joseph's stash for the first time. Those moments were thrilling, yes, but they were also born from fear and longing: the need to feel something, anything, that told me I was alive and in charge, even if only for a moment.

The truth is, I grew up feeling like I had to earn love. I wanted it so badly that I would entertain anyone who gave me a sliver of attention, no matter how small. My Tío Joseph called me a "Prima Donna," teasing me for being vain, moody, and proud. At the time, I didn't understand; now, I see he was trying to hold up a mirror to the ways I was seeking love and approval, even if I didn't know it.

What I didn't understand then was that I was learning how to live in a different way—a calm, structured way that wasn't flashy or loud, but steady and strong. It took years for me to see that the chaos I carried in me, the constant need for validation, the anger and sadness, were all wounds from feeling uprooted and unwanted. But living with them, observing their quiet resilience, I began to understand the value of stability, of care, and of being truly seen without needing to perform.

Chapter 23

Say you, say me; say it for always
That's the way it should be
Say you, say me; say it together
Naturally
Say You, Say Me by Lionel Richie

When December arrived, we were given a two-week winter break from school. My brother and I returned to Los Angeles to visit my parents and my little sister, who had stayed behind for Christmas. It was our first time home since leaving in June of 1985.

We traveled by Greyhound bus, just the two of us. During the visit, we went to the old county jail to see my Uncle Richie. I hadn't seen him in about eight months. The waiting room was crowded, as usual, until his name was called over the intercom and we were led into the visiting area.

The visit felt unfamiliar. There were no other inmates or visitors present, and my dad sat with us on the same side of the room. Until then, every jail visit I remembered had been to see my father. This time, we were there for my Tío Richie.

He entered the visiting area and sat behind the glass partition, picking up the phone as my dad did the same. They exchanged polite greetings before Tío Richie asked to speak to me. My dad handed me the phone, and I hesitated.

Something about my uncle seemed different to me. I can't fully explain it now, only that I felt unsettled. My dad handed me the phone, but I hesitated. When I looked at my uncle, he seemed different. I don't know if it was just my imagination, but I wasn't seeing my Tío Richie anymore—I saw something else. His eyes, his expression, his entire countenance frightened me. He must have noticed the fear in my eyes because he spoke gently and said, "Don't be scared. It's just me."

Through the glass partition, he asked,

"How do you like living in El Paso?"

"It's okay," I replied. "I'd rather be in L.A."

He laughed softly and said, "Yeah, I know."

Then he grew serious. "Listen, I'm sorry all of this happened. You're going to hear things, but always remember that I love you guys."

He asked how it was living with Tío Joseph and Tía Sofía. I answered honestly, in the way teenagers do, that it was fine—but that I wished I were home with my parents. After that, the rest of the visit faded quickly from my memory.

While in Los Angeles, I spent time with friends, visited my grandparents who lived next door, and stopped by my old middle school to see my former English teacher, Mr. Rivera.

Returning to El Paso meant returning to routine—school, chores, and expectations. Soon after, I came down with a severe case of the flu. Even with a fever, I was expected to keep up with my responsibilities. One evening, exhausted and sick, I laid down instead of joining the family for dinner. Later, my Tía came into my room and reminded me that it was my turn to wash the dishes. I got up and did it, though I felt worn down and unseen.

Not long after, the night terrors I had experienced as a child returned. I was fourteen by then, old enough to feel embarrassed by them but unable to stop them.

One afternoon after school, still weak from illness, I took a nap while home alone. During my sleep, I slipped into one of these episodes. I telephoned my grandmother, convinced someone was trying to harm me. She rushed over and found me crying and disoriented, unaware of my surroundings. My grandma came to my rescue so quickly. I will never forget how I felt so scared alone and terrified. Once I was fully awake, I felt bad that I had put my grandma through such a scare.

Another night, I woke up screaming, convinced that people were trapped inside the television and needed help getting out.

Thoughts

Looking back now, I can see that the girl I was during that winter lived in a state of quiet suspension. I had been moved away from home, away from my parents, and away from everything that made me feel anchored. Los Angeles wasn't just a place—it was where I understood who I was. El Paso felt temporary, as though my real life was waiting somewhere else for me to return.

I was observant then, perhaps overly so. I noticed shifts in tone, changes in faces, and what went unsaid. I didn't yet have the words for discomfort or fear, only the instinct to pull inward and watch carefully.

When I saw my uncle in that visiting room, what unsettled me wasn't something I could name—it was simply the feeling that something familiar had altered, and that I was expected to accept it without question.

At fourteen, I was exposed to realities that belonged to adults: jail visits, apologies without explanations, warnings about things I might hear but not fully understand. No one sat me down to explain any of it, and I didn't know to ask. I learned instead how to absorb, how to listen, and how to stay quiet.

What I understand now is that I felt invisible more often than I felt neglected. There was food on the table, rules to follow, chores to complete. Even when I was sick, life went on. I did what was expected of me, not because I was strong, but because it seemed easier than asking for care I wasn't sure I would receive.

The night terrors returned during that time, though I was far past the age when such things are forgiven. I felt ashamed of them then. Now I see them differently. My mind was doing what I could not—releasing fear, confusion, and grief in the only way available to it. In sleep, I cried out for protection, imagined being pursued, and believed others needed rescuing. I was asking, in the language of dreams, for safety and reassurance.

I wasn't broken. I was overloaded. I was a child trying to carry separation, illness, silence, and responsibility all at once. I didn't know how to make sense of what I was feeling, only how to endure it.

With distance and time, I can look back at that girl with tenderness. She did the best she could with what she had. She survived not by understanding her world, but by holding herself together until she was old enough to look back and finally make sense of it.

Chapter 24

1986 Halley's Comet and
Carless Whisper by George Michael Wham!
So I'm never gonna
Dance again, the way I dance with you

In March of 1986, during spring break, my Tía Ruth took us camping at Old Hueco Tanks State Park, just outside El Paso. The desert smelled like dust and sun-warmed stone. We stuffed sleeping bags into the trunk, wrestled with tent poles, and laughed at how little we knew about what we were doing. It was the first time we had gone camping with her—my cousins Rudy, Ruby, and Gloria, my brother, and me—and it felt like freedom.

We spent our days hiking over rock formations and slipping into cool, shadowed caves. At night, the air dropped fast, carrying the crackle of firewood and the sharp scent of smoke. We sat around the campfire, wrapped in blankets, waiting for Halley's Comet to streak across the sky. Someone swore they saw it first. Someone else said we'd missed it. Either way, we stayed up too late, telling stories, our faces glowing orange in the firelight.

When spring break ended, I returned to school and was voted Duchess for the ROTC Military Ball. It should have felt like a reward. Instead, it became a problem.

My grades weren't where my Tía Sofía thought they should be. She and my Tío Joseph decided I wouldn't be allowed to attend, even though I was part of the court. I went to the school counselor, my stomach tight, and explained everything. She let me use the office phone to call my mom at work—long distance. I knew My mom was still working, printing invoices for a manufacturing company. Back then, you didn't make those calls lightly. You knew they cost money before you dialed.

"I'm not allowed to go," I told my mom. "They won't let me."

That afternoon, when I stepped off campus and saw my Tía Ruth waiting in the car, I felt it immediately. Trouble.

At my grandparents' house, I was sent to the detached room in the backyard. The space smelled faintly of dust. My Tía Ruth followed me in, her jaw set.

"You upset your parents," she said, holding a belt. "Pull down your pants. Bend over."

She didn't ask why I'd called. I didn't try to explain. I did what I was told. The belt landed four, maybe six times—each one sharp and final. When she finished, she scolded me for causing problems, for making things harder than they needed to be.

Then my grandfather came home.

He stepped into the room and took in the scene. His voice was low but firm.

"No," he said. "You don't do that."

He told her she was wrong—for hitting me and for scolding me.

"She had every right to call her parents," he said. "Good or bad, they need to know what's going on with their child."

No one had ever spoken up for me before.

I started to cry. My grandfather pulled me into his arms. He smelled like sweat and aftershave, like a man who had worked all day and still had gentleness left. He didn't tell me to stop crying. He didn't minimize it. He understood what it was to miss your parents, to live divided between families.

People talk about my grandfather's temper, the man he once was. We never knew that man. The grandfather who raised us had a softened heart.

My father sent my mother to El Paso to make sure I was allowed to attend the Military Ball. My mom and little sister came with me. After years of being bullied in elementary and junior high school, being chosen felt unreal. The ball was held in the high school cafeteria, which smelled faintly of floor wax and leftover lunch trays. White streamers hung from the ceiling, trying their best to disguise the room.

We waited in a hallway until the court was ready. My palms were damp. When the music started, we were introduced and escorted in. We took our places for the ceremony, after the ceremony "Careless Whisper" played. A boy named Adrian stepped forward.

"Would you like to dance?" he asked.

He held me carefully, swaying to the music.

His arms felt safe. He would hold me like that for the next two years.

They called it puppy love, first love.

We were young enough to believe forever was possible.

Chapter 24

We started dating in late April. Adrian was two years older, still in the
tenth grade because school didn't come easily to him. We were both in
ROTC. We both went to summer school. Back then, our high school
even had a smoking section—a square of concrete where students stood
with cigarettes between their fingers. Times were different.

My grades improved. My rebellion didn't stop. I skipped classes, then
whole days. I wrote excuse notes for myself—and for Adrian. Once,
during summer school, we skipped to go to the dollar movies with friends
who had a car. I don't remember the movie. I remember sitting close in
the dark, the thrill of getting away with something.

My Tía and Tío didn't allow me to date. Sneaking off during school
hours became the only way we could be together. When summer school
ended, Adrian and I took a break.

Now, looking back, I see what I couldn't then. I manipulated the
situation between my Tía and Tío and my parents. I played them against
each other—and I won. My Tía and Tío were my guardians. They fed me,
clothed me, and tried to keep me on the right path.

All the adults should have stood together.

That moment marked a turning point. Not because of the ball or the
boy, but because I learned how power could shift—and how easily I could
use it. None of us knew what we were doing. We were all learning as we
went.

Thoughts

I can see her clearly now—the girl I was then—standing between
households, rules, and expectations, trying to make sense of where she
belonged. At the time, I didn't have the language for it. I only knew that I
missed my parents in a way that sat heavy in my chest, and that being
good never quite guaranteed safety. Love felt divided, conditional,
something that could be withdrawn if I failed to meet the moment.

When I was chosen for the Military Ball, it felt like proof that I
existed beyond the margins. After years of being overlooked or mocked,
being seen mattered more than I understood. Losing that felt unbearable,
like being erased all over again. So I reached for my mother—not to
manipulate, but to be rescued. I didn't yet know the difference.

The punishment that followed didn't teach me accountability. It
taught me silence. It taught me that explanations didn't matter, that

obedience was safer than honesty. And then my grandfather stepped in and changed something fundamental. He didn't just stop the moment—he named my feelings as real. In doing so, he gave me something I didn't know I needed: permission to trust my own experience.

Adrian came into my life at a time when I was aching to be held without judgment. Being with him felt like relief, like rest. What I called love then was really safety—being chosen, being wanted, being treated gently in a world that often wasn't.

I didn't understand then that I was learning how power worked. I learned that adults could be turned against one another, that rules bent under the weight of love, that attention could change outcomes. I told myself I was just trying to breathe, but those lessons followed me. Skipping school, forging notes—those weren't acts of rebellion so much as experiments in autonomy, ways of testing how far I could go without losing connection.

Looking back, I don't judge that girl. She was navigating absence, authority, and longing with the tools she had. The adults around me were learning too, doing their best in a situation none of us had prepared for. But I can see now that this was a turning point—the moment innocence gave way to strategy, when need quietly learned how to disguise itself as behavior.

I wish someone had helped me understand why I was acting the way I was. But understanding came later, with time, distance, and mercy. And that, too, became part of the story.

Chapter 25

In this country, you gotta make the money first.
Then when you get the money, you get the power.
Then when you get the power, then you get the women.
– Tony Montana in Scar Face

The summer of 1986 was like many summers since I was eight years old, we spent that summer with my Tía Ruth, my cousins Gloria, Rudy, and Ruby, and my brother. My Tía Ruth had planned a trip to California for us, but there was a catch—we had to raise as much money as we could. She helped us organize bake sales at swap meets to earn pocket money for our summer activities. She also helped us secure a spot at the swap meet so we could sell old items.

We gathered every old, unused item we had and labeled them with prices. We baked cupcakes in every flavor we could think of. My Tía had us walk around the swap meet in pairs—usually Gloria and I together, and my brother with Rudy. There were two reasons for this: one person handled the money while the other sold cupcakes, and it was also for safety.

We had to be there very early if we wanted to make good money. Early arrivals meant better sales, so we always made an effort to get there at the break of dawn. We loaded up my grandpa's truck, and my Tía Ruth drove us to the swap meet, also known as the flea market. We spent several Saturdays selling old items and cupcakes until we had enough money to drive to California in an old white Chevy Nova—if I remember correctly, it was a 1978.

Once we had enough money saved, we were off to California, all excited. I like to think we raised enough money on our own, but now, as an adult, I realize we had help along the way. Whatever the case, I was thrilled to introduce my cousins to my East LA friends.

On the way, we stopped at my Tío Robert's house. At the time, he was married to Brandy, and they had a four-year-old daughter named Shelby. They lived in a two-bedroom house with a living room, dining room, TV room, and enclosed screen porch. My Tía Brandy's favorite color was red. She had some ruby-red vases, which she claimed were very expensive, along with beautiful sofas, a wall-sized mirror, a glass coffee table, and matching end tables. We were told to be very careful because everything was expensive and we were not allowed to sit in the living room. Every room felt luxurious. My Tía Brandy had a talent for making a room look upscale through her décor. Whenever I visited, I often felt inferior, as if she wanted to convey that she had "arrived" and was better than us. Hence, the many "you can't do this" or "don't touch that" rules.

Shelby, my cousin, was a spoiled little brat. Pampered and indulged, she could do or have anything she wanted and often acted disrespectfully toward others, including her parents. She addressed them by their first names—Brandy and Robert—rather than "Mom" or "Dad," occasionally calling my Tío Robert "Pinky," short for Pink Panther. Her room had a queen-sized bed and every toy imaginable. I thought Gloria had lots of toys, but Shelby took the cake. My brother and cousins and I were in awe of the collection of toys and knickknacks she had amassed at only four years old. She talked back, yelled, and threw temper tantrums until she got what she wanted.

My Tío Robert had a job, though I wasn't exactly sure what it was. I suspected that he also sold drugs on the side, specifically cocaine. On top of a chest of drawers in their bedroom, I noticed scales with powder residue—familiar to me from my Tío Richie selling marijuana.

We stayed at their house because it was the midpoint between El Paso and Los Angeles, allowing my Tía Ruth to rest. We set up a tent in their backyard where the kids would sleep for the night. My Tío Robert had a bar in his TV room, with bottles of liquor in all shapes and sizes—bourbon, rye, gin, cognac, scotch, ranging from small flasks to large demijohns and carboys. We were allowed to stay up late watching TV with him. By this time, Scarface with Al Pacino was available on VHS, which he owned. A VHS player at that time cost between two and four hundred dollars—a true status symbol.

We stayed up late watching Scarface. "Say hello to my little friend!" During this time, many of my Tío Robert's "friends" stopped by to pick up "something." My brother and I exchanged knowing looks each time, silently acknowledging we understood what was going on. The next morning, we were back on the road again.

<u>Thoughts</u>

In retrospect, I feel that my Tío Robert and Tía Brandy fell prey to the mindset of chasing the American Dream—hence the lure of easy money through drugs. When I was a teenager in the 1980s, the American Dream meant becoming wealthy. Most people I knew aspired to wealth, even if only in theory. It's a great concept, but chasing money for its own sake often leads to emotional debt.

I remember my Tío Richie, looking through the newspaper, saying he would one day be rich and famous. I often wonder if that mindset led to disappointment and frustration, and eventually, lashing out at the world and at God. My cousin Shelby also comes to mind when I think of the risks people take for money—stealing family photo albums, selling family photos and forged letters, selling memorabilia, appearing on TV shows demanding payment, even losing relationships for the love of money.

Accumulating wealth is not easy. There are no shortcuts. It requires hard work every day, 24/7/365 days a year, with full commitment. Even then, the pursuit can feel endless, as desires for large houses, fast cars, or luxury goods can leave one questioning, "Is it all worth it?" The answer is often no. Money alone does not guarantee happiness, and overworking for it can lead to emotional exhaustion.

I used to play the game of "I'll be happy when…"—when I get married, have a baby, lose ten pounds. The same applies to money. Many believe that achieving a financial goal will solve all problems, but it rarely does. Reasons include:

There is never enough money. If money alone brought happiness, lottery winners would be the happiest people on Earth. Studies show lottery winners are more likely than the average American to file for bankruptcy within a few years.

The more money we make, the more we spend, sometimes even committing criminal acts to obtain it. This creates an addictive cycle.

Money is a tool, not a destination. It provides access to things we need or want—clothes, food, transportation, housing, education, medical care—but it should not be an idol.

Obsession with money often leads to comparison, dissatisfaction, and a negative impact on self-esteem and happiness. This is why the Bible warns that the love of money is the root of all evil. When we love money more than God, it becomes an idol. God says, "Seek ye first the kingdom of God, and his righteousness, and all these things shall be added unto you" Matthew 6:33 KJV. He will provide, even if the provision seems ordinary Psalm 37:25 KJV.

Looking back, I realize that even as a child, I was watching everything—absorbing details most kids would overlook. I noticed the way my cousins behaved, the differences in how they were treated, the luxuries of Tía Brandy's house, and the subtleties of adult interactions that I didn't fully understand. I was curious, constantly observing, trying to make sense of the world around me. Even then, I had a sense of right and wrong, of fairness and injustice, though I didn't yet have the words to articulate it.

There was a tension in my mind that summer, a mix of excitement and unease. I was thrilled to be part of the California trip, to be with my cousins, to experience the thrill of early mornings and hard work at the swap meet. And yet, I was also aware—vaguely, instinctively—that the world was larger and more complicated than my small, orderly life at home. I saw indulgence and entitlement in Shelby, the youngest cousin, and I felt a mix of awe, envy, and discomfort. I knew instinctively that her behavior—her tantrums, her disregard for others—was unacceptable, yet it seemed to go unchecked. That, too, left a mark on me.

I was processing contradictions, even if I didn't yet have a name for them: hard work versus easy money, rules versus privilege, respect versus entitlement. I noticed patterns in adult behavior too—Tio Robert's mysterious "friends," the late-night comings and goings, the signs that money and power could corrupt. I didn't speak about these things aloud, but I understood them in my own quiet way.

Emotionally, I was stretched thin between awe and fear, excitement and caution. I compared myself to others, wondering why some children were given so much while we worked so hard for so little. And yet, even in that comparison, I began to form a sense of gratitude and pride—for my family's guidance, our hard work, and the experiences we earned through our own effort.

Perhaps most importantly, I was beginning to think about values. I realized, in the subtle, unspoken ways that only children can, that wealth alone did not equate to happiness. I saw how obsession with money and privilege could twist behavior, create rifts, and distort one's sense of self. And in my own small, careful observations, I started to form an idea of the person I wanted to be: curious, moral, self-aware, and cautious about the seductions of money and status.

Even as a child, I was learning to navigate a world of contrasts. I was forming my own moral compass, quietly taking notes on what worked, what didn't, and what I wanted to carry forward into my own life. That summer, with all its chaos and excitement, was more than a trip—it was an early lesson in awareness, ethics, and the complexities of human nature.

Chapter 26

**If I could turn the page
In time then I'd rearrange just a day or two
Close my, close my, close my eyes
But I couldn't find a way
So I'll settle for one day to believe in you
Tell Me, Tell Me, Tell Me Lies by Fleetwood Mac**

When we arrived in Los Angeles, the city hit me all at once—the smell of hot asphalt mixed with exhaust and something sweet, like melting ice cream in the sun. The sidewalks seemed endless, lined with palm trees that swayed lazily in the breeze, and the air carried a warmth that made your skin tingle. I finally got to introduce my cousins to my friends, and it was a small thrill to watch them navigate my world. My brother introduced Rudy to his friends, and the boys disappeared into a haze of video game bleeps and glowing screens, laughing and shouting as if they'd known each other forever. I wandered behind them, listening, watching, feeling the city pulse under my feet.

One morning, my Tía Ruth surprised us. She told us she was taking Rudy and Gloria to Disneyland, leaving us with our parents. They tried to keep it a secret, worried we'd be upset. I remember a pang of jealousy mixed with excitement for them. When they drove off my parents took us to the beach, we were left with the salty, briny smell of the ocean and the rhythmic roar of the waves at the beach. The sand stuck to my bare feet, warm and coarse between my toes, while the water lapped at our ankles, cool and foamy. The wind carried a faint scent of sunscreen and seaweed, tangling with the laughter of kids chasing seagulls along the shore. It wasn't Disneyland, but it was ours, and for a few hours, it felt like paradise.

We also went to visit my Tío Richie. The last time I had seen him, a shadow clung to him, one I didn't understand, something dark that made him frightening. This time, he looked better—or maybe it was me. Perhaps my world had gotten messy enough that the fear I once felt had dulled, or perhaps I simply chose to see the man behind the shadow.

One afternoon, my Tía Ruth took us to a thrift store. The instant I stepped inside, the air was thick with the scent of old fabric, mothballs, and leather polish. Rows of clothes hung like a jungle, bursting with patterns and colors, each piece whispering possibilities. I ran my fingers over the fabrics, imagining each outfit as a declaration of identity. I found baggy Dickies, striped polo shirts, high-waisted skirts, and jackets with worn-in patches. The smell of aged cotton mixed with the faint tang of perfume bottles left behind by previous owners—it was intoxicating. For the first time, I could see myself in clothes that felt alive, clothes that spoke louder than I ever could. I tried on a gold chain and let it catch the fluorescent thrift-store lights; it gleamed, and for a moment, I felt fierce and untouchable.

Even though I had never been part of gang, I was fascinated by it. In Southern California, it was everywhere: the street corners, the murals, the lowriders gliding like slow-moving shadows down the avenues. Hispanic gangs had their own rules, their own style, distinct from the African American crews that also claimed corners of the city. From pancake makeup to bracelets and hairspray-drenched hair, to the stiff creases of Dickies and the oversized polos, everything about their look was intentional, commanding, magnetic. I studied it all—the Cholas especially.

They were warriors in their own right, strong, stylish, and unafraid.

When we returned home with my new attire to match my inner identity, my grandmother and Tía Sofia were unimpressed. Their disapproval hit harder than any chola glare ever could. "No way," they said. "You're not wearing any of this." My new identity, my carefully curated thrill of self-expression, was dismissed in a single sentence. I felt the knot of disappointment twist tight in my stomach, the way it had twisted so many times before in my life when adults around me decided who I could be.

Still, I couldn't stop thinking about the Cholas. They lined their lips with cherry lip liner, plucked their brows thin, and teased their permed hair high with Aqua Net, creating stiff, asymmetrical bangs that caught the sunlight. Baggy polos draped over cropped tops, Dickies belted high, gold jewelry clinking with every movement. They cruised in lowriders—Impala, Chevelle, Monte Carlo—shiny paint catching the California sun, music blasting oldies from open windows, jelly bracelets stacked thick on wrists, Chinese Mary Jane shoes completing each outfit. Every detail was intentional, a declaration of strength, pride, and style.

Cholas weren't just about clothes. They ran neighborhoods, protected their men, and held the streets together with quiet authority.

After seeing *Scarface*, my fascination only grew. Their world felt dangerous, yes, but alive, beautiful, and powerful. I wanted that confidence, that boldness, that ability to walk through life on your own terms. Trying on those thrift-store clothes, brushing my fingers over gold chains, spinning under the fluorescent lights—I felt a small spark of it, a taste of freedom. Even when my family said no, the spark remained, tucked somewhere deep inside me, waiting.

Los Angeles, with its heat, its streets, its thrift stores and beaches, showed me a world I wanted to touch, to understand, to claim. Even from the outside, even in stolen moments, it gave me a sense of who I could become—a girl learning to step boldly into her own identity, one thrifted outfit, one sun-bleached sidewalk, one wave-lapped beach at a time.

Thoughts

I realize now that, as a teenager, I was trying to reinvent myself—not just in how I looked or acted, but in who I believed I was. Deep down, I was hiding from the truth of myself, from the parts I didn't yet understand. I wanted to carve out an identity that felt separate, defiant, independent. Looking back, I see that this rebellion wasn't just against my aunts and uncles—it was against the inner voice of God calling me to the truth of who I really was.

At the time, I didn't know it, but I was under attack in the area of my identity. The Bible warns us to "protect your heart above all else, for it determines the course of your life" (Proverbs 4:23 NLT). And here, the word "heart" isn't talking about the organ that pumps blood—it's talking about the center of who we are, the thoughts and beliefs that shape our lives. In other words, what I believed about myself would determine the path I walked.

In my own life, those beliefs were messy and conflicted. I struggled with rejection and abandonment. I carried the weight of thinking I was "wrong," that I was somehow defective or unworthy. Those thoughts governed how I acted. I anticipated failure because I assumed it was inevitable. My heart, instead of being a place of security and truth, had become a breeding ground for disobedience and defiance. I sought control where I could find it, and I found it by resisting authority. Living under the direction of Tía Sofia and Tío Joseph felt suffocating; it was one of the first real lessons in humility I had yet to learn. Control would remain a lifelong challenge for me.

But this struggle was bigger than family dynamics. Without Jesus, I had no true anchor, no guide to discovering who I was or who I could become. The Bible says our enemy, Satan, seeks to "steal, kill, and destroy" (John 10:10 King James Version). I felt it in the negative thoughts that crept in, in the subtle ways I believed lies about myself, and in the temptations to numb my pain with things that would never satisfy. He was trying to make me someone I was not, to steal my joy, and to keep me from stepping into the identity God had planned for me.

The antidote, I've learned, is simple in theory but profound in practice: immerse yourself in God's Word, cling to His promises, and let His truth shape who you are. When I believed the lie that my worth depended on other people, I found Psalms 139:14 KJV whispering back to me: *"I am fearfully and wonderfully made."* When I thought my pain was too heavy to bear, Psalm 34:18 KJV reminded me: *"The Lord is near to the brokenhearted."* And when I felt unlovable, Romans 5:8 KJV reminded me that *"while we were still sinners, Christ died for us."* These verses weren't just words on a page—they were lifelines to the me I couldn't yet see for myself.

Even with these truths, it took me years to internalize them, to allow them to reshape my heart and mind. I made mistakes, I rebelled, I sought validation in all the wrong places. But gradually, over time, I began to understand that my identity was not defined by the authority I resisted, the mistakes I made, or the approval I longed for. My identity was—and is—rooted in Christ. In Him, I am loved, I am purposed, I am treasured.

Looking back, I see that every misstep, every act of defiance, and every moment of doubt was part of the journey. I was learning, slowly and painfully, that without God, I could never truly know myself. But with Him, I could. And even now, years later, that understanding still shapes every choice I make and every version of myself I continue to discover.

Chapter 27

I think I'm beginning to understand why Boo Radley's stayed shut up in the house all this time... It's because he wants to stay inside. How to Kill a Mocking Bird by Jem Finch

The August of 1986 marked my fifteenth birthday—a coming-of-age year in Hispanic culture, whether anyone named it or not. My mom had returned to El Paso, and we stayed with my grandmother's sister Julia in Anapra City, New Mexico. A small group of family gathered to celebrate me. My second cousin Rosa, at the time a professional cake decorator, made a beautiful two-tier cake. I remember the way everyone crowded into the house, the warmth of being noticed.

Not everyone was there. My grandparents, Tía Ruth, Tía Sofía, and Tío Joseph were absent. I noticed. I always noticed. Still, my brother and I built something rare that summer—real relationships with not just our first cousins, but our second cousins too. Those bonds endured. I still carry them.

That fall, I started tenth grade. By then, the clothes Tía Ruth had bought me in Los Angeles—the clothes that made me feel like someone new—were gone. Tía Sofía had made me get rid of them. Instead, she took me to Kmart and asked a question no one had ever asked me before: *What size do you wear?*

I didn't know.

I had never bought new clothes. We tried on size after size until one fit just right. She put everything on layaway, and by the time school started, it was paid off. For the first time, I walked into school wearing clothes that were mine alone—new, crisp, untouched. They smelled clean. That mattered more than style or price. I was the first person to exist in them. Many kids never think twice about that. I did.

School began to click too. Pay attention. Do the work. Turn it in. Get a grade. My grades improved, and with them, something unfamiliar bloomed—confidence. Tía Sofía noticed. Her approval mattered more than I wanted to admit.

Boys noticed too. Mike was the kind of boy parents love—clean-cut, polite, neatly dressed, working after school at a grocery store. When he showed up at the door, my Tía was impressed. We talked outside, about school and family and plans. But eventually he told me about the weed. Then the cocaine. Mischief I could handle. Drugs crossed a line.

I pulled away slowly. He disappeared. My Tía kept asking. I kept shrugging. When my younger cousin asked, I told her the truth. That clean image was a mask. The questions stopped.

Adrian came back into my life soon after. He struggled in school the way I had. Together, we improved. Tía Sofía allowed us to date—but only if his parents chaperoned.

That condition led us across the border.

If you drive into El Paso on Interstate 10, you pass between worlds. To one side, the University of Texas at El Paso rises in Tibetan-inspired architecture. To the other, homes cling to rocky hills, smoke drifting into desert air. Two cities. Two countries. One invisible line.

Juárez wasn't dangerous yet—not the way it would become. My grandparents had roots there. As a child, I crossed the border every week: Coke bottles, barbershops thick with aftershave, quince fruit, open-air markets buzzing with sound and color. Back then, I thought Juárez was dirty, old—a reminder of where my family came from.

At fifteen, I saw it differently.

On weekend nights, like so many El Paso teens in the 1980s, I crossed the bridge to Avenida Juárez. Five dollars to park. A short walk. Loud music. Cheap drinks. Dancing. Clubs packed with kids from every high school—white, Hispanic, Black. Rich kids. Poor kids. Parents unaware that their children were drunk in alleys at three in the morning.

We danced to The Cure and New Order. SaraWalk offered "Drink and Drown"—five dollars, unlimited alcohol. I was still a high school student. I felt grown. Sophisticated. Untouchable.

Adrian's parents loved Juárez too. They chaperoned us the way adults did then—loosely. We'd pick a meeting spot, usually a restaurant, believing food could sober anyone up. They went one way; we went another. We danced, drank, laughed, and watched for each other. The police watched us too. Step out of line and you could end up in a paddy wagon until your friends scraped together bail or a bribe.

We rarely strayed from the Strip, but danger was never far.

I didn't know then what Juárez would become.

By the mid-1990s, cartel wars erupted. In 1994, the bodies of young women began appearing in the desert—first a few, then dozens, then hundreds. *Las Muertas de Juárez.* Their murders remain unresolved. Gangs preyed on girls, trafficking them across borders. Some never came home. Some were never found.

I now realize how easily I could have been one of them.

I crossed that bridge so many times. I drank. I trusted strangers. I believed nothing bad could happen to me. But God was watching over me—even when I wasn't watching over myself. *But God.* That phrase holds more weight now than it ever did then.

Years later, my husband and I crossed the bridge for a long-overdue date night. Avenida Juárez was quiet. No drunk teenagers. No soldiers. The clubs of my youth were gone. The border was no longer invisible—it was hardened, guarded, dangerous.

I loved the city. I grieved it.

Juárez taught me something I didn't yet have language for: that freedom without protection is an illusion, and identity without grounding is fragile. I was searching for myself everywhere—across borders, in clothes, in boys, in rebellion—while God was quietly keeping me alive long enough to find Him.

<u>Thoughts</u>

At fifteen, I lived inside contradiction. I wanted to belong, but I was afraid of being fully seen. I longed for structure, yet bristled against authority. I craved safety, even as I edged closer to danger. At the time, none of this felt confusing or conflicted. It felt necessary—like instinct.

I had learned early that love could be unreliable. Adults moved in and out of my life, and the rules changed depending on who was in charge. I adapted the only way I knew how. I learned to control what I could and reinvent what I couldn't. If I could shape how others saw me—through clothes, confidence, or quiet rebellion—then maybe I wouldn't have to face the parts of myself that felt unwanted or disposable.

I wasn't chasing chaos for the thrill of it. I was chasing agency. New clothes mattered because they gave me a sense of ownership over my own body and identity. Juárez mattered because it offered freedom from supervision, a place where I could feel older, bolder, almost untouchable. Boys mattered not just for romance, but because being chosen felt like proof that I was worth choosing at all.

At the same time, I carried a low, persistent belief that something about me was fundamentally wrong. That belief dulled my sense of danger. When you already feel expendable, risk doesn't register the same way. I assumed bad things happened to other people—people who made worse choices or mattered less—because somewhere deep down, I believed I was already living on borrowed grace.

Spiritually, I was exposed in ways I couldn't yet name. Scripture tells us that the heart determines the course of a life, and my heart was bruised and unguarded, searching for definition. Lies slipped in easily. *You're on your own. You're grown enough to handle this. You don't need protection.* They sounded like strength. They felt like freedom. In truth, they were quietly leading me toward harm.

And yet, I wasn't reckless in the way people often imagine. I still had boundaries. I refused drugs. I stayed close to my friends. I paid attention. These were fragments of wisdom—small mercies, really—evidence that God was already at work, even while I resisted Him. Grace was operating long before I had language for it.

I didn't know I was being preserved. I thought I was just being clever.

Looking back now, I see a girl who wasn't trying to destroy herself. She was trying to define herself before someone else did. She was running from shame, loneliness, and the fear of not belonging, unaware that identity isn't something you seize through rebellion or proximity to danger. It's something you receive. And in His mercy, God gave me time.

Chapter 28

**the scars that cannot be visibly seen hurt the most,
the scars that cannot be visibly seen take the longest to heal.
so i will take my time with my healing
because my heart deserves relief,
and my mind deserves peace
Sour Honey & Soul Food by Billy Chapata**

Toward the end of my tenth-grade year—1986 to 1987—I began to unravel. At the time, I would not have called it that. I would have said I was bored. Restless. In love. Rebellious. But the truth is, my world felt unstable, and I was trying to manufacture relief.

My tío Richie's incarceration had shaken everything loose. Our family fractured under the weight of it. In the name of protection, we were separated—siblings divided, parents distant, new homes assigned. I was placed in a different household with new routines, new expectations, new rules that did not feel like mine.

My parents had promised it would only be for a year.

Two years later, we were still living apart.

No one explained much to us about the case. Silence was supposed to protect us. Instead, it left space for fear to grow unchecked. A friend would sometimes bring me the newspaper so I could read updates about Richie's court proceedings. I would scan every line, hungry for information, trying to piece together a story no one would tell me.

But there were other things no one talked about either.

I felt abandoned. Invisible. Angry.

Angry at Tío Richie—for what he had done to me, for what he had done to all of us. Angry that because of him I could not return to Los Angeles to live with my parents. Angry that his arrest had rearranged my life like furniture no one asked permission to move.

I was angry at my parents for not protecting me, even though I knew they were drowning in their own chaos.

And I was angry at God.

I didn't understand how He could allow something like that to happen and then expect me to remain soft and faithful.

I didn't have language for any of that at fifteen. What I had were behaviors.

I learned how to lie in ways that were harder to detect.

Before caller ID existed, I would phone my Tía and tell her I was home, safe at home. In reality, I was at Adrian's house. Alone.

Lying gave me control. If I could shape the story, I could shape the outcome. I learned how to omit details, how to coordinate versions of events, how to stretch the truth without snapping it. The lies became smoother. Easier. They created small pockets of freedom inside a life that felt dictated by other people's mistakes.

Then came shoplifting. Earrings. Makeup. Purses.

I stole clothes from an aunt and jewelry from a cousin. Family.

It wasn't about the objects. It was about the surge—the brief spike of power when I walked out of a store unnoticed. For a few seconds, I was in charge. I had taken something. I had decided something.

Sleep became another form of relief. If I could not fix my life, I could at least shut it off. I took sleeping pills whenever I could get them. Unconsciousness felt safer than being awake inside my thoughts.

At night, I would sneak out to meet friends at the canal near my Tío and Tía's house. Sometimes we skipped school entirely. We'd walk back to my Tía's house while she was at work, push the coffee table aside, turn the stereo up loud, and dance to oldies in the living room.

We weren't drunk. We weren't high. We were just laughing.

For a few hours, movement replaced heaviness.

I never invited them over when my tía was home. Just by the way they dressed, she would have disapproved. Some of them were drawn toward gang culture. I hovered near it, close enough to feel its pull, far enough to pretend I wasn't part of it.

And then there was Adrian.

We ditched school together, walking to his house or mine when it was empty. Sometimes we stayed close to campus, hiding under a nearby bridge, talking and kissing for hours. Thomas Manor Park became ours. We made plans like all teenagers in love—marriage, a house, forever.

Adrian was my first true love.

Being with him felt like oxygen. When I was with him, the noise inside me quieted. That, too, was manufactured relief.

But while I was trying to feel better, my grades slipped again. I wasn't failing the way I had in ninth grade, but they weren't what my Tía expected. Every report card felt like proof that I was disappointing someone.

That's when I discovered another way to quiet myself.

It happened accidentally at first. I was helping my Tía cook when my forearm brushed against the hot edge of a pan. The pain was sharp and immediate—but what followed surprised me. A warm rush spread through my body. A strange calm.

It felt better than kissing.

For the first time, I realized that physical pain could drown out emotional pain.

After that, I began burning myself deliberately. Heating metal until it glowed. Pressing it against my skin. Returning to the same spot again and again. The first burn always brought the strongest wave of relief. Picking at the scab extended the sensation, though it never quite matched that initial surge.

Once, I bent a wire into the shape of an R, heated it, and pressed it into my forearm like a brand.

The scar is still there.

I also pierced my own ears with a needle heated over a lighter, threading string through the new holes. Four additional piercings in each ear. Another mark. Another way to claim my body.

If my world was unstable, at least I could control what happened to my skin.

When I got caught misbehaving, I was sent to stay with my grandparents for a week at a time.

I slept on the floor in their bedroom.

At four in the morning, my grandmother would gently wake me. The kitchen light would already be on. The air would smell faintly of coffee. She tied her apron with practiced hands and began making homemade flour tortillas for my grandfather's lunch.

Three cups of flour.

A palm of salt. A pinch of baking powder. A scoop of lard.

She never measured. Her hands knew.

I would press my fingers into the dough. It was soft and warm, yielding under my palms as we kneaded it together. The rolling pin moved back and forth across the wooden table—steady, rhythmic, almost soothing. The radio played a Spanish-speaking minister every morning.

Chapter 28

My grandmother listened closely, nodding occasionally, absorbing each word. I heard the radio, but I didn't listen.

The tortillas puffed on the hot comal, filling the kitchen with the smell of toasted flour and home. My grandmother moved with quiet purpose. There was stability in her motions. Order. Tradition.

In that kitchen, everything had its place.

I didn't.

My tía Ruth drove me to school during those weeks. On the way, she tried to talk to me—really talk to me. She reached for my heart with gentle questions.

But by then, I had armored it.

I mistook hardness for strength.

Softness felt too dangerous.

If I couldn't feel, I couldn't break.

<u>Thoughts</u>

Reflecting no one noticed anything—except that I was always getting in trouble. I was grounded, scolded, punished. Sometimes I was sent to stay with my grandparents for a week at a time, as if distance itself might fix me. Looking back, I can see that I was living in a constant state of emotional whiplash—pulled between craving structure and needing escape, between guilt and defiance, longing and numbness.

At fifteen, it felt like survival.

From the distance of adulthood, I recognize it as exhaustion.

I felt displaced. Home was no longer one steady place; it had fractured into multiple households, multiple authorities, multiple versions of who I was supposed to be. I never fully settled anywhere. I learned to adjust quickly, to perform, to adapt. My behavior wasn't careless—it was strategic. I was trying to stay one step ahead of instability, to manage chaos before it managed me.

Whenever I was in trouble, the solution was to send me to my grandparents' house. The adults in my life believed the one person who could reach me was my Tía Ruth. They thought proximity to her—and to my grandmother's steady routines—would soften me.

But if I wasn't listening, even to her, then it was just time passing.

One of my deepest regrets is that I never learned how to truly listen the way my grandmother did. I heard people, yes—but I didn't listen.

Back then, I thought I already understood everything. She would sit at the kitchen table, listening to the minister on the radio, then turn to explain what he meant. I would nod. I would let her speak.

But I wasn't listening.

There is a difference.

Hearing is passive. Listening requires humility. Hearing coexists with distance; listening creates connection. My grandmother was trying, in her quiet way, to hand me wisdom. When I reach back now to retrieve the pearls she offered, there is only silence—not because she didn't give them, but because I wasn't open to receiving them.

Beneath everything I did was a belief I rarely spoke aloud: something was wrong with me. Not that I made mistakes—but that I was the mistake. That belief shaped how I interpreted everything. It lowered my sense of worth and made consequences feel deserved, even inevitable. When I was sent away, when I slept on the floor, when I was woken before dawn, I didn't experience those moments as correction. I experienced them as confirmation.

This is what someone like me gets.

And yet there was a contradiction I couldn't name. Even as I resisted authority, part of me craved containment. The early mornings. The ritual of making tortillas. The steady cadence of a preacher's voice on the radio. Those routines offered what my life lacked: rhythm, predictability, a beginning and an end. My body felt relief there, even when my mind rolled its eyes.

I didn't know how to trust calm.

Emotionally, I had learned to shut down—but I was never empty. When Tía Ruth tried to reach past my defenses, I hardened. Not because I didn't feel, but because I felt too much. Vulnerability seemed dangerous. To open myself was to risk disappointment, misunderstanding, abandonment.

Silence became my armor.

No one suggested counseling. No one asked what might be happening beneath the surface. I walked around with burns on my forearms, new piercings, sleeping excessively. I chased affection in all the wrong places. In my own way, I was crying for help—but my language was misbehavior. Yes, I was rebellious. Yes, I had an attitude. Yes, I was difficult.

But no one stopped long enough to ask why. And when they did, I didn't have the words. I didn't understand myself well enough to explain myself.

Anger and resentment were the only emotions I knew how to access quickly. Over time, I began to see the adults in my life as impossible to please. What's the point? became my silent refrain. If I was going to be wrong no matter what, I might as well stop trying.

If someone called me into their bedroom and closed the door, my stomach knotted instantly. Even now, decades later, when someone says, "Close the door so we can talk," a flicker of that old dread rises up: What did I do wrong?

Labels are powerful things. I carried the title of "problem child," and eventually I grew into it. Young people often live up—or down—to the names they are given. I never felt fully valued. What I was feeling, what I was enduring, did not seem to matter.

Faith surrounded me—in my grandmother's rituals, in the sermons humming from the radio, in the language of the adults who loved me— but it hadn't taken root. God felt like another authority watching me fail. I was angry at Him for allowing what had happened to happen. I heard about grace, but I did not feel protected by it.

Still, something was being planted.

Even in resistance, seeds fall.

The adults in my life were doing the best they could inside a storm none of us knew how to navigate. Much of their attention was consumed by Richie—his trial, his behavior in court, whether he had commissary money, whether he had called. His crisis eclipsed everything else. Even my pain.

I wrote to him regularly. It's difficult to reconcile that now. In the beginning, he was just my Tío Richie—like a big brother. He wasn't infamous to me. He wasn't a headline or a cautionary tale. He was the person who had hurt me. He was the reason my life had been uprooted. And somehow, he was still family.

That contradiction lived quietly inside me.

What I was really longing for back then wasn't freedom from rules.

It was to feel chosen. Protected. Seen.

I didn't want fewer boundaries.

I wanted belonging without conditions.

Chapter 29

These eyes have seen a lot of loves
But their never gonna see another
One like I had with you
These Eyes by The Guess Who

Toward the end of the 1986–1987 school year, I got into a fight at school with a girl I thought was my friend. I had caught her making out with my boyfriend, Adrian. The betrayal from both of them burned deep. When I saw her alone in the hallway one day, something in me snapped. I was already looking for a fight.

I rushed at her. I grabbed her hair with one hand and punched her in the face with the other. I let go of her hair, grabbed her blouse, and pulled her toward me, tearing the fabric. When she stumbled back toward me, I shoved her, and she fell to the ground, caught off guard. I climbed on top of her and kept punching until teachers rushed in and pulled us apart.

We were both taken to the assistant principal's office. He wanted to call my Tía Sofia, but some teachers who knew my living situation convinced him not to. Later that evening, Adrian came by to apologize. His concern for my well-being felt sweet, and somehow, everything was forgiven.

I was given one week of SAC—Student Assignment Center— basically in-school suspension. I reported to a classroom behind the school buildings, where I sat in an isolated cubicle. My teachers sent my assignments there, and I completed them alone. We were taken to lunch before the regular lunch periods and weren't allowed to socialize. Then it was back to the cubicle and more work.

Thanks to my teachers, my Tío Joseph and Tía Sofia never found out about the fight. If they're reading this now—well, now they know. Sorry, Tío. Sorry, Tía.

As the summer of 1987 began, Adrian and I grew closer. School was out, and as the oldest, I was left to care for my two younger cousins while my Tío and Tía went to work. They were having new carpet installed in the house and asked us to move as much furniture as possible from the living room and bedrooms and place it outside under the attached carport.

I was fifteen. My cousin Rudy was twelve, and Ruby was eight. We were in charge of the chore.

Adrian, who was seventeen at the time, called and asked what we were doing. I explained that we were moving furniture outside because new carpet was being installed. He said, "Sounds like you guys could use some help." I told him we could. About thirty to forty-five minutes later, he showed up with two of his friends.

We got all the furniture moved out in no time. They brought pizza, and we ate, laughed, and joked around for a while. After they left, we cleaned up and erased any evidence they had been there. We swore we wouldn't tell.

When my Tía and Tío got home, they were so impressed that we had done everything ourselves. We took all the credit — and milked it for all it was worth. We played up how exhausted we were from the "laborious" work of the day. I lay on the floor in the empty bedroom I shared with Ruby when Rudy came in, closed the door, and we both giggled with glee over getting one past them.

Tia Sofia was a hawk — smart, intuitive, and always watching. She took motherhood very seriously, constantly making sure we didn't do anything wrong. That vigilance was her way of showing love, and I believe it came from growing up without her own mother. Her care operated at a level I wasn't used to, and at times it felt suffocating. If we had tried to pull anything past her today, with caller ID and security cameras, we never would have gotten away with it. Still, many of the things I was doing went unnoticed — or at least unspoken.

One summer afternoon, while my Tío and Tía were at work, Adrian came over. We had been dating about a year by then. My cousins were watching television in the living room while Adrian and I slipped into my bedroom. I was wearing a turquoise sleeveless summer romper. We locked the door, turned on the radio, and started making out, but this time it went further.

We had sex. It was my first time.

He was gentle and loving. People say you never forget your first time, and that has been true for me. We were so young, and I have never forgotten him. My eyes would go on to see many loves, but never another quite like the one I had with him.

My first sexual experience was significant because I had never willingly participated in sexual activity before. I had been sexually abused as a child, but there had been no penetration. In that sense, I still considered myself a virgin.

We had been together for over a year, and I loved him very much, but it was nothing like it's portrayed on TV or in movies. Many of us build up an imaginary idea of what first-time sex is supposed to be like, and reality often doesn't match that image. No one's first experience is exactly the same. Sometimes it's smooth and romantic; other times, it's awkward.

As tender and special as my first time was, it stirred up many mixed emotions — even nightmares. The saddest part was that I had no one to talk to. No one knew. I felt alone and confused.

That was when my negative behavior escalated to a new level. I stopped hiding what I was doing. It became blatant, almost as if I wanted to be found out.

Thoughts

Looking back now, I can see that girl was not living in emotional safety. She was living in survival mode.

She carried childhood sexual abuse in her body, even if she didn't yet have the language to name it. Her early attachments had been unstable, and although the love she later lived under was real, it was also watchful and intense. My Tía's vigilance came from care, but to a nervous system already shaped by trauma, constant watchfulness does not always feel like safety — it can feel like being observed, measured, one mistake away from losing love.

So that girl learned to hide.

She learned to protect herself.

She learned to carry her emotions alone.

Not because she wanted to be secretive or distant, but because she didn't know another way to exist.

And yet, when I think of the woman described in Proverbs 31, the one clothed in strength and dignity, the one who works willingly with her hands and cares for her household, the person who comes to mind is my Tía Sofia. For so many reasons. She was a woman of excellence, hardworking, full of initiative. She chose to help raise me. She was my aunt by marriage, not by blood, yet she loved me as if I were her own. She made sure we were clothed warmly in winter, managed her home with care, gave to others, shared wisdom, and carried a deep reverence for Yahweh. Her husband and children thought the world of her — and so did I, even when I didn't know how to show it.

My rebellion and defiance had nothing to do with her or my Tío Joseph. The home they tried to create for me was as close to perfect as they could make it. I see that now. At the time, I did not. I was already carrying too much. Trauma from my childhood had shaped me into someone defiant, indifferent, resentful, and self-deluded about my circumstances. I had been exposed to things too early — spiritual confusion, fear, unhealthy influences — while also carrying the unspoken shame of sexual abuse at the hands of my Tío Richie. I lived with a false sense of guilt, as if somehow it had all been my fault, as if I had brought it on myself.

Adrian entered my life in the middle of all that.

He was never just a boyfriend. He represented choice — my first experience of intimacy that was not taken from me. He represented gentleness, being wanted, and a soft place to land away from the chaos inside me. Being with him felt like stepping into control of my own body for the first time. On the surface, it looked like a teenage love story. Beneath that, it was something deeper: *I finally chose this.*

But trauma does not disappear just because a moment is tender. The body keeps its own memory. After the sweetness came confusion. Mixed emotions. Nightmares I couldn't explain. Shame that didn't seem to match what had happened. I didn't understand how something loving could stir up pain. That inner contradiction — pleasure tangled with fear, closeness wrapped in old echoes — was enormous, and I faced it alone.

That was the real problem: there was no emotional container.

I had no one I felt safe confiding in. No adult I believed could hold the truth without judgment. No language for trauma. No understanding that past abuse can resurface during first consensual intimacy. So all those feelings — love, guilt, fear, longing, confusion — stayed trapped inside me.

And feelings that have nowhere to go will always find a way out.

That was when my behavior began to change. I can see now that the acting out wasn't random. It was communication. When I stopped hiding and became blatant, when it seemed like I wanted to be caught, it wasn't rebellion for fun. It was closer to this: *If someone finally sees how "bad" I am, maybe they'll finally see how much I'm hurting.*

Risk became a release valve. A form of self-punishment. A cry for someone to step in. A way to make the outside world match the chaos already living inside me.

My relationship with Tía Sofia made everything more complicated. She loved fiercely, but she was strict, watchful, emotionally intense. For a girl already wired for hypervigilance, that could feel suffocating. It felt like there was no room to make mistakes, no safe space to bring messy feelings. So I split my life in two: the good girl at home and the secret girl everywhere else. That split bred shame, and shame is gasoline on risky choices.

If I could give words to that girl's inner world, it would sound like this:

I love him, so this must be okay.

Why do I feel strange after something that was supposed to be special?

I can't tell anyone.

Something must be wrong with me.

If I get in trouble, maybe someone will finally notice.

The truth is, I wasn't reckless because I didn't care. I was reckless because I was carrying more than I could hold — a trauma survivor, a lonely teenager trying to feel loved, trying to feel ownership of my body, carrying emotions I didn't know how to name.

My behavior wasn't the real problem.

My silence was.

And silence is where pain learns to turn itself into action.

Chapter 30

We never put the past behind us, but we carry it on our shoulders and carry it with us. And we need to have strong shoulders to not feel the weight of it and move forward.
— Bruce Lee.

As the summer of 1987 was coming to an end, the beginning of my junior year was beginning. My Tía let me go to Kmart with Adrian. She told me to pick out clothes for school since I was starting my junior year. My Tía met us there and took care of putting everything on layaway. This was the second year she had bought me clothes, but this time I knew what size I wore.

At that time, my mom and little sister had moved to El Paso. They were living in my grandparents' converted garage. My mom was collecting food stamps and welfare while she lived there. My grandmother required her to buy food and cook for herself, my brother, and my sister. It was as if my grandmother was trying to teach my mom how to be a mother.

You would think that living with her in-laws would have made my mom try harder to control her drinking, but it didn't. You would think she would try to control her anger and stop physically abusing my brother and sister, but she didn't. Many times, I overheard my grandmother and my Tía Sofia or Tía Ruth talking about things my mom had done while drunk. It made me angry. I couldn't understand the hold alcohol had on her.

When I went to my grandparents' house to visit, I purposely avoided the garage so I wouldn't see or talk to her. I was angry. She should have been doing everything she could to reunite her children under one roof. Instead, I gave her the silent treatment. I was mean. I would get angry and cuss at her, demanding she get her life together.

School started. I figured out how to keep my grades up while still ditching school. Adrian and I skipped more and more. We often went to his house, where we spent the day having sex. Other days we would ditch half a day and go to my Tío and Tía's house.

My shoplifting increased. One weekend, I stayed in Anapra, New Mexico, with my Tía Julia. I stole two of her dresses and a necklace from one of my adult cousins who lived down the street with her father, my grandmother's brother, Jose.

In October, shortly after that, my Tía Sofia and Tío Joseph decided to travel to Los Angeles to visit my Tío Richie. They couldn't leave us alone, so they asked Tía Julia my grandmother's sister to stay with us for the week.

Instead of making it easy on my elderly Tía, I turned my misbehavior up another notch. Adrian walked me home while my aunt and uncle were gone. Some friends from school came over, and we hung out outside, talking and listening to music.

Later that week, Adrian walked me home again. We went into my bedroom, which I shared with my little cousin Ruby. We closed the door and had sex. When I came out, I saw Tía Julia sitting on the sidewalk outside, smoking a cigarette. I had no shame, no respect — not for her or anyone. I asked her if she could give Adrian a ride home. She did.

During that week, she discovered I had stolen her dresses — they were hanging in my closet.

When Tío Joseph and Tía Sofia came home from Los Angeles, everything exploded. I wasn't called in for a "talk." I wasn't sent to my grandmother's to make tortillas. What I had done went beyond that. The only thing they said loud and clear was that, after two years, they were tired. Tía Sofia told my cousin Ruby they were trying to figure out what to do with me because they couldn't handle me anymore.

As they searched for other arrangements, I quietly packed my belongings in trash bags and took them, little by little, to a friend's house nearby. Within three days, I had moved out. No one noticed — not even my younger cousins. I left notes in my cousins' drawers telling them I loved them and that my leaving had nothing to do with them. I stayed with a friend named Kate from ROTC.

One afternoon, while changing classes at school, I saw my uncle leaving the office. I had continued going to school while staying with Kate. Soon after, the police showed up. I was called into the office. As I walked in and saw them waiting, my mind raced to all my shoplifting. I was sure I had been caught.

I had learned early that encounters with police were bad. I feared them. Little did I know they were there because my Tío and Tía had reported me as a runaway. They took me to Child Protective Services.

I was assigned a social worker. She interviewed me alone and asked several questions. One of them was whether I had ever been molested.

For the first time in my life, I said yes. She asked by whom, and I told her my uncle Richie. She wrote it down, and that was it. No one ever mentioned it again. I didn't know what to think.

I stayed at a runaway shelter for two weeks. My uncle Joseph came to sign paperwork saying he was no longer my guardian. I assumed he was angry about what I said, but no one spoke to me about it. After two weeks, my mom picked me up. I stayed with another high school friend until my mom could find a permanent place for us in El Paso. The abuse was never brought up again, so I stayed quiet.

Looking back now — I can't help but wonder how much my childhood shaped the choices I made.

I teach in a prison. I stand alone in a classroom with twenty-five male inmates, preparing them to return to society and make better choices.

Today, I asked how many children they had. Together, they had forty-six. Then I asked how many had a parent who was incarcerated while they were growing up. Several hands went up.

I asked if that had impacted them. To my surprise, some said no — that their choices were solely their own.

That response stayed with me. I'm not saying people should blame their parents. In the end, the crimes they committed were their choices. But to say their upbringing had no impact, while sitting in prison, stunned me. Even more shocking was their belief that their incarceration would not affect their own children.

I often wonder what impacted me most. My father's addiction and incarcerations? My mother's alcoholism? The domestic violence? The physical abuse? The verbal abuse? The molestation? The abandonment that I felt?

Parents' choices leave lasting marks — good or bad. That realization is why I feel such urgency with my students. My parents' actions affected me and my siblings. I believe, in many cases, the oldest child carries the most — I know I did, and so did my son.

Each day as I walk through the prison gates, I pray, "Lord, here I am. Use me. Let me be a light in a dark place. Let me be a living testimony of Your goodness. Speak through me. What message do You have for them today?"

Thoughts

Looking back now, I understand that the girl I was back then wasn't wild without reason. She wasn't simply rebellious, promiscuous, or angry. She was a child trying to survive in a life that never felt safe.

At the time, I thought I was furious with my mother. Furious that she drank. Furious that she hit my siblings. Furious that she didn't fight harder to pull us back together. But beneath that anger was something I didn't yet have language for — grief. I was mourning the mother I longed for but never truly had. Rage was easier than heartbreak. Anger felt powerful. Grief felt unbearable.

So anger became my armor. If I stayed mad, I didn't have to admit how deeply I felt unwanted.

I didn't understand then how profoundly abandonment shapes a child. When the people meant to protect you become the ones who hurt you — or the ones who vanish — something inside rearranges itself. You stop believing you are worth protecting. You stop expecting tenderness. Survival replaces growth.

No one spoke about the molestation. Maybe some suspected pieces and chose not to see the whole. But my body knew. When a child's boundaries are crossed and nothing is done, confusion takes root. You grow up uncertain about what your body is for, what love should feel like, where your worth begins and ends. I didn't think in those words then, but I lived them. My body felt like the only thing anyone seemed to value.

Sex felt like closeness. It felt like control. It felt like choosing instead of being chosen for. What I see now is that I was trying to reclaim something that had been taken — to rewrite a story that had already wounded me. I wasn't chasing recklessness. I was chasing agency.

The stealing, the ditching school, the disrespect — they weren't random acts of defiance. They were signals. I didn't know how to say, "I am hurting," so my behavior said it for me. I was asking, without knowing how to ask, "Will someone see me? Will someone stop me? Will someone care enough to fight for me?"

But hurt children are often labeled trouble before they are understood.

I used to wonder why I felt so little shame at times. Now I know numbness is its own survival skill. When too much happens for a child to process, feeling shuts down. Consequences blur. The future feels abstract, almost imaginary. You live in the moment because nothing has ever felt secure enough to promise you tomorrow.

So I leaned into the role that was handed to me — the bad kid. If I was already the problem, then rejection couldn't surprise me. I would leave before I could be left. I would harden before anyone could break me.

That is why I packed my things into trash bags and disappeared quietly. No dramatic exit. No pleas to stay. I had already learned that expressing need rarely changed anything. Leaving without asking felt safer than risking one more unanswered cry.

Now I see that nearly everything I did was an attempt to meet needs I couldn't name. I wanted to feel wanted. I wanted control. I wanted to matter. I wanted the pain to stop. I wanted someone — anyone — to fight for me.

I wasn't self-destructive because I didn't care.

I was self-destructive because no one had convinced me I was worth protecting.

Understanding this doesn't excuse my choices, but it gives them context. It allows me to look back at that angry, reckless, aching teenager with compassion instead of shame.

She wasn't trying to ruin her life.

She was doing the only thing she knew how to do.

She was surviving.

Dear Rosie,   2/6/88
        Hi babe. whats up? Hope your doing great. Say hi to ████ for me when you see him. I sent a letter to you at an address you gave me. It was a short letter. I think it was sent to your boyfriends house. Any way. I want you to write me soon o.k. Your dad was suppose to visit yesterday but this other stupid woman beat him to it. Stupid because I had told her not to come. I go to the roof twice a week and box. I hit a punching bag. So how's school? Dont get mad but Im just answering your letter now. I didnt know where to send the letters. Write back and let me know if you got this one. Hey so whats with the Vida Loca? I thought you were gonna join the army. So Adrian told you that your family was wierd and terrible huh? ha ha Aint that the truth. Well for some of us I guess. When you go to Juarez be careful dont trust anyone over there not even the cops.

Even if you dont talk to ████ or ████ stay in touch with ████ and ████ cause I hear they miss you. Have you heard from Roxanne? heh. I start trial March 22. Yeah I still get visitors. Take some pictures for me and send em ok? Do you talk to ████? Dont be a stranger and write. Maybe when you guys get a phone we can talk. Are you still going around with adrian? Me - Im still here reading sleeping and the usual. When do you think you can come visit me? Id really like to see you. You going to school? How do you get there and what school is it? Ha I bet your saying he asks alot of questions. I think of you often. Take care girl I love you lots.

I got a nosy Nose :)

Yr uncle

Chapter 31

Under One Roof

My mother got a job as a home health care worker while she was still living with my grandparents. She had applied for housing through the Housing Authority of the City of El Paso and had been placed on the waiting list. Until her name rose to the top.

She came to the runaway shelter and took me out. I remember the way she signed the paperwork—her handwriting rushed but firm, as if speed alone could fix what had already broken. She spoke to the grandmother of my friend, and I moved into their crowded house.

Like many Hispanic families I knew, their home held more people than bedrooms. My friend lived with her grandmother, three siblings—two sisters and a brother—an uncle, and his girlfriend. The television was always on. Someone was always cooking. Someone was always arguing. Privacy didn't exist, but neither did silence.

I was still going to school. Still dating Adrian. For reasons I didn't fully understand, I stopped shoplifting. I stopped taking the sleeping pills. Maybe I was tired of numbing myself. Maybe I was beginning to believe that something better might be possible.

That Thanksgiving, I spent the holiday at Adrian's house. I watched how his family passed plates across the table without tension clinging to their hands. I studied the easy way they laughed. I wondered if living under one roof like that automatically made things whole.

After school, my friend's brother, Leo, began lingering near me. We stayed up late watching television, our shoulders brushing beneath the hum of the house. Attention felt like warmth. Warmth felt like safety. One night, it went further than it should have. I wasn't in love. I was lonely. At that age, the two can feel identical.

Around that same time, my mother finally dared to leave my grandparents' house. She followed my example in quiet rebellion, carrying out small bundles of clothes—hers and my sister's—a little at a time to avoid confrontation.

One of her clients, Mr. Chacon, lived alone in a three-bedroom home. He allowed my mother and sister to stay there. My brother refused to leave my grandparents. He said he wasn't going anywhere.

When my mother moved, she transferred my sister to the elementary school near Mr. Chacon's house. Everything felt temporary, like we were waiting for something official to declare us safe.

When my mother left, my father returned from Los Angeles to El Paso, determined to find her. The love between them has always been hard to explain. It survived separation, addiction, pride, and public scandal. It was never steady, but it was stubborn.

By December, I was staying with my mother and sister at Mr. Chacon's house. Her name had begun moving up the housing list. They were requesting the deposit for an apartment which was $150—money she did not have.

Some things hadn't changed. She was still drinking. Money slipped away in small, invisible leaks.

At school, I had a friend named Rachel who had access to her grandmother's checkbook. She had been writing checks for various things, as if consequences were theoretical.

I asked her to write one for $150.

I told her my mother needed it so we could move into our own place. So we could bring our family back together under one roof. I said it like that was the same thing as fixing us.

Rachel wrote the check without hesitation.

I remember staring at the blue ink of her signature. It looked official. It looked like salvation.

My father somehow found us. He took my mother to cash the check. I watched her hands as she folded the receipt and placed it in her purse after paying the deposit. Her face didn't glow with relief the way I expected. It looked guarded. As if she knew something I didn't—that an address does not erase history.

That winter inside Mr. Chacon's house was cold. He kept the wall heater on in the front room, which he had turned into his bedroom. He slept in a hospital bed and moved between that room and the nearby bathroom in his wheelchair. The rest of the house stayed unheated.

At night, the air in our rooms felt metallic and thin. I slept under two blankets and a coat, the fabric scratchy against my chin. During winter break, I read *Flowers in the Attic* by V.C. Andrews, burrowed beneath layers of wool and polyester. Children trapped in a house full of secrets—it felt less like fiction and more like recognition.

I told myself that once we were all together again, things would be different. Warmer.

When the apartment finally became available, we moved into the Alvarez Apartments Projects—a three-bedroom, one-bath, two-level apartment just under a thousand square feet. The largest place we had ever lived.

The first night there, I walked through every room slowly.

The apartment smelled like fresh paint and something faintly chemical, like new beginnings wrapped in plastic. The linoleum floors were cool beneath my bare feet. The walls were an uneven shade of beige, but they were ours. The refrigerator hummed loudly in the empty kitchen, echoing against the hollow space. Every sound felt amplified.

My mother stood in the living room holding a dishtowel she hadn't yet used. My sister spun in a slow circle, claiming corners with her eyes. For a moment, no one argued. No one accused. No one slammed a door.

It felt like standing inside a pause.

We arranged mattresses on the floor that first night. The air was warmer than Mr. Chacon's house, but not by much. I lay awake listening to the small noises—pipes ticking, someone turning over, my mother coughing softly in the next room.

I waited for something to happen. For an argument. For proof that this wasn't real.

Nothing happened.

And yet, beneath the quiet, I felt it: a thin, invisible line of tension running through all of us. We were together, but we were careful. Like guests in our own lives.

My brother chose to remain with my grandparents, visiting on weekends so he wouldn't have to change schools. We had been separated for two and a half years. Being under one roof again felt like victory. It also felt unfamiliar.

We had grown in different directions. We had survived different things. The arrest of my Tío Richie. The media stories that twisted our name. The years of instability. We carried those experiences into the apartment with our boxes.

The first few weeks were gentle. Everyone tried. Voices stayed soft. Doors closed quietly. We behaved as if forgiveness were automatic once walls surrounded us.

Later, I would understand this as the honeymoon period—the fragile calm after upheaval.

But reunification is not the same as healing.

An apartment cannot undo what silence has built. Square footage does not dissolve mistrust. Proximity does not guarantee peace.

I walked the two miles to high school each morning, forty-three minutes there and forty-three minutes back. My sister stayed at her new elementary school. My brother slept in a different house during the week. We were together, but not entirely.

Slowly, the careful politeness began to thin. Old habits surfaced in small ways—sharp tones, unopened mail, evenings that stretched too long. The walls held our voices, but they did not soften them.

Still, that first night remains suspended in my memory—the smell of paint, the hum of the refrigerator, the way we all stood still in the living room as if afraid to disturb the moment.

We believed being under one roof meant we were whole again.

We didn't yet understand that healing requires more than an address.

But for that night, possibility was enough.

Thoughts

I understand why we believed that apartment would save us. After years of separation—garages, borrowed rooms—having an address felt like redemption. We thought stability could be measured in square footage. We thought being under one roof meant we were repaired.

But healing is quieter and more demanding than that. It asks for truth. It asks for accountability. It asks us to sit in rooms together without pretending the past didn't happen.

What we had that winter wasn't healing—it was hope. And sometimes hope is the only bridge available. We crossed it the best way we knew how, carrying our wounds like luggage we weren't yet ready to unpack.

Chapter 32

Reunited, and it feels so good
Reunited 'cause we understood
Reunited by Peaches & Herb 1978

New Year's Eve, 1988. My father was still in town.

That night Adrian was allowed to come over to our new apartment to celebrate. Even now, I remember how significant that felt. Permission in our house was unpredictable. It arrived without explanation and disappeared the same way.

Outside, fireworks cracked in the winter sky. Inside, my parents opened their first beers.

One drink became two. Two became several. Laughter thickened. Their words began to overlap and sharpen at the edges. The smell of alcohol mixed with cigarette smoke and whatever my mother had cooked earlier that evening. By the time midnight approached, the celebration had shifted into something familiar and dangerous.

As tradition would have it, my mother began picking at my father. A comment. A jab. A grievance resurrected. My father answered back. Their voices rose like rival sirens.

Then the bedroom door slammed.

The argument intensified behind it—muffled shouting, something crashing against the wall, a heavy thud. The kind of sounds you learn to interpret without ever wanting to.

Adrian and I went into my bedroom. My sister went to her room to sleep. I turned on the radio and raised the volume, hoping music could drown out violence. The DJ's voice crackled through the static. A love song played. The irony did not escape me.

Adrian stayed the night.

In the morning, sunlight crept across the linoleum floor as if nothing had happened. My parents said nothing about the fight. Nothing about the noise. Nothing about the fact that a teenage boy had spent the night in my room.

They were not concerned in the slightest.

At my tío and tía's house, this would have been a scandal. A disgrace. A betrayal of rules written in stone.

But in our home, chaos created strange freedoms.

This was the freedom I had longed for.

Unsupervised. Unrestricted. Unquestioned.

Was it appropriate? Probably not.

But my parents believed everyone made mistakes. What mattered, they said, was what you did after you realized you'd made one. They talked through consequences with us in long, winding conversations—sometimes sober, sometimes not. Looking back, I see that even in their dysfunction, they were teaching us something about responsibility.

Still, I was beginning to understand something else.

I was learning what love wasn't.

In January, my father returned to Los Angeles to be close to my Tío Richie. His departure left the apartment quieter—but not calmer.

Then February arrived, and with it another loss.

Adrian's parents announced they were moving to Wilmington, California.

I remember the way the air felt when he told me—thin, like something had been pulled out of it. Adrian didn't want to go. He wanted to stay in El Paso. One afternoon he refused to go home at all.

His father eventually came to our apartment. He spoke to my mother first. Then he spoke to me. By then he had heard enough about me to form his opinion. I could see it in the tightness of his jaw. He didn't like me very much.

As a parent now, I understand that. I wouldn't have liked me much either.

Adrian left with his family. For a while, we wrote letters. Blue ink on lined paper, folded carefully into envelopes that carried promises across state lines. My mother had finally gotten a phone, and sometimes we called each other, stretching the cord as far as it would go for privacy.

He promised he would come back.

He promised we would get married.

But I had grown up watching promises evaporate.

He went to California. He never finished school. He started working instead. In every letter he repeated the same vow: I'll come back for you.

I wanted to believe him.

But I had already learned that love can leave without warning.

At home, the fragile peace between my mother and me began to dissolve.

She was drinking heavily again.

And I was no longer a little girl.

For reasons I still struggle to explain, when she drank, she could not see me as I was. The alcohol blurred time. She reached for me the way she used to—pulling my hair, slapping at my face, grabbing my arms as if I were still small enough to overpower.

One night she grabbed a fistful of my hair and tried to drag me across the living room floor.

The floor burned against my knees. Instinctively, I hit her hands to make her let go.It was never about defiance. It was never about trying to dominate her. It was survival. The moment she released me, I stopped. I never tried to strike her back.

But something fundamental had shifted. I was no longer afraid.

The neighbors called the police more than once. Red and blue lights would flicker against our walls, turning our living room into a stage of exposure.

Then one night, instead of threats or lectures, an officer did something unexpected.

He opened a small pocket New Testament Bible.

Standing in the middle of our disheveled living room, he began reading from Romans.

"There is no one righteous, not even one."

His voice was steady, almost gentle. My mother sat on the couch, mascara smudged, shoulders slumped. The air still carried the sour scent of beer.

"For the wages of sin is death, but the gift of God is eternal life…"

The words felt foreign in our house, like light entering through a crack no one had noticed before.

He read from John: "For God so loved the world…"

He explained that Christ died while we were still sinners.

That salvation wasn't earned. That it was offered.

My mother's voice, when she finally spoke, was small.

"What do I need to do to be saved?"

The officer turned to Romans again. Confess with your mouth. Believe in your heart.

Right there, in the wreckage of another fight,
my mother bowed her head.
"Lord, I'm a sinner. Please forgive me. I know You died for my sins and rose again. Jesus, come into my life. Be the Lord of my life. Thank You for saving me."
I watched her carefully.
I had seen her cry like that before. I had seen her rage before.
But this was different. There was a softness there. A surrender.
The officer told her to call
Victory Outreach Chapel on Ochoa Street.
He left us with a phone number and a quiet room.
Something holy had stepped into our chaos.
Not perfectly. Not instantly. But undeniably.

My mother began going to church. And we followed.
The shouting didn't disappear overnight. The drinking didn't evaporate like magic. Change came slowly, unevenly. But there was now a place we went on Sundays where no one screamed. A place where hands were lifted instead of raised in anger.
Looking back now, I see how that year reshaped me.
Adrian's promises taught me that love can be sincere and still not endure.
My parents' fights taught me that passion without restraint is not devotion.
My mother's surrender taught me that even the most volatile heart can soften.
I was learning what love wasn't—
and slowly, painfully, what it might be.
Not control. Not chaos. Not abandonment.
But grace that enters a room when no one expects it.
And stays.

Thoughts

When I look back on that year now, I no longer see it only through the eyes of a teenage girl losing her first love or defending herself in a living room filled with sirens and Scripture. I see it as the year God began introducing Himself quietly into the fractures of our family.

Not through perfection.
Not through instant transformation.
But through interruption.
A police officer with a Bible.
A prayer whispered between tears.
A church on Ochoa Street that became a refuge instead of a battleground.

Adrian leaving taught me that not every promise is meant to last. My mother's spirit kneeling taught me that brokenness is not the end of a story. Faith did not erase our dysfunction overnight, but it planted something sturdier beneath it—a possibility of change.

As an adult, I understand now that God did not wait for our house to become peaceful before entering it. He stepped into the noise. Into the smoke. Into the shame. And He began the slow, patient work of rebuilding from the inside out.

I was learning what love wasn't.

And in the most unexpected way, I was beginning to learn what grace looks like when it refuses to leave.

Chapter 33

Adversity is like a strong wind. I don't mean just that it holds us back from places we might otherwise go. It also tears away from us all but the things that cannot be torn, so that afterward we see ourselves as we really are, and not merely as we might like to be
— Arthur Golden

The Winds

In El Paso, there is one thing you can count on when spring begins to appear: **the winds.**

They do not ask permission. They arrive like a warning.

The sky turns sepia. The Franklin Mountains disappear behind a moving wall of dust. Tumbleweeds—dry, skeletal, relentless—skitter across highways like creatures fleeing some invisible predator. Sand rattles against windows. The air tastes like chalk. Power lines sway and hum. Trees bend until they nearly kneel. After a hard gust, you might drive past a house and see an aluminum shed flipped upside down in someone's yard, as if the wind had reached down and rearranged someone's life for sport.

Spring in El Paso has a way of exposing what isn't anchored.

That year, as the desert winds battered the city, another storm was gathering—this one inside my mother. And without knowing it, I had struck the first match.

The Letter

I wrote to my best friend in Los Angeles.

It was an attempt to reach backward, to reclaim something that once felt steady and safe. I mailed the letter to the last address I had for her, praying it still belonged to her. I filled the first page with pleasantries— updates about our new home, the desert, school. But as my pen moved across the paper, something inside me began to loosen.

I told her I missed her.

I told her I felt alone.

I told her I didn't have anyone I could confide in.

I wrote about arguing with my mother. About Adrian moving away.

About the nightmares that had returned, uninvited and vivid.

And then, almost as if my hand knew what my mouth had never dared to say, I wrote the sentence that had been living in my body like a splinter:

My Tío Richie molested me.

Even now, I am not sure why I wrote it. Maybe it was the first time I allowed the truth to exist outside of my skin. Maybe I was journaling without realizing it. Maybe I was simply tired of carrying it alone.

It was the first time I had ever put that pain into words.

I folded the letter carefully. Sealed it. Mailed it.

And waited.

But she had moved.

The envelope came back stamped **Return to Sender**.

While I was at school, it made its way into my mother's hands.

She opened it.

She read it.

She kept it.

I did not know any of this at the time.

What I know now is that she hand-carried the letter to my grandmother. They read it together. And neither of them said a word to me about it.

Not that year.

Not the next.

It would not surface until 1991.

I remember exactly where I was when I found out. I was standing in my grandmother's bedroom—like she had been waiting for the right moment, and that moment had arrived and I felt cornered.

"We saw the letter," she said, my grandfather in the room.

The room went still. My chest tightened as if the wind had rushed in and stolen all the oxygen. My ears rang. I felt exposed—like someone had taken my diary, stood in the middle of a crowded street, and read it aloud.

They had known.

They had read my confession.

And they had said nothing.

In that silence, something inside me shifted permanently. It was not just betrayal I felt— erased—my truth, my voice. The truth had been acknowledged privately, then buried publicly. My pain had been handled like contraband.

Chapter 33

When my friend never responded, I assumed the letter had been lost. Or worse, that she no longer cared about me the way I cared about her. I never imagined my words had been intercepted, absorbed, and sealed away by the very people who should have protected me.

Outside, the winds roared against our house. Sand hissed against the windows like a whispered warning.

Inside, something in me hardened.

The Plan

If I could not control what had happened to me, I would control what happened next.

I was in the eleventh grade. The future no longer felt abstract—it felt urgent. High school was almost over. I needed an exit. A structure. A mission.

I had stayed in ROTC throughout high school, partly because of discipline, partly because my father's voice still echoed in the crevices of my mind. So I made my decision.

I would join the United States Army.

I would become a soldier.

I would "Be All I Can Be."

The delayed entry program sounded perfect. I would attend basic training between my junior and senior year, return to finish high school, then graduate and report to AIT. After that, I would go to my duty station. And once I was settled, I would send for my nine-year-old sister.

I would rescue her.

I would remove her from my mother's care and give her the stable home we had never known. I would show her that the way we had been living was not normal. I would build the family we should have had.

I was sixteen.

And like most sixteen-year-olds, I believed I knew everything.

The danger of youth is not ignorance—it is certainty. I was certain I understood life, sex, drugs, pain, and love. I was certain I was smarter than my parents. They had ruined their lives; I would not ruin mine. I would do better. I would be better.

And in a moment of breathtaking arrogance, I essentially told God:

Thank You for Your efforts these past sixteen years, but I'll take it from here.

Bible says in Proverbs 14:12 KJV, "There is a way that seems right to a man, but its end is the way to death." At sixteen, that verse felt less like wisdom and more like a dare. Proverbs 16:18 KJV warns, "Pride comes before destruction, and an arrogant spirit before a fall."

I did not yet understand that pride had wrapped itself around my wounds and convinced me it was strength.

Looking back now, I see something my sixteen-year-old self could not: God had not failed me. People had. And instead of grieving that truth, I tried to outrun it. I mistook control for healing. I mistook independence for maturity. I mistook escape for salvation.

My plan was not just ambition—it was desperation disguised as discipline.

March of 1988 found me determined, defiant, and deeply naïve.

I did not know how quickly life would test every promise I had made to myself.

Life is an unforgiving teacher. The most important lesson I was about to learn would not come from school, church, ROTC, or even the Army. It would come from experience—the kind that humbles you without asking permission.

At sixteen, I thought I knew everything.

What I did not know was how much I did not know.

I did not know that not everyone who smiles is safe.

I did not know that you never truly know someone until you live with them.

I did not know that if a man hits you once, he will likely hit you again.

I did not know that pride and pain can dress themselves up as confidence.

Spring always brings the wind to El Paso.

That year, it brought my reckoning.

The dust eventually settled over the desert.

The consequences did not.

<u>Thoughts</u>

When I think about that spring now, I no longer see only the wind. I see a sixteen-year-old girl trying to hold herself together with plans.

I understand her better than I used to.

For years, I judged her harshly. I called her arrogant. Rebellious. Dramatic. I quoted Scripture at her in my mind as if verses were verdicts. But maturity has softened me. I can see now that what looked like pride was often pain wearing armor.

She had written one honest letter in her life. One. And when it came back to her house, it did not bring comfort—it brought silence. That silence shaped her.

When my mother intercepted that letter and never spoke of it, something sacred fractured between us. Not because she read it—but because she did not say, *Tell me what happened. Tell me how you're hurting.* Even now, I try to imagine what she must have felt reading those words. Shock. Guilt. Fury. Denial. Perhaps she carried her own storms and had no shelter to offer mine.

I no longer need to villainize her to validate myself.

But I also no longer minimize what happened.

The truth is this: a child reached for help, and her hand was not taken. So she made a plan instead.

I smile gently when I remember the boldness with which I informed God that I would be taking over my life. I can almost hear Heaven's quiet patience. I thought surrender was weakness. I thought dependence was failure. I did not yet understand that healing is not built through control— it is built through truth, safety, and time.

What I know now is that God was not absent in those years. He was present in ways I could not recognize. He was present in my survival. Present in the fact that I wrote the letter at all. Present in the restless ache that refused to let me accept dysfunction as normal. Present in the dream to rescue my sister, even if my methods were naïve.

The winds in El Paso still come every spring.

They still rattle windows and bend trees. But I have learned something about storms: what is deeply rooted can withstand them. And what is not anchored must either be rebuilt or released.

At sixteen, I thought strength meant never bending.

Now I know strength sometimes looks like telling the truth.

Like grieving what was lost.

Like forgiving without excusing.

Like surrendering the illusion of control.

The girl who wrote that letter was not foolish.

She was brave.

And though the winds howled around her, they did not carry her away.

Chapter 34

"Be All You Can Be".
The Army's iconic recruiting slogan 1980 to 2001

Between Names

The United States Recruiting Office sat one block from our apartment, as if escape had opened an office and was waiting for me to walk in. It was late **March of 1988.**

I told the recruiter I wanted to begin the Delayed Entry Program. Like the slogan promised, I wanted to "be all I could be." I didn't know what that meant. I only knew I couldn't keep being this girl—angry, restless, ricocheting between arguments and apologies, between church pews and slammed doors.

She scheduled my ASVAB for early April and offered to pick me up. The test would be downtown at the federal building, and there was no other way for me to get there. My mother didn't have a car, and even if she had, she hated driving. At the time, she was trying to "do the church thing," which I supported because I needed something steady in the house—even if it was fragile.

Adrian and I were still writing letters, still talking on the phone, still tethered by long-distance promises. Nothing between us had ended. It had only stretched.

The morning of the test, I dressed like I was headed to a kickback, not a government building that might determine my future.

Turquoise Converse.

Turquoise Levi's.

A white button-up layered over a tank.

My hair fell to the middle of my back, feathered and blown away from my face. My eyeliner was thick and sharp. My lashes were dark and dramatic. Big silver hoops swung from my ears like punctuation marks.

I looked like a girl who belonged somewhere loud—not in a federal building about to take a test about discipline and destiny.

When the recruiter pulled up, there was already one person in the passenger seat and two in the back. I made four. We introduced ourselves casually, each of us pretending not to be scared.

While we stood outside waiting to be let in, I noticed a young man inside watching me through the glass. His gaze didn't waver. When we finally entered the testing room, he sat beside me.

More than once, I felt his eyes on me. When I looked up, he smiled—steady, confident. I tried to focus on the exam, but I could feel him there like heat. Even in the reflection of the window, he was watching.

After the test, he asked for my number. Asked if I wanted to do something sometime.

The recruiter dropped me off and waited until I walked through the door before driving away.

I didn't know it then, but I had just stepped into another enlistment.

A few days later, I was on the phone with Arturo several times a week. Soon he was coming over.

My mother didn't like him from the start.

One Friday evening, while we waited for a nearby church family to pick us up, I asked if Arturo could join us. They didn't mind.

My mother did.

He came anyway. Afterward, he said there were too many hypocrites. He couldn't understand how men who claimed to love God still had needle marks on their arms while lifting those same arms in praise.

I didn't argue.

I didn't know how to defend faith yet. I only knew how desperately I needed something to believe in.

Arturo was nineteen. He'd dropped out in ninth or tenth grade. He said he'd been on the football team until a tattoo on his forearm got him kicked off.

That was his version of events.

But he was attentive in a way that felt new. When I told him I had to be at El Paso Community College at four in the morning to apply for a program with limited spots, he didn't hesitate. My friend Cindy stayed the night, and Arturo arrived before dawn. I had my paperwork organized in a neat stack.

We made it in time.

I was accepted.

Then the clerk studied my documents.

Chapter 34

My birth certificate read Rosalinda Rodriguez.

My Social Security card read Rosalinda Ramirez.

She explained that both documents had to match exactly. They would hold my spot—but only briefly.

Later that day, my father called to ask if I'd gotten in. I told him about the problem and said I needed him to notarize paperwork so I could change my birth certificate.

After a pause, he asked, "What would you have to do if you changed your name on your Social Security card instead?"

"All I'd have to do is go to the Social Security office with my birth certificate and fill out a form," I said. "I'd change Ramirez to Rodriguez."

"Do that," he replied gently. "It's easier. I know, and you know, that you're my daughter. Whether your name is Ramirez or Rodriguez, you're my daughter."

My heart cracked—but quietly.

Ramirez was my biological father's name—the man on the other end of the phone, claiming me in that moment.

Rodriguez was my mother's maiden name—the name I had carried most of my life, the name that had marked me as hers when she stood alone.

And there I was at sixteen, standing between two last names like they were two different lives.

"Okay, Dad," I said.

I went alone to the Social Security office and changed my name from Ramirez to Rodriguez.

I told myself it was practical. Efficient.

But it felt like erasing something sacred. Like rewriting a story that hadn't been properly finished.

During our courtship, Arturo brought me stars and moonlight—and promises.

He told me I was the one meant for him. That he would take care of me for the rest of my life. That I wouldn't have to struggle anymore.

The talk was so good I believed him.

I was still writing Adrian. Still unfinished. But Arturo was present—solid, immediate. He saw how my mother treated me. He witnessed her hit me. He said he owned a house in Socorro, left to him by his stepfather, deed in his name. His mother and sister lived there.

He spoke like a man offering rescue.

I was a girl desperate to be rescued.

The talk was so good that I slept with him.

After nearly a year of unprotected sex with Adrian without getting pregnant, I had convinced myself I couldn't. So protection never crossed my mind.

There are dates you never forget.

May 2, 1988—the first day of my last menstrual cycle before my first pregnancy. At the time, I didn't know it would be the last.

On Mother's Day weekend, my father sent for my mother to visit him in Los Angeles. She wouldn't return until Tuesday. I was left in charge of my sister. My brother was still living with our grandparents.

When the cat's away, the mice will play.

Arturo came over.

He spent the night.

When my mother returned, she found out.

She called Adrian and told him everything.

Less than a week later, Adrian was sitting in our living room, summoned like evidence in a trial I hadn't agreed to. My mother and I argued about her interference, about her exposing me. Then Arturo showed up at the door.

I had to tell him about Adrian—that it wasn't over.

The night unraveled fast.

Even after I told him we were done, Arturo refused to leave. I closed the door on him. He slept on the back porch. In the early morning hours, my mother—moved by pity or guilt—let him inside to sleep on the sofa.

Upstairs, I lay in bed with Adrian.

Downstairs, Arturo slept.

Less than ten days earlier, I had been in Arturo's arms. Now I was in Adrian's again.

I wasn't choosing love.

I was choosing whichever version of escape felt safest in the moment.

In the morning, Arturo left empty-handed.

He wanted me to go with him.

Adrian practically moved in.

My mother began drinking again and stopped going to church. The fighting between us escalated—sometimes turning physical. Adrian and I fought too. When I told him I wanted him to leave, he grabbed my arms and shook me, yelling that he loved me, that he wasn't going anywhere unless I went with him.

I felt myself splintering.

I wanted the Army.

I wanted Arturo.

I wanted Adrian.

I wanted to leave.

I wanted my mother sober, gentle, whole.

I wanted someone else to decide.

When I told my mother I wanted Adrian gone, the argument turned physical. In the struggle, she lunged at me and bit my upper arm.

Her teeth broke the skin.

The bruise bloomed purple and green over the next few days, shaped like a crescent moon. I wore long sleeves even in the heat. No one asked about it. Or maybe they did, and I shrugged.

Violence in our house was both visible and invisible at the same time.

My father called. Nothing changed. My Tío Richie called. Nothing changed.

And there I was—trapped between names, between men, between futures.

The Army offered a uniform.

Arturo offered rescue.

Adrian offered history.

But none of them offered peace.

I was trying to choose a future before I even knew who I was.

And beneath all of it—quietly, invisibly—my body had already begun making a choice of its own. I was more tired than usual. My breasts felt tender. A faint nausea brushed against my mornings and disappeared before I could name it.

Something was shifting. I just didn't know how much.

Thoughts

Looking back now, I see that none of those choices were really about love. The Army wasn't about patriotism. It was about structure—about order, about someone telling me what to do so I didn't have to keep guessing. Arturo wasn't a knight; he was a wounded boy speaking fluent fantasy. Adrian wasn't stability; he was familiarity—proof that someone had chosen me once before.

What I was chasing wasn't romance. It was relief.

Years later, I can see that season for what it truly was—not recklessness, not rebellion, not even passion, but hunger. I was hungry for safety, for certainty, for someone to choose me and stay. Every man in that chapter carried a different promise: escape, rescue, belonging, love. None of them could give me what I was actually asking for.

The name change may have been the clearest foreshadowing of all. I thought it was small—just paperwork, just ink. I didn't understand then how often I was already reshaping myself to survive—switching names, loyalties, futures—trying to anchor myself to whatever felt safest in the moment. I didn't yet know how much power there is in a name, or how often women like me are taught to surrender parts of ourselves to keep the peace.

Identity doesn't come from paperwork.

And rescue doesn't come from romance.

When I look back, I don't see a girl making bad choices. I see a girl doing the best she could with the tools she had. A young woman standing at the edge of adulthood, pulled in four directions, mistaking urgency for love and endurance for devotion.

Faith, at that time, was still a borrowed language. I knew how to sit in church, how to bow my head, how to listen—but I didn't yet know how to hear God speaking directly to me. Still, even then, there was something holy in my longing. Something sacred in my desire for a life that was larger, safer, truer than the one I was living.

That chapter didn't end with clarity. It ended with pressure—names, bodies, futures colliding. But it planted a quiet truth I would only understand years later:

Confusion is not failure.

Wanting more is not sin.

Chapter 35

So much for your promises
They died the day you let me go
Caught up in a web of lies
But it was just too late to know
Shattered Dreams by Johnny Hates Jazz

The summer I learned I was pregnant was the summer I learned how far I could walk.

After Memorial Day weekend, I returned to school for the final week before summer break. It was the end of my junior year. Everything around me seemed to be winding down—classes, routines, the fragile sense of normalcy I had tried to maintain.

Looking back now, I realize that sometimes life begins to change quietly before we understand what is happening. A door begins to open somewhere behind us while we are still looking forward, believing the path we are on will remain the same.

On Tuesday, May 31, 1988, during lunch, I noticed bruises blooming across my left upper arm. I stared at them, trying to remember how they had gotten there. Slowly the memory returned: Adrian grabbing my arms, shaking me.

I showed my friend Cindy. Her expression shifted immediately.

"You can't go back there," she said.

Cindy walked over to the row of payphones outside the school—this was long before cell phones—and called her mother. I stood nearby, listening while she explained the situation. She asked if I could stay with them for a while.

Her mother said yes.

Then I picked up the payphone and called my own mother.

My voice trembled as I told her Adrian had bruised my arm. I said that either he leaves, or I would not be coming home.

She answered calmly.

"Adrian can't just get up and leave."

I hung up the phone.

Standing beside that payphone, I understood something without fully naming it: sometimes the door you thought would protect you is already closed.

I decided I would stay with Cindy until I could sort things out.

Unlike the previous time I had run away, I had not prepared. I had no suitcase, no clothes, no plan.

For the next three days I borrowed clothes from Cindy and her sister.

On June 2, I expected my period.

Instead, there was only a faint spotting.

This is the lightest period I've ever had, I thought.

It lasted only two days. At sixteen, I did not yet understand the quiet ways life can announce itself.

Once school was out, I called Arturo. I told him I was staying with a friend at the Kennedy Apartments—the projects.

He came by later that afternoon.

There were specks of spray paint on his arms and shirt.

"What happened?" I asked.

"I've been working on something," he said.

We stepped outside to talk.

He told me to give him a couple of days so he could talk to his mother. When I went back inside, Cindy's mother asked who he was.

"My second cousin," I said quickly.

Later, Cindy's mother called my own mother. That was when my mother told her Arturo was not my cousin, but my boyfriend.

I was furious.

I had lied to Cindy's mother, and suddenly that lie had collapsed.

I knew I could not stay there anymore.

So I called Arturo.

I told him I would move in with him and his mother.

Looking back now, I see how many doors I was walking through without realizing what waited behind them.

The weekend after I moved in with Arturo, I told him I needed to go back to my mother's apartment to get my belongings.

He called his brother-in-law to come with us.

When we arrived, Arturo and I entered through the front door. His brother-in-law waited by the back door in case Adrian tried to run out.

Inside, the apartment was quiet.

I grabbed a trash bag from the kitchen and crept upstairs.

My mother's bedroom door was closed, music blaring inside. My sister's room was closed. The bathroom light was on behind a shut door.

I slipped into what had been my bedroom and began throwing clothes into the trash bag as quickly as I could.

Then the bathroom door opened.

Adrian stepped out and saw me packing.

He began begging me to stay.

I ignored him and ran downstairs with the bag.

He followed.

But when we reached the dining room, he stopped.

Arturo was standing there.

Adrian lunged toward the table where a knife sat.

"Go ahead," Arturo said. "Pick it up."

"Stop!" I shouted. "Let's go."

And we left.

Sometimes leaving is not brave or dramatic. Sometimes it is simply the act of stepping through a doorway and not turning back.

Soon after that, I began feeling sick.

My stomach churned constantly.

Every day I felt nauseous, and often I vomited.

Finally, I went to Planned Parenthood.

The nurse confirmed it.

I was eight weeks pregnant.

My due date was February 23, 1989.

I remember walking out of the clinic feeling as though the ground beneath me had shifted. There I was, sixteen years old, already walking farther down a road I had never imagined.

That was also when I began to see Arturo differently.

Very quickly I learned that he struggled to hold a job longer than a few months. I also discovered he smoked marijuana—and sometimes injected heroin.

During our courtship, I had never suspected any of it.

At sixteen, I believed I understood the world.

Now I understand that youth often walk with confidence down roads it cannot yet see clearly.

That summer I found a job through a youth program for teenagers from low-income families.
I worked as a filing clerk at Ysleta High School.
Every morning I woke up at 4:30 a.m., got ready, and began walking.
The nearest bus stop was three and a half miles away.
It took an hour and fifteen minutes to get there.
Seven miles a day.
Thirty-five miles a week.
The first bus arrived at 6:20 a.m., and then I transferred to another that stopped in front of the school.
Sometimes someone would pull over and offer me a ride.
I always accepted.
Looking back now, I realize how vulnerable I was.
Many of the drivers were men who began recognizing me.
A group of men from a notorious gang offered me rides several times.
A year later, in February 1990, those same men were arrested after sexually assaulting an undercover police officer.
She had been raped at gunpoint.
I think about that often—the thin distance between safety and danger that I walked each morning.

My job involved answering phones and filing documents. The school basement had flooded in earlier years, so many records needed to be reorganized. After eight hours of work, I took two buses home and walked another hour and a half.
The walk always felt longer in the evening.
Fatigue settled into my legs like stone.
But I kept walking.
At the time I believed I was simply walking to work.
Now I know I was walking toward survival.

One afternoon I stopped in a small store near the shopping center by my job. I needed mascara but was trying to save money for the baby.

Makeup was expensive.
I picked up a package with two tubes and slipped it into my purse.
When I walked toward the exit, an alarm exploded behind me.
Two employees grabbed my arm and took me to the back room.
They emptied my purse and found the mascara.
"I'll pay for it," I said.
They refused.
They called the police.
I showed the manager my prenatal vitamins and clinic card.
It didn't matter.
The police handcuffed me and placed me in the back of the patrol car.
At the station they put me in a holding cell.
Eventually I lied again and said my cousin could pick me up.
The cousin was Arturo's sister.
When Arturo arrived, he laughed at me for getting caught.
The store manager never pressed charges. He only wanted to scare me. And it worked.
I never stole another thing again.

Later that summer I learned Adrian had returned to California, and my sister had gone there to spend the summer with my father.
My mother was alone.
I went to visit her.
Feeling sick and exhausted, I laid down and fell asleep.
While I slept, she went through my purse and found my prenatal vitamins.
Soon my father began calling, demanding that I get an abortion.
"You're going to drop out of school," he said.
"You'll be on welfare, living in the projects with a bunch of babies."
Eventually I stopped answering his calls.
He didn't speak to me for nearly a year and a half.

Then my uncle Richie called collect.
His voice was gentle. "Your dad told me to call you, he is pretty upset about you getting pregnant, he's having a cow" he laughed
"I know, Tío" I said.

"What's your plan?" he asked.
"I'm having my baby," I said. "And I'm going to graduate."
"Babies cost money," he said kindly.
"Have you thought about diapers? Childcare?"
"No," I admitted. "But I will figure it out."
"Let me know if I can help you, take care of yourself" he said.
At sixteen, hope often looks like stubbornness.
Sometimes that stubbornness is the only thing that keeps you
walking forward.

Living with Arturo slowly revealed the truth about him.
I found plastic bags of marijuana in the house and burned bottle
caps scattered across the bedroom dresser.
Then one afternoon I saw him outside with his friends.
Through the window I watched him roll up his sleeve.
Then I saw the needle.
That was the day I learned something important.
You never truly know someone until you live with them.

This lesson was the hardest.
Whenever I did not respond the way Arturo wanted, he responded
with violence.
Punches. Slaps. Dragging me by my hair.
He did not care that I was pregnant.
One night he beat me and raped me.
Afterward I ran out the house down the street
until a car slowed near the corner.
I hit the hood with my hands.
They stopped.
I jumped into the back seat and begged them to go.
They drove me to my mother's house.
But I told her nothing.
Silence was another road I had learned to walk.

Eventually Arturo arrived.
My mother opened the door and let him in.
He looked at me.

"Let's go home."
I hugged my mother and left with him.
He always apologized afterward.
He always promised it would never happen again.
And I believed him.
Because I was sixteen.
Because I thought love meant enduring.
Because I did not yet know that some doors should never be walked
through twice.

By the fall, I would begin my senior year.
And somewhere inside me, another life was growing quietly.
Every morning, I woke before dawn and began walking those long
miles to the bus stop.
The road stretched ahead of me in the dark.
Cars passed. Dogs barked behind fences.
The desert air held the cool silence of early morning.
I walked carrying everything I knew and everything I did not yet
understand.
Seven miles a day.
Thirty-five miles a week.
A sixteen-year-old girl walking down a long road with a secret life
growing inside her—still believing, somehow, that if she just kept moving
forward, she would eventually find her way out.

<u>Thoughts</u>

I was a teenager—pregnant, living inside a relationship shaped by
drugs and fear—and I didn't have language for any of it.
I mistook survival for love.
I confused apology with change.
I believed that if I worked hard enough, stayed quiet enough, wanted
goodness badly enough, the road would eventually soften beneath my
feet. I didn't yet understand how power works—how addiction bends a
house around it, how violence doesn't begin with fists but with
permission, small and quiet and learned.
Being young did not mean being weak. It meant being unprotected.

What I carried was more than a child. I carried responsibility heavier than my years. I carried it while walking miles each day—literally and spiritually—because walking was the only way I knew how to move forward.

Each bus stop.

Each stretch of pavement.

A place where I waited for my life to begin.

Now, from where I stand, I can say this with clarity and compassion:

None of it was my fault.

Not the drugs.

Not the violence.

Not the staying.

I was a child navigating adult consequences without a map.

And still, I graduated.

Still, I kept my child.

Still, I lived.

What amazes me now is not that I survived.

It's that something in me—quiet, unnamed, untrained—

kept choosing life.

Even when love was distorted.

Even when safety was temporary.

Even when hope looked like nothing more than a long road and the belief that if I kept walking, I might someday reach myself.

That girl did not know how strong she was.

But I do.

When I think about that summer now, I don't first see the bruises or the fear. I see the road. I see a seventeen-year-old girl walking before dawn, one hand resting lightly over her stomach, believing that movement itself could save her. She didn't have language for abuse. She didn't understand addiction or power or trauma. She only understood forward.

So she kept going.

What I know now is this: endurance is not the same as love, and silence is not the same as strength. But walking—choosing not to collapse, choosing not to disappear—that was strength all along.

I once believed I was surviving by accident.

I understand now I was surviving on instinct.

And somewhere between those bus stops and that diploma, between fear and fierce determination, I began becoming the woman who would one day look back at that girl with tenderness instead of shame.

She thought she was lost.

She was, in truth, already on her way.

Chapter 36
The Long Walk

August came quietly; the way change often does—without knocking.

I had been saving money from my paychecks, folding each bill with intention, smoothing the creases as if I could press certainty into them. Every dollar felt like a key I might need later. I didn't know which door it would open, only that I would need one.

My sister had just returned from California, glowing because my dad had bought her a Walkman radio and cassette player. It felt like a small miracle you could hold in your hands. Music without wires. Freedom that fit in your pocket. When she showed it to me, her eyes were bright in a way I hadn't seen in a long time. For a moment, it felt like light had stepped into the room.

One afternoon, I took the bus to visit my mom and asked if we could go to Kmart. I told her I wanted to help buy school clothes for my sister. She agreed.

Inside the store, under the humming fluorescent lights, I became the one choosing jeans and shirts, holding them against my sister's shoulders the way Tía Sofia had once done for me. I imagined her walking through the school doors feeling new, feeling seen. There is something holy about helping someone else step into a better version of themselves. I didn't have the language for it then, but I think God was already teaching me how to mother.

During that same trip, I bought maternity clothes for myself—soft waistbands, fabric that stretched instead of resisted. I held them in my hands for a long time before placing them in the cart. I was stepping through a door I had not chosen, carrying a life I had not planned, trusting that somehow there would be ground beneath my feet.

I never told my mom about the abuse I was experiencing at Arturo's hands. Silence was my oldest skill. I had learned it young and practiced it well. Silence can feel like safety when you are a child. It can feel like survival. But silence is also a locked room.

By late August, as my senior year approached, I had registered for school and taken my senior pictures. In those photographs, my smile was steady. No one could see the weight I carried just beneath the surface.

Chapter 36

I signed up for WIC and registered at Thomason General Hospital, where I would deliver my baby. My prenatal care came through the county clinic—another waiting room, another clipboard, another set of forms asking questions I didn't always know how to answer. Nothing in my life came easily or without paperwork. Even help required proof.

To prepare for school, I practiced the route: an hour-and-fifteen-minute walk to the bus stop, then two buses. The desert mornings were cool then, the sky still lavender before sunrise. I walked past fields and quiet houses, my breath visible in the early air. Some mornings I prayed without realizing it—counting my steps like rosary beads.

Please let me finish.

Please let the baby be healthy.

Please open a door.

This was my senior year.

I refused to change schools. They offered to send me somewhere else—an alternative school for pregnant teens—but I declined. I would not be moved aside. I wanted to graduate where I had begun. Proving my father wrong became my fuel, but beneath that was something deeper: I needed to prove to myself that I could walk through a door without breaking it.

When my pregnancy began to show, I was called into the nurse's office. I told them I was due in February. They offered options. I chose to stay.

Once a week, I met with other pregnant girls in folding chairs inside the nurse's office. We compared due dates and cravings, swollen feet and quiet fears. That's where I saw Rachel again—the same Rachel who had once written checks for me when I had nothing. I learned she had been pregnant too, hiding it from nearly everyone.

We had been carrying more than we knew—each of us a secret vessel, walking the same hallways, pretending to be lighter than we were.

Some of my teachers were told. Sgt. Byrd and Mr. Ware had known me for years. They did not lecture me. They did not shame me. They made room.

I often fell asleep in Mr. Ware's afternoon class, exhaustion pulling me under like a tide. Sometimes I would wake to find a hall pass on my desk, his quiet permission to rest in the nurse's office. No questions asked. Mercy can be small and still change everything.

I still remember him—white-haired, slight in stature, enormous in my heart. Looking back now, I see how God placed people along my path like steady doorframes—something to lean against when I was too tired to stand alone.

One weekend, my sister offered to let me borrow her Walkman for my morning walks.

When she placed it in my hands, it felt sacred. I remember the weight of it, the soft click of the cassette sliding into place, the foam padding cool against my ears before the music began. The first time I pressed play and stepped into the early morning dark, it felt as though the world had opened.

Music made the miles bearable.

When "Don't Worry, Be Happy" played, I turned the volume up and sang into the empty road, my voice rising into the pale desert sky. The song felt almost like a whisper from heaven—simple, steady, repetitive, as if joy itself were knocking at my chest.

Don't worry.

Be happy.

I didn't know much about theology then.

But I knew what it felt like to be carried for three minutes at a time.

One afternoon, Arturo asked to borrow the Walkman.

I hesitated. It wasn't mine.

Fear answered for me.

I said yes.

He sold it.

I never got it back.

Telling my sister was harder than losing the music. When she looked at me, disappointment flickered across her face—but she didn't yell. She simply nodded. Forgiveness can be quiet. It can sound like nothing at all.

By early October, I was running out of bus money. I asked my mom if I could stay with her during the week. She agreed. My walk went from thirty-five to twenty-three miles a week.

Still, it saved me twelve miles.

Survival is often a math problem.

Faith is believing the numbers will stretch.

Around that time, my Tío Richie called from Los Angeles County Jail while I was back in Socorro with Arturo. My mom's phone had been disconnected, so he called Arturo's house. I accepted the charges.

He asked how I was. Asked about the baby. Asked if I was ready.

Tio Richie: Hey good thing I caught you, how are you?

Me: I'm good Tío, how are you?

Tio Richie: You know, court, boring, still in county the only good thing about it is the pretty girls. Don't listen to everything they say about me.

Me: I don't Tío

Tio Richie: How are you and the baby doing? Are you ready?

Me: Tío, I am good but I could use some help.

Tio Richie: I am going to send you five hundred dollars; do I send it to your mom's address?

Me: No Tío, send it to me here at this address.

Tio Richie: Don't tell anyone

Me: Okay Tío thank you.

Don't tell anyone. He said and I didn't.

Weeks passed. By mid-November, I was five months pregnant. One afternoon, Arturo's mother told me a letter had arrived from my Tío. Inside was an unaddressed money order for five hundred dollars. I asked her to hold onto it. It wasn't just cash. It was proof that someone, somewhere, believed I could make it.

A few days later, when I told my mom I was going to the store to use the payphone and call Arturo, she stopped me.

"Don't call him tonight," she said.

"Do you have to call every day? Your feet look swollen.

You need to rest."

Something in her voice felt off. I went anyway.

That's when I learned the truth. My parents had gone to Arturo's house, convinced his mother that I had sent them for the money order. She believed them. The money was gone. My parents took it.

That was the moment rage found its voice.

I won't explain rage the way I once tried to. It doesn't need poetry.

It is heat. It is a locked door kicked open after years of pressure.

I screamed. I kicked the wall. I broke what I could reach.

When my father arrived, the door opened —

the years came spilling out at him.

"You left us," I said. "You promised it would only be months.

Now you take from me, you steal from me."

The money wasn't just money. It was diapers. Blankets. Preparation. It was safety for my son. They said they had used it toward a crib on layaway. Something inside me fractured.

Then the door opened again.

My Tía Ruth stood there.

"¿Qué pasó, mija?"

Her voice was not loud. It didn't have to be.

When she wrapped her arms around me, the rage collapsed.

Not because I had won.

Not because anything was fixed. But because someone was steady.

"This much anger isn't good for your baby," she said softly.

She didn't defend my parents. She didn't defend me.

She simply said, "They're going to give it back."

Her faith felt older than the moment.

It felt like something anchored beyond us.

A few days later, the money returned—four hundred and forty dollars, he kept sixty to replace my sister's Walkman.

I spent it slowly. A bassinet. Small shirts. Receiving blankets. Bottles. Diapers. I bought everything for a boy.

Doctors didn't tell you the gender then—but I knew.

Sometimes a mother knows before the world confirms it.

Thanksgiving came I spent it with Arturo and we stayed behind while his mother visited family. That night, I said something sharp. Something meant to wound.

He beat me. This time, I fought back.

When his mother forced the door open, my eye was already swelling.

The bruise was truth rising to the surface.

Evidence that refused to stay hidden.

I packed my things.

She drove me through the dark desert night to my mother's house.

I stood at the door with a bag and a bruised eye.

When my mother opened it, she didn't ask questions.

She stepped aside.

Chapter 36

That was the first time I understood that a door can be an act of grace. The next day, I told her the truth.

She said, "Of course you can stay."

No lecture. No condition. Just room.

And now, looking back, I see it clearly:

Rage breaks doors.

Violence forces them.

But faith waits.

Faith knows which doors are not meant to be kicked open.

Faith knows when to close one quietly behind you.

Faith knows that protection does not always look like power—it often looks like surrender.

I did not leave that season unmarked.

But I was not abandoned.

God did not stop every blow.

He did not prevent every loss.

But He placed door after door in front of me—some to walk through, some to shut, some to survive behind.

And though I did not yet know how to pray without anger,

He was already teaching me how to walk toward light.

The baby would come in February.

I would graduate in June.

There were still doors ahead I could not see.

But for the first time, I understood this:

I did not have to break them to pass through.

Thoughts

When I think about that year now, I no longer see only the bruises, the miles, or the slammed doors.

I see a young girl learning, slowly and imperfectly, that survival is not the same as strength—and that strength is not the same as faith.

Back then, I thought faith meant being rescued. I thought it meant the money not being taken, the Walkman not being sold, the blow never landing. But faith, I would learn, is quieter than that. It is the door that opens after midnight. It is the aunt who steps into the room without judgment. It is the mother who says, "Of course you can stay," and means it.

I did not know how close I was to breaking. I only knew I had to keep walking.

And somehow, even in my rage, even in my fear, even in my stubborn pride, God kept placing thresholds in front of me—small chances to choose differently, to leave, to return, to begin again.

I crossed them one by one.

Not gracefully.

But alive.

Dear Rosie,   11/6/88

Hi what you doing? Got your letter. Thanx. Hope your doing ok. I'm 50-50. Try and make up with your dad you know cause I know he's not feeling too good about what happened down there either. I almost grew up with you so I know about the problems you had. Remember 71st? I used to go outside to smoke dope and you used to go out there too. Hope everything works out for you and Arturo.

I don't know what to tell you about your situation with your mom. Maybe its a good thing high school is almost over for you right? Be sure and throw my letters away. I don't wanna get in trouble with your folks. I'm glad to see you doing good in school. Maybe after you finish college or the army you can make it without anybody elses help. But at your age, you should get help. Fuck everyone who gives you a hard time.

Yeah back in 1873 you were 3 or 4 right? I was 13. Anyway. I'm stoned right now, it happens. I hope and wish for you the best regarding your baby. I guess I'll stop here. Stay in touch — at least once a month. In December, I'll be sending you something at the [redacted] address. Don't tell your folks

or anybody else you got it from
me. When you get it in the mail
call Jamie (213) ████ ████ and let
her know if you got it. Love
you lots. Yr tio
Rich

P.S. Also when you get it tell
████ that you got it by telling
him you got the birthday card
that way I'll know for sure
you got it. And write me too
As you can see I worry
about these things. ve

Chapter 36

Though it's been a while now
I can still feel so much pain
Like a knife that cuts you, the wound heals
But the scar, that scar remains
Every Rose Has Its Thorn by Poison

1989

New Year's Eve arrived the way it always did—loud on television, quiet in our apartment.

My mom was babysitting someone else's kids that night, which meant she was drinking. That was the arrangement. She watched the children of younger mothers in the projects if they bought her alcohol in return. It wasn't said out loud. It didn't need to be.

My sister and I sat on the couch, watching *Dick Clark's New Year's Rockin' Eve*. Confetti fell on the screen. Strangers cheered. Time counted itself down.

Just before midnight, there was a knock at the door.

I went downstairs and opened it.

He stood there, smaller than I remembered, his shoulders slumped, his face tired. He said he was sorry. He asked if I would go with him. I told him no—my mom wasn't home. His eyes dropped to my stomach. He told me I looked beautiful, that my belly was big now. He asked if he could hug me. I let him.

For a moment, he held me. Then he said goodbye and walked away. The door closed. The year turned. Something inside me shut quietly, without sound.

In January 1989, my dad showed up with a car for my mom. It was strange—she hated driving. Her hands shook on the steering wheel. Her anxiety rose the moment the engine started. We used the car for groceries and errands, but mostly it sat there, parked and still, like time paused around it.

On Wednesday, February 8, Arturo came to see me. He stayed the night. We slept together.

The next morning—Thursday, February 9—I skipped school to go with my mom. We needed groceries. We needed the registration sticker for the car.

While getting dressed, I noticed something wasn't right. I couldn't hold my urine. I kept leaking. I rolled toilet paper and tucked it into my underwear, embarrassed, uneasy, trying not to imagine what it meant.

At the registration office, while we waited, I told my mom. She didn't say much. Her silence felt heavy, as if she already knew the answer and was waiting for time to say it for her.

Afterward, we went to the grocery store. We moved down every aisle slowly, choosing what we would need for the month. Cans clinked. Bread went stale in my hands before it even reached the cart.

Then the cramp came—low, sharp, undeniable.

At 11:30 a.m., I told my mom I was having a strong menstrual cramp.

She looked at me and said quietly, "I don't think that's a menstrual cramp."

We paid and headed home. On the way, her nerves took over. She stopped at a convenience store and bought a pint of vodka before driving the rest of the way.

Arturo was still there when we arrived. He helped carry in the groceries. By then, the cramps were closer together. My mom began timing them, watching the clock. Arturo laughed nervously, pacing, unsure where to put his hands or his fear.

By 1:30 p.m., the pain was no longer something I could talk around.

"These contractions are too close," my mom said. "It's time."

Arturo grabbed my hospital bag and loaded it into the car. He walked me to the passenger side and buckled me in. Then, standing there, he said he was too nervous to be any help. He said he was going home. He told my mom to call him when the baby was born.

There wasn't time to argue. Time had already decided.

The drive to Tigua General Hospital was only a mile and a half. Five minutes. Every second stretched.

We checked in and were rushed to a labor room. The contractions intensified. My mom was still drunk—her speech thick, the smell of alcohol clinging to her breath as sharp as antiseptic.

A doctor came in and asked if I would mind if interns observed the delivery.

"No," I said. I didn't care. Pain stripped everything else away.

My mom leaned in.

"Rosie, you don't want interns watching you. Really?"

"I said no—I don't mind."

She went to find the doctor and told him I was fine with it.

In the delivery room, I placed my feet into cold metal stirrups. The doctor told me to push like I was having a bowel movement. I pushed. Time broke into pieces—breath, pressure, heat.

When my baby's head crowned, I asked my mom to stand on the other side and tell me what was happening.

In that moment, she seemed to sober up.

She cried when she saw his head.

"One more big push," the doctor said.

And then he was here.

"It's a boy."

They placed Jimmy on my chest at 3:46 p.m.

He weighed seven pounds, two ounces.

He was warm. Solid. Real. The clock could not take him back.

They took him to clean him, gave me something to help me relax, and I drifted into sleep while the doctor delivered the placenta.

When I woke up, my mom was still there.

She told me my baby was fine.

We were just waiting for a room.

Waiting had become familiar.

Throughout my pregnancy, Arturo often doubted that the baby was his. I didn't blame him.

During arguments, he would say, "Maybe that baby isn't even mine."

I stayed quiet. I prayed.

Every day, the same prayer:

God, let my baby look exactly like his biological father.

On Thursday, February 9, God answered me.

When Arturo walked into my hospital room with his mother and little sister, I was holding my son. The moment they saw him, they squealed. There was no question. No doubt. My baby looked exactly like Arturo.

He held his son and smiled—wide, unguarded, certain.

I didn't say anything.

I just thanked God quietly, holding the weight of my answer,

knowing that being delivered doesn't always mean being kept.

Time kept moving.

But for that moment, my son stayed.

<u>Thoughts</u>

I understand now that I learned about time that day—not from a clock, but from my body. I learned how quickly someone can leave, and how little that stops what is coming. I learned that birth does not wait for certainty, sobriety, or courage. It arrives anyway.

For a long time, I believed God answered prayers only in ways that proved something—proof of love, proof of belonging, proof that I hadn't imagined the pain. That day, my prayer was answered plainly, almost practically. My son looked like his father. The doubt stopped. The room exhaled.

But adulthood taught me that answered prayers do not guarantee protection. They don't promise presence. They simply meet you where you are and leave the rest for you to carry.

When I think back to that day, I don't remember the fear as much as I remember the weight of my son on my chest. The way time slowed just long enough for me to breathe him in. Long enough to know that something had been given to me—something real, something mine.

My faith grew quieter after that. Less about asking. More about noticing.

I no longer ask God to stop people from leaving. I ask for the strength to stay—steady, awake, present—when it matters most.

And sometimes, when I need reminding, I return to that moment at 3:46 in the afternoon, when time paused long enough for a boy to arrive, and for me to begin.

Dear Rosie   3/11/89

  Just a small note to let
you know I got yr letter, to wish
you and yr baby well, and to
let you know that I'm thinking of
you. Say hi to yr mom and ████
for me. I'll enclose a small note
for ████ also. Thank you for
the birthday card. I haven't been
able to call home cause I'm on
restrictions. They wont let me use
the phone. But hope all's going good
with you. Say hi to Jimmy for
me. Have you recieved my letters
to you? Are you going back to
school now? Write when you can
ok. Love you lots. Yr tio .C.

Chapter 37

**We got something to believe in
Even if we don't know where we stand
Only God would know the reasons
But I bet he must have had a plan
'Cause you were born to be my baby
And baby, I was made to be your man.
Born to Be My Baby by Bon Jovi 1988**

A new chapter. A new life. And in the quiet, unannounced way that truth often arrives, this life would eventually change everything.

High school maternity leave was only two weeks. Two weeks to recover, to adjust, to pretend that motherhood could be folded neatly back into a teenage schedule. Before I could even return to school, I had to report to the WIC office—to register my baby, to prove on paper that he existed, that I existed now in this new role.

The weather forecast warned of rain. The night before my appointment, I called Arturo and asked if he could borrow a car to take us. He said yes.

That morning, I bundled my baby carefully, layer by layer, protecting him from a world that already felt too sharp. We waited. And waited. The minutes crept closer to my appointment time, but Arturo never came. Finally, with no other choice, I grabbed an umbrella, pulled on a coat, and took the bus.

We barely made it.

After the baby was examined, they examined me. They adjusted our benefits—numbers on paper standing in for survival. I attended a nutrition class that lasted an hour, my son cradled against me, his small weight anchoring me to the chair. When it was over, we boarded the bus again and rode home through the rain.

When we arrived, Arturo was standing at the front door—angry.

He yelled at me for taking the baby out in such terrible weather.

"What kind of mother takes a baby out in the rain?"

Then his voice sharpened into something colder.

"If this is the kind of mother you plan on being, I'll take the baby away from you. I'll get a lawyer."

My mother wasn't home.

I tried to ignore him, focused only on getting inside. The front door was locked. I asked him to hold the baby while I checked the back door. It was open. I let myself in, then walked back to the front to let them both inside.

When I opened the door, he was gone.

Gone—with my baby.

I ran around the building, then through the apartment and back out again, screaming at the top of my lungs,

"He stole my baby! My baby!"

Fear hijacked my body. My heart slammed so hard it hurt. I was shaking, dizzy, unable to breathe properly. I was so terrified I wet myself. Neighbors poured out of their apartments, drawn by my cries. And then I saw him—walking back toward us, my son in his arms.

I ran to him and took my baby back without a word.

Something in me locked into place that day. A hard, permanent knowing. I would never again assume safety. I would verify it.

From that moment on, I never trusted Arturo to be alone with my son again.

Every morning after that, I found myself back at school. I got myself ready, then packed the diaper bag. I placed my son into his stroller, and together we walked two miles to the home daycare. I left him there— along with the stroller—then walked the rest of the way to school.

At the end of the day, I walked it all again. Back to the daycare. Back home. Every step felt deliberate, my body sore, my mind always alert. Walking became my discipline. My proof. As long as I kept moving, we were still okay.

My Tío Richie sent more money, but this time he sent it to my Tía Ruth. Whenever I needed any of it, I would call her with the amount and meet her at a bakery near my mom's house. She would hand me the cash, ask how I was doing, then drive away.

That money made survival possible. I bought a stroller. Pampers. My class ring. My letterman jacket. I paid the daycare in advance for the rest of the school year. Each purchase felt like laying another plank beneath my feet.

Every other weekend, we stayed in Socorro with Arturo, his mother, and sister. During those visits, he would let me sleep through the night, waking to feed the baby himself. Once, I woke to find him sitting in his mother's rocking chair, talking nonsense to our son. The baby stared up at him, wide-eyed and calm.

It was a precious sight, but it unsettled me.

When prom approached, I wanted to go. I wanted one last night of pretending my life still looked like everyone else's. Arturo said prom was immature. He said he was too grown for that.

Mike was still my friend. He offered to take me—he still had a crush on me. I declined. I stayed home with my baby while my friends danced through their final school night. I told myself this was what choosing responsibility looked like.

Graduation came quickly.

With invitation in hand, my mother, my sister, my son, and I went to my grandmother's house. I hadn't seen her or my grandparents since I ran away from my tío and tía's home. It mattered to me that I invited them. I needed them to see that I had done something good—that I was still capable of finishing what I started.

On Monday, June 5, 1989, I graduated from high school.

During the ceremony, Arturo held my son while he cried with colic. My baby was almost four months old. And I made it.

My grandmother and cousins surprised me by showing up. To celebrate, we went to the dollar movie. Beforehand, we stopped at a grocery store—Big 8—to buy popcorn and drinks to sneak into the theater inside the diaper bag.

As the cashier scanned our items, I asked if they were hiring.

"Yes," she said.

I asked for an application before she could finish the sentence.

The next day, June 6, I filled it out. I asked my mom and sister to watch the baby while I turned it in. The store was less than a mile away— a short walk, but one I took seriously. I introduced myself to the manager and handed him my application.

A week later, I returned.

On June 13, I asked to speak with him again. He took me upstairs to his office. I asked about the status of my application.

"What's your name?" he asked.

"Rosalinda Rodriguez."

He shuffled through a stack of papers, found my application, and studied it.

"Memorize this list," he said, handing me a sheet. "Come back in a week. Be ready for a test."

It was a list of produce codes. Every fruit and vegetable had its own number. I studied day and night. I put my baby in the stroller and walked to the store four times that week. I stood in the produce section, touching each item, whispering its code under my breath like a prayer.

On June 20, I returned and told the manager I was ready.

He called the head cashier and instructed her to test me in the produce aisle.

Exactly two weeks after graduating, I was hired.

Gratitude washed over me—not as relief, but as resolve. I didn't feel rescued. I felt accompanied. As if every step I had taken had been seen.

Now I needed childcare.

There was no way I would leave my baby with my mother. In our apartment complex lived an older woman everyone called La Cristiana— the Christian lady. I walked to her door and knocked. She already knew me from the police calls, from the way trouble sometimes echoed in the projects.

I told her about the job. I asked if she would watch my son while I worked. I told her I would pay whatever she asked.

She agreed without hesitation.

That night, I held my baby and thought about the distance still ahead of us—the hours, the miles, the discipline it would require. I didn't know where the path ended.

But I knew how to walk it.

And for now, that was enough.

Thoughts

At seventeen, I did not yet have language for what my life required of me. I only knew that stopping was not an option. By then, I had already learned how quickly love could turn conditional, how adults could fail you, how safety could vanish without warning. Motherhood did not arrive as a beginning so much as a reckoning—it demanded that I become the one thing no one had reliably been for me: steady.

I believed then that endurance was the highest form of strength. That if I could just keep moving—keep walking, keep showing up, keep putting one foot in front of the other—I might outrun the chaos that had followed me since childhood. What I did not understand was that endurance alone is not freedom. It is only the first layer of it.

The day my baby was taken from my arms, even briefly, something fundamental shifted. Fear rearranged my instincts. Trust became something earned slowly, reluctantly. I learned that vigilance is not paranoia when danger has already introduced itself. It is wisdom shaped by experience. I did not grow hardened. I grew precise.

By the time I graduated, found work, and arranged childcare, I had already lived several lifetimes of responsibility. I had navigated violence without a map, dependence without protection, and faith without certainty. I had learned how to ask for help without begging, how to accept provision without surrendering my agency, how to stand on my own while still reaching outward.

My faith, even then, was quiet. It did not shield me from harm or lift me out of struggle. It met me in the ordinary acts of survival—the knock on a stranger's door, the courage to walk into an office and ask for work, the discipline to memorize codes while rocking a baby to sleep. Looking back, I see now that grace often appeared not as escape, but as enough.

I did not know I was building a foundation. I thought I was simply trying to survive the day. But each step—each mile walked, each boundary drawn, each decision made with my child in mind—was teaching me who I could be. Not the girl who endured everything quietly, but the woman who learned to choose herself and her child deliberately.

I am older now, and I understand that what carried me forward was not just strength or faith or love, but the convergence of all three. Survival taught me how to walk. Faith taught me why to keep going. And motherhood taught me where I was headed.

I was not saved all at once. I was shaped—step by step—into someone who could finally believe that a life built with care could also be a life built with hope.

Chapter 38

**"My mother was my role model before
I even knew what that word was."
— Lisa Leslie**

I had only been working for about a week when Arturo's mother called me at work. Her voice was flat, almost practiced, as she told me Arturo had been arrested and was being held at the El Paso County Jail.

On my next day off, I took the bus downtown. The jail rose from the sidewalk in dull gray blocks, heavy and sealed, a building meant to keep people in and the world out. A line had already formed—mostly women—waiting their turn. Without thinking, I stepped into it. I had stood in lines like this before, years earlier, holding my mother's hand. That memory settled into me like a bruise I hadn't realized was still tender.

The women around me talked easily about their men—the charges, the time, who might be home soon. Their voices blended together, casual, practiced. When it was my turn, I handed the officer my ID and the form with Arturo's information. Then I sat in the waiting room, plastic chair against my legs, my thoughts drifting backward despite myself.

When his name was called, I rode the elevator up. He was already seated behind thick Plexiglas, the phone hanging beside his face. I sat on the small metal stool and lifted the receiver. He smiled—wide, familiar, the same smile that had always come before apologies.

"What happened?" I asked.

He told me about friends, a store, shoplifting. How the police had detained them. How they had almost let him go—until they ran his name.

"They found a warrant," he said.

"For what?" I asked.

"Domestic violence." He said it lightly, as if it belonged to someone else. "The victim's name was Rosalinda Rodriguez."

The words hit harder than I expected. Every time he beat me and left, I had called the police. I had shown them the bruises, the red marks blooming and fading on my skin. They wrote their reports and walked away. No follow-up. No calls. Nothing. Until now—until I was sitting across from him, my past finally named out loud.

"What happens now?" I asked.

"Now you need to drop the charges and get me out," he said. "You got me into this."

Something in me shifted—not loudly, not dramatically. Just enough.

"Okay," I said slowly. "But I'm in control now. You don't get to tell me what to do."

He felt it. I saw it in his eyes. He leaned forward, softened his voice, smiled again. He apologized, repented, promised change—the same words rearranged, polished, repeated. I listened until the emptiness of it all bored me. Then I hung up the phone, stood, and walked out. The door closed behind me with a quiet finality.

At my mother's house, I went upstairs first. My baby slept peacefully, unaware of how close I had come to repeating a life I knew too well. Downstairs, my mother sat at the dining room table. The radio hummed softly. She was drunk, nursing a beer, a cigarette burning between her fingers. Smoke curled through the room as I sat beside her.

"What did he say?" she asked.

"He wants me to bail him out," I said. "He wants me to drop the charges."

She took another drag and exhaled slowly, already laying out instructions—bail bondsman, court, paperwork. Her voice moved steadily forward while my mind went somewhere else.

If I get him out, I will end up like her.

If I stay, my son will grow up the way I did.

The radio played. Smoke rose. My baby slept upstairs.

No.

No.

No.

I didn't bail him out. I didn't drop the charges. I didn't go back to see him.

Ten days later, he knocked on my door, released on a personal recognizance bond. He told me jail had changed him, that it opened his eyes, that he was never going back. I wanted to believe him. When he asked to see our son, I let him.

In late July, my baby became seriously ill—bronchitis and pneumonia. He was admitted to the hospital, and I didn't leave his side. Arturo stayed a couple of days. When my grandmother and my Tía Ruth came to visit, I introduced them to him. Their disapproval was immediate, unmistakable. Arturo noticed it too and stepped out, closing the door behind him.

"So that's your baby's father?" my grandmother asked.

"Yes, Grandma."

That look again—the one that needed no words. We made small talk until they left. When Arturo returned, he complained about being judged. I barely heard him. The doctor came in soon after, examined my son, and said we could go home the next day. Relief loosened something tight in my chest.

After the hospital, we stayed at my mom's house. I took a few more days off work. When I returned, I noticed Arturo helping less and less financially, even as he asked more of me—wanting me to spend nights with him at his mother's house. I began using work as an excuse. He didn't like that.

One afternoon he stopped by, and I told him I had to work the next day. "Next weekend," I said, "I'm off. I'll go with you—but bring a bag of Pampers for the baby."

He hesitated, then agreed. He hugged me and left.

The following weekend, he knocked right on time—empty-handed.

"Are you ready?" he asked.

"Did you bring the Pampers?"

"No, but we can stop and buy some."

"That wasn't the deal," I said. "You bring Pampers, I go."

"Come on, baby."

My voice didn't shake. "No."

I turned away, walked inside, and closed the door. He left.

Motherhood teaches hard lessons. I learned many early, but none as difficult as the ones I learned at sixteen—when I thought I knew everything about life. I'm grateful now that I don't.

That day, I didn't open the door. And that made all the difference.

<u>Thoughts</u>

I did not understand it then, but something older and steadier than fear was beginning to speak to me. Not loudly. Not in answers. Just in the strength it took to say no and mean it.

For years I believed survival meant endurance—that love was proven by how much pain you could tolerate without leaving. That was the faith I had inherited, learned by watching and by surviving. I believed cycles were inevitable, that the lives handed to us are the lives we live. But that day, when I closed the door, another kind of belief took hold. One that said my life was not meant to be a repetition. One that said my son was not meant to inherit silence.

I did not call it God at the time. I only knew that something unseen was asking me to choose differently, and that I was finally listening.

Looking back now, I can see it clearly: that moment was not only mine. It was an interruption. God was already at work, long before I had language for Him, pressing against the inheritance I thought was fixed. He was not asking for courage so much as consent—to stop, to choose, to turn.

When I closed the door, I did not know I was breaking a cycle. I thought I was only refusing one man, one demand, one night. But God sees farther than we do. What felt small to me was decisive to Him. In that quiet act of obedience, something ancient loosened its grip.

Faith, I have learned, does not always arrive as comfort. Sometimes it arrives as clarity—the kind that costs you what is familiar. That day, God did not remove the fear. He simply made it possible for me to walk through it without surrendering myself or my son to it.

I didn't walk forward with certainty. I walked forward with resolve. I did not walk away because I was strong. I walked away because God made a way where I could finally see it.

He did not promise me ease. He offered me freedom.

And freedom, once chosen, does not belong to one generation alone.

Rosie,
    Hi. Happy Birthday.
May you have many
more to come and hoping
they are real happy days
for you. Say hi to
your son for me. And
of course to ███,
yr mom Chavela, yr dad
Julio and ███.
    Take care.
            With Love
            yr Tío
            Rich

May your birthday become
a garden of joys and well wishes
that grow with the seasons!

Dear Rosie,   Aug 26 89
        Hiya. Glad to hear from you.
Say hi to Jonathon for me and
also ▓▓▓ ▓▓▓ ▓▓ Julian lets
see did I forget anyone. Oh yeah
yr boyfriend AA. Thank you for
the picture of yr son. His real
cute. Also thanx for the graduation
card. Congratulations on that and
don't feel bad about yr job.
Over here in CA they get
paid good. Plus your getting
experience right! I'll try and write
▓▓ and ▓▓▓ back but it
might take awhile as I'm real
lazy. Did you get your apartment?
My trial? The jury is still
deliberating. I'm waiting. If you
get a phone send me the #.
Ok? Take care of yrself
cause I care. Love you

Chapter 39

Free at last, Free at last,
Thank God almighty we are free at last.
— Martin Luther King Jr.

I thought freedom would feel clean. Like fresh air. Like stepping outside after being locked in a room too long.

Instead, it arrived smoky—uncertain, stinging my eyes, clinging to my clothes even when I tried to shake it off.

I accomplished my goal. I stayed with Arturo until I graduated and got a job. By September 1989, that chapter was over. What came next was unclear, but for the first time, no one was telling me where to go or what to do. I told myself that was freedom.

I started going out with friends from work. I was still dressing like a chola then, still wearing my armor on the outside. There was one guy I began hanging out with—the first man I dated after Arturo. His name was Xavier. He was timid, quiet, a grocery bagger while I worked as a cashier. We dated about a month. Of course, that included sex.

He fell hard. He talked about marriage, about children, about a future that sounded thick and hazy to me, like smoke filling a room. I didn't feel what he felt. He was a distraction—something to stand between me and the silence Arturo had left behind.

One afternoon, Xavier came by in his truck and asked if I wanted to go for a ride to Sierra Blanca. By this time my dad had returned a was living with us although he barely speaking to me. I asked my parents if they would watch my son for a couple of hours. They agreed. I didn't realize how far it was—about an hour and a half of road unspooling ahead of us.

We talked. We listened to the radio. Cigarette smoke drifted out the window as the miles blurred together. I let myself believe this was normal. Harmless.

When we finally arrived, I noticed another truck pulled over to the side of the road. A man sat inside, smoking. The ember of his cigarette flared in the dusk. Xavier told me to wait in the truck. He walked to the back, opened a tool compartment, and pulled out a brown package wrapped in plastic. He handed it to the man. The man handed him a thick wad of cash.

In that moment, the smoke thickened.

I understood.

I had crossed into something illegal, dangerous, something that didn't ask for my consent before pulling me in. Whatever the charge would have been called, I knew what it meant: I was now complicit.

When Xavier jumped back into the truck, I exploded. I yelled. I punched him. My hands shook as if trying to beat the smoke out of my lungs. I couldn't believe what had just happened. That was the end. There was no future here, no excuse large enough to cover what I had seen.

Soon after, he was arrested. He wrote me letters from jail, pledging his love. I never wrote back. Some fires burn themselves out. Others just leave residue.

While I was learning how close I had come to ruining my own life, a much larger reckoning was closing in on my family.

Toward the end of September 1989, my Tío Richie was convicted on all forty-three charges—thirteen counts of murder, five attempted murders, eleven sexual assaults, and fourteen burglaries. The penalty phase of the trial was set to begin. After his conviction, my dad returned to El Paso and stayed there, waiting. Life continued in the meantime, heavy with unspoken dread.

Arturo showed up again, as if summoned by habit. He knocked on the door. My dad and brother were in the living room watching TV when I stepped outside. My dad, still not speaking to me, told my brother the visitor was for me.

Arturo stood there empty-handed.

"Did you bring the diapers?" I asked.

"No," he said. "I wasn't sure which ones or what size."

"So did you bring the money so I can buy them?"

"No. You see, if you come with me—"

I stopped him. I didn't need the rest. I already knew. He wanted me to go with him, to his mom's house, to give him what he'd always taken before.

Before, he had forced me.

Now, I refused.

"You used to make me do things I didn't want to do," I said. "But you can't anymore. I don't want to go with you, and I don't want to have sex with you."

The slap came fast and hard, like a spark. My face burned. I screamed. Smoke exploded in my chest.

My father and brother ran outside—my dad holding a bat. Arturo took off, jumping into a car and disappearing down the street.

That was the end. I never went back.

The slap hurt—but strangely, it cleared the air. My dad started talking to me again. The silence between us thinned. For the first time, I wasn't choking on excuses or fear. Arturo was gone for good.

I told myself I was free. But freedom, it turns out, doesn't mean you suddenly leave old worlds behind.

There were others. Louie, another bagger—we went on two dates before I learned he was the father of my friend Rachel's baby. That ended quickly and safely, kept at arm's length.

In high school, I had a close friend named Audrey. She lived in the same projects I did and got hired as a cashier at the store. We went to keg parties, house parties. Cigarette smoke, weed smoke, exhaust smoke—it all blended together. Drugs were always there, hovering like fog. I told myself the smoke kept finding me. I didn't yet understand how much I was still standing in it.

Freedom was being negotiated everywhere in my life—but not for everyone.

On November 7, 1989, my Tío Richie was sentenced to death in California's gas chamber.

That night, I came home late from my shift at the grocery store, my eight-month-old son asleep in my arms. I walked into the living room and saw my father standing in front of the late-night news. I stood beside him, holding my son, watching.

On the screen, guards escorted a man in ankle and wrist shackles to a waiting van. He spoke to reporters.

"Big deal," he said.

"Death always went with the territory. See you in Disneyland."

"Qué pinche agüite," my father muttered, cigarette dangling from his fingers.

I laid my son down and stared at the television. It had taken four years to convict and sentence him. In those same four years, my life had been completely rearranged. In 1985, I was a child in Los Angeles. Now I was eighteen, in El Paso, a mother with an eight-month-old baby. And the man I had grown up with had been sentenced to die in a chamber filled with gas.

As my father paced the room, cigarette smoke curling around him, I kept thinking about what Richie had said—see you in Disneyland.

My earliest memory of him was there. Disneyland. A parade. Characters marching past. I couldn't see through the adults' legs, so I tugged on his hand. He lifted me onto his shoulders. My hands wrapped around his neck. My chin rested against the soft peach fuzz of his jaw. His hair smelled like Flex shampoo. I felt safe. Elevated. Protected.

See you in Disneyland.

There I was, celebrating my freedom from Arturo and the abuse I had survived—while my tío would never know freedom again.

The smoke lingered.

My father paced, cursing under his breath, cigarette after cigarette, while I stood there holding memory in one arm and release in the other, learning that freedom doesn't always arrive as air.

Sometimes, it arrives as smoke—and you have to decide whether you'll keep breathing it or finally step away.

Thoughts

Looking back, I understand that what I called freedom then was really the absence of one particular danger. I didn't yet know how to recognize safety, only how to flee harm. Smoke was familiar to me—the way it burns your eyes, how it lingers in fabric and hair long after the fire is gone. I mistook that familiarity for normalcy.

What I was learning, slowly and without language for it, was how cycles repeat when they aren't named. Violence doesn't always announce itself. Sometimes it arrives as distraction. Sometimes as love. Sometimes as nostalgia dressed up like Disneyland.

My faith did not rescue me in a single moment, and it did not erase what had already happened. It worked more quietly than that. It taught me to pause. To notice when the air was thickening. To believe that a life without smoke was possible, even if I had never seen one modeled.

I didn't step into clean air all at once. I took shallow breaths at first. I backed away in inches. But I learned this much: freedom isn't proven by how fast you run—it's revealed by what you no longer return to.

And that understanding, hard-won and slow, became the beginning of my way out.

Chapter 40

**Nobody owns life, but anyone
who can pick up a frying pan owns death.
— William S. Burroughs**

Relentless as ever, Arturo found me at work.

The store smelled like warm plastic and floor cleaner, the air buzzing with fluorescent lights. The register chimed each time I scanned an item, a small bell announcing transactions that meant nothing to me. I was counting change when I felt him before I saw him—his presence heavy, familiar, pressing against the ordinary rhythm of my shift.

He could no longer knock on my mother's door. He knew better than that. My father would have beaten him without hesitation. So instead, he came to the one place I couldn't escape him.

He told me he had gone to rehab. That he was clean now. That he wanted to make amends.

His voice was careful, practiced. He asked if I could find it in my heart to forgive him. If I could give him another chance. He said I was the best thing that had ever happened to him, besides my baby. He said I was a good woman. That he shouldn't have treated me so terribly.

The words piled up between us, heavy and insistent, like he could stack them high enough to block my exit.

I listened, nodding, my hands moving automatically—coins into the drawer, bills smoothed flat. A customer waited behind him, shifting their weight. Life went on.

When I spoke, my voice didn't shake.

"I'm glad you went to rehab," I said. "Thank you for the apology, and for thinking so highly of me. But we want different things in life. No hard feelings. I think it's best we go our separate ways."

The sentence landed clean and final, like a door closing.

Later, I learned the truth.

What he called rehab was the El Paso County Jail.

Arrested October 23, 1989.

Released November 9, 1989.

Rehab? Right.

Dating became my distraction. My way of staying in motion. I went through men quickly—faces, voices, hands that never stayed long enough to matter. Working as a cashier made it easy. Conversation flowed. Compliments opened doors. I was friendly—maybe too friendly. A smile and a little attention could turn into a date by the end of a shift.

But none of them were men I could build a life with. None were husband material. None were father material. Most were good-time guys, light and temporary, unwilling to carry any weight beyond their own pleasure.

One evening, we stood at the bus stop—my mother, my sister, my baby, and me—huddled together under a fading sky. The pavement still radiated heat from the day. A man struck up a conversation. He introduced himself as Joe, early thirties, easy smile, calm voice.

He told us about the ministry he was involved in—Victory Chapel—and how God had changed his life. When the bus arrived, we boarded together. The diesel engine groaned as we pulled away, and Joe kept talking—about faith, about salvation, about redemption that could lift a man out of his past.

He handed us some pamphlets and invited us to his church.

My mother gave him our address. If he could give us a ride, she said, we'd be happy to attend.

When we got off at our stop, we said goodbye, certain we'd never see him again. We walked home, the moment already slipping behind us.

But a couple of days later Joe showed up at our door.

My mother invited him in out of politeness, though she had no real interest in the Bible. I went upstairs, grabbed mine, and brought it down. We stepped outside, the evening air cool against our skin, and talked about scripture—about meaning, about what it meant to be saved.

In December, I finally accepted his invitation to church. The sanctuary hummed with music, voices rising together. Praise and worship wrapped around me, warm and steady. I saw Joe out of the corner of my eye—eyes closed, one hand raised, singing like nothing else existed.

I closed my eyes too. And I prayed.

Lord, why can't you send me just one good guy? One who doesn't smoke, doesn't do drugs, who works, who doesn't disappear with his friends. I'm tired of these men going nowhere. Can't you just send me one good guy? Is that too much to ask?

It was an honest prayer. Quiet. Spoken under my breath. I forgot it almost as soon as it left me.

At the time, I believed the right man could fix my life—that love could carry the weight I was tired of holding alone. I wanted someone willing to go to any length for me, someone who understood that relationships required effort, even when it wasn't easy.

I didn't yet understand how dangerous it was to confuse rescue with love.

One afternoon, during my lunch break, I walked home instead of buying food. The house smelled stale when I walked in—alcohol and something burned. My mother was drunk. Not the quiet kind. The restless, agitated kind. The kind looking for someone to fight.

I told her I was on my lunch break. That I'd cook something quick and be gone. She didn't like my answer. The insults started coming fast and sharp. I turned to the stove, focusing on the pan, on the heat, on the sound of food hitting metal. My back was to her.

I didn't see what she picked up.

When we first moved in, we had used gray cement cinder blocks to prop up mattresses—no bed frames, just survival. My father had recently bought a metal frame, leaving four blocks downstairs.

Heavy. Solid. Unforgiving.

She lifted one.

Fifteen-five pounds of cement raised over her head. Over mine.

Time narrowed.

Just as she started to bring it down, my brother walked in.

"What are you doing?" he yelled, grabbing the block from her hands.

I turned around.

I saw her face.

I saw the rage.

My mother tried to kill me.

The weight of that knowledge settled into my chest, undeniable and final. In that moment, something inside me shifted. I understood, with absolute clarity, that staying was no longer an option.

One way or another, I had to get out.

Thoughts

For a long time, I misunderstood weight. I thought love was something you carried for other people—their addictions, their anger, their broken promises. I thought strength meant absorbing blows and calling it endurance. I thought faith was asking God to send someone strong enough to lift the load from my hands.

But the day my mother raised a cinder block over my head; I learned the difference between weight and truth.

Some things are not meant to be carried. Some dangers are not trials to be endured. No amount of faith asks you to stand still beneath a falling stone.

Looking back now, I see that God was not in the block, or in the men I hoped would save me. God was in the moment it did not fall. In the breath I took after. In the quiet understanding that staying would cost me my life.

Faith, I've learned, is not about waiting for rescue.

It is about knowing when to step out of the way.

Chapter 41

Yeah, C.C. Rider
Girl, see what you have done
Yes, yes, yes, C.C. Rider
See what you have done
C.C. Rider by Chuck Willis 1957

In 1990, Audrey, Tony, my son Jimmy, and I began in a small two-bedroom apartment—one bathroom, a narrow kitchen, and a living room that had to hold everything. The rent was three hundred dollars a month. Four miles from my mother. Three from my job. Far enough to feel grown, close enough to fall back if I had to.

Tony had a car when he could spare it. When he couldn't, the bus ran from early morning until night, a thirty-minute ride that stretched longer when you were young, tired, and holding a baby who depended on you to know where you were going.

At first, it felt like a beginning. It rarely stays that way.

Tony's cousin John moved in next door with his common-law wife and their baby. She traveled back and forth between El Paso and Los Angeles, collecting welfare in both places, gone for days at a time. When she left, the apartment filled with noise—music shaking the walls, beer bottles lining the counters, the buzz of a tattoo gun cutting through the air. Smoke settled into the curtains. Laughter stayed too long.

Audrey and I were usually the only women there. She was spoken for. I wasn't. I told myself I was careful. John was in a relationship—there would be no future to manage, no promises to keep. When his girlfriend was gone, we slipped into something borrowed and easy. A kiss here, a touch there. Temporary, I told myself. Like a song you didn't plan to remember.

Joe came next. Church invitations. Rides to work. Hands that lingered. He was in his mid-thirties; I was eighteen. Something in me stiffened around him, even as I kept him close. I didn't want his body. I wanted what he provided.

The morning Joe couldn't take me to work, I stood at the bus stop outside the Circle K, my son wrapped tight against my chest. My father had taught me to watch my surroundings, and I did. A small pickup pulled up. A man jumped out, bought beer and cigarettes, then looked at me. When he asked if I wanted a ride, I said yes before fear could catch up.

That's how Loren entered my life—at a bus stop, between routes.

Soon I was seeing Joe, John, and Loren, each one pulling on a different version of me. Loren brought drugs and recklessness. John brought jealousy he had no right to claim. Joe brought generosity I didn't know how to receive. Men wanted loyalty from me while offering none in return.

Music filled the spaces between us. Oldies played endlessly, their longing sweet and familiar. Chuck Willis became my favorite—his voice heavy with want, his songs full of roads that never quite led home. The cassette felt like mine in a way nothing else did. Loren kept asking for it. I kept refusing.

John had a tattoo gun and offered to use it. My son was the only thing that felt permanent, so I let John carve his name into my shoulder. The needle buzzed. It hurt. When I saw it in the mirror the next morning, it was crooked, wrong. John told me to scrape the scab off, said it would fade. It didn't.

One night in early February, Loren stayed over while my son slept in the next room. I wasn't on the pill. I told myself I'd been careful before. He didn't pull out. Anger came too late to change anything.

The next morning, Joe knocked on the door. Loren whispered for a ride. I asked. Joe gave it, knowing Loren had spent the night. In his mind, I belonged to him. In mine, I was surviving—using rides, money for diapers, whatever kept me moving.

Then Xavier showed up. Jail hadn't softened him. When I refused to take him back, he punched through my bedroom window, glass shattering across the floor. A boundary broken, again.

Joe fixed the window later that day. Bought the glass. Made it whole. When he left, he never came back.

Weeks later, Loren asked if I'd gotten my period. I shook my head. He left without a word. I never saw him again.

A few days later, our apartment was burglarized. Cigarette ashes in the toilet. The seat left up. Nothing of mine was taken—except my Chuck Willis cassette.

Audrey blamed me. Tony blamed me. They moved out. I moved back in with my mother, carrying my son, my body marked with a name that would never leave me, understanding too late that everything I thought was temporary had been teaching me about permanence all along.

<u>Thoughts</u>

I did not understand then how quickly a life can teach you, its patterns. I thought I was moving forward, choosing freely, surviving one day at a time. I did not yet see how often I stood in the same place, waiting for something to arrive and tell me who I was going to be.

I learned early that some things enter your life easily and leave just as quietly. Others take something with them when they go. There were losses I could name and others I only felt afterward, when the rooms sounded different, when silence replaced what had once been familiar.

I believed damage could be undone if you acted quickly enough, if you followed the right instructions, if you were willing to endure a little pain. I did not yet know that some marks are not meant to be erased, that they exist not to shame us but to remind us of what we loved fiercely and without condition.

There were men who mistook my endurance for devotion, my need for survival for consent. I allowed it because I did not yet know the difference. I thought care was proven by what you were willing to tolerate. I thought repair meant things would return to how they were before.

What I know now is that repair is not the same as restoration. Something can be fixed and still be changed forever. Something can be made whole and still ask you to leave.

I carried a child through all of this, believing I was protecting him from my confusion. In truth, he was protecting me—anchoring me to a future I had not yet learned how to imagine. Loving him taught me what permanence really was, long before I had the language for it.

I did not walk away cleanly. I did not leave without loss. But I did leave with something harder to destroy than what I lost: the beginning of discernment. A quiet knowing that my life was not meant to be entered and exited without care. That I was not meant to keep waiting for harm to announce itself before I moved.

Faith, when it finally reached me, did not arrive as answers. It came as restraint. As the strength to stop saying yes when my spirit had already said no. As the slow understanding that survival was never the end of the story—only the place where the story finally began.

Chapter 42

If you don't like something, change it.
If you can't change it, change your attitude.
— Maya Angelou

I received my first income tax return and decided it was time for a change. Not just a small one, but a visible one, something I could put on my body and step into, something that might convince the world I was no longer who I had been. I believed, with the kind of logic you build when you're tired of repeating the same story, that the men I kept drawing toward me were responding to what I wore, how I carried myself, the version of me I allowed to be seen.

So I made a plan. New clothes. New hair. New makeup. A car—my first. Stone-washed, high-waisted jeans with tapered legs had replaced the Dickies. Dresses layered over leggings softened my outline. Jean jackets still clung to me, familiar and worn. Piece by piece, outfit by outfit, I tried to dress myself into a different future. As if fabric could shield me. As if looking changed might mean I *was* changed.

In early March of 1990, I went to the clinic for a pregnancy test. It came back negative. I told the nurse I was sure I was pregnant. She instructed me to return in a week or two. I left knowing she was wrong. My body had already spoken. I felt certain this baby would be a girl, though I didn't know where that certainty came from—only that it arrived uninvited and stayed.

At work, Audrey stopped speaking to me. No explanation. Just silence. The kind that stretches across a room and presses against your chest. Without anyone to share my thoughts with, each shift felt heavier. I was living with my mother again, and mornings brought waves of nausea that left me folded over the sink. Smells turned my stomach. Fatigue clung to me. This pregnancy was different—quieter, more insistent, as if my body had learned how to whisper instead of shout.

When I returned to the clinic, the test was positive. A blood test confirmed it. The truth settled in like cold—sudden, numbing, impossible to ignore.

I scheduled an abortion.

At the time, my reasoning felt unavoidable. *I can't do this again.* I wasn't married. I wasn't stable. I was earning minimum wage and barely managing to survive. My father had only just begun speaking to me again, and that fragile reconciliation felt like thin glass—I was afraid of shattering it. Another child felt less like a blessing and more like a weight I could not carry. I told myself God would understand—or perhaps I convinced myself His silence meant permission.

My friends April and Grace drove me to the clinic and dropped me off. Inside, everything felt cold—white walls, metal chairs, voices kept low, as if even sound understood this was a place for quiet decisions. We were shown a video explaining the procedure and its effects. Then came the paperwork. I signed my name as if it were just another form, another errand. A pen scratching across paper, trying not to tremble.

I was a single mother, back in the projects, living with my own mother again. I counted what I had and what I lacked, over and over, like if I did the math enough times it might change. There was no room left—no money, no space, no certainty.

Still, my hand hesitated before the final stroke of my name.

Just for a second. Long enough to notice. Not long enough to stop.

I signed anyway.

I sat there waiting, cold creeping up my spine, wishing for speed, for quiet, for the moment to pass—while another part of me wanted time to stretch, to stall, to interrupt what I had already set in motion.

When they called me back, I undressed from the waist down and climbed onto the exam table. I couldn't stop shivering. A nurse placed a blanket over my shoulders, a small mercy. The doctor spoke gently, explaining what would happen, grounding his voice in reassurance. He said something that stayed with me: *Women's bodies are made to get pregnant. Sometimes the timing just isn't right. This isn't your fault.*

I held onto those words like they might carry me through.

Like they might make this simpler than it was.

I wanted to believe him.

I wanted something clean—an answer without edges.

I asked him to tell me each step as he worked, as if naming things could keep them from unraveling me. My hands rested on my lower abdomen, aware of the slight curve forming there.

Already a shape. Already a presence.

Then the machine came on—a low, steady hum. It filled the room, steady and indifferent, continuing no matter what I thought, no matter what I felt. I focused on the doctor's voice. On the nurse's presence. On anything that sounded human.

Because the truth was, I had already made the decision.

This was just the part where I had to live inside it.

The procedure was brief—intense, uncomfortable, but short. The nurse stayed close, her presence steady when my thoughts were anything but. I stared at the ceiling, willing myself not to think too far forward, not to think too far back. Just stay here. Just get through this.

When it ended, the machine fell silent. The sudden quiet felt heavier than the sound had been.

The quiet that followed felt different. Not relief. Not peace. Just absence.

I felt my body go still. An emptiness settled in—not dramatic, not loud. Just hollow. Like something had been decided long before this moment, and now my body was catching up to it.

They had me dress quickly, as if clothing could return me to myself. Someone told me I was strong. Resilient. I nodded.

Because what else was there to say?

Strength didn't feel like strength.

It felt like continuation.

In recovery, I sat in a soft chair with a heating pad and ginger ale. My body cramped, but my mind stayed somewhere just out of reach. Instructions were given. Prescriptions written. I was told I could leave when I was ready. Ready.

April and Grace were waiting, and we drove home mostly in silence. I watched the world pass by outside the window—cars, people, ordinary life moving forward without hesitation. It felt strange that everything kept going exactly as it had before.

The medication that followed made my body feel foreign, heavy, unsteady. Cramps came in waves, my body already trying to empty itself, as if it knew before I was ready to admit it.

My mother was in the kitchen when I walked in. She studied my face and said I looked pale. I told her I was having menstrual cramps. She accepted the answer and didn't ask anything more.

Silence, again, doing its quiet work.

The next morning, I woke up feeling normal. The nausea was gone. The exhaustion lifted. The bleeding had slowed. My body moved on with the efficiency of something well-practiced. I got dressed. I went to work. Life resumed its shape.

And that might have been the hardest part.

How quickly everything returned to ordinary.

How easily the world made room for what had happened by not acknowledging it at all.

There was sadness, yes—but I folded it into reason. Told myself it was necessary. That it wasn't the right time. That survival sometimes asks for choices you don't fully understand until much later.

I repeated it until it sounded true.

I didn't feel punished.

I didn't feel forgiven.

I felt quiet.

But underneath that quiet, something had shifted—

not loudly, not all at once,

but enough that I would carry it forward,

even when I pretended I wasn't.

It was early April of 1990.

<u>Thoughts</u>

I did not lose my faith that spring. It simply went quiet.

For a long time, I believed faith had to sound like certainty—like declarations, like obedience, like knowing the right thing and doing it without hesitation. But what I carried out of that clinic was not disbelief. It was memory. And memory has its own way of praying.

I remember the cold most clearly. The way it lived in that building, in the waiting room, in my bones. The way a blanket felt like grace without explanation. I remember getting dressed afterward, pulling my clothes back onto a body that felt both familiar and altered, as if fabric could restore what had been undone—or at least help me stand upright and walk forward.

I remember the silence. How no one asked me what God thought. How no one told me what I should feel. How even God, it seemed, did not speak in that moment. And yet, years later, I have come to understand that silence was not absence. It was restraint. A holy withholding of commentary when my life was already heavy with consequence.

I did not hear forgiveness then.

But I also did not hear condemnation.

Faith returned to me slowly, through remembering rather than resolving. Through the understanding that God had been present not in my certainty, but in my endurance. Not in the decision itself, but in the way I survived it. In the way my body healed. In the way I kept going. In the way I learned—much later—to hold complexity without breaking myself open on it.

I no longer believe faith requires clean edges. I believe it lives in the places where we did the best we could with what we had, even when that best still left a mark.

What remains with me is not an answer.
It is the memory of being held—briefly, imperfectly, quietly—by something I could not name at the time. And that, I have learned, was enough to bring me back.

Chapter 43

**A hero is someone who has given his or her
life to something bigger than oneself.
— Joseph Campbell**

Soon after, while I was still working as a cashier, a young soldier came into the store. He went first to the floor manager and the head cashier. They greeted him with an ease I noticed immediately, their voices warm, approving his personal check without question. He was with his parents, walking just behind them as they grocery shopped. I felt his attention before I understood my own. He lingered in the aisle directly across from my register, then turned and caught me staring.

When his parents were ready to pay, I overheard him say he wanted to go through my line. Heat rushed to my face as I pretended not to hear. As I scanned their groceries, he stood straight in front of me, shoulders squared, haircut sharp, boots planted wide like he was used to being steady. He made small talk—how long had I worked there, what were my plans.

I told him the truth. I wanted to buy a car. Maybe in the fall, I'd start college. When he asked what I wanted to study, I said social work— delinquency prevention. He listened closely, as if these answers mattered. I finished ringing them up and cashed his check. Then he was gone.

Wednesday was my day off. I had a hair appointment—no more feathered-back hair. I wanted something cleaner, more deliberate. Thursday was also my day off. My son was fourteen months old and had outgrown nearly everything he owned. My dad came with me to shop for him, and afterward we stopped at a car dealership. There was an old 1978 Chevy Maverick I wanted to see. I asked my dad to come with me.

The car ran well. My credit was decent. I put money down and financed the rest—one hundred and fifty dollars a month. It felt like movement. Like proof I could make something hold.

When I returned to work on Friday, everyone told me the same thing: the young soldier—Nathan—had been looking for me. I had reported early that morning, so my lunch break came at ten. I went home, as I always did. When I returned, he had already stopped by again.

At eleven in the morning, he finally came through my register holding a six-pack of wine coolers. He smiled like we were already familiar and said I was very hard to find. I noticed his bloodshot eyes, the time of day, the alcohol—but I let it pass. I asked if something had been wrong with his purchase earlier in the week.

"No," he said. He had come back to ask me out.

He told me he was on leave, visiting family, and returning to his duty station on Sunday. He asked if I would go out with him that evening. Before answering, I told him I had a fourteen-month-old son.

"Bring him along," he said, without pause.

I gave him my address and told him what time I'd be ready. When he pulled into the apartment complex, I saw him park and rushed out the door with my son on my hip. I didn't let him walk to the door. I didn't want him to meet my parents, yet.

We went out to eat, then to a drive-in movie. El Paso still had them then. My son fell asleep against my chest as the screen flickered. We watched *Look Who's Talking*. Nathan told me pieces of his life—how he'd grown up in El Paso, graduated from a local high school. His parents were high school sweethearts. There were nine children in his family. One of his brothers had been shot at thirteen.

After high school, he worked as a stocker at the grocery store where I had once worked. Then he enlisted in the Army, quitting when he left for basic training. He was stationed at Fort Campbell, Kentucky. He was gentle with my son, adjusting the blanket when it slipped, lowering his voice when the baby stirred.

At the end of the night, he asked if he could see me again on Saturday. I told him the same thing I had before—that my son would come with me.

Saturday night, after work, he picked us up again. Again, I didn't let him come to the door. We ate and watched another movie at the drive-in. By then, I had learned not to give myself away too quickly. Waiting had taught me something—how desire sharpened in restraint, how men tried harder when access wasn't immediate.

That night, Nathan asked me to go back with him to Fort Campbell.

"I can't," I said. "I just met you."

"We'll get married," he said.

The words landed between us, heavy and unreal.

"What?" I asked.

"We'll get married," he repeated.

I told him I needed time. He said I wouldn't have to work, that I could go to school and get my degree. The car idled. My son slept between us. I stared at the darkened screen of the drive-in, the last credits gone.

"I need time," I said again.

"I'm coming back in July," he said. "We'll get married then."

What I thought—but didn't say—was that certainty spoken too quickly felt less like promise and more like persuasion.

On Sunday morning, before he left, we met once again. We went to a nearby swap meet. He bought us matching shirts that said *El Paso*. My son tugged at the fabric, sticky with juice. We ate together before he dropped us off. Once more, he said he would come back in July. Once more, he said we would get married.

This time, I said it out loud.
"If you come back, I'll marry you."

But inside, I didn't believe he would.

Later, I learned that when he returned to Fort Campbell, he went out with friends, met another girl, and spent the entire weekend with her.

Thoughts

I can see now what I couldn't then: how certainty felt like shelter to a woman who had learned to live without it. How quickly spoken promises sounded like structure, like walls that might finally hold. I mistook confidence for safety, speed for devotion. I believed that if someone chose me fast enough, firmly enough, the choice itself could make us real.

I was not naïve—I was tired. Tired of waiting, of holding doors closed with one hand while balancing a child on my hip with the other. I wanted a future that looked solid, legible, approved. A uniform. A plan. A man who said *we* without hesitation. What I did not yet understand was that love is not proved by urgency, and commitment is not measured by how little time it takes to offer it.

I was learning, slowly, that what lasts speaks more softly.

And still—he did come back.

Not in the way I had imagined in those quiet, guarded corners of myself, where hope was something, I rationed carefully—but he returned just the same. And by then, I understood something I didn't yet have language for at nineteen: that a man's return is not always proof of his promise. Sometimes it is only proof of his ability to circle back.

What I had mistaken for certainty in him was, in truth, urgency. What I had felt in myself—hesitation, caution, the instinct to wait—was not fear, but wisdom still forming.

At that age, I thought love announced itself loudly. That it arrived with declarations, with plans already spoken into the future tense—*we'll get married, I'll come back*—as if saying something firmly enough could make it solid.

But life taught me differently.

Love, the kind that holds, does not rush to convince. It stays. It is consistent in ways that don't need performance. It does not ask you to gamble your stability on someone else's timing.

And when he returned, I was no longer standing in the same place he had left me. Something in me had already shifted—not because of him, but because I had begun, quietly, to build a life that did not depend on whether anyone came back.

That was the real turning point.

Not his return.

Mine.

Chapter 44

some gives protection, some needs protection.
— Furqan Haider

Once I had my 1978 Chevy Maverick, I drove myself to my grandmother's house more often. I liked the way the door closed there—solid, final. Inside, things were steady. Quiet. A place where words weren't wasted.

It was there I told her about Nathan. About his intention to marry me. I asked if it was alright for him to call me at her house since my mother didn't have a phone. She said yes. When my grandmother said yes, it meant the line would stay open and no one else would listen.

My cousin Gloria still lived there. My grandmother cared for my youngest cousin, Jas. Gloria and I took the kids to the park, pushing swings, watching time move forward without us. She was still in high school. I already had a child. Every other Saturday, I sat near the phone and waited for it to ring.

By May 1990, it was my second Mother's Day. A card arrived. Inside it, a simple ring—my initial etched into the metal. I hadn't expected it. We hadn't known each other long. I turned the ring in my fingers, feeling its weight, how easily it fit.

Every other weekend, I waited by the phone at my grandmother's table. The same chair. The same sound of the receiver lifted from its cradle. Routine can feel like safety when chaos has taught you to accept less.

On the night of June 4, pain woke me—sharp, insistent. Downstairs, my parents were still watching television. When I told them, my father stood immediately. *We have to take her to the emergency room.*

My sister—eleven—was woken to watch my son, sixteen months old. The door closed behind us. The hospital lights were unforgiving. Appendicitis. Emergency surgery. No time to think.

Afterward, my mother stayed until I was out of surgery. When I woke, she told me she had to go home—to the children. I stayed five days. Recovery required stillness. No driving. No lifting. My father drove me wherever I needed to go. For once, I let myself be taken care of.

My parents still didn't know about the ring.

Chapter 44

Nathan returned in early July, during the last two weeks of my medical leave. He was focused. Certain. Marriage was not a question to him. To me, it felt like a door already opening.

I told myself I had nothing to lose.

That thought settled easily inside me. I had already learned how to endure. I had already learned that love arrived with conditions. I had a child. A history. As long as I didn't have another baby, I told myself, I would be fine.

Nothing to lose.

On Sunday, July 1, Nathan knocked on my front door. We spoke outside. Later, he picked us up. Over the next few days, we filled in the blanks—memories overlapping, silences mistaken for understanding. We agreed to go through with it.

I asked only one thing: that he tell his parents. I would tell mine.

When I told my father I was getting married on Friday, July 6, he laughed. Told me to go shower. *Vete a bañar.* A dismissal disguised as affection.

My mother believed me. Especially when I said it aloud: I had nothing to lose.

I told my grandparents next. I introduced Nathan and asked them to come to the courthouse, to stand as witnesses. They said yes. Inside the house, my Tía Ruth greeted me warmly. She said I looked better. Stronger.

When I told her I was getting married, she blinked and stood up. *Let's meet him,* she said.

She asked Nathan everything—age, work, plans, intentions. She asked the questions no one had ever asked for me before. I felt, briefly, shielded.

The next night, Nathan took me to his parents' house. Everyone was there. The table was full—pots, pans, tortillas stacked warm and soft. They sat together, passed dishes, talked about their day. I watched, stunned. I thought families like this existed only on television.

When the conversation turned to us, his sister asked why the rush. Nathan stiffened. The subject was dropped. The table returned to laughter. His mother asked about my son. Told him to call her Grandma. Just like that. I felt something open in my chest—hope, maybe. Or hunger.

Later, Nathan showed me the wedding rings. Pawn shop gold. Thin. Ordinary. I slipped mine on and told myself again that I had nothing to lose.

<u>Thoughts</u>

Looking back now, I see how easily I confused structure with safety. How completely I believed Nathan—and his family—were better than me. His certainty. His table. I mistook order for love and placed myself beneath it.

I believed the best about him because I believed the worst about me.

That belief—that I had nothing to lose—was not courage. It was inheritance. A lesson learned early and repeated often: take what is offered, don't ask for more. Childhood abuse had trained my sense of worth, teaching me to accept what arrived without question. Silence became consent. Endurance masqueraded as faith.

I didn't yet know that some doors open because you push them— and others because you don't believe you deserve to keep them closed.

Even now, those old thoughts sometimes return. When they do, I remind myself of what I could not see then: I was created with intention. Formed carefully, not accidentally. I am not an afterthought. I am worthy of gentleness. Of goodness. Of love that does not require pain as proof.

Chapter 45

Wedding bells
Goin' to the chapel and we're gonna get married
Goin' to the chapel and we're gonna get married
Gee, I really love you and we're gonna get married
Goin' to the chapel of love
Chapel of Love by The Dixie Cups

July 6, 1990, was not the kind of day most girls dream about.

There were no grand declarations of love, no long courtship, no slow unfolding of certainty. It was more like, "We're going to the courthouse, and we're going to get married." And if I'm honest, love wasn't really there, how could it be if I only known him for seven days.

My thoughts were practical, almost detached: What do I have to lose? I was no longer a virgin. I already knew the pain of domestic violence. If he beat me, I believed I could survive it. I had survived before. I would survive again.

The one thing I was certain of was this: I would not bring another child into something that might not last.

What we did have was chemistry. Yes—chemistry.

That invisible force that feels like destiny but is often just biology telling a convincing story. Any good science teacher will tell you that during courtship, the brain floods with chemicals. First comes lust— driven by testosterone and estrogen. Then attraction—fueled by dopamine and norepinephrine—making you feel alive, energized, almost euphoric. You lose your appetite. You lose sleep. You mistake intensity for love.

And finally, attachment—the most dangerous of them all. The one that convinces you this could last forever. That bond is fueled by oxytocin and vasopressin—the same hormones that help a mother bond with her child. And we had that. Or at least, we believed we did.

My future mother-in-law, Olivia, decided to host a dinner to celebrate our marriage. She asked me to invite my parents so they could meet the family. I told her my mom would bring chile con queso and tostadas—corn chips.

That morning, I told my dad again about the wedding.

He still didn't believe me.

As I stood in the kitchen preparing the chile con queso, I told my mom about the dinner. I made one simple request:

"If you come… please be sober." I meant it.

I would rather have been embarrassed by her absence than humiliated by her presence.

At the courthouse, I invited my grandparents to witness the ceremony. My grandfather, sadly, was not feeling well and couldn't attend. My grandmother came, and my Tía Ruth stood in his place, taking pictures—small, quiet snapshots of a moment that felt bigger than it should have been.

And just like that…I was married.

No music. No aisle. No pause to breathe.

Just a signature—and a life changed.

When we arrived at my in-laws' home, the smell of enchiladas filled the air. Warm. Welcoming. The kind of home I wasn't used to. As I carried in the chile con queso, I explained that my mom had sent it with me because she wasn't sure if she would make it.

Even then—eighteen years old, almost nineteen—I was still covering for her. Still protecting her. Still carrying her.

We were just about to begin serving food when someone walked into the kitchen and said, "Someone's here." My heart sank before I even turned around. It was my mother. My sister.

My brother—only sixteen—driving them there.

A cold wave of dread washed over me as I saw her stumble into the living room. She was drunk. Not just a little. Fully loaded.

My chest tightened. My stomach dropped.

I felt the heat of embarrassment rise up my neck. She saw my face immediately and said,

"You're my first one to get married. I was going to come."

"But Mom…" I whispered, trying to keep my voice steady,

"Did you have to come like this? Didn't I tell you not to come if you were going to be like this?"

She ignored me. Just like she always did.

She walked into the kitchen and asked my mother-in-law if she needed help, as if everything were normal.

And Olivia—sweet, gracious Olivia—saw right through me.

She leaned in close and whispered,

"It's okay… don't worry."

Then she gently rubbed my back.

That small act of kindness felt foreign.

Because I wasn't used to being protected.

We sat and ate. My mother laughed, talked, filled the space with noise that didn't belong. And after a while, she, my brother, and my sister left. The house exhaled when they were gone.

That night, we went to a local nightclub. My husband's brother joined us, and my new sisters-in-law babysat my son.

For a moment—just a moment—I let myself believe I had stepped into something better. The night felt special. Like maybe this life could work.

The following week was filled with paperwork, changing my last name, updating documents, stepping into a new identity before I had fully understood it. We had only been married a week when he returned to his duty station to prepare for my son and me to join him.

So I went back. Back to my mother's house. Back to the same walls.

While I waited, my mother and I got into one of our many arguments. But this time, it escalated. This time, she threatened me.

Something shifted in my father when he heard. Concern replaced distance. He asked my grandmother if I could stay with her until I moved to Kentucky. It was temporary. Just a couple of weeks.

My grandmother had a small room in the backyard—built by my grandfather out of gray cinder blocks. No air conditioning, no heater, no bathroom.

But it was quiet and quiet felt like peace.

After everything, peace felt like a gift.

One day, after dropping my son off with the babysitter, I stopped by my mom's house before work. I had a pounding headache and needed something to drink to take some aspirin.

I knocked. No answer. I knocked again.

When my mom finally opened the door, something felt off.

But I didn't question it.

I walked straight to the kitchen.

"I have a bad headache," I said. "I just need something to drink."

I poured juice. Reached for aspirin.

For a moment, everything felt normal. And then I turned around.

My mother stood there—smiling.
And then he stepped into the room.
Adrian. The air left my body.
My heart dropped so fast it felt physical. The glass slipped from my
hand and shattered on the floor, juice splashing across the tile.
I covered my face. I just got married, what did I do?
He walked toward me slowly, gently, as if I might break.
And maybe I would have.
He pulled my hands away from my face.
I didn't resist. Then he wrapped his arms around me.
And everything else faded.
For a moment—a dangerous, fragile moment—I forgot everything.
I forgot the courthouse. I forgot the vows.
I forgot the life I had just chosen.
All I felt was him. And a thought slipped in, soft but undeniable:
This is where I belong. I broke.
Tears came fast, uncontrollable. Not just for him—but for
everything. For the confusion. For the timing. For the part of me
that hadn't let go. We didn't speak. We didn't need to.
Some connections don't end just because life moves forward.
Some linger. He held me like he understood the war inside me.
When he pulled back, he wiped my tears and said softly,
"It's okay… I know."
Those words unraveled me. Because I didn't know.
I didn't know how I could be standing in two truths at once:
Married…and still here.
He told my mom he would be back.
We walked out together.
At my car, I handed him the keys without thinking.
We sat there for a moment before driving.
Talking—but not about what mattered most.
I remember the way he looked at me.
Steady. Certain. Like nothing had changed.
And that certainty shook me. Because it made me feel seen.
He drove me to work. Walked me inside.
When we embraced again, I didn't want to let go.
He looked at me and said,

"I will always love you. There will never be another one like you."

And I believed him. That was the problem. I believed him.

I stood there as he walked away…feeling something inside me split in two. One part of me had just stepped into a new life. The other part was still standing in the doorway of the old one. And I didn't yet know which version of me would win.

<u>Thoughts</u>

For a long time, I believed choosing stability over love meant choosing wisdom. Survival had taught me to trust what stayed, what closed the door softly and did not ask too much of me. Love, by contrast, had always arrived loud, unannounced, and costly. I learned early that longing could undo a life faster than violence ever did. So I chose what looked safe. I chose what would not disappear in the night.

But survival is not the same thing as peace.

Years later, I ran into him by chance—no warning, no preparation. He was single. Older. Still gentle. He told me, from a respectful distance, that he has always loved me. That there had never been another quite like me. He did not reach for my hands. He did not ask me to undo my life. He simply named what has never fully left.

And I realized something then: love does not always demand to be chosen to remain real. Sometimes it just waits—quiet, intact—outside the door you closed because you had to.

I don't regret choosing stability. It kept me alive. It gave my child a future. But I no longer confuse endurance with devotion, or safety with fulfillment. Longing was never my enemy. It was only my reminder—of the woman I might have been if I had learned earlier that love does not have to hurt to be true.

Some doors must be closed to survive.

Others stay with you, even when they are.

Dear Rosie,   Sep '90
            Recieved yr letter dated
Aug 1st Wishing you Jimmy all
the best. Thank you for the
pictures. So that's yr husband
huh? I wish you all the
happiness in the world. I hope
you two or three I mean including
Jimmy will be very happy. I'm
glad you found someone to be
your liking.
            Be prepared for anything in
Kentucky. There's alot of racism in
this country right now Just be
loud + proud. Think positive too.
Be sure and write me always
ok? Don't be a stranger. keep in
touch. So your last name now
is ▬▬▬ huh? ▬▬▬ in English ¨
As for myself Rosie, its the
same every day. Nothing changes
in here I went to court
yesterday. How thrilling huh? ¨
I immediately recognized where you
were in one of the pictures where yr
standing under a tree. Its at North
Loop and Tomaland Do they still have
that drive in there? Take Care Babe.
    All my Love - y too Rich

Chapter 46

Shame thrives in silence.

1990 Half a world away, the Middle East reached into my life and rearranged it. At the end of July, my husband called to tell me his unit had been placed on alert. The word itself felt temporary, almost harmless. But then the orders came—mobilize, deploy—and the ground beneath me shifted. I was still in El Paso, still dreaming of leaving, and suddenly history had decided for me.

My father and I flew to Clarksville, Tennessee, to collect what my husband could not take with him. His car. A television. Boxes of the life he was leaving behind. We spent a few quiet days there with him and one of his friends. Time moved strangely—compressed, careful—as if we were all trying not to disturb the moment too much. Then my father and I turned west, the car heavy with belongings, the road stretching endlessly ahead.

We drove for hours, crossing states like pages in a book I hadn't chosen. In Memphis, I asked my father if we could stop. I had always loved Elvis. Not the man exactly, but the myth of him—the idea that someone could come from nothing and still be remembered. We didn't have the money to go inside Graceland, but I didn't mind. Standing outside the gates was enough. I saw the pink Cadillac. I pressed my fingers to the iron bars. I wrote my name on the rock wall as a promise: *One day I'll come back.* Then we got back on the road.

In Arkansas, we stopped for gas. The back seat was full—boxes, the television visible through the open door. I noticed the police car watching us, but I didn't say anything. I had learned early not to announce fear. We filled the tank, bought drinks and snacks, and pulled back onto the highway. Minutes later, red and blue lights bloomed behind us.

My father pulled over without a word. The officers separated us— him to the front of the car, me to the back. Questions came easily to them. Where were we coming from? Where were we going? Who did the television belong to? They compared our answers. I watched their faces, careful, still. With my father's record, this was familiar terrain. We knew the rules. Say only what's asked. Yes, sir. No, sir. Don't offer yourself up.

Eventually, they let us go. We merged back onto the road like nothing had happened. My hands didn't stop shaking until miles later.

We passed through Dallas at night. Everything was closed, but my father wanted to stop anyway. Dealey Plaza sat quiet under the dark sky, history resting behind barricades and plaques. My father stood there, reverent. He loved history. Loved knowing where things had happened, even if he couldn't enter the buildings themselves. I followed him, silent, learning again how to stand in places that were not meant for me.

When we returned to El Paso, I was still living with my grandparents. It was my father who suggested I apply for housing—use my maiden name, explain my situation. I did what I was told. A caseworker came. She looked around. Apparently, it was worse than I realized. Within weeks, I was placed in a two-bedroom apartment in south central El Paso.

The Sherman Apartments sat in the middle of everything people warned you about—gangs, drugs, violence spilling into the streets. My son was not yet two years old when we moved in, mid-October 1990. I told myself it was temporary. I told myself it was better than where I'd been.

While my husband fought a war, I enrolled in business college. Clerk typist. It sounded practical. Safe. I worked part-time at the grocery store and went to school full-time. The neighborhood Christian Lady continued to babysit my son. We wrote letters back and forth. Sometimes he called. Once a month, he sent five hundred dollars, and I learned how to stretch it thin. The days were long. The nights longer.

Temptation was everywhere. Doors opened easily. Invitations came without effort. I said no, not because I was strong, but because waiting had become my specialty. Eight months passed. Then he was coming home.

In April 1991, my husband returned from Desert Storm. We packed our things. I left school before finishing my certificate. Following him back to Fort Campbell felt more important than anything I had started on my own.

Before we left, I stopped at my grandparents' house to say goodbye. My grandmother called me into her bedroom. My grandfather followed and closed the door behind us. She told me my mother had brought her a letter—one she still had. She asked me if what it said was true.

I asked what the letter said.

She told me I had written to a friend in Los Angeles.

That I had said Tío Richie raped me.

I knew the letter then. Patty. The one I never heard back from.

I told my grandmother he didn't rape me. I said he touched me. I said he made me touch him. I said the things a child shouldn't have to say aloud to be believed. So I spoke it fluently.

She looked at me and said, "I don't believe you. You never said a word."

She said she didn't believe me because I had never said a word.

I understood then that silence had always been the safer language.

So I stopped speaking.

My grandfather sat beside her, pale and quiet, listening. He never said anything. Neither did I. I learned, in that room, what silence was worth. And how easily it was inherited.

Thoughts

Years later, I understand that silence was never the absence of truth. It was a language I was taught fluently and early. It lived in closed doors, in lowered voices, in the way adults looked away and called it peace. Silence was not emptiness—it was instruction.

I mistook it for strength for a long time. For loyalty. For survival. I believed that enduring quietly was the same thing as being good, that saying nothing was a kind of protection I owed to everyone but myself. Silence kept families intact. Silence kept questions from forming. Silence kept me moving forward without asking where I was going.

But silence also taught my body to remember what my mouth would not say. It settled into my shoulders, my breath, my sleep. It followed me across state lines, into marriages, into rooms where I stood politely at the edges, waiting for permission that never came. I carried it with me the way others carry heirlooms—unexamined, unquestioned, heavy.

Only much later did I see silence for what it truly was: not virtue, not grace, but a bargain. Safety in exchange for myself.

This telling is not loud. It does not shout or accuse. It does not undo what happened in that room or on that road or in those years. But it breaks the contract silence asked me to sign over and over again.

I am no longer fluent in that language.

And that, finally, is how I know I survived.

Chapter 47

Not a Surrender, but a Stand

With a small U-Haul trailer hitched to the bumper of a 1986 Cutlass Supreme, loaded with everything my son and I owned, we drove to Clarksville, Tennessee—922 Power Street. I believed I was arriving somewhere new, but I didn't yet understand how much of myself I was leaving behind.

The red dirt at the baseball fields stunned me. I thought it had been painted that way. I had never seen earth so raw, so exposed. Later, I would realize it was simply honest soil, unashamed of its color.

We drove straight through. I stayed awake at the wheel while my husband and my baby slept. I didn't mind. I was barely twenty, alert with hope, buoyed by the belief that a new city and a new state could remake a life. Somewhere off Power Street near Fort Campbell Boulevard, we found a small trailer park and rented a furnished two-bedroom trailer. It was modest, temporary—but it was ours.

We went to K-Mart and bought what little we needed. Plates. Towels. The bare minimum to make a place livable. Setting it all down felt ceremonial, like planting stakes in the ground. We began our life together on four hundred eighty-three dollars every first and fifteenth, and somehow it held us. This was home. My home.

A few nights later, after dinner, after my baby slept alone in his own room, I ran a bath. I sank into the warmth and stayed still. The water wrapped around me, and for the first time in years, I felt safe enough to notice how far I had come. The heat loosened something I had kept tight for a long time. In that small bathroom, God found me again.

I didn't speak aloud. The prayer rose quietly, the way truth sometimes does.

Lord, You've been chasing me for a very long time, and I don't know what You want with me—or why You would want someone like me. But I know You've been good to me. Lord, I give up. I'm done running. I'm in a new state, a new place. I don't know anyone here. If You want me to go to church and serve You, You'll have to show me where...

Romans 2:4 (New Living Translation)

Don't you see how wonderfully kind, tolerant, and patient God is with you? Does this mean nothing to you? Can't you see that <u>his kindness is intended to turn you from your sin</u>?

All my life, God had been faithful—patient even—while I resisted, hid, and ran.

Less than twenty-four hours later, a knock came at the trailer door. A little girl stood there, holding flyers for a week-long church revival. I stared at the paper in my hands, stunned by how quickly surrender had been met.

I had avoided God for years. And the moment I stopped running, He answered.

I went to the revival. My spirit was exhausted, parched from endurance, and it drank deeply. Every time the doors opened, my son and I were there. One night, walking back to the car, I noticed my husband was walking away from the car.

"What are you doing here?" I asked.

"I've never heard of church going on this many days," he said. "Or this late."

He had walked nearly a mile—just to be sure we were where I said we were.

After the revival, the assistant pastor visited and invited me to a class for new believers. I went. I read my Bible. I learned how to sit still long enough to listen. I took a job as a cashier at Arby's. Slowly, quietly, my life widened. I left my son with a neighbor while I worked.

My husband didn't like the change. Not the church. Not the work. Tension crept in, sharp and familiar. Arguments filled the small trailer. Some nights, I imagined taking my son and boarding a Greyhound back to El Paso. I didn't say it out loud. I didn't need to. The thought itself was loud enough.

I hadn't called my grandparents since I left El Paso. The last conversation with my grandmother had left me unsettled in a way I didn't yet have language for. Four months later, standing in the middle of my new life and questioning whether I could stay, I felt an ache to call her.

Someone else answered.

My grandfather had died.

The timing felt deliberate, like a hand on my back. My husband arranged for me to fly home. He stayed behind with my son. Later, I would understand why he hadn't wanted me to take the baby with me. He was afraid I wouldn't return.

My grandfather had been sick—colon cancer. He had hidden it, even as his body failed him. When he collapsed, it was already too late.

When I arrived, I stayed with my in-laws the first night. The next day at my grandmother's house, my Uncle Robert and Aunt Brandy arrived with my cousin Shelby. I spoke with my Tío Richie on the phone.

"Hi, Tío."

"Hey, Sweetie. How are you? How's everyone?"

"Tío, everyone is so sad. No one knew he was sick. I'm so sorry."

He began to cry. "Let me talk to Ruth."

At the funeral home, my grandmother asked one of the girls to kiss him goodbye. She refused. Then she looked at me.

I leaned down and kissed my grandfather's forehead.

It was cold. Shockingly cold. The chill traveled through me, and with it came an old recognition—the same coldness I had felt so often from my grandmother, the same distance that had shaped my childhood into something careful and quiet. In that moment, loss and memory collapsed into each other. I understood that love could exist beside absence, that warmth was not guaranteed by proximity.

Later that night, women gathered in a back room, speaking of how well the funeral arrangements were carried out. When my Tía Sophia prepared to leave, I walked her out. When I returned, the tone had shifted. Someone began speaking badly about her.

Something in me rose.

I said she was a good woman. I said she deserved better than careless words. My voice did not shake. I surprised myself. Faith had not made me smaller or quieter—it had made me steadier. The surrender in that bathtub had grown a spine.

The room went silent.

No apology followed. That was the last time I spoke to her.

I did not yet know how to name what was happening inside me. I only knew this: I had arrived, surrendered, awakened, endured loss—and somewhere in the cold and the fire, I had begun to speak.

<u>Thoughts</u>

For a long time, I misunderstood faith. I thought it meant endurance without resistance, silence mistaken for grace, obedience confused with love. I had learned to yield so completely that I disappeared inside the yielding.

But that season taught me something different. Faith was not what asked me to shrink. It was what asked me to stand. It did not require my silence—it gave me my voice. It did not excuse harm—it named it. What rose in me then was not submission, but clarity.

Looking back now, I see that the prayer I prayed in that bathtub was not an act of giving up. It was an act of claiming myself. Faith did not soften me into compliance; it steadied me into truth. It became the quiet force that allowed me to say *no* without apology and *yes* without fear.

I did not find God by disappearing.
I found Him when I stopped running—and finally stood still.

Chapter 48

Under Watchful Eyes

August 1991, I returned home, and over the next year and a half our life tightened around my husband's jealousy. He began going to church with me, sitting beside me in the pew, his arm heavy across the back of the bench. Sometimes I watched him watching the preacher and wondered what he was listening for. I could never tell if his devotion was aimed upward—or sideways, always tracking me.

He invited his friends over to the trailer, men from the base, loud with laughter and boots still on. When my husband became absorbed in conversation, it never failed—one of them would turn his full attention to me. Not a glance. A stare. Long enough that I felt pinned in place, as if movement would confirm something I didn't want named. Another liked to stand too close, his hand resting on the counter beside mine, his shoulder brushing my arm. I learned to keep my eyes down, my hands busy. I learned where to stand so I could disappear into corners.

I never told my husband. Silence had taught me how to survive. I was afraid he wouldn't believe me. Worse, I was afraid he would believe them instead.

When he picked me up from Arby's, where I worked, he would stare down my male coworkers, his jaw set, his eyes hard. I felt it before I saw it—the shift in the room, the sudden awareness of being watched. The next day, I would hear about it: how scared they looked, how he'd shown them. Fear, I learned, could be worn proudly if it belonged to someone else.

During that time, I enrolled in a junior business college to earn my associate degree. I sat in classrooms with fluorescent lights and clean desks, trying once again to reach for knowledge, hoping it might give me a language for what I couldn't yet say.

Our weeks settled into a rhythm. School and daycare and the base. Saturdays for scrubbing floors and grocery lists. Sundays for church— morning service and evening service, the same songs, the same prayers. Occasionally we went fishing at the Cumberland River. We stood side by side along the bank, watching the water move past us, as if stillness might eventually pass for peace.

Clarksville, Tennessee was a season of growth, at least by appearances. I was twenty; he was twenty-four. I stopped working to focus on school. About a year in, I decided I wanted another baby.

That was when I learned he didn't. Not really. He was content with the three of us, with my one child. The decision felt already made, as if I were being informed rather than asked. Jimmy was three. He needed a sibling—I believed that as fiercely as I believed anything. At church, in the nursery at First Assembly of God, there was a little girl named Mary. My son would watch her and say he wanted a little sister just like her.

In February 1992, my husband finally relented. I stopped taking my birth control pills. Three months later, I knew I was pregnant. I didn't need confirmation—I knew. A girl. I felt it immediately, the way some truths arrive whole. Jimmy and I whispered names to each other, trying them out like secrets. When I asked my husband what he thought, he shrugged, already elsewhere.

My first Christian friend and mentor was a woman named Julie. A stay-at-home wife and mother, she moved through the world with calm purpose, a living embodiment of Proverbs 31. One afternoon, while I stood at the sink washing dishes, the television murmured behind me. Jimmy played next door with friends. The sound was supposed to be background, something to keep the house from feeling empty.

Then I heard the words *child sexual abuse.*

I turned off the water. Sat down. The room seemed too narrow, as if everything else had stepped back. The Oprah Winfrey Show had become something else entirely.

One moment from that day has stayed with me ever since. I can still see myself sitting on that couch, clutching kitchen hand towel in one hand and tissues in the other, crying harder than I ever had before. God met me there—in the middle of my kitchen, through a daytime talk show in 1992. She said, *"No matter if you had a crush on that uncle, that cousin, that family friend—and no matter how your body may have reacted to that touch, because God created our bodies to respond in certain ways—"* She paused, letting the words land. *"It was not your fault. He was a grown man. He knew better. You were just a child in a bad situation."*

I began to cry until my face burned and swelled.

The words broke something open. I cried until my chest ached, I sobbed until my face was swollen and red. I cried for all the years I had kept the secret locked inside me. I cried for every year I had stayed quiet, for every time I had learned to survive by not being seen.

When my husband came home, dinner wasn't ready. He saw my face, wrapped his arms around me, and asked if I was okay. I wasn't ready to tell him how God had spoken to me that day.

Not long after, my husband received orders to Berlin, Germany. We were to report by November 10, 1992. At the time, it was just a date on paper. Later, I would understand how dates can watch you long before you understand them.

My brother was graduating in June of 1992, but with a month-long leave planned in October before the move, money was tight. He decided to join the Navy. Another departure. Another uniform.

I didn't want to go to Germany. I had been granted a scholarship for the following year of college. My husband told me I could stay, finish the year, and follow him later. I considered it. Then I did what I had always done. I put my life on hold and went with him.

The Army packed our belongings into two shipments. We drove our car to St. Louis, where it would be shipped overseas. Before that, we decided to spend a month in El Paso.

When I wrote to my mother to tell her I was coming home, I felt certain it would be the last time I would see her. In my mind, the ending was holy—Christ returning, glory breaking open the sky. I didn't imagine the quieter ending waiting instead that she would die two years and five months later.

That month, I saw my mother sober two days.

One of them was the last day.

She sat across from me, clear-eyed but tired. I told her this would be the last time I would ever see her—and that I had only seen her sober twice. She said nothing.

As we waited for the airport shuttle, I told my husband I wasn't happy about going to Germany. That I was only going because he was.

He looked straight ahead. He said nothing.

Thoughts

I understand now what I couldn't then: that the day truth reached me through a television screen was not the same day I learned how to live it out loud. The words I heard that afternoon named my innocence, but they didn't yet give me a voice. Faith met me there—real and undeniable—but it did not immediately make me brave. I learned I was not to blame, yet I still believed love meant staying, meant following, meant not choosing myself too loudly.

My mother's sobriety came and went the same way truth did in those years—brief, fragile, easily lost. I watched her clearly only in flashes, just as I watched myself. I mistook endurance for devotion, silence for righteousness. Even as I stood firmer in what I believed, my life kept moving in the direction of other people's decisions.

What repeated was not the pain itself, but the quiet. Silence changed its shape—sometimes it was fear, sometimes obedience, sometimes faith misunderstood—but it always asked the same thing of me: to wait, to follow, to be still. It would take years before I understood that belief does not require disappearance, and that choosing is not the opposite of faith.

11/3/71

Hi Rosie,

Good to hear from you. Wishing you and yr family the best. Say hi to Jimmy for me. I've tried calling you but the lines never seem to connect. So Jimmy is 2 now huh? Of course he's smart, yr his mom. And I know yr smart. So you got an office job huh? Sounds like alot of money goes thru yr hands. And thats always good.

I'll try calling you on a weekend soon ok? No, they don't read my letters. They just go thru them to make sure there are no drugs. But you can ask me whatever you wish, unless you want to wait till I call you on the phone. It's up to you Rosie. Yes, I heard yr mom's mother died. Sorry to hear about that. I wrote yr mom a letter. So hopefully I'll see you next year if your in the area right?

's been ok I guess. I wake up and its the same thing as yesterday and the same tomorrow. Really boring. My trial is set for May of next year. Tell yr dad to visit my mom more often. The food here is terrible. I get lots of letters and pictures. ███ wrote me. She's all grown up now huh? Do you read books? Love you ok. Take care of yrself and say hi to ███ and again to Jimmy for me.
love, yr bro
Richie

Hi Rosie,   9/10 92
          Wishing you Jimmy and ████
the best. What are you doing? Mo? Well
I'm watching dumb tv. I'm tired of watching
tv. Don't like it too much. Never did.
Thank you for the great pictures. I
really enjoyed them. Sorry that I haven't
called you. They only give me one hour
on the phone a day. I've been having
to call my lawyers, family, and
the media big time. But hopefully I'll
be then talking w/ the ~~media~~ media
and my lawyers soon. Then I'll call you.
Hate calling you collect though.
          Good luck on becoming a
computer secretary Rosie. I know you'll make
it. Jimmy sure grew up fast huh? Maybe
one day I can see him. I'm glad to
hear you doing well. You work at
Arby's huh? Mmm.... wish I had
one of their triple quadruple whatever
burger they got. The food in here
is bad- big time! I talked to ████
on the phone the other day. I should
of joined the Army like ████ did. Maybe
I wouldn't be here. I still don't know
exactly when the show is airing. Might
be the 19th or the 17th. I got a new

lawyer and I'll be going to trial maybe next year. Do you go fishing in that lake you mention? You look pretty in that dress. It's in one of the pictures you sent. Are there a lot of people where you live? Did you see "Inside Edition" on "Friday"? They had something as usual – it was stupid. You said you might be up here sometime & when? I'll be able to visit again in Oct. After Oct 18 that is. Tues and Sat. only 1–3pm in on the 7th floor.

Tell ██████ I read an M-16 & Just kidding. That is yr husband's name right? ██████ What are the people like there where you live? Assholes like everywhere else? Ha Well girl, you take care of yrself ok. Write when yr able. I think of you often.

Yr bro w/ Love

Richie

Chapter 49

What the Hands Remember

We arrived in Berlin, Germany, in early **November of 1992.** I was nearly eight months pregnant. The Military Guest House felt temporary but kind—clean floors, quiet hallways, doors that closed gently behind us. My husband reported to base each morning, and my son and I stayed behind, holding our breath in a place that did not yet know our names.

The Army assigned us a sponsor—someone to show us how to live here. How to ride the buses. How to read maps without understanding the language. We learned that a military ID could open doors, could grant permission to move through a civilian world that was not ours. My son held my hand tightly on those first bus rides, his fingers small and warm in mine, as if he understood how much depended on staying connected.

Weeks passed. Housing was assigned. Our household goods arrived. Boxes opened like evidence of another life—plates, clothes, furniture— proof that we existed somewhere before this. We were given a three-bedroom apartment with one and a half baths. Across an ocean, in a city I could not pronounce correctly, we prepared our home to receive our second child.

In the 1990s, mothers waited until birth to learn the baby's gender. I didn't need a test. I knew. I knew in my hands and in my heart, in the way my body carried her weight. My daughter would be born the following January, in Berlin.

One afternoon, walking to the Military Exchange, I saw a familiar face moving toward me through the crowd. The world slowed.

"Bonnie?" I said, unsure.

She turned. Recognition bloomed. We laughed and hugged, our hands gripping each other as if to confirm this was real. In a foreign country, someone from my past had found me. We picked up our friendship where it had once been set down, unfinished.

The day my daughter was born was a Saturday. My husband was home. We had gone grocery shopping, our hands full of bags, our minds still in the ordinary. When we returned, the contractions began—soft at first, then closer together. We put the groceries away. I called Bonnie. We dropped off my son. Then we drove to the hospital, hands gripping the steering wheel, the door of the car closing behind us like a sentence ending.

Eight hours and twenty-four minutes after the first contraction, I held my daughter Julia Marie. She weighed eight pounds, two ounces—a full pound more than her brother. She had a full head of dark hair. When my husband held her, she wrapped her tiny hand around his pinky finger, and I watched something in him soften and surrender.

For six weeks, he tended to nearly everything except feeding. I had decided to breastfeed—something I had wanted with my son but couldn't manage then. I was younger, still in school, unaware of pumps and stored milk and options. This time, I was home. This time, I let my body do what it knew. My daughter drank and slept and rested in my arms, her small hand opening and closing against my skin.

When she was six weeks old, my husband returned to work. Soon after, he was sent to the field for a month. Just like that, I was alone in a foreign country with a four-year-old and a two-month-old baby.

The military wives checked on one another, gathered in each other's homes. I listened more than I spoke. Their stories moved easily—two-parent homes, stability, childhoods without fractures. I nodded, hands folded in my lap, unsure what to do with the distance I felt between us.

Around this time, faith found me at a bus stop.

I was wearing a shirt that said *God Loves You*. A woman noticed and asked if I was a Christian and where I worshipped. I told her I was looking. She told me about the Christian Servicemen Center.

My heart lifted. My husband and I began attending. The pastor was Tom Phythian, and his wife, Cathy. They were gentle, the kind of people whose presence quiets a room. They took us in without questions, without expectations. Over time, they became like parents to us. Looking back now, I believe they were placed in my life deliberately—especially for me.

And still, something in me was unraveling.

Some people are slow to anger. Others ignite quickly. When anger has nowhere safe to go, it waits. It gathers. It erupts.

I had become a walking storm.

My son Jimmy stood closest.

"Clean your room," I would say.

Fifteen minutes later, it was still a mess. He was playing. I lost control. Toys flew from shelves. My voice rose sharp and loud. He cried. My hands moved before my thoughts could catch them.

Milk spilled once—just a small glass, white spreading across the floor. I reacted as if something sacred had been broken. I raged. I struck. I left marks I could not take back.

Afterward came the silence. The kind that presses in. The kind that tells the truth.

At least when my mother hurt me, she was drunk. She could blame the alcohol.

I was sober. I was a wife. A mother. I had no excuse. No language for what was happening inside me. I knew it was wrong. I did not know how to stop.

Before Germany, I had been fine. Here, with everything stable, everything quiet, memory had room to breathe.

Pastor Tom and Cathy had fostered many children—children whose lives bore the same fractures as mine. One afternoon, when I finally spoke about my abuse, Cathy took my hands in hers.

"There is something you must believe," she said.

"What?" I asked.

"Abuse of a child is never the child's fault."

The question I had carried since childhood rose to my lips. *Why?*

"I don't know why," she said. "But I know who does. God saw it all. He was there with you."

That night, my daughter slept in her crib, her hands curled into themselves. My son slept behind his closed door. I stood in the quiet hallway, listening to the house breathe, my own hands empty at my sides.

For the first time, I wondered—not why it had happened to me— but what it would take for it to stop with me.

Thoughts

Decades later, when I think of Berlin, I don't picture the city first. I remember small things instead. The weight of a child asleep in my arms. A spill on the kitchen floor. A hallway at night, hushed except for breathing behind closed doors.

Time has given me language I didn't have then. It has also taken away the need to defend myself or condemn the woman I was becoming.

I can see her now with more mercy. She was not cruel by nature. She was overwhelmed by echoes she didn't yet recognize—by memories that lived in the body long before they found words.

I understand now that safety had always been something my hands searched for. Holding on. Pushing away. Learning, too late and too urgently, the difference between protection and harm. What I passed down was not intention, but inheritance. What stopped it was truth.

That truth arrived quietly. It didn't erase the past or excuse it. It simply named what had never been named. And once named, it loosened its grip.

My children are grown now. Their hands are their own. Sometimes I watch them gesture as they speak, reach for what they love, turn the handles of doors I once feared would never open. The cycle did not end in one moment, or even in one season. It ended slowly—through listening, through repair, through choosing, again and again, not to look away.

Faith did not return to me with answers. It returned with memory. With the understanding that God was not waiting on the other side of perfection, but standing in the room the whole time—present in the quiet, present in the learning, present in the long work of becoming someone new.

And when I stand still long enough now, in moments of ordinary waiting, I sometimes feel it again—not the rage, not the fear—but a steadiness. A sense that the past no longer speaks the loudest.

The doors are open.

The house is quiet.

My hands are finally at rest.

Dear Rosie,   12/20 92
            Hi. Wishing you and your family
the very best. How is Jimmy? Is he
growing up faster than you expected?
Merry x-mas and Happy New Year. I
wish you ████ and ████ all
the best in the world ☺ I got
    yr card. I hope yr happy in
    yr new house. As for me, I might
be going back to San Quentin in
late January. So I might not be here
incase you intended to visit. I might be
here a week out of every month.
We — my lawyer and I are still
working out the details.
                What's going on in your
life? Are you happy? Hope so. Thanks
for calling my mom now + then.
She gets lonely all by herself
there. Although I'm sure you run
into the answering machine now
+ then huh? Send some pictures. ☺
I think of you often. I'll try calling
you soon ok?
                Love Always ♡
                yr tio
                Richard

Dear Rosie,   3/18 93
        Hi! :) It was really great
hearing from you I just got yr
letter a few day's ago Thank you
for the pictures Your daughter Julia
Marie is beautiful. May she have
a long and happy life, As for the
book- I have this author in New
York who's doing it. His name is
Phil Carlo. He knows movie stars
like Tony ~~Danya~~ Danya and Robert
Deniro. His gonna put it on the
auction block and 31 publishing houses
are gonna bid on it. That should
be in about a month.
            I'm sure your aware
of how ill yr mom got. I write
████████ and yr dad and they
tell me shes at home doing a
bit better. I hope she gets well.
Buy Jimmy a punching bag. You
know us mexicans grow up to
be great boxers. and that
proffesion pay's well. I don't write
to ████████ ████████ or ████████ cause
they don't write me. Only ██████ is
real good about writing me. I
do write to ████ now and then.
Well it is sad concerning yr

2.

parents. Habits especially old ones are hard to break. I'm sure you'll agree they weren't the best parents but they weren't the worst either. Well "Current Affair" cancelled the interview w/ yr dad & me. Maybe later they said. But I did come out on "Inside Edition" Feb 26. How's ▮▮▮▮▮ doing? Tell him I said hi. Is he ever gonna be stationed somewhere in the Orient? I always wanted to go there.

I just got an awesome toothache. Yeah I still have em. I outa pull em all out and gum my food. ha. Well Rosie take care and know I'm thinking of you and wishing you and yours the best.

Love Always
yr tio
Richie

Rosie R.
E-320th 7A
Unit 26783 Box 1508
APO AE 09235

Hi Rosie,

Received yr letter dated 4/1. Say hi to Jimmy and ▮▮▮▮ for me. And of course Marie too. :) So maybe if Jimmy popped two punching bags already, that means hes a born boxer. When I get some money hopefully this month ill send you some so you can buy him one of those expensive ones. Send me a picture of yrself ok? Who told Jimmy Jesus doesnt like the Halloween holiday? He may be right ha ha. I didn't know that the same doctor that delivered Jimmy is taking care of yr mom. My mom tells me she's doing 50-50. Or at least thats what Julio tells her. I sent 200 to ▮▮▮▮ so she could take her walkman out. Out of where I dont know. :) Did I tell you she sent me a school picture of herself and she looks all grown up. Well not really, but she looks 15 yrs old and real pretty.

As for me I'm doing ok. Its really boring in here. They call jail "the brig" in the army right? ha ha. Theres a guy 2 cells down that went crazy. Catatonic actually. He just stares at the walls. He don't eat much. Have you seen any good movies lately? Well, ill let you go. Take care ok and write soon.

Love Always,
yr tio
Rich

Chapter 50

When Silence Looked Like Love

June 1993.

I was still breastfeeding my daughter—barely five months old—when my husband came home after being gone nearly a month. My body had not yet finished giving, and already it was being asked again.

I wasn't on birth control. Condoms were our method, fragile as promises. My son had been conceived in the space of a sentence I had heard before:

I'll pull out. I promise. Don't worry.

I did worry. I remember saying it out loud, not angry—just certain.

"You know I'll get pregnant."

He didn't pause.

"That's fine. One more kid is fine."

As if "fine" were something my body could negotiate with.

A few weeks later, sick with gastritis and a familiar dread, I sat on the crinkling white paper of an exam table while the room smelled faintly of antiseptic and metal. The doctor's eyes shifted, just slightly, before he spoke. Suspicion turned into fact.

Pregnant again.

There was no celebration in me. No soft joy rising up. Only the weight of it, settling low and heavy. I was already living like a single mother. Another child didn't feel like a blessing—it felt like confirmation.

Confirmation that I would continue alone.

That summer, when Berlin was warm and alive with tourists and street musicians, I met Emily, who lived upstairs. Her children were older—nine and eleven—and she seemed unburdened by fear. She took a liking to my daughter, stopped by when I wasn't feeling well, held the baby while I rested.

With her, the world widened.

We rode the U-Bahn and buses, sometimes the double-deckers, moving through the city as if motion itself might save us. Trains became my quiet ritual—the doors sliding open, the hum beneath my feet, the promise that something could change even if I didn't yet know how.

I loved watching the platform recede through the window. I loved the illusion of forward motion.

Emily wasn't afraid of getting lost. I admired that about her. I had been lost for years but had never learned to wander on purpose.

We stood beneath the Brandenburg Gate, history rising around us—stone that had once divided a country now posing as unity. We visited the Kaiser Wilhelm Memorial Church, its broken tower left standing after the war, a wound preserved on purpose.

I stared at it for a long time.

How strange to call ruin a memorial.

How much silence can be mistaken for peace?

Emily invited me to travel with her—to Poland, to Prague. I never made it to Prague, but even the invitation mattered. It suggested a version of me who could say yes.

I was living in Berlin. In Europe. I was still young.

The city was beautiful.

For a while, so was my life.

By early autumn, the air sharpened. I was still attending church. My faith hadn't disappeared, but it had gone quiet. I wasn't walking, I was crawling.

Pastor Tom and Cathy took me in gently. They taught me about daily prayer, about reading Scripture not as punishment but as nourishment. That fall, I went with them to Christian retreats and conferences in Garmisch-Partenkirchen. The town was small and snow-covered once winter arrived, known for skiing, the mountains rising like witnesses.

I loved the cold there—the way it clarified things.

The air felt honest, almost severe.

The meetings mattered. But so did the silence between them.

I believed God was asking me to endure.

I mistook stillness for holiness.

Late that year, while my husband was away for training again, I was alone with my children when the phone rang.

El Paso.

My sister. My father.

My mother was in the hospital.

She wasn't doing well.

I stood there, the receiver pressed to my ear, the distance unbearable.

I couldn't get in a car. I couldn't board a train. I couldn't cross the ocean between us. For the first time, the trains I loved felt like a cruelty—capable of carrying me everywhere except where I needed to go. My first thought wasn't of my mother.

It was of my sister. Fifteen years old.

I called the doctor—he had once been mine when I was pregnant with my son. His voice was steady, practiced.

Cirrhosis of the liver.

If she stopped drinking now, he said, she might live another ten years. Then he added something that lodged inside me:

"She's thirty-nine. But the inside of her body is seventy."

Seventy.

A body aging faster than time. A life collapsing inward.

He asked about a man who had been with her—a man who wanted to know if it would be okay for her to have one beer occasionally.

"That's my dad," I said.

"He asks because she'll say the doctor said it was fine."

Later, I called her brother. Then her father—my grandfather.

I told them what was happening.

They said there was nothing to be done.

Nothing.

I hung up angry, the silence afterward louder than the call itself. Silence had always been our family's language—thick, inherited, impossible to translate.

When I finally spoke to my mother, I begged. I told her she had to stop drinking. I told her she was needed. That she had a granddaughter she hadn't met. Another grandchild on the way.

"Mom, Marci still needs you."

All she said was, "I know."

Two words that felt like watching a train pull away from the platform—close enough to see, impossible to stop.

She was released from the hospital. We told ourselves the scare might be enough. We wanted to believe in turning points.

We had always wanted to believe in turning points.

By January 1994, orders came down. The base was shutting down. We were being moved to southern Bavaria, to a small town called Amberg, between Vilseck, Grafenwöhr, and Hohenfels—training bases.

The upside was that my husband would be gone less.

The trains would stop taking him away so often.

We couldn't get housing on base. Instead, we were placed in a four-bedroom apartment in Amberg, forty-five minutes from his duty station. Thirty minutes from the others. Distance measured in drives. In waiting.

We found a Servicemen's Center where we worshiped. Pastor Frank Alcorn and Sandy led us. I stayed close to Scripture then. When I read daily, my rage episodes eased.

Silence helped—or so I told myself.

Somewhere during that time, I absorbed the idea that discipline meant a belt, or a small piece of wood. It was good, I reasoned, because I no longer used my hands. My hands were for love.

But when rage came—and it did—the line between correction and harm blurred. Even that happened quietly.

Children learn to read quiet more quickly than shouting.

They feel it in the air pressure of a room.

They memorize the shift in breath.

I told myself I was breaking cycles.

I did not yet see the ways I was repeating them.

My marriage grew heavier.

When my husband was angry, he punished me with silence.

Two days. Five. Sometimes fourteen.

Often I didn't know why.

I learned to inventory myself automatically:

Did I kiss him when he came home?

Did I kiss him before getting out of the car?

Did I hold his hand while we drove?

Did I kiss him goodnight?

During sex, was I engaged enough?

Did I speak too kindly to another man at church?

I kept my hair long because he liked it that way. I wore little makeup so I wouldn't draw attention.

I followed rules that were never spoken aloud and accepted them as reasonable—righteous, even.

I told myself this was love.

I told myself endurance was faith.

The truth was simpler and harder:

My self-esteem was small.

And I believed his "normal" upbringing made him better than me.
Silence had trained me well.
I understand now what I couldn't then.
I believed God lived in quiet suffering because that was the only
place I had ever been taught to find Him.
I mistook control for order.
Silence for peace.
Endurance for holiness.
Airplanes and trains carried me across countries, across seasons of
my life—but I was rarely the one choosing the destination. I thought faith
meant standing on the platform while everyone else boarded, convincing
myself that waiting was obedience.
What I know now is this:
Faith does not require you to delete parts of your past, your pain, or
your identity to be worthy of that faith..
Love does not demand silence.
And a body—pregnant, nursing, exhausted—is not something to be
overridden by promises or punished by quiet.
God was never asking me to disappear.
He was waiting for me to speak.

Thoughts

When I look back on that year now, I don't see weakness the way I
once did. I see a young woman in motion—crossing borders, nursing
babies, navigating foreign streets—who had never been taught that she
was allowed to choose where she stood.
I thought survival was the same thing as faithfulness. I thought
staying was the same thing as loving. I thought silence made me holy.
But silence is not holiness.
It is often just fear, dressed in Scripture.
I did not yet know that agency can grow slowly, like muscle after
injury. I did not yet know that God's voice is not found only in
endurance, but also in boundaries. Not only in sacrifice, but in truth.
The trains I loved so much were never meant to carry me away from
myself. They were reminders that movement is possible. That destinations
can be chosen. Those platforms are not permanent addresses.

If I could reach back through time, I would sit beside that young mother on the crinkling paper of the exam table, or on the cold bench of a Berlin station, and I would tell her this:

You are not difficult.

You are not ungrateful.

You are not faithless for wanting tenderness.

You are allowed to speak.

And the moment you do, even if your voice shakes, that is not rebellion.

That is the beginning of freedom.

2-10-94

Dear Rosie,

Hi girl. Missed your letters! I just got your letter. It took a month. I'm doing fine. Say hi to Jimmy for me. Didn't you have another baby? Well, today's the day yr leaving Berlin. Hope you get this letter. Have you visited concentration camps? Took any pictures? Say hi to ████ for me. I sent you a letter before I left Frisco telling you I was moving. Guess you never recieved it. The reasons that you like to move are good. It's always good to move to a new place where noone knows you. Something I should of done in L.A. ha. Have you been to any other cities in Europe beside Germany? Give a hug to Jimmy for me and give him a belated birthday greeting from me to him. How was his day yesterday? So he starts school in Sept huh? When are you coming back to the States Rosie? Do you miss mexican food? I've read a few books. I'm gonna start 'Along came a Spider'. I've seen 'the Unforgiven' 'Hard Target' and 'Kalifornia'. They were all good movies. Have you seen any good movies? Send me some pictures. No I didn't feel the earthquake. Most of them (the bad ones) are down in L.A. I'll probably go to trial in Frisco this year or next. I go outside + the food's better here. I can't use the phone here though. I stay in contact w/ yr family though. So you saw huh? that's good. Well, I'll end here. Thinking of you. Yr tio Richie.

USA 29
Airmail
Rosie
E 320 th 7A
Unit 26 783 Box 1508
APO AE 09235
TAMAL CA
94974

Chapter 51

Before the River Moved

March 1994, once in Amberg, Germany—a small town, contained by its own quiet. It felt like a waiting room—narrow streets, steady rhythms, everything paused just long enough to notice your own thoughts. It was there that we folded ourselves into church life. Not casually, but completely. We tithed. We attended every service. We hosted Bible studies in our home, men and women filling our living room, Bibles open, coffee cooling in their cups. My husband loved books as much as I did, and together we devoured Christian mystery novels, turning pages late into the night. Faith, for us, was something you lived inside.

Around that time, we ran into one of my husband's friends from basic training—Brazil—and his girlfriend, Marianne, a German Catholic. Friendship came easily. Over conversation that stretched long and honest, I shared the gospel with her. She received Jesus as her Lord and Savior without spectacle, just a quiet yes. I invited her to church, and she came, but I could feel her longing. She wanted a church that spoke her language—not just spiritually, but literally.

As my due date—March 31, 1994—approached, my body felt like it was standing at a threshold that refused to open. I was ready. More than ready. But the date came and went. There was no military hospital nearby, so I was scheduled to deliver at a German hospital. Each Sunday I waddled into church, heavy and uncomfortable, greeted with the same question: *"Still no baby?"* I smiled, but inside something tightened. Waiting had begun to feel like failure.

Each day stretched thin. I questioned God quietly, the way you do when you don't want to sound ungrateful. I opened my Bible and kept returning to *Joshua*—the story of crossing into promise after so much wandering. I underlined verses about courage, about stepping forward when the river was still in front of you. Still, there were no answers. Only waiting.

On Wednesday, April 6, I had a routine doctor's appointment. That morning, contractions began—low and insistent. My husband was already at work. I called him, told his supervisor, and waited again. When he came home, we packed quickly. Along with the hospital bag and diaper bag, I slipped my Bible and the book I was reading titled *Joshua* inside. Seven days overdue, I felt emptied out, as though all my strength had already been spent just getting to this moment. We left our two children with a neighbor.

At the hospital, they checked me and rushed me into the delivery room. I was already ten centimeters. They told me to lie down, to push the way they instructed. The pain in my back was unbearably sharp, consuming, impossible to reason with. I said I couldn't do it that way. I needed to sit up.

They were not pleased.

And then they left.

The room emptied—the sound of shoes, the click of the door. I sat on the delivery table, exposed and stunned, my arms wrapped around my husband's neck like a lifeline.

"They left me," I whispered.

"I'm right here," he said. "I haven't left."

I pushed. I could feel our son crowning, my body taking over where my mind could not. When my husband called for help, the room filled again—hurried voices, movement, and equipment. They brought a horseshoe seat, laid fresh mats on the floor. Sitting upright, grounded, I pushed our baby into the world.

Daniel Robert was born at 2:35 p.m. on a Wednesday in April 1994, in a German hospital in Amberg.

When they placed him in my arms, I waited for the rush I had known before—for joy to break over me like light. Instead, something heavy slid into my chest. It wasn't sadness exactly. It was absence. A hollowing. I held him, but felt oddly distant, as though I were watching myself from the doorway.

They moved me to a shared room. My baby—nine pounds, six ounces—was taken to the nursery. My husband left to tend to our other children at home. The door closed behind him, and the room went quiet.

That was when it hit.

Not all at once, but like a shadow spreading. My arms felt too light. My body felt foreign, emptied and unfamiliar. I stared at the wall and wondered why I felt nothing where something enormous should be. Guilt followed immediately—sharp and accusing. *What kind of mother feels this way?* I turned my face toward the pillow and cried silently, afraid the sound might make it real.

I prayed, but not in sentences. Just fragments. *God, I can't hold this. I can't do this.* And then, just as suddenly as the heaviness had settled, it loosened its grip. Not gone—but lifted enough to breathe.

The next day, my husband returned with our children. Jimmy and his sister leaned over the bassinet, curious and solemn. A doctor came in and asked if I wanted my tubes tied. I was twenty-two years old, with three children. They said I qualified. My husband believed three was enough. A part of me felt a door closing—softly, but finally. Reluctantly, I agreed.

German hospitals understood something American ones often did not: mothers needed rest. Every mother stayed five days. The next day, I had the tubal ligation. When my husband and children left that evening, my roommate and I began to talk—her limited English, my limited German meeting somewhere in the middle. She was surprised by my age, by my children.

When she saw my book—*Joshua*—and my Bible beside it, she asked if I was a Christian.

She was too.

The next day, Marianne came to visit. I introduced her to my roommate, and the two women connected immediately. My roommate invited Marianne to her Christian German church—the one Marianne had been praying for.

Only then did I understand the waiting.

God had delayed my son's birth not as punishment, but as passage. A crossing. The appointment was not for me, but for Marianne. I had simply been standing at the door.

On Sunday morning, I begged the doctor to release me early so I could go to church. He said if I walked the wing a few times and my body cooperated, he would consider it. Then my newborn developed a fever. In this hospital, babies stayed in the nursery. When they told me, something in me rose up—clear and unafraid. I insisted on staying with him.

I prayed over my son. I woke my roommate and asked her to agree with me. Then a thought came—*undress him*. Simple. Certain. I knew it was the Holy Spirit.

The nurse was not pleased when she walked in. I asked her to take his temperature again.

It was normal.

We were released that Sunday morning—just in time to walk through another door and into church.

<u>Thought</u>

Years later, I understand that motherhood is not only made of beginnings, but of endings we agree to without fully knowing their weight. Some doors close loudly—with arguments, ultimatums, certainty. Others close the way mine did: with a signature, a hospital room, a sense of relief braided with grief.

At twenty-two, I believed choice was something you made once and then lived inside forever. I didn't know yet how often choice returns, asking to be re-understood. I loved my children fiercely. I still do. But love does not cancel the longing I continued to have for the next twenty years, and faith does not erase the ache of what might have been.

I think now of doors—how God sometimes holds them open and sometimes lets them close without explanation. Not as punishment. Not even as loss. But as passage. I walked through many of those doors without turning back, believing obedience meant not looking sideways.

Only later did I learn that quiet closures leave the longest echoes— and that God, patient and unafraid of our questions, remains on both sides of every door.

Dear Rosie,   5/2 94

    Hi. Wishing you and your family the very best! Congratulations on yp new born son Daniel! I'm very happy for you. Thank you for sending the card. I'm doing ok I guess. Could be worse I suppose. How are all you doing? Say hi to Jimmy and ████████ for me. I sent you a letter to your old address. You probably never got it right? I've been getting in trouble here alot lately. Thru no fault of mine. But it's like the saying goes, when it rains it pours. When & if you write back and I hope you will, tell me all of what you've been doing w/ yourself. Where do you live now? When are you coming back to the states? Did

I hope all of you are happy forever. Your dad is in New Jersey working and yr mom + ▬▬▬ are doing ok. They write me now + then. Seen anything good on tv or at the movies? You probably rent stuff right? Hope yr not feeling depressed cause they say that's what happens when women have babies. Keep your chin up.
 Love Always
 Your tio
 Richie

Rosie,   7/14

    Hi wishing you the best. Say hi to everyone for me. You have a beautiful family. Except for ▮▮▮. Thanx for the pictures. Do you go to the beach? I saw on tv that the German army went on a parade in France. They got snubbed for the D DAY festivities. Your kids are cute. I'm sure your a proud mom. Yr letter is dated 6/12. ▮▮▮ writes to ▮▮▮ He's doing ok. ▮▮▮ came to visit this weekend. Thanx for answering my nosy questions. Na You have a big house. I heard on the news that in England the media is not allowed to report anything in a criminal trial. They get thrown in jail if they do and the defendant goes free. Wish I was in England. Have you heard about this OJ thing in Germany? I saw The Fugitive and some movie about the Civil War. So you like to read Religious books huh? Are you religious? I'm listening to the radio right now. I'm going to court this month. Can you believe after almost 10 years I'm still going to court! Where were you in Aug 85? Come this Aug 31 It will have been 9 years since my arrest. Heard of the rock band the Scorpions? They come from Germany. Send more pictures if you can ok Rosie? Love Ji

SAN QUENTIN
STATE PRISON
Rosie
HHC 14 Inf.
Unit 28211 Box 1182
APO AE 09173

9/24/94

Dear Rosie,

Hi. I got yr letter. Its dated 8/23. How does Jimmy like kindergarden? Did you write ▮▮▮ and tell her to be careful? Cause I think she'd listen to you. ▮▮▮ is at my mom's house. He's there till Oct 10. My mom's brother died. Jose. I don't know if you knew him. Yeah that Sally R. show is a rerun. I don't see that dumb blonde anymore. yeah, I do think he's guilty. OJ that is. he him still awaiting for trial for one murder in San Francisco. Maybe next year. ▮▮▮ yr husband should tell people he don't know me but I appreciate him trying to stand up for me but its best this way. So Shindlers List was ok huh? I heard you were going to Washington cause one of yr kids is sick? what's up? I hope everythings ok. write soon

Love you
yr tio Richi

Chapter 52

**No storm, not even the one in your life, can last forever.
The storm is just passing over.
— Iyanla Vanzant**

In the summer of 1994, my daughter became sick.

It started with ear infections—one folding into the next—until illness felt woven into the fabric of our days. Then came the vomiting spells, sudden and violent. We learned to prepare for them the way other mothers prepared for outings. Extra clothes. Extra towels. Readiness.

The military hospital had no answers. Eventually, they sent us to a German hospital in Amberg. My daughter was admitted for testing, and I stayed with her, sleeping in that humming, fluorescent quiet, where time loosens its grip and fear keeps watch.

A pastor came to visit.

My husband called.

"The pastor's here," I told him.

There was a pause. Then suspicion crept into his voice.

"What is he doing there?"

"I don't know," I said. "I'm on the phone."

He hung up.

The pastor stayed. He listened. He prayed. He placed books in my hands, as though words themselves might steady me. The phone rang again.

"Why is he still there?" my husband demanded.

It was hard to speak with someone listening in the room, hard to explain faith to jealousy. Before I could finish answering, the line went dead again.

The pastor anointed my daughter's head with oil and prayed for her healing. His hands were gentle. Certain.

The next day, test after test came back normal. Allergy panels. Bloodwork. Everything negative. We were discharged.

From that day forward, my daughter never had another vomiting spell. Not one. No more ear infections. No relapses. Healing arrived quietly, without explanation—and stayed.

That fall, I spoke with my Aunt Polly, my mom's sister. She told me my mother had been asking her for money, and that she often sent it. I told my aunt what I already knew—that my mother was likely drinking again. That money did not help her. It armed her. And my sister was still at home.

When my mother found out I had intervened, she cut me off. Her silence was sharp and intentional. Late in 1994, I stopped hearing from her entirely.

At the time, I didn't regret it. Silence, for once, felt protective.

Later that year, my husband attended the Christian retreat I loved so deeply. We traveled south, crossing into Bavaria, to Garmisch-Partenkirchen—a town held in place by mountains. The retreat lasted a week. Worship. Fellowship. Voices rising from many directions, many lives.

On the way home, we took a detour. We drove to Neuschwanstein Castle, rising impossibly from the Alpine foothills near the Austrian border. Stone against sky. White against green. I learned that Walt Disney had drawn inspiration from it for Sleeping Beauty's castle. Standing there, it felt like belief itself had architecture—something solid enough to be built, high enough to be seen from far away.

By early 1995, my letters with my Tío Richie had shifted. I began writing to him about God. About memory. About childhood. Our words crossed states, countries, an ocean—yet he felt close, as if distance were only geography, not presence.

He asked about Germany. About my children. I told him what Americans often brought home—cuckoo clocks, armoires. I told him I didn't want those. I wanted a table that seated six. Something meant for hands passing plates. Something that stayed.

He offered to help pay for it.

Despite everything—despite what he had done and what people believed about him—there was good in my tío. I learned to hold that truth without denying the rest.

In February, the call came. My mother was back in the hospital.

This time, the doctor did not soften his words.

"I think it's best you come home," he said.

"I don't think she'll make it."

My heart dropped anyway.

Even when love is complicated, loss is not.

The next day—February 9, 1995—my son turned six. His birthday passed under the weight of phone calls, forms, and waiting rooms. We moved through systems that required patience when I had none. Everything felt slow. Bureaucratic. Cold. I wanted motion. I wanted a plane.

That night, before we could leave, I called my Tía Ruth.

"She's gone," she said.

My mother had held on as long as she could. Before she died, she asked my aunt to tell me she was sorry. That she loved me.

Even now, remembering it pulls tears from places I thought were dry. Grief doesn't vanish. It waits.

My mother died on my son's sixth birthday. She died on her grandson's birthday. She had been there when he was born, and she chose that day to leave. I choose to believe it was love—reaching forward, not backward.

When we arrived in El Paso, my brother apologized. He told me the doctors kept reviving her, and that he finally said no. That letting her go was the only mercy left.

As he spoke, I looked at him and wondered when the boy I once protected had become a man capable of that kind of courage. I hugged him. I cried. His arms held me steady.

My father arrived from San Francisco, drawn back by death the way he had once been held there by loyalty. Preparations began. Family came in from Los Angeles. The house filled with voices and memory.

At the viewing, I noticed the funeral director had chosen coral lipstick for my mother. I leaned toward my sister.

"She'd hate that," I whispered.

My mother always wore red. Always. Bright, unapologetic.

Color as declaration.

I hadn't seen her in three years. As I stood there, I remembered 1992—when God had quietly shown me that the last time I saw her alive would be the last. This was the completion of that knowing.

The rosary began. My father sat in the front pew. I sat beside him, holding his weakened hand—the same hand that had once been stabbed, the same hand that led him to the nurse's office where he met my mother. My sister sat on his other side. My brother next to her.

Midway through the prayers, I turned around.

Every pew was full. People stood shoulder to shoulder along the walls, filling the doorway, spilling into the hall.

My father whispered, "Did anyone come?"

"Yes," I said softly. "Turn around."

When he saw them, he lowered his head and wept.

His hand tightened around mine.

She had been difficult. She had been dangerous.

But she had been loved.

And somehow, in the same season—one child healed, one mother gone—I learned that grace does not arrive evenly. It arrives where it is needed most, and it asks us to carry the rest.

<u>Thoughts</u>

Years later, I understand that faith did not rescue me from contradiction—it taught me how to stand inside it. That season held both a healed child and a dying mother, mercy arriving in one room while grief waited in another. I had believed faith would bring order, clarity, and protection. Instead, it asked me to hold what could not be reconciled. Even jealousy—sharp, watchful, suspicious of grace—stood at the bedside with us. It could not tolerate a pastor's presence, could not trust a prayer offered freely, could not see healing without fearing loss of control.

But faith was quieter than jealousy. It did not argue or defend itself. It simply stayed. It rested its hand on my daughter's head, and later tightened its grip around my father's trembling fingers. It did not explain why one life was spared while another ended, why love sometimes healed and sometimes only survived. It only taught me this: that God was present in both rooms, and that believing did not mean choosing between them. It meant carrying healing and loss together—without answers, without certainty—and learning that even there, I was not alone.

Dear Rosie,   6/1/94

Hi. Wishing you and your family the very best. I'm doing ok I guess. Isn't ████████ an MP or something? I'm probably wrong. Did you get my last letter to you. I got yours. It doesn't have a date on it. I'm watching Star Trek. So that's Jimmy, Robert and Marie huh? Do you have a big house? What books do you like to read? Have you visited the concentration camps the Nazis had?

So no more kids for you huh? Three is good. Your gonna have your hands full for sure!" If you come back to the states come visit me. That's if I'm still around. Send me some pictures. My mom's not feeling too good. I think tomorrow is yr dad's birthday. Or maybe yr mom's? Not sure. Glad to know your doing great cause you deserve it! Gonna go now. Love you.

                    Yr tío
                    Rick

Chapter 53

Goodbye to you my trusted friend
Together we climbed hills and trees
Goodbye my friend, it's hard to die.
Seasons in the Sun by Terry Jacks

The Funeral—February 1995

On the day of the funeral, we drove to the cemetery down Alameda Street in a van my sister-in-law had loaned us. My husband drove. I sat in the passenger seat, watching the street slide past the window, storefronts blurring together.

"I know it may sound bad," I said finally, breaking the quiet. "But in the back of my mind all these years, I kept worrying about my mom and my sister. Is my mom okay? Is someone walking her to the store? What if she falls? What if she's too drunk to catch herself?"

The words I hadn't planned to say rose anyway.

"Her dying feels like a weight has been lifted."

He didn't correct me. He didn't judge me. He looked at me with tenderness and said nothing. The van hummed beneath us. In that silence, I wept.

We went first to the funeral home. The air inside was still, thick with flowers and polish. We said our final goodbyes. When they moved to close the coffin, my father stopped them.

He needed one more moment.

He took off his T-shirt and draped it across her torso. My mother was only forty-one, but early in their marriage she used to wear my father's shirts as pajamas, especially when he was away in jail. Cotton softened by years. Familiar. Intimate.

My brother, my sister, and I understood immediately. Love, history, survival—all folded into that simple act.

We cried as they closed the coffin.

We climbed into the funeral home limousine and followed the hearse to Mount Carmel Cemetery, where my mother was buried beside my grandfather. The priest spoke. His words floated past me. My sister played Seasons in the Sun by Terry Jacks. The song hung in the air, sweet and unbearable.

People came forward one by one. Hugs. Kisses. Hands clasping ours. Flowers placed gently on the coffin. Faces blurred together into a single expression of condolence.

When the undertakers were ready to lower the coffin, we did not move. When my grandfather died, we made a promise: we would never leave our loved ones until we saw them lowered into the ground with dignity and care. We did not want jokes. We did not want haste. We wanted reverence.

They hesitated. They were afraid one of us might throw ourselves onto the coffin. My brother spoke calmly.

"We just want to make sure she's lowered properly."

After a pause, they agreed—if we stepped back.

As we walked to a safe distance, a woman approached my brother. She smiled politely.

"I knew your mother," she said.

"We were good friends." He nodded.

She looked at my sister and me.

"Which one is Rosalinda?

Your mother said Rosalinda would hit her."

My brother didn't raise his voice.

"Excuse me, ma'am," he said. "If you truly knew my mother, you'd know she was a violent drunk. She beat us. And if my sister ever hit her, it was in self-defense. Thank you for your condolences."

There was nothing more to say.

The woman turned and walked away.

My brother slipped his arm around my shoulder and guided me back.

We sat in silence and watched as they lowered her into the ground.

I wish I could say her death healed us. It didn't. It felt as though time folded in on itself, as if we were children again—three, eight, and ten, small—clinging to one another, protecting each other from a world too eager to divide us.

My brother stood tall, our protector. But when I looked into his eyes, I still saw the baby brother who once stretched across my lap when I was barely more than a child myself.

My grandmother—my father's mother—held a small reception at her house. People came and went, murmuring condolences. In one of the bedrooms, whispers passed from ear to ear. Each whisper sent someone else toward the phone.

Eventually, one reached me.

"Tío Richie is on the phone. He wants to talk to you."

I picked up the receiver.

"Hey, Tío."

"How are you holding up, Sweetie?"

I couldn't speak. My eyes filled. The silence answered for me.

"I'm so sorry about your mom," he said.

I cried. Soon, I heard him crying too.

"I wish I was there," he said. "I wish I could have done more. When we were kids, your mom and I used to watch scary movies together. Did she ever tell you that?"

"Yes," I whispered. "She loved you."

"I know," he said. "I wish—"

The weight of it all pressed down on me at once.

"Tío, I have to go," I said. "The baby's crying."

It wasn't true. But it was the only way out.

"Who do you want to talk to next?"

"Your brother. I love you."

"I love you too."

I placed the receiver beside the phone.

I passed the message along and sat in my grandmother's living room, taking my brother's place. The room held too many versions of my life. This was where we used to sneak around at night and find my grandmother asleep on the couch, startling us.

This was the window I once stared out of as reporters swarmed the house when my Tío Beto arrived.

This was where I invited my grandparents to my high school graduation.

Where I introduced them to the man who would become my husband.

Now I sat there wondering what would happen to us next—my sister, my brother, my father. We had spent so long worrying about my mother. Now she was gone.

What were we supposed to worry about now?

The next day, we went to my mother's apartment in the projects, where she had lived since December 1987. My brother told me he was seeking guardianship of my sister and planned to move in with her.

My father walked down the stairs, my two-year-old daughter leading him by the pinky, toddling carefully from step to step. He was returning to San Francisco the next day.

My sister told me to take whatever I wanted from my mother's room. I took one of her blouses. A sweater I still have them both. What I kept were her books. Two Bibles and her Big Book from Alcoholics Anonymous. She had gone into detox. She had tried the steps.

The pages were worn and marked. Scriptures underlined. Notes folded into the margins. One Bible was Revised Standard Version. The most marked was her King James Version Bible.

Inside, I found the letter I had written to her.

I don't know what her death means. I only know she tried. And that, in the quiet she left behind, I am still trying too.

Thoughts

Years later, when I look back on that day, what I remember most is not my mother's coffin, or the words people said, or even my grief. I remember my brother. How he stood between us and the world without being asked. How he spoke when silence needed a spine. How he held the line when old stories tried to rewrite us.

We were no longer children, but we were not whole either. And somehow, he knew what was required. Not tenderness. Not explanation. Protection.

He did not save us from loss. He saved us from being broken apart by it.

That was the role he stepped into that day—not because he wanted it, but because someone had to. And because, long before we had language for it, he had already learned how to stand guard over what mattered most.

3/22/ ‑ os 95

Dear Rosie,

Thank you for the x-mas card. I did get it finally. I hope you and yr family are doing well. I hope yr trip back went well. I sent you a letter about a month ago. Did you get it? Say hi to Jimmy, Marie, Robert and ask. [redacted] for me. I talked to yr dad. He's doing ok. He's in Frisco. I haven't spoken to [redacted] or [redacted]. How are they doing? It's raining real hard over here. I'm glad yr aunt came out of her illness ok. Sounds like she was in a bad situation back then. Those doctors don't know what's going on most of the time. Have you seen any movies lately? Send me some pictures please. How involved was [redacted] — the gulf war? Did you ever take that vacation to Cornish? I haven't seen Schindlers list yet. I saw the mask. It was ok. Do you see any tv over there? I hear yr mom was buried next to my dad. Did you get them all that ok? CA is really getting hard on prisoners. They took away weight lifting equipment, pornography magazines, and conjugal visits. Is there a lot of crime there? Let me know if you move ok? When are you coming back to the States? Where will you move to if you do? Stay in touch

love you
yr bro
Rob

CLYDE McPHATTER
29
USA
USA 03
SAN QUENTIN
STATE PRISON

Chapter 54

¹⁷ If the God we serve exists, then he can rescue us from the furnace of blazing fire, and he can rescue us from the power of you, the king. ¹⁸ But even if he does not rescue us, we want you as king to know that we will not serve your gods or
worship the gold statue you set up.
Daniel 3:17–18 CSB

We returned to Amberg, Germany after another week of tying up loose ends following my mother's death. Grief traveled back with me, folded into our luggage like an extra garment I could not unpack. I resumed my life there as though nothing had shifted, but something inside me had.

My husband returned to work. I returned to routine.

I was a stay-at-home mother then. Wednesdays and Sundays we were at church. Tuesdays were men's Bible study. Thursdays were women's Bible study. One Saturday each month, I volunteered with our church's prison ministry at a nearby German prison. Letters resumed between my Tío Richie and me—thin blue aerograms crossing the ocean, carrying inked fragments of connection.

From the outside, my life looked steady. Structured. Faithful.

Inside, I was tired.

Motherhood in a foreign country carried a particular loneliness. I did not speak the language fluently. My family was across an ocean. I loved my children fiercely, but I carried a quiet determination to do everything right—to be patient, attentive, godly, composed. I wanted to prove to myself that I could build something stable, even if I had not grown up inside stability myself.

1995 pressed in from every direction.

My husband was approaching the end of his enlistment. He hoped to reenlist, but that door did not open. Instead, he requested a one-year extension so we could prepare financially for civilian life. The Army approved it, but uncertainty hovered over us like the low German clouds—never storming outright, never fully clearing.

At home, life unfolded in the unpredictable rhythm of raising three small children.

My oldest son was six when I began teaching him to bathe himself. After I scolded him one afternoon about properly washing behind his ears, he decided to correct his mistake by stuffing slivers of bar soap deep inside both ears.

We ended up at the walk-in clinic.

I remember sitting there thinking, I am failing at this. How do other mothers make this look so easy? I felt constantly on guard, as though one misstep would prove I was unfit for the sacred work entrusted to me.

Soon after that episode, the children were playing in their room while I lay down for what I told myself would be only a few minutes. Exhaustion crept over me quickly. Then—

Running feet.

Laughter.

A door slam.

And a scream.

My two-year-old daughter's cry sliced through the apartment. I ran down the hallway to find my fourteen-month-old son clutching his hand. Blood streaked his fingers and dotted the floor.

I scooped him up, my heart pounding against his small body. In the kitchen I rinsed his hand under cool water, trying to steady myself while he cried. At the German emergency room, X-rays revealed a fractured distal phalanx in his right middle finger. Because he was so small, they couldn't splint it. They stitched the torn skin where the door had crushed him.

On the drive home, I braced myself. I was certain my husband would blame me. He didn't. Still, I blamed myself enough for both of us.

The stitches healed. My son remained an explorer—undaunted, undeterred, still reaching into the world with fearless hands.

Chocolate cake has always been my weakness.

One quiet evening, after the children were in bed, my husband and I sat watching television. I enjoyed a generous slice of chocolate cake with a tall glass of milk. When I finished, I carried my plate to the kitchen but left the empty glass on the floor beside the sofa.

The next morning, as I prepared breakfast, eighteen-month-old Robert picked up that forgotten glass and toddled toward the kitchen. The floor changed from carpet to ceramic tile at the threshold. His older brother saw him and reached from behind to grab it.

The glass slipped.

It shattered.

Robert fell.

He tried to catch himself with his hands.

I lifted him quickly, scanning his arms, his chest—no visible cuts.

Relief washed over me.

I sat him on the sofa and returned to sweep up the shards.

Then a quiet thought pressed against me:

Check his eyes.

I brought him into the light and saw it—something in his eye. Assuming it was a tiny fragment of glass, I carried him to the bathroom sink and flushed his eye with water, holding his small eyelids open while he cried.

When I looked again, it was still there.

I called my friend Connie to stay with the other children. I called my husband and told him to come home immediately.

Again, I carried my child into the German emergency room.

The staff examined him, speaking rapid German. What I understood, pieced together from gestures and fragments of vocabulary, was this: he had a cut on his iris. I needed to walk to another clinic nearby.

They pointed. So I walked.

I stepped onto the sidewalk of a town I barely knew, holding my son tightly against my chest. I did not know the street names. I did not understand the language. I did not know how far it was.

Thirty minutes passed.

Fear rose slowly at first, then all at once.

I began to cry—not softly, but loud.

"God, are You there? Do You see this? My son is hurt.

I don't know where I'm going.

If You are real, I need help right now."

There I was—in a foreign country, on a sidewalk, demanding something from a God I could not see.

I stopped shouting.

I kept walking.

Within moments, a man approached me. He spoke German words I did not understand but he gently took hold of my elbow and guided me down the street. He led me directly to the entrance of a clinic. Before releasing me, he spoke to a blonde German woman waiting outside.

She placed her hand lightly on the small of my back and led me inside. After speaking with the receptionist, she turned and looked straight into my eyes.

"Gott ist gut," she said softly.

God is good.

Then she walked away. Tears streamed down my face.

Inside, someone finally spoke English. The cut on Robert's eye was severe. He needed specialized surgery at the University Hospital in Erlangen near Nürnberg.

We were transported by ambulance.

Surgery followed quickly. Then waiting.

I sat alone in that sterile room, suspended between fear and surrender. When they told me he was stable and out of surgery, I felt something loosen in my chest.

As I waited, I sensed that same quiet prompting again:

Go to the main entrance.

I stepped outside just as my husband pulled up in our little red 1989 Hyundai Excel.

God is good.

Robert and I remained in Erlangen for six days. Then he developed a stomach virus—vomiting, diarrhea, increasing lethargy.

He stopped urinating.

The doctors were specialists in ophthalmology, not pediatrics.

I raised concerns; they focused on his eye.

The next day he was worse.

I called my husband.

"If they won't transfer him, I'm leaving. Be ready."

When the doctors arrived for rounds and praised his eye's progress, I told them plainly that my son was dangerously ill and needed pediatric care in Amberg. They resisted. I did not.

They arranged the transfer.

At Amberg Hospital, the pediatrician examined him and said that if we had waited another day, he likely would not have survived the dehydration.

They inserted an IV immediately.

She suggested I go home to rest.

I refused.

I would not leave him. Not now. Not after walking this far.

Within days he improved.

Then came another kind of crisis.

Due to a processing error, the Army stopped paying my husband.

For a month and a half, there was no paycheck.

I remember standing in front of the refrigerator one evening, staring at half a gallon of milk, a package of hot dogs, and a nearly empty carton of eggs. I counted the coins in my purse on the kitchen table. I calculated whether we should put gas in the car or buy groceries first.

I felt that familiar tightening in my chest—

the fear of not having enough.

Neighbors dropped off a bag of groceries.

Someone from church left diapers at our door.

An envelope appeared with a small amount of cash tucked inside.

It was never extravagant. It was always enough.

One night during that season, I dreamed that my son Jimmy sat atop a washing machine, legs crossed neatly like a kindergartener. His hands were folded in his lap. When I approached him, he opened his palms and said,

"Mom, you know God has you in the palm of His hand. Don't worry. The money will be there at the end of the month."

I woke up and told my husband. I wrote out the budget.

I filled in each check. He hesitated.

"I have faith for both of us," I told him. "Mail them."

He did. And by the end of the month, the deposit came.

Thoughts

Looking back now, what stays with me is not only the surgery or the provision or even the words spoken on that sidewalk.

It is the walking.

The walking without understanding.

The walking without certainty.

The walking while afraid.

The walking anyway.

I did not know the language.

I did not know the streets.

I did not know how everything would work out.

I only knew to keep moving forward, holding what mattered most close to my chest.

That year in Germany, I learned that faith does not always feel triumphant. Sometimes it feels like walking blind down a foreign road, tears drying on your face, hoping the next turn will reveal what you cannot yet see. And sometimes, if you keep walking, it does.

I am no longer the young mother standing on a German sidewalk, shouting at the sky.

Time has gentled some of my urgency. It has also clarified it.

When I think back to that year in Amberg and Erlangen, I don't see myself as heroic. I see a woman stretched thin—grieving her mother, raising small children far from home, trying desperately to hold everything together with competence and faith. I see how tightly I gripped outcomes, how quickly fear rose when I sensed something slipping beyond my control.

What I did not understand then was that faith was not the absence of fear. It was movement in spite of it.

I thought strength meant never doubting. Now I know strength often looks like questioning God on a sidewalk and continuing to walk after the questions echo unanswered. It looks like insisting on a hospital transfer when your voice shakes. It looks like writing checks with more hope than certainty and placing them in the mailbox anyway.

That season shaped me in ways I could not have named at the time. It taught me that provision rarely arrives early—but it does arrive. It taught me that motherhood would repeatedly push me to the edges of my control. And it taught me that walking blind is sometimes the only way forward.

I no longer need dramatic signs to believe that God is near. I have learned to recognize Him in quieter ways—in steady breath, in stubborn courage, in the ordinary mercies that meet us just in time.

If I could stand beside that younger version of myself, I would not tell her to worry less. I would simply tell her this:

Keep walking. You are not as alone as you think.

Dear Rosie,   12-27.95
         Hi. I wrote this letter
a long time ago but it got
returned for lack of a
better address. I got yr
card today. Wishing you
and your family a happy
new year. Will ██ be going
to Bosnia? How are you
doing? I've seen yr dad.
He's doing fine. He's working
in S.F. I've had a cold
trying to get over it. You
have friends there you drink
coffee with? :) Everyone
down here is ok except
Ignacio my mom's brother
and Miguel, my aunt
Maggie's husband. He's
real bad off. Anyway
send some pictures of
yrself to me ok.
                    Love Yr tio
                    Rudy

Chapter 55

What the Springs Released

Forgiveness did not arrive in my life as a virtue.

It arrived as a way to survive.

As our lives slowly returned to something resembling normal, our time in the Army began drawing to a close. Around that same season, I formed a friendship with a woman from Czechoslovakia. One afternoon she invited me to visit her hometown—Karlovy Vary, a spa city known for its healing springs in what is now the Czech Republic.

Water rose everywhere there. Springs bubbled up from stone, warm and mineral-rich, as if the earth itself refused to keep what would poison it. Steam lifted into cold air. Visitors walked slowly beneath the colonnades, porcelain cups in hand, sipping what the ground had released.

Healing did not look dramatic. It looked patient. Persistent.

I walked those streets amazed—not only by the beauty of the country, but by the quiet goodness of God in my life. Something long trapped inside me was beginning to loosen.

I did not yet have language for what was happening. Only the sense that healing, like water, needed a way out.

God does not waste longing.

February 26, 1996

As my faith grew, I became bolder—not louder, but braver. I began writing letters to my Tío Richie. Real letters. Page after page. I wrote about repentance. About forgiveness. About God's love. About my memories.

The letters became my springs.

In them, I released what I had held for years. Words I had swallowed as a child rose to the surface. What I had buried began to breathe.

One day he wrote back. He acknowledged that he had molested me. He apologized. Then, almost immediately, he turned away from it— deflecting toward a lighter, funnier memory from our past, as if humor might soften the truth.

Still, something had shifted. The acknowledgment mattered. The apology mattered. Forgiveness, which I had already begun practicing in private, suddenly had something to stand on.

People often ask how I managed to get him to admit it. They imagine some perfectly crafted sentence, some spiritual argument that cornered him. But it was nothing like that. In one letter I wrote something simple, almost careless:

It's funny the things kids remember when they're small. I remember lying in bed, pretending to be asleep—but I wasn't. Do you understand what I'm trying to say?

That was all.

Deep in my heart, love still existed for my Tío Richie—an inconvenient, stubborn love that had survived what it should not have. I had forgiven him long before he admitted what he did. The letters were not about forcing confession; they were about release.

God does not waste longing—not even the longing to be free of what nearly destroyed you.

I wanted him to know forgiveness was already there. And I wanted him to know that if I, so human and limited, could forgive him, then there was a greater One who could forgive far more than either of us could name.

I wanted him to experience the love of God not as theology, but as rescue—the way I had. A God who met me not after the pain, but inside it. A God whose love did not erase the past, but refused to let it be the end of the story.

The same way I remembered the frightening moments of my childhood, God remembered my childhood desires too.

In April of 1996, my German Christian friend Marianne and I traveled to Paris—the city of love, the city I had dreamed about as a girl without ever believing I would see it.

When our tour bus stopped at a small French restaurant, I stepped onto the sidewalk and felt disappointment flicker through me. My husband had not wanted to come. I carried that quietly, like so many other disappointments.

The air smelled like rain and espresso. My coat felt heavy against my shoulders, damp from the mist. Traffic hummed behind me, and somewhere nearby dishes clinked against porcelain as waiters cleared café tables.

But standing there, something else took its place. God had brought me anyway.

I glanced at the bus parked across the street. A strange feeling washed over me—familiarity without memory. The sky was overcast. I looked down at the wet cobblestones glistening beneath my shoes, then turned to my left.

Down the street stood the Eiffel Tower. Café umbrellas lined the sidewalk. Flower shops spilled color into the gray afternoon.

And suddenly I knew.

I was standing inside a photograph from my middle school world geography book—the exact angle, the same street. A picture I had stared at as a twelve-year-old girl, imagining a life larger than the one I had been given.

I cried right there on a Paris street. Not because it was Paris—but because God remembered something so small. A child's longing. An insignificant wish I had forgotten I ever made.

God does not waste longing.

He remembered when I did not.

People ask how I could continue to love my abuser. How I could write him. Cry with him when his father died. Mourn with him again when my mother died.

The answer is not complicated, but it is costly: love.

Love was not sentiment. It was a decision. A daily refusal to let what happened to me become the authority over who I would be.

Forgiveness did not mean forgetting. I remembered everything. I remembered how ugly it was. I remembered how it altered my body, my silence, my understanding of safety. When I cut my finger, it still bleeds.

But I decided the past would no longer be my master.

You can let what happened to you enslave you to bitterness, or you can choose to survive it. Survival, I learned, requires release.

What that experience gave me—unwanted as it was—became a tool. Not to excuse what was done, but to help pull others out of the ditches where they find themselves trapped. To show them there is a line they can cross.

On one side of that line is unforgiveness: bitterness, repetition, a life lived looking backward.

On the other side is a different choice. You ask for help. You open your hands. You let healing begin, even when it is slow and incomplete.

Chapter 55

This was only the beginning of mine. I still had a long way to go. But a crack had formed in the wall I had built, and through it love and joy began to seep.

Like water through stone.

Before leaving Germany on August 10, 1996, we visited Dachau.

Flowers bloomed everywhere—reds and yellows against green grass—but the air was heavy, dense with memory. Gravel crunched beneath my shoes. The buildings stood quiet, orderly, unspeakable.

Even here, life had returned.

Even here, something had survived.

Later that year, we returned to El Paso, Texas.

I had many conversations with my grandmother about what had happened. She wanted me to travel to San Francisco, to confront him in front of her. Our conversations followed the same pattern.

"Tell me, "She would ask, "did he really do that to you?"

"Yes, Grandma. I have no reason to lie."

"Then why didn't you tell someone?"

Who was I supposed to tell? A father lost to jail and addiction? A mother lost to alcohol? Who, Grandma, was there?

"You could have told me," she said.

"When you came in the summers."

I looked at her hands—folded, certain, untouched by doubt.

I had always felt small next to her. The family's difficult one.

The black sheep.

No, I don't think I would have told her.

Some silences are taught.

Some are inherited.

Some are enforced by fear.

But even then, something in me had already begun to rise.

Like water finding its way through stone.

God does not waste longing.

Not even the longing to speak.

Thoughts

For a long time, being the black sheep felt like a verdict—proof that I was difficult, disobedient, ungrateful. I understand now that it was never weakness that set me apart.

It was strength.

It was my refusal, even as a child, to pretend that what happened did not happen.

Forgiveness did not make me small. It required more strength than silence ever did. It asked me to hold truth without letting it harden me, to choose release without denying the cost. I learned that forgiveness is not a gift we give to those who hurt us—it is a boundary we set for ourselves.

I did not forgive to restore what was broken. I forgave so that brokenness would not become my inheritance.

Looking back now, forgiveness no longer feels like something heroic. It feels practical. Necessary. Like breathing.

It did not excuse what happened. It did not make it smaller. It did not make me safer then. What it did was prevent the past from owning my future.

Would I choose it again? Yes.

Not because it was easy. Not because it was fair. But because bitterness would have chained me to a room I no longer lived in. Forgiveness unlocked the door.

What I know about silence now is this: silence protects what harms you. It rarely protects you.

As a child, silence felt like survival. As a woman, I learned that breaking it was.

I used to think forgiveness meant pretending something did not hurt. Now I know it means telling the truth about the wound and choosing not to let it define you.

Water rises. Longing rises. Truth rises.

And when it does, it makes a way where there was none.

Like the springs in Karlovy Vary, what rises must be released—or it will poison the ground it comes from.

Forgiveness was never about him.

It was about letting my life keep moving.

Forgiveness does not mean that I condone what was done to me. It does not erase the past, nor does it pretend the wounds were small. Forgiveness is something else entirely. It is the quiet decision to loosen the grip that pain once held over my life.

For a long time, I struggled with the idea of loving those who had hurt me. Loving people who do not seem to deserve it feels almost impossible. Yet I have come to understand that those who wound others are often the ones most starved for grace. They carry their own brokenness, their own chains.

The love that God pours out into the world is not measured by who deserves it. It is unconditional, steady and undeserved, given freely even when we have nothing to offer in return. That kind of love has a healing power.

It reaches us in the places where shame has taken root. It finds us when we are trapped in our dependencies, our addictions, our compulsions—when we feel too damaged, too flawed, too unworthy to be loved at all.

And still, God reaches for us. Again and again.

Accepting that love—allowing it to enter the places we once tried to hide—is where healing begins. It is the foundation of recovery. It is the quiet miracle that reminds us that no life is beyond redemption, and no heart is beyond repair.

Dear Rosie,   Jan 29.96

Hi. Wishing you the best. As for me I'm trying to maintain. Yr dad is fine. He watched the Super Bowl w/ Doreen at her house yesterday. I was thinking of you the other day. I hope your family is doing well. Yr letter's dated 1-10. Did you finally get the money from ████ pay check? I do get sick alot huh? I did test negative for HIV last year. My immune system is down cause of where I am, the bad food, and all the stress I go through. So the Straubing Prison is a U.S prison run by US gov't? Who are the guards- the U.S. marines? Have you seen "Dead Man Walking" w/ Sean Penn? It's suppose to be real good. They executed 2 guy's in the U.S. One by firing squad and one by hanging. They're suppose to execute someone here on Feb 23. Did ██ watch the Super Bowl? What you wrote about god does make sense. Do you ever feel frustrated and like your giving up on being your faith? My tia Juana, my dad's sister died last week. My toe is fine. Thank you for asking. Your dad does think about you. He asks me all the time if I've heard of you. Maybe

O.J. did do it and get a break like you say. ☺ He's trying to sell a video now. The book is coming out in May or June. Don't know if it will come out in Germany. It's not gonna be too nice. I cain't control that. I hope yr not too upset at what is written. They don't want to give me phone or contact visits here. They probably think I'm too evil. ☺ But you've known me a long time and I'm cool. ne Send me some pictures ok? My mom mentioned something about a policeman – related to ██████? I didn't understand what she wrote. In Houston? Anyway– write when you can. I heard you called El Paso. Did you hear ██████ pregnant? When are you coming to the USA? Take Care ok?

Love,
yr tio
Richi

Dear Rosie, ♡   2/26/96

     Hi. Wishing you the best. I got your letter today. Always good hearing from you. Hope you and the kids + ▅▅▅▅ are doing well. Thank you for the birthday card. I got it today. Right on time huh? Can you read my writing ok? Doreen sees yr dad more than me. I told her to tell him about the postcard. Saying you wanted to hear from him and that his aline is I saw him last about 3 weeks ago. He does call home often though Sometimes he calls-mad at my mom. I don't know I guess he gets frustrated sometimes. I know him losing your mom was devastating to him. You got my letter quick! How did you get it so fast? They must of flown it in a B-52 huh? Ever seen that movie Under Seige? Its good! Its about crooks who take over a Navy ship. Stars Steven Seagull! I'm not sure if that's how you spell his name. They executed a guy here named Bonin 3 day's ago. He raped + killed 14 boy's. It was in 1980 when he did it. He was known as the Freeway killer.

2

He would dump their bodies off different freeway's. Before they executed him, They asked him which freeway he wanted to get dumped on. ha That's a joke but you might not think its too funny. Sorry! I hardly know you now. I suppose yr still the same but different too huh? I hope we can meet and see in each others eyes again. Someday, will you visit? Why I think of you? Cause memories are all I have. I figure I died in 1985 when I got busted. So my day's w/ you and yr family were some of the best I realize now that no matter what problem's there are in life as long as yr free and got yr health everything is cool! I'd like to buy you that table you want if you'll allow me. I sent you 50. Let me know if you get it and I'll send you more. I sent a bit cause I don't want it to get lost in the mail. Can you cash money orders? How much does the table cost? The prisoners in the german prison that you write of sound interesting.

③

Did you ever see "Midnight Express"? That's what it was about. An American smuggling drugs and landing in a Turkish Prison where he got raped. Does anyone other than yrself see my letters to you? There's talk that Johnny Depp might play me in a movie someday ha. Your dad was for Pittsburg too. I've always been a Cowboy from As for receiving God's gift well thank you babe. I mean, its.... I'm pretty set in my ways. I keep an open miNd though and I do read what you write me. I don't think I can change. Maybe I'm possessed. ☺ Do you believe in such a thing? Did I send you a small picture of me? I'm sending one in here. If you already have it send this one back ok? Maybe you need to come see me. I don't see how I can ever chaNge Rosie. My emotions, feelings, ideas, are just too iNgrained in me I've lived w/em for years. It's like an old coat I can't/don't want to get rid of. Miguel + Ignacio are doing lots better. When are you going to send me pictures? Do you watch American

(4)

tv? I like The X-Files and The Simpsons. Yeah – yr dad needs a woman. He say's He'll never find one like Chanela. I don't even think his trying. You remember my Cadillac huh? I loved that car. I still have dreams that I'm riding around in it." I'm locked up. Most of the prisoners on death row here are. We're Not walking around the prison. Do the ones in Germany get to walk around the prison? Oh – sorry – I got sidetracked. Yes sweetie, I know you were pretending to be asleep. I don't know what to say. Anyway, sorry about those times. Remember when you chased me w/ a knife? ☺ Like I said earlier in this letter even though we had bad times I loved you then as I love you now. ████████ – a policeman? Yikes! I believe your father is talking to ████. The one who got mad at her was ██. Yr right, yr dad should be <u>taking</u> responsibilities

In between the lines, there was something that sounded like an apology. Not the kind that arrives clearly and without hesitation, but the kind that hides behind uncertainty.
He said he didn't know what to say about those times.
Then he added, almost as an afterthought,
"Sorry about those times."

(5)

He's never been ~~much~~ much for those anyway! My whole family is kaput in the head. ha ha. Including me of course! I wish I could have been there for you when you needed me in your life. Like when you had that abortion. As you ~~know~~, I was having a hard time at dealing w/ life myself! ██████ probably will be happy w/ her baby. I'll try and help her in any way I can. I'm glad life is treating you good. I'll send you a copy of the book. Its free. Your not going to like it one bit though. It went out of control. Fucking P.C. went crazy w/ it. He wouldn't listen to me. Your dad's name is Ruben. Most names are changed. Your not in it though. Thank goodness. Its called N.S. He (P.C.) embellished it. Made mountains out of mohills. It doesn't mention ██ or █████ either. Its out in May Hardcover $22.95. Like I said though, I'll get you a free copy. I'll end here. Love you lots. Write soon.

Up + o ♡
R.L.

Dear Rosie, ☺   4/19/96
          Hi. Wishing you the best along
w/ yr family. Say hi to ██████ for
me. I'm having my fiance call you
or maybe she already did. I think
I have yr phone #. If not, send it ok?
I got yr letter. Thank you for the
pictures. They were sweet. Looks like
you were having a good time in one
picture. You look a lil bit pale in
another, but you look good in another
As you know incoming and outgoing
mail is opened + inspected. There's many
things I'd like to write you about
but I can't. Sometimes other prisoners
get my mail by mistake. So it's a
messed up situation. But it hasnt
happened for a long time. Thats why
I can't discuss certain things and so
I have to wait till you come and
visit ok? There's another guy here on
death row w/ the same name as me
but w/ a different number. When I
was in the Frisco jail, women would
write him thinking it was me. He
would write back pretending to be
me, ha. He got caught though. Anyway,
I'm glad to hear some of yr

2

financial problems went away. Hope
I'll be able to help you out
later this year. So that's what
happened in 87 w/ you and my
parents huh? Yikes! I didn't know
that. Thanks for telling me. I got yr
March 8 letter along w/ the pictures.
Who sent it back to you? San Quentin?
Tell me again when yr coming
back to the states. When you come,
will you be bringing your car and
furniture? Where do you think you'll
live? Very strange that you had
kidney problems in March cause I
started having them myself around
that time. I'm taking antibiotics right
now and I'm waiting for some X rays
to be done to see if I have kidney
stones. The Indians believe in one
god called Great Grandfather. They
believe that one person can suffer
so that all his relatives will
not suffer. That's just what some
Indian guy said to me on the
yard outside. Have you read
the paperback book by Lindecker?
If you want to come see me, I

3

need to send you a visiting form.
You fill it out and send it back
to this prison and they'll let me
know when yr approved. I'll send
one to ▆▆▆ too if you want. The
kids would need a picture I.D.
I'd like to meet and see you
very much. It's been a long time.
Tell ▆▆▆ I didn't see "Blood in
Blood out." So I really can't say
if they potrayed San Quentin correctly.
But it is very violent here. yr
table costs mucho dinero. ☺ Yikes!
But it's real nice. I did get
the clippings of them. I'll pay half
for it but it's gonna be a few
more months before I'll be able to
help you w/ it. I do want to help
you w/ it and other things too. It's
no problem. Or at least I'm hoping it
won't be. ☺ They are going to execute
someone else here on May 3rd. I
haven't seen yr dad but I know
he's around. Yes I do remember
the time at Leo's house. But for
certain reasons, I want to continue
those discussions in person. I hope

4

you understand. But if it's cool w/
you, I'd prefer you keep all that
private. It would just cause
too many problems like you said.
It would be ok w/ me if you
wrote a book, but it's real hard
to get it published. Yeah — I remember
when I used to send you +
to the store to buy me apple
juice and candy. :) I'd forgotten
until you mentioned it. I do
know who James Dobson is.
Well, I know of him. I know he
interviewed Ted Bundy. Have you
met my girlfriend Doreen? She's real
nice. She can tell you alot about
what's going on over here. She gives
rides to yr dad and stuff. If she
can't call you then maybe you
can call her - collect - no problem.
As for the crimes I'm convicted
of - well again - I can't get into
that in a letter but when I see
you we can talk ok? Jeffrey Dahmer's
father wrote a book. I will end —
here. Thinking of you. Love + kisses :)
yr

Tucked between ordinary lines, he said something that shifted the ground beneath me. He wrote that it would be okay with him if I chose to write a book. Not that I should. Not that I must. Only that I could. And in that small allowance was something I had never been given before — space to speak without betrayal. In the letter, he told me that if I ever decided to write a book about what happened, he would be alright with it.

Chapter 56

But she caught me on the counter (It wasn't me)
Saw me bangin' on the sofa (It wasn't me)
I even had her in the shower (It wasn't me)
She even caught me on camera (Nah, it wasn't me)
She saw the marks on my shoulder (It wasn't me)
Heard the words that I told her (It wasn't me)
Heard the scream get louder (It wasn't me)
She stayed until it was over.
Honey came in and she caught me red-handed.
It Wasn't Me by Shaggy

April 1997, we bought a house on the outskirts of El Paso. By then, we had already lived there for almost a year, but the house did not feel like arrival. It felt like a place I was bracing inside. My grandmother's questions about the molestation had not softened with time. They sharpened. Each conversation felt less like concern and more like cross-examination, as if the truth needed to be repeated until it broke or I did.

I finally spoke it where she could not interrupt me—on paper.

I wrote to my tío Richie and told him he needed to tell his mother what he had done to me. I told him that if he didn't, I would go public. I would go on talk shows. I would take a lie detector test. I would pass it. *You know that*, I wrote. I told him she wanted the truth. It was time.

Weeks later, he went crying to her. He did not confess what he had done—he confessed his fear. He told her he was afraid that if the accusation followed him into the prison system, he would be killed. The danger he described was not mine. It was his.

In March 1998, my grandmother came to my house. She had never done that before. My aunt came with her. My aunt knocked and asked me to step outside because they wanted to talk. She was driving a truck with a front bench seat. My grandmother slid into the middle, making room for me, and I climbed in.

The truck became a small, enclosed courtroom.

She didn't ask how I was. She didn't ask what had happened to me.

She asked, "How could you write to your Tío and threaten to go on talk shows?"

I told her I was trying to get her the truth she said she wanted.

She told me she wanted me to go with her to San Quentin and repeat the accusation in front of him. Then her voice changed. She told me that although I called myself a Christian, no real Christian would lie like that. She said instead of God in my heart, I had the devil. Then she said she hoped that every problem she had suffered with her own children would come upon mine—ten times worse.

Ten times worse.

My aunt interrupted her, her voice breaking through the cab of the truck. *How can you say that? They're innocent.*

I knew then that nothing I said would matter. Truth had already cost me everything it was going to cost.

I leaned forward, kissed my grandmother on the cheek, told her that I loved her and that all I ever wanted was to be accepted by her with that I stepped out of the truck.

I walked away shaking, my legs barely steady enough to carry me back inside my house.

I did not know where to put what had just happened. I could not understand how a woman who had raised children could wish harm on mine. The following day I prayed as I walked to my car, my voice barely more than breath. *Lord, what do I do? I don't know what to do.*

I don't remember where I was driving, only that the radio was set to 1590 AM. When I turned the key in the ignition, the preacher's voice filled the car:
"Having a form of godliness, but denying its power. And from such people turn away."

For me, it was not subtle. It was instruction.

That day, I chose distance. I chose silence where there had only been punishment for speech. I did not speak to my grandmother for eighteen years, and I stopped writing to my Tío Richie there was no need.

Over time, my father would ask me if it was true. I showed him the letter my tío had written me—the apology, the admission. My father always said he believed me. And then, later, he would ask again. Each time felt like being quietly retried. If he believed me, why did I have to keep proving it?

The asking wore me down.

Around the same time, my husband still did not want me to work. He said the children needed me too much. My oldest was nine, our daughter five, our youngest four. We compromised: I could go to school if everything else remained kept up with—house, children, order.

I enrolled part-time at community college in the fall of 1998. My days became a tight rotation of driving, cleaning, studying, cooking, folding, helping, repeating. I lived inside a schedule that left no margin for error. Exhaustion settled into my body like a second skin. I earned permission to grow by proving, daily, that nothing else would fall apart.

When the house was finally quiet at night, I opened my books. Sometimes my hands shook from fatigue. Sometimes resentment stirred beneath obedience, but I swallowed it and kept going. Silence, I had learned, was often safer.

On the days I cleaned houses, I worked for an elderly man named Mr. Whitecotton. He lived alone and spoke to me kindly. In those hours, driving from one place to another, I felt briefly unpoliced—moving through the world without explaining myself.

By the summer of 1999, I had completed my first year of college. My husband was working as a security guard at a military hospital. There was a new female hire. Somehow, every story from his day included her. There was a lightness in his voice I hadn't heard directed at me in a long time.

One night, he came home with a mark on his neck. He said his coworkers had been roughhousing. I told myself I believed him. Still, something in me stayed awake.

We celebrated nine years of marriage that July.

Not long after, the dreams began.

In the first dream, I saw him kissing her in a bathroom stall. I woke startled, turned over, and prayed without words. In the second, they were in an empty hospital room, hands roaming freely. I woke up again and whispered, *Lord, what is happening?*

In the third, they were walking hand in hand through the hospital garden, kissing openly. This time, I woke up to my husband asking what was wrong.

I told him everything. As I described each dream, I watched his face drain of color. He didn't deny it. He didn't need to.

When he finally spoke, he said it was nothing—just kissing.

"Oh," I said. "I didn't know we were allowed to do that. I guess I have some catching up to do." I got dressed. I woke the kids. I left.

I drove to my friend Pam's house. She fed my children breakfast while I sat there hollowed out. Later, we took the kids swimming. We went out for pizza—paid for with the money we had been saving for my husband's new truck. That day, I decided he didn't deserve it.

When evening came, I drove home. My hands shook on the steering wheel, but I reminded myself: *I am not the one who should be ashamed.*

I told him to get the kids ready for bed. I said I was going out. *I have some catching up to do.*

I dressed carefully. Makeup. Hair straightened to my waist. A short skirt. Black nylons. Heels. Armor.

I drove to the movie theater. Bought popcorn and a large Coke. I watched every preview, every trailer, then the movie *Wild Wild West.* When it ended, I stayed until the credits finished and the lights came on.

I was the only one left in the theater.

I sat there because I did not want to go home.

Eventually, I did.

<u>Thoughts</u>

Years later, I understand that the truck and the affair were not separate wounds—they were echoes of the same lesson being enforced.

In the truck, I told the truth and was condemned for it. I was called evil, disloyal, and unchristian. Love was offered only if I agreed to be silent, only if I carried the weight without naming it. The door of that truck closed on the possibility of being believed.

With my husband, the betrayal came later, but it followed the same pattern. What I knew was minimized. What I felt was inconvenient. I was expected to absorb the damage quietly and keep the structure intact. When I finally stood up—when I drove away, when I spoke—it was treated as excess, as rebellion, as if my response were more dangerous than the harm that caused it.

Both moments taught me this: truth is often punished most harshly by the people who benefit from your silence.

For a long time, I thought leaving was weakness. I thought endurance was faith. But now I know that getting out of the truck, getting in the car, sitting alone in that movie theater—those were not acts of spite or drama. They were early rehearsals for survival.

I did not leave because I stopped loving.

I eventually left because I finally understood that love without truth is not love—it is control.

And I chose, at last, to step out.

Dear Rosie   6-22-98

Hi. Sorry I've not written I hope you and your family are doing well. I got thrown into the hole I'm having alot of problems right now. I had hoped to help you out financially so you could come visit this month but I was unable to. Maybe later this year hopefully, unless you can make it on your own it would be good to see you. I'm in big trouble here it seems. They're reading all my mail and such. Well I started reading the bible a month ago but it too got confiscated, I'll probably get it back soon. There's alot of tension and violence in the prison. They are gonna execute 2 guys next month. Hope your kids are doing well. Well, I just wanted to drop a line, if you can't reply I understand I know your busy. You know you can always call Darren. Bye for now.

yo tio
Paul

He told me he was reading his Bible. Back then, I believed faith meant safety. Sometimes people hold the Bible in one hand while hiding something else in the other. I did not reply.

Chapter 57

Should I stay or should I go now?
Should I stay or should I go now?
If I go there will be trouble
And if I stay it will be double
So you gotta let me know
Should I cool it or should I blow?
Should I Stay or Should I Go by The Clash

He was sorry. Yes, I knew he was sorry—a sorry *mother trucker*—was my first, unguarded thought.

He wanted to work things out. He reached for the oldest line in the book, the one men seem to borrow from each other when the truth is too heavy to carry: *"I'm sorry, babe. She meant nothing to me."*

Nothing.

I looked at him and said, "Really? All of this for nothing?" Then, quieter but sharper, "If she means nothing, I want to hear you say that in front of her. And me."

He stared at me. "What?"

"Ask her to meet you for lunch in the hospital cafeteria," I said. "I'll be there. Then you can tell her—right in front of me—that whatever was going on meant nothing. That it's over."

He hesitated. Then, reluctantly, he agreed.

The day of the meeting, I made sure my hair was perfect. My makeup precise. I wasn't walking in wounded—I was walking in armored. Whatever she thought she had on me, she didn't.

I entered the cafeteria and spotted them sitting together in a booth by the window. Sunlight poured across the table, bright and ordinary, as if nothing sacred had been disturbed. I walked toward them, pulling from a place I hadn't needed in years—my nerve, my edge, my old street sass.

My husband greeted me. She did too. I couldn't tell how much he had told her before I arrived.

I placed a brown paper bag on the table.

"Look," I said evenly, "I'm not here to fight for him. If you want him, you can have him. I even brought a celebratory gift for the two of you."

I opened the bag.

Cash—for a motel room, so you don't have to sneak around in bathroom stalls.

Condoms.

Latex gloves—so the next time you jack him off, your hands won't get dirty.

And cheap wine—20/20 M.D.—because a cheap bitch deserves cheap wine.

"I'm out."

I turned and walked away before either of them could speak.

I had won the moment—but lost the marriage I thought I had.

I drove to Lincoln Park, a place from my childhood, familiar and quiet. I sat on a bench and the armor drained out of me. My chest tightened until breathing felt shallow and deliberate. My hands shook in my lap. I pressed them together, willing them to be still.

I wasn't angry yet. I was unmoored.

Nothing felt solid beneath me anymore, not him, not the life I thought we had, not even myself.

I cried until my body hurt, until my breath stuttered and slowed.

I had never felt so alone.

The questions came next.

If I could find what I had done wrong, then maybe the pain would make sense.

I blamed myself—for his affair, for his indiscretion, for his sin.

I took inventory of everything.

I had done right, as if obedience should have earned me safety.

He didn't want me to work, so I didn't.

He didn't want me to cut my hair, so I didn't—

it fell all the way to my waist.

The house was clean.

The laundry done.

Dinner on the table by 5:30 p.m.

The children cared for.

Where did I go wrong?

I wondered if this was karma. When I was younger, I had been involved with married men. Was this payment coming due? Had I missed something on an invisible list of rules?

The questions tightened into a loop I couldn't escape:

Did I kiss him enough? Touch him enough? Listen enough?

Was I too quiet? Too visible? Too friendly? Too much?

Not enough?

If this was my fault, then I still had control.

That was the lie I clung to.

I gathered myself and drove home. I cooked dinner.

It was on the table by 5:30 p.m. He walked in. We sat. We ate.

I thought of my grandmother and wondered if she had ever felt this same quiet betrayal. How had she lived with it?

How had she endured loving someone who wounded her?

For the first time, I understood her differently.

We went to marriage counseling through our church for the next year. Another couple was assigned to us. They had survived something similar. We were given exercises. Homework. Steps to follow.

One Sunday during service, the pastor said, "Greet one another."

A woman approached me. She took my face in her hands, looked straight into my eyes, and said, "This situation is not about you. You didn't do anything wrong. This is about him—and his heart."

Then she hugged me.

I stood frozen.

No one had known the thoughts I whispered to God on that park bench. I hadn't said them out loud to anyone. And yet, there they were— named, uninvited, undeniable.

Her words stayed with me. They carried me.

I tried to push forward, but something in me had shifted. The old version of myself tugged at me, restless and awake. I thought I wanted revenge.

But what I wanted wasn't revenge—it was proof that I still existed.

I took back what I could. Everything he had prohibited, I reclaimed.

"These nine years," I told him plainly,

"I did everything the way you wanted. And look where it got me.

You cheated. Now I'm going to do what I want."

I cut my hair. Added highlights. Changed how I dressed, how I moved through the world. I started going to the gym. I stayed in community college—day classes when available, evening classes when they weren't.

When I had night classes, he asked me to call when they ended. At first, I mistook it for concern. But if I lingered—talking to classmates or a professor, the questions came fast and sharp. He knew my driving time by heart.

That's when I saw it clearly.

The affair hadn't just broken trust—it had exposed a structure where my silence had been mistaken for devotion.

It wasn't just jealousy. It was control.

The betrayal hadn't destroyed me—it had revealed me.

I no longer trusted him. But worse, I didn't trust myself. I hadn't seen it coming. How could I trust my own judgment again?

I had given him everything—my secrets, my wounds, my joys.

I had been an open book. The damage he caused didn't stop at the surface. It bruised something deeper.

Resentment settled in. For years, I had shaped myself around his comfort. Now the certainty I once had—

he will never leave me—was gone.

I grieved as if someone had died. I mourned the trust I had given freely. The marriage I believed in. The future I had imagined.

I wrestled with the same question day and night:

Should I stay or should I go?

If I left, would these nine years have meant nothing?

If I stayed, could trust ever be rebuilt?

Avoidance became my refuge.

Counseling didn't seem to change much—but I showed up.

Life kept moving. Y2K came and went.

In January 2000, our pastor suffered a massive heart attack. My son took it hard. The pastor had always given him time—listened to him with the same attention he gave adults.

We stopped counseling. I tried to forgive. Tried to move forward.

For our ten-year anniversary, we went to San Francisco—just the two of us. When we returned, Mr. Whitecotton became ill. He had no family in El Paso, so I became his.

I took him to the VA. He asked me to drive his Lincoln—my Ford Taurus barely worked, couldn't go over forty-five miles an hour, had no heat or air-conditioning. Still, it got me where I needed to go.

I checked on him twice a day. Made sure he ate. Took his medication. At breakfast, I cooked while we talked about everything. If I wasn't careful, I lost track of time. He offered to pay me. I refused.

He was kindness without conditions.
A quiet reminder that care did not have to cost me myself.

<u>Thought</u>

Years later, I can see that moment more clearly—not as the end of my marriage, but as the end of my disappearance.

At the time, I thought the affair shattered me. What it actually shattered was the story I had been living inside: that love required my vanishing, that obedience was devotion, that silence was strength. I had mistaken endurance for virtue and control for care. I didn't awaken all at once. There was no clean turning point, no sudden freedom. The awakening came in fragments—in a woman's hands on my face at church, in the sound of scissors cutting my hair, in the quiet relief of realizing I could take up space without asking permission.

I used to believe betrayal meant I wasn't enough. Now I understand it meant I had been too much of what I was never meant to be—smaller, quieter, more pliable than my own soul could tolerate.

Looking back, I don't judge the woman I was. She was surviving with the tools she had. She kept dinner on the table. She kept the marriage standing. She kept the children safe. But survival is not the same as living.

What changed was not my appearance or my defiance—it was my clarity. I stopped trying to earn love by disappearing. I stopped confusing control with commitment. I began to trust the part of myself that had known, even when I tried not to listen.

That awakening did not make my life easier. It made it truer.

And once I saw myself clearly, I could never again pretend that vanishing was the price of being loved.

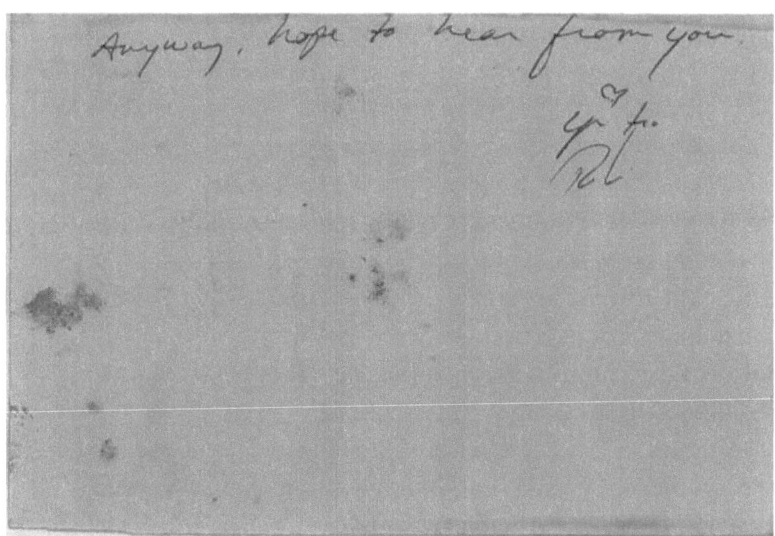

This was the last letter I ever received from him.

Chapter 58

**I know all the things you do, and I have opened a door for you that
no one can close. You have little strength,
yet you obeyed my word and did not deny me.
Revelation 3:8 NLT**

Mr. Whitecotton recovered, and when he did, he decided to move closer to his family. I helped him sell his house and pack his belongings, sorting through the residue of a life lived mostly alone—old furniture, paperbacks with cracked spines, the quiet evidence of endurance. Caring for him had become woven into my days so gradually that I didn't recognize it as preparation. But God often trains us in ordinary rooms before asking us to stand in harder ones.

My church practiced deliverance ministry—a subject that makes people uneasy. I understand why. I would not have believed in it myself if I had not lived it in my own body.

During my young adult years, I had wandered far from God. I entertained and engaged in things I knew were against Him: sex outside of marriage, pornography, horror films, dark music. The spirit guide I had encountered in sixth grade—the one I once dismissed as imagination, had never fully left. I also became deeply involved in astrology and horoscopes, a form of divination I did not yet understand as dangerous.

What I came to see, slowly and painfully, was that I had left doors open. The enemy does not enter where there is no access. Doors cracked through ignorance or pain become entryways. What we excuse becomes permission. God's protection had never abandoned me—but I had stepped beyond its boundary.

During prayer, ministers gathered around me. Hands rested on my shoulders. Voices rose. And from somewhere inside me, something answered back—uninvited, unmasked.

"No."

Fear surged through my body. I wanted out. I remember thinking, *If I can just get to the doors, I can leave.*

At that exact moment, every door in the church began to rattle violently—metal shuddering against frames—yet not one of them opened.

The apostle praying over me stopped.

She looked at the pastor and the other minister.

"Did you hear that?"

"Yes," they said.

They kept praying.

I stayed.

That was the first threshold. The first time I learned that obedience is not the absence of fear, but the refusal to run when fear demands the exit. When it was over, there was no spectacle. No collapse. Just a quiet release—as if something that had followed me for years finally lost its grip.

Freedom did not announce itself. It simply made room for breath.

The summer of 2001, nearly eleven years into marriage, we took our first family vacation. We rented a van and drove west—Disneyland, Hollywood, the Walk of Fame, Grauman's Chinese Theatre. Then Pismo Beach, where our children ran into the waves, laughing, fearless. For a few days, life felt open again, like a road with no immediate turnoffs.

We ended in San Francisco, where my dad was living at the time. The Golden Gate Bridge, the Maritime Museum—landmarks meant to remind you that endurance can also be beautiful. When we returned home, I believed, briefly, that we had arrived at steadier ground.

In September, that illusion collapsed.

I was getting the kids ready for school, the television murmuring in the background, when Charles Gibson mentioned a plane hitting one of the Twin Towers. I froze. Watched. Tried to understand what my eyes were telling me.

After dropping the kids off, I went to the gym before class. Every machine stood empty. Every person was gathered in front of the televisions, watching the world fracture in real time.

I called my husband at Fort Bliss Army Hospital, where he worked.

"Did you see?"

"Yes," he said. "It's on everywhere."

He was still in the Army Reserves. His unit was placed on alert. He was hopeful—he had always loved the Army, always believed that door might open again. But this time, I wouldn't follow.

"I'm not leaving until I graduate," I told him.

I had quit school twice before to follow his career. I had believed his calling mattered more than mine. After the affair, something in me had closed for good. I was done stepping backward through doors I had fought to open.

In the spring of 2002, Mr. Whitecotton returned with his son. I invited them to dinner and cooked his favorite—chile rellenos. We talked, laughed, remembered. Before he left, he handed me a set of keys.

A green 1999 two-door Chevrolet Cavalier.

He placed the paperwork in my hands and told me the title would be mailed in my name.

I had been worried about transferring to the University of Texas at El Paso—forty-five minutes away. My old car barely made it past forty-five miles per hour. No air conditioning. No heater. I had been praying quietly, telling God I didn't know how I was going to manage.

I hadn't asked for a car. But God had heard my thoughts.

Mr. Whitecotton laughed, remembering our slow drives to the VA. He told me he didn't know how he would have survived his illness without my help. My husband thanked him and stayed quiet.

When I held those keys, it felt like more than transportation.

It felt like permission. Like God saying, *You may go forward now.*

That car carried me across a threshold I had once believed was closed.

I transferred to UTEP in the spring of 2003. I was terrified. It went anyway. The campus was larger. The classes were harder. The workload heavier. Each morning, I turned the key and drove myself into a life I had almost abandoned.

That summer, urgency overtook me for reasons I still cannot explain. I enrolled in eight accelerated classes—four in June, four in July. My two youngest attended a YWCA program. My fourteen-year-old son found a job bagging groceries at the Fort Bliss commissary.

My days were relentless: drop-offs, lectures, pick-ups, dinner, laundry, homework. I often finished assignments at three or four in the morning.

Then there was the professor.

I noticed the pattern before I named it—women receiving lower grades than men. My friend Mike and I turned in identical assignments. Same work. Different names. Different grades.

When I confronted the professor, he said, "Bring me the fellow's paper so I can lower his grade."

The pressure rose in my chest, the same old instinct to retreat, to disappear quietly and call it peace. I recognized it. I had felt it before, in a room where doors rattled and none of them opened.

I stayed.

I gathered evidence. Copied graded papers. Marked discrepancies. And I knocked on the door of the Math Department dean—an office not designed for women like me to enter with authority.

I walked in anyway.

The dean agreed. There was clear discrimination. The professor was mandated to allow retakes and adjust grades. By the following fall, he no longer taught that course.

That class was required for my degree. I survived.

But more than that—I learned something essential.

Some doors must be shut for our protection. Others must be opened with courage. And once you are given the keys, you do not return them.

Thoughts

Years later, I understand that what I was learning was not just faith or endurance, but authority. No one hands a woman her voice fully formed. It is earned—through staying when it would be easier to leave, through speaking when silence is rewarded, through walking into rooms that were never meant to receive her.

Womanhood, as I came to know it, was not submission to closed systems, but discernment about which doors deserved my knocking and which ones needed to be shut for good. Faith did not make me smaller. It taught me where my boundaries were—and how to defend them.

I no longer confuse obedience with disappearance. I know now that when a woman learns to stand in her own life without asking permission, her voice carries weight.

I still hold the keys.

Chapter 59

The Lord is my strength and my shield;
in Him my heart trusts, and I am helped.
Leviticus 26:1-46 ESV

The fall of 2003 marked my final year of college—the year I would complete my student teaching. I had been preparing for this moment for as long as I could remember. It felt like stepping into the light after years of effort, finally able to see what all that work had been for. I was ready to practice what I had learned, ready to stand in front of a classroom and claim the title I had been working toward.

By the summer of 2004, I was taking my very last class.

At the same time, my daughter Marie—eleven years old—had been in ballet since she was five then one afternoon she came home rubbing her thigh, saying it hurt. I barely paused. I assumed it was soreness, the ordinary ache of muscles being asked to stretch and strengthen. It seemed harmless, temporary—something that would pass.

Looking back now, I know how quietly catastrophe can begin. Sometimes it enters a life as nothing more than a child rubbing her leg after dance class.

On the final day of class, I stopped by a middle school to drop off my résumé. As I pulled away from the campus, distracted and rushing, I crashed my car. The green 1999 two-door Chevrolet Cavalier—gifted to me by Mr. Whitecotton—was totaled in an instant.

My husband picked me up, and still shaken, I went on to class anyway.

I wasn't going to let anything stop me from finishing. I had come too far.

In July 2004, I earned my Bachelor of Interdisciplinary Studies in Math and Science from the University of Texas at El Paso, stitched together through scholarships and grants. I became highly qualified in Math and Science and earned my Texas Education Agency certification.

It felt like standing under a bright light—exposed, proud, hopeful.

But even as one light turned on, another began to flicker.

By early August, my daughter's pain had spread from her thigh to her entire leg. Sometimes she dragged it when she walked, as if her body had forgotten how to move forward evenly.

I began to watch her more closely.

Worry crept in quietly, like dusk—slow and undeniable.

Doctor appointments followed one after another. Pediatrician. Orthopedic specialist. A children's neurologist who admitted he didn't know what was happening. Answers never came—only referrals, waiting rooms, and the tightening of my own breath as each visit ended without clarity. The medical bills piled up. Between co-pays, deductibles, and medications, we fell behind.

One evening, the lights in our house went out.

My son Jimmy was fifteen then. He tried to make it lighter. We lit candles—more than a few—and he joked about how many we had.

"Mom," he said, smiling,

"if we get one more candle, we'll qualify as a Catholic church."

I had always loved the smell of candles.

But now they weren't comfort or decoration.

They were survival.

Small flames holding back the dark.

We didn't tell anyone our electricity had been shut off.

But our neighbor noticed.

She knew my daughter was sick. She saw the darkness inside our house. Without asking, she paid the bill and the reconnection fee.

The lights came back on.

Once again, God came through—not with spectacle, but quietly, through another person's hands.

Looking back, I see how often grace arrives that way—not as thunder, but as someone standing at your door with light when you have run out of your own.

The neurologist suggested physical therapy while we waited to see a more experienced specialist, Dr. Lavine.

By then, my daughter was using a wheelchair.

One leg was completely unresponsive; the other was weakening.

Soon her right arm followed. She struggled to lift it, to trust it.

Because she had lost her balance, the physical therapist recommended water therapy.

In the pool, my daughter floated, buoyed by something that held her when her body no longer could.

Watching her move through the water felt like watching someone learn how to breathe again.

During one session, the therapist said, "So it started in one leg, and now it's affecting both legs and one arm."

I nodded. We were still waiting for answers.

"It seems like whatever this condition is," she continued, "it's traveling."

She paused before adding gently,

"It could affect her breathing. You need to be prepared if that happens."

The air left my lungs. I had to face a fear I had been avoiding: my daughter might stop breathing.

I practiced drawing slow breaths, as if my calm could somehow teach her body to keep going.

In the middle of all this, I received a call offering me a job at Cordova Middle School—the same campus where I had dropped off my résumé just before my accident.

I was hired as an eighth-grade science teacher.

Nearly all the students came from low-income families, many carrying burdens far heavier than their backpacks.

I hesitated.

I explained my daughter's condition to the principal.

She listened.

She accommodated.

I accepted.

By September, my daughter—Marie—was eleven years old and could no longer walk.

The doctors still didn't know why.

My brother began researching our family history, searching for clues.

Then one night, Marie woke us, gasping for breath.

We rushed her to the emergency room, fear riding in the backseat with us.

The specialist we had been waiting to see—the one for a second opinion—was on call that very night.

What were the odds?

Marie spent nine days in the ICU.

The room hummed with monitors and quiet alarms. Tubes and wires surrounded her small body. I learned to watch the rise and fall of her chest the way other mothers watch the tide.

Each breath became something sacred.

I counted them the way I once counted candles.

When she stabilized, she was moved to a regular room.

I worked during the day. On lunch breaks, I drove to the hospital.

My husband stayed during the day; I stayed at night.

I got ready for work in the hospital bathroom, smoothing my hair beneath fluorescent lights before stepping back into a classroom.

It was exhausting.

It was relentless.

And yet, she remained hopeful.

She cried sometimes—who wouldn't? —but she laughed too.

I told her to notice what she still had: laughter, sound, breath. Even as I said it, I wondered how close we had come to losing all of it.

The diagnosis finally came:

Miller Fisher syndrome, a rare variant of Guillain-Barré.

The doctor recommended IVIg treatments.

We signed immediately.

Life settled into a fragile rhythm.

Marie returned home on homebound instruction. Teachers came during the day. My husband adjusted his schedule to work night schedule; I kept teaching.

She returned to physical therapy, her muscles weakened, relearning movement inch by inch.

One afternoon, as I pushed her wheelchair down the hallway after therapy, children's artwork lining the walls, I found myself praying.

I thanked God for my education, my job, my marriage, my family.

I thanked Him that my daughter was improving—that she was still breathing, still here.

I even thanked Him for the affair—because we were doing better now, or so I believed.

We had just celebrated fourteen years of marriage.

And then, quietly, unmistakably, something rose within me.

He's doing it again.

I pushed the thought away.

I didn't want to see it.

I needed the light to stay steady.

While we waited for Marie's pool session, she asked,

"Mom, do you call the house in the mornings?"

"No," I said. "Why?"

She told me about the phone ringing. About her dad's voice.

About the woman on the other line.

About how he told her to hang up.

"She calls every day," Marie said. "At the same time."

The truth took my breath away.

I had ignored the warning.

And now it had come through my child.

When I confronted my husband, he said it was just a friend.

My heart knew better, but I clung to doubt like a candle in a drafty room.

My siblings and I traveled to California soon after.

We visited our ninety-three-year-old grandfather in

East Los Angeles. Family stories filled the air.

I confronted an old wound, forgave an old name.

My brother asked questions about our history.

I spoke with an older cousin—a woman grounded in faith.

I told her everything.

She listened quietly, then said, "You already know.

You just don't want to see it. But you must face it."

We drove home in silence.

When I walked back into our house, the lights were on.

My daughter was breathing.

But something inside my life had already begun to go dark.

The truth was no longer hiding.

"She is not your friend," I told him.

"You are cheating again.

And I told you what would happen if you did."

<u>Thoughts</u>

I understand that truth is a kind of light God does not allow us to unsee. Scripture says what is hidden will be brought into the open, and I have learned that this is not punishment—it is mercy. It does not arrive gently. It does not ask permission. Once it appears, it exposes—and in exposing, it rearranges everything it touches.

I had learned to live by candlelight—accepting what was barely enough, calling survival peace, calling endurance love. I told myself that if the house was lit again, if breath returned to the body, if the crisis passed, then the cost had been worth it. I mistook partial restoration for healing. But borrowed light always flickers. It cannot hold against what God insists on bringing into the open.

When the truth finally revealed itself, it was not cruel. It was clarifying. It did not destroy my life; it showed me the shape of it. What I lost was not marriage, or faith, or hope—but illusion. And illusion, I would later learn, is not covenant. It is not love.

I once believed forgiveness meant dimming the light so everyone else could stay comfortable, mistaking silence for grace. Now I know forgiveness begins with truth. It means standing fully illuminated and refusing to deny what has already been revealed.

Truth does not always heal immediately. Sometimes it burns first. Light stings before it warms. But it is the same light that separated chaos from creation, the same breath that restores life where it seemed impossible. Once you have stepped into that light, faith is no longer about surviving the dark—it is about walking forward with open eyes, unafraid of what can now be seen.

Chapter 60

Ever since you found yourself in someone else's arms
I've been tryin' my best to get along
But that's okay
There's nothing left to say, but
Take your records, take your freedom
Take your memories, I don't need 'em
Take your space and take your reasons
But you'll think of me
You'll Think of Me by Keith Urban

Ten days later—Wednesday, November 10—I came home from work to a house already emptied of him. The silence told me before my eyes did.

He had spent the entire day packing. Every drawer hollowed. Every surface cleared. The bedroom television gone. His military gear gone. Even the small things he never used but still claimed as his. The house felt stripped down to its bones, like it had been waiting all day to exhale him.

A week earlier, he had been set to move out. I had changed my mind. I asked him not to go. *Please don't leave. Let's work things out.*

He didn't hesitate. "I want to leave. I'm not in love with you anymore. You've gotten too skinny. I don't desire you."

I stood still. I learned that day how quickly a body can armor itself. I didn't let him see how much it hurt. I watched him load the truck. I listened to the engine start. Then I stood in the doorway as the sound of him leaving disappeared down the street.

The house closed around me.

I went into the bedroom and lay on the bed, the quiet pressing against my ears. I cried out to God—not politely, not carefully. I cried until my chest ached and my throat burned. And then, without warning, a calm settled over me. The crying stopped. The silence softened. I slept.

Sometime in the night, the front door opened. My sister let herself in, the way people do when they know words won't help. She came into my room and lay down beside me. She didn't ask questions. She just held me. And the tears came back.

In the days that followed, I learned how loud an empty house can be. I learned how every room remembers who used to be there. I went to work anyway. My daughter returned to school—she could walk again just as her father walked out of our daily life. My boys carried their grief differently, but it lived in them all the same.

I kept writing in my prayer journal. I had always written things there I couldn't say out loud. My husband used to take it, sneak away, and read it. I caught him more than once. Those pages had never been safe.

On November 15, 2004, I wrote:

> *Lord, I am so angry at myself for loving him. The kids cry every night for him, and he says leaving was the best thing—for him. Even little Robert sees how selfish this is.*
>
> *Heal their hearts, Lord. They are holding so much anger. They love their father, but at home they don't think he's that great anymore. Grant them love that doesn't harden into bitterness.*
>
> *Robert said after getting off the phone with him, "You know, Mom, I think Dad is only a billionth great. How can things go well between you and Dad if he was seeing another lady?" Out of the mouths of babes, truth is spoken*

The phone became its own kind of reckoning. It rang when I wanted silence. It stayed quiet when I needed proof we still mattered.

Thanksgiving came, and he hadn't spoken to us at all. I took the kids to Los Angeles to be with my family. Before we left, I forwarded the house phone to my cell—unable, even then, to fully cut the cord.

While we were gone, it rang. He asked to speak to the children.

I handed the phone to my daughter.

Afterward, he asked for the boys.

She covered the receiver.

"Dad wants to talk to the boys. What do I tell him?"

"They're at the park."

"What park?" he pressed.

She hesitated. "We're in Los Angeles, Dad."

When he spoke to me, his voice sharpened. He accused. He threatened. He said words meant to scare me. The phone felt heavy in my hand, like it could bruise.

"Go ahead," I said. "Do what you've got to do."

When we returned to El Paso on November 29, the house was exactly as we'd left it—still quiet, still holding its breath.

Chapter 60

A couple of weeks later, the kids asked to spend the day with their dad. He picked them up. When the door closed behind them, the silence rushed back in.

I lay on my bed and told God I was tired of living. Not angry.

Just tired.

The kind of tired that empties you out. And then the phone rang.

I didn't answer.

It rang again.

When I finally picked up the receiver with one hand and a bottle of pills in the other, it was my friend Pam from church. She said God had put me on her heart and told her to call. She asked how I was.

We talked for hours. I cried. I laughed.

The house listened as my voice came back to life.

That night, I chose to stay.

I never told her that her obedience interrupted something that might have ended me.

Later, at work, I talked too freely to someone who listened too easily. I was lonely. I was vulnerable. I mistook attention for care. When Christmas came and the kids went with their father for a few hours, I agreed to lunch with him—thinking proximity might feel like repair.

It didn't.

I moved too fast into something new, desperate to fill the rooms of myself that had gone hollow.

The house was no longer empty.

But it still wasn't whole.

Thoughts

I understand what carried me through that season.

The phone taught me that silence is never neutral. Sometimes it wounds. Sometimes it saves. A ringing line can be a threat or a lifeline, depending on who answers it—and whether you do.

The journal taught me that truth needs a body. Words written in secret still matter. Even when they are violated, even when they are read by someone who means to control them, the act of writing is a form of standing upright. It was the first place my voice learned to return to itself.

And the house—empty, echoing, stripped bare—taught me that absence tells the truth faster than presence ever did. You can't pretend in a quiet room. You either fill it with lies, or you learn to live honestly inside it.

I survived because I kept answering, kept writing, kept staying.

Voice didn't arrive all at once. It came in fragments—through a phone call, through a notebook, through rooms that refused to be numbed. That was the beginning.

Chapter 61

Someday I'm gonna run across your mind
But don't worry, I'll be fine
I'm gonna be alright
While you're sleeping with your pride
Wishing I could hold you tight
I'll be over you
And on with my life
You'll Think of Me by Keith Urban

My divorce was finalized in **May of 2005**.

We stood before the judge at the county courthouse, waiting for a door to close. The room felt small, official, final. Even though I was already talking to someone else, my heart was crushed. Tears streamed steadily down my face throughout the entire proceeding—so much so that the judge stopped and gently asked if we wanted to pause, if perhaps we were not ready to go through with it.

I wanted to tell him that some doors close even when you're not ready. Some shut because staying inside them is no longer survivable.

I tried to hold my tears back. I couldn't.

When it was over, my husband walked me to my car. We sat there with the doors closed, the world sealed out, and talked about everything that had led us here. Before he got out, he said,

"Maybe in the future we can get back together.
I'm just not ready to be married right now."

Then he stepped out, closed the car door, and walked back into the courthouse to file the papers that made it final.

I was thirty-three years old. Divorced. A single mother. My children were sixteen, twelve, and eleven. Every responsibility stood waiting on the other side of that door.

My father was still in San Francisco, California. He was worried— but not enough to come home. Worried enough to call every day, his voice traveling through the phone like a hand knocking gently, repeatedly.

One day he said, "Tío Richie is worried about you. He wants to know—if he wrote to you, would you write him back?"

"Did he come clean with his mother?" I asked.

"No," my dad said.

"He wants you to come visit him so he can talk to you."

"No, Dad," I replied.

"I'm not opening that door. Not until he tells Grandma the truth."

I had never imagined my life would narrow and split like this. And as if the divorce itself were not enough, many of the people who should have stood beside me chose not to follow me through it.

Friends from church—people who had once welcomed me inside—closed ranks and turned away from me and my children. Somehow, they decided I was wrong for divorcing him. That I should have forgiven more. Stayed longer. Endured.

I felt doors quietly closing all around me. Conversations ended sooner. Invitations stopped coming. I could feel who they sided with, and it wasn't me.

I held onto my faith, but there came a moment when I knew I could no longer attend that church. Walking away left me exposed, standing outside a structure that had once given me shelter.

By July of 2005, I stepped into another relationship.

I did not knock on God's door. I did not open the Bible or sit in pews. I walked through the first open doorway that offered warmth.

I started seeing Romero.

In the beginning, everything felt gentle and promising, as beginnings often do. He didn't speak English, but my children liked him well enough. He worked as a custodian at the same school where I worked. He was charming, generous with affection, quick with endearment words that unlocked something tender and desperate in me.

He sent me flowers. He made me feel chosen. His Mexican chivalry and romantic gestures felt intentional, attentive. He was eleven years older than me, liked going to the gym, and we often went together—something my husband had never wanted to do.

When I was with Romero, I felt protected, as if he stood between me and the world. Yet when he wasn't there, doubt slipped in through the cracks. I wasn't sure which door I was walking through—only that I couldn't go back to the one behind me.

The day of my divorce proceedings, Romero invited me out to eat. When we arrived at the restaurant, I stayed in the car, my hand resting on the door handle, unable to move. He leaned over and wrapped his arms around me, and I cried into his shoulder until my body gave out.

He didn't ask why. Some grief announces itself without explanation.

Inside, the restaurant felt quiet, as if we had entered with something sacred and broken.

That same July, my ex-husband began coming around again, helping with repairs to the swimming pool. After a trip to California with my children, I returned to find a small bouquet of flowers waiting for me, along with a limited-edition copy of one of my favorite movies, *Gone with the Wind.* He had never brought me flowers in the fourteen years of our marriage.

I stared at them, angry. *Now* you're knocking? Three months later?

My birthday fell on a Wednesday. Romero bought us dinner, and we celebrated at home with my children. His car was parked outside, a quiet declaration. My kids baked me a cake and sang "Happy Birthday." I turned thirty-four. They cleaned the kitchen and disappeared into their rooms.

Romero and I sat on the sofa, talking. The blinds were still open when the doorbell rang. When I opened the door, my ex-husband stood there holding flowers and a gift bag.

"I came to wish you a happy birthday," he said.

"Thank you," I replied, not stepping aside.

"May I give you a hug?"

I hesitated, then agreed. He hugged me briefly, turned, and walked away. I closed the door behind him.

When I returned to the sofa, Romero said quietly,

"I think he's having second thoughts."

"You're probably right," I said.

The phone rang almost immediately. It was my ex-husband—angry now, upset that another man sat in the house we had once shared, on the furniture he had bought, eating from plates that belonged to a life he had already left.

I let him finish.

Then I asked, "Seeing me with another man—does it hurt?"

"Yes," he said.

"The medicine doesn't taste good," I replied. "The hurt you're feeling now is the same hurt I felt. The difference is that you did it while we were married—not once, but twice. I did it once, after the door was already closed."

I hung up the phone.

That night, something shifted. Not because a door opened—but because I finally locked one.

And for the first time since the courthouse, I stood on the inside of my own life.

<u>Thoughts</u>

Today I understand that the hardest doors to close are the ones we once begged to be opened. At the time, I thought strength meant keeping every entrance unlocked—being forgiving, available, patient enough to wait for people to decide whether I was worth staying for. I believed love was proven by how much I could endure.

It took years to learn that boundaries are not acts of cruelty.

They are acts of clarity.

Some people only want access without accountability. They knock when they feel lonely, when regret gets loud, when the house they chose no longer feels like home. But an open door does not obligate you to let them back inside.

I also learned that faith does not always live in sanctuaries. Sometimes it lives in the quiet courage to walk away from places that confuse obedience with silence and sacrifice with worthiness.

Being the one who closes the door often looks like failure from the outside. It looks like abandonment. It looks like rebellion. But from the inside, it feels like breath returning to the body.

I did not close that door to punish anyone.

I closed it so my life could continue forward—uninterrupted, unafraid, and finally my own.

Chapter 62

Waiting at the Bridge

When I first met Romero, he was good to me and good to my children. I wish I could point to the exact moment when that goodness shifted, when something essential bent out of shape. But it didn't happen all at once. It arrived the way fog does—thin at first, almost polite.

I think it began when he started "living with me." I put that phrase in quotation marks now because even then, it never felt solid. His version of living together came with conditions. He stayed with us Monday through Friday morning. By the time the weekend arrived, he belonged somewhere else.

Romero had a spot at a swap meet in Ciudad Juárez. He collected used items—things other people had let go of—and resold them across the border. He said he needed to focus, to get his business going. Focus, I learned, often meant distance.

Friday mornings developed their own quiet ritual. Romero would move through the house with a small bag, gathering what he needed for the weekend. The zipper closing sounded louder than it should have in the kitchen. By the time I looked out the front window, his truck was already backing out of the driveway, the engine fading down the street. The house settled into a different kind of silence once he left.

On Saturdays he stayed with his nephew in a studio apartment behind his house in Juárez. Romero said it was easier that way. Crossing the bridge could take hours. The explanation was always practical, always reasonable. Logistics wrapped themselves around absence until it looked necessary.

When I asked if I could go with him—help him, be part of his routine—he waved the idea away. He already had a system. I would only get in the way.

Any time I questioned why he didn't come home on weekends, the conversation flipped. I was insecure. I was projecting wounds from my past. I was punishing him for my ex-husband's infidelity. Somehow, my asking for presence became proof of my instability.

The bridge loomed quietly in the background of my life, not just the physical crossing between countries, but the space where explanations lived. He was always just across it. Close enough to justify waiting. Far enough to remain unreachable.

In 2006, gas prices rose sharply. To save money, I bought a used four-door 1993 Honda Accord. It wasn't glamorous, but it was reliable. At that point in my life, reliability felt like luxury.

That same summer, my seventeen-year-old son told me he wanted to join the United States Army. He wanted to follow in the footsteps of the man he had called Dad since he was two years old—my ex-husband. Because he was still a minor, he needed both parents' signatures.

I took him to see his biological father Arturo, whom he hadn't seen since he was very young. My son stood there, taller than the memory his father held of him, asking for permission to leave.

His father looked at me and asked if I was okay with it. I said yes. I believed it was a good thing.

The papers were signed. My son entered the delayed entry program. He left for basic training that summer, returned to finish his senior year, and then left again for advanced training.

Years later, I would look back on that moment and feel the weight of it settle differently. At the time, I didn't know how many kinds of leaving I was already practicing.

By then, the warmth I once felt with Romero had faded. Not vanished—just thinned. The relationship no longer felt healthy, but I couldn't yet name why. There was no single bruise, no clear offense. Only a low-grade tension, like driving with the check engine light on and convincing yourself it could wait.

I tried to leave him indirectly. I told myself I would get a job closer to home because the cost of gas had become a hardship. It was true—but not the whole truth. I hoped that changing my circumstances might give me the courage I lacked.

I found a teaching position nearby. My life filled quickly. I taught eighth grade, coordinated the science fair, coached cross country and track, served as science department head, and sat on hiring committees.

On paper, I was thriving.

Romero's schedule didn't change. Monday through Friday morning he was present. Friday through Sunday night he was gone.

Weekends became something I learned to build around. My children were busy with their own lives. My daughter, despite ongoing health struggles, marched in the high school band. My oldest son played football. My youngest ran cross country. I stayed busy on purpose—Friday nights under stadium lights, Saturdays at meets, watching my son disappear down the course and return breathless.

I told myself this was independence.

I told myself this was modern.

I told myself I didn't need him as much as I sometimes felt I did.

After graduating high school, my oldest son left home. He was stationed at Fort Bragg. Another door closed quietly behind someone I loved.

Romero was no longer the man I had first dated. Occasionally I caught glimpses of that earlier version—just enough to keep me hoping. When I tried to talk about what had changed, he twisted the conversation until I was apologizing.

His anger came in bursts. He yelled. He threw things. These moments weren't confined to private spaces; they happened in public, without warning. Doors slammed. People stared.

I learned to make myself smaller in advance.

The day I bought my first brand-new car—a 2007 Honda Accord— should have been a celebration. Romero came with me to the dealership.

During the final paperwork, the salesperson asked if I wanted GAP insurance. I asked him to explain it.

As he spoke, Romero interrupted.

"You don't need it."

"I want to hear what he has to say," I replied.

Again: "You don't need it."

Then the salesperson asked a simple question.

"Who will be making the payments?"

Something ignited. Romero stormed out, slamming the door so hard it echoed through the showroom. The moment collapsed in on itself. My excitement curdled into embarrassment.

Later, somehow, this too was my fault. There were many moments like that—milestones soured, joy interrupted.

Each time I finally drew a line, Romero would pack his things, load them into his truck, and leave. Then he would come back.

He apologized. He promised change. He was charming, persuasive. And once I let him return, the cycle reset. Chaos dressed itself up as reconciliation.

He often said he would never marry again.

He had already been married twice. He didn't want a third.

Eventually, I tried one final strategy—not to keep him, but to end it.

I told him I wanted marriage someday. I told him I wanted to return to church. I said that this half-life—this coming and going—was contrary to the Word of God.

It was the first time I spoke the truth without cushioning it.

Looking back now, I see how emotional abuse entered my life without announcing itself. It crossed bridges disguised as work. It hid in weekends framed as practicality. It took the front seat in cars I paid for. It slammed doors loudly enough that I learned to brace before they closed.

For the first time, I understood that waiting had become a habit— and habits can feel like love when you live inside them long enough.

I spent years standing at the edge of that bridge, believing love meant waiting for someone to cross back.

I didn't know then that love doesn't require you to wait indefinitely, to explain your loneliness, or to apologize for wanting someone to come home. I only knew that something in me had begun to wake up—and that this time, when the door finally closed, it would be mine to shut.

Thoughts

For a long time, I believed abuse would announce itself loudly. I thought it would arrive in the form of obvious cruelty, something unmistakable that anyone could see. What I did not understand then was how quietly emotional abuse can enter a life. It rarely begins with shouting. More often, it begins with small distortions: conversations that leave you doubting yourself, absences explained so reasonably that you begin to question your own expectations.

Romero did not arrive in my life as an angry man. He arrived kind, attentive, and good to my children. That is what made the change so difficult to see. The shift was gradual, almost invisible. By the time the tension became undeniable, I had already learned to explain it away.

Looking back now, I understand that emotional abuse often hides inside ordinary routines. It disguises itself as practicality, as stress, as misunderstandings between two people trying to make things work. Nothing was broken all at once. There were no rules posted, no ultimatums spoken aloud. Instead, my world grew smaller by degrees.

I learned to wait.

I learned to explain myself.

I learned to measure my needs against someone else's comfort and call that compromise.

I mistook distance for independence and tension for normal disagreement. I believed that if I were more patient, more reasonable, more understanding, the ground beneath me would stop shifting. At the time, I thought patience was a form of love. I believed loyalty meant enduring confusion without asking too many questions.

What I could not see then—but understand clearly now—is that emotional abuse rarely begins with the intention to harm. It begins with imbalance, with control disguised as certainty, with one person slowly learning they can shape the reality of another.

What I lived through did not look like harm at first. It looked like adjustment. It looked like loyalty. It looked like giving someone the benefit of the doubt again and again until doubt became something I directed inward.

Only with time did I understand that erosion can be as damaging as impact. That being diminished slowly still counts as being diminished. And that leaving—when you finally do—is not a failure of endurance, but an act of return.

And yet, even inside that fog, something in me remained awake—a quiet voice that noticed the distance, that questioned the explanations, that refused to fall completely asleep inside the waiting.

It took time before I trusted that voice.

But it was already there.

I didn't lose myself all at once.

I misplaced myself in small, reasonable ways—

until I decided to come back.

Chapter 63

**Me and Mrs. Jones
We got a thing going on
We both know that it's wrong
But it's much too strong to let it go now
Me and Mrs. Jones by Billy Paul 1972**

March 2008, I married Romero in Las Vegas, Nevada, against my intuition and the counsel of friends who loved me, especially Julie and Estela. They warned me plainly. They told me the relationship was unhealthy. I heard them, nodded even, but I kept walking forward, as if the decision were already made and all I had to do was step through the door.

I told myself a story that felt holy enough to justify everything: once married, God would bless us. Once married, I would no longer be living in sin, and God would change him. Marriage, I believed, was a kind of threshold—cross it, and grace would follow.

What I didn't understand then was how easily a door can close behind you.

Not with a slam.

But softly.

Almost politely.

Our home quickly became a place of tension and confusion, marked by screaming arguments that left me vibrating long after the noise stopped. I didn't yet have language for what was happening. I only knew that I was always bracing myself, always listening for the next shift in the air.

The cycle came in waves: anger, cruelty, fear—followed by affection, humor, apologies. He could be charming, attentive, even compassionate. Those were the moments that pulled me back in, the ones where I convinced myself I had misread the last explosion. I learned to stand in doorways waiting to see which version of him would appear.

During his rages, he threw whatever he could reach—cell phones, remotes, picture frames, shoes. He tore photographs, broke my things, destroyed the small proofs of my life. Each broken object felt like another room I was no longer allowed to occupy.

One morning, as I was leaving for work, he demanded that I find a paper he needed. I told him I didn't have time and that I would look for it when I got home. He followed me out the door, yelling while my daughter and I stepped into the car.

I started the engine and pulled out of the driveway.

That's when he picked up a rock.

It was heavy, solid, deliberate. He lifted it as if to throw it at me. I stopped the car, shifted into park, and looked straight at him.

Go ahead.

For a moment, the world held its breath. Then he dropped the rock. I drove away, hands shaking on the steering wheel, wondering how close I had come to something irreversible—and how I had ended up standing on that threshold at all.

Another time, we were in Ciudad Juárez, driving separate vehicles. My son Robert was with me. An argument started, but I decided not to step into it. I drove toward the line to cross back into the United States. While we waited, he pulled up beside us and motioned for me to let him cut in front.

I shook my finger *no* and gestured for him to go to the back.

He tried to ram my car on the driver's side.

The first time, I pretended it didn't happen. The second time, he came so close that fear finally reached me. Still, I didn't show it. I had learned that fear was another door he knew how to use.

At home, he blocked doorways so I couldn't leave. He stood between me and the exit, telling me I was too sensitive, that I exaggerated, that I was the problem. When I tried to explain how his behavior made me feel, he laughed—or twisted the conversation until I found myself apologizing.

Somewhere in all of this, my faith began to thin. I didn't walk away from God in defiance. I drifted. I kept stepping through doors that promised relief or peace or quiet, and I stopped noticing how many I had closed behind me. Prayer became tentative, then occasional, then mostly silent. I told myself God understood.

Then came the calm periods—the gentleness, the apologies, the illusion of change. I would lower my guard. Let him back in.

But it was always the same room, rearranged.

In 2009, my former mother-in-law Olivia, whom I had remained close to—was diagnosed with colon cancer. I spent every free moment with her. She was family in the truest sense, a constant in a life that had become increasingly unstable.

One weekend, shortly before she died, she was admitted to the ICU. Romero decided not to go to Ciudad Juárez to work because he said he wasn't feeling well. That morning, as I got ready to leave for the hospital, he asked, "Aren't you going to stay with me?"

"No," I said. "You didn't stay home to be with me.

You stayed because you're sick."

"So where are you going?" he demanded.

"To the hospital," I said. "Olivia is on her deathbed. You're not."

I walked out.

For the first time, he didn't follow me.

That October, the evening news reported that San Francisco police had linked my uncle's DNA to the 1984 murder of nine-year-old Mei Leung. I stood frozen as the report played, tears streaming down my face.

The last time he molested me was December 23, 1983. One hundred nine days later, he murdered a child.

Now there was proof. DNA.

Surely now, I thought, my family would believe me. Surely now someone would call, apologize, open a door that had been sealed for decades.

The call never came.

Instead, I collapsed inward. I drank too much. One night after meeting coworkers at a bar, I realized on the drive home that I couldn't see clearly. I pulled over, put the car in park, and passed out. I woke to a police officer knocking on my window. Somehow, I was spared.

Another night, celebrating a friend's departure, I drank until I was vomiting in a restroom. I had my children come get me. I was unraveling, reaching for exits wherever I could find them.

That's when Mendez appeared—quietly, like a side door I hadn't noticed before. He was the father of a student in my Science Fair Club. Divorced. Kind. He looked at me one afternoon a little longer than necessary. We talked the next day. He asked me out. I told him I was married.

It didn't stop him.

Chapter 63

We exchanged numbers. When Romero left on Fridays, I met Mendez at restaurants, then at his house. When his children were there, he texted once they were asleep. My children were teenagers. I went anyway.

This wasn't confusion. This wasn't accidental.

It was an affair—sexual and emotionally intimate. A door I walked through with my eyes open because, for the first time in a long while, no one was yelling on the other side.

Olivia's health declined quickly. She was placed on hospice so she could die at home, surrounded by family. My oldest son flew in from Fort Bragg. She was the woman he called Grandma, bloodless but bound by love.

At home, the fighting resumed. I was spending too much time with my former in-laws.

This time, I didn't retreat.

I stood with them, the family who had known me since I was eighteen, who treated me like one of their own. On the day of the funeral, I prepared the food for the reception. I was enveloped by love and acceptance, a feeling so steady it startled me.

That night, when I returned home, the yelling started again. Objects flew. The old familiar chaos rose to meet me.

I turned around.

I walked back out the door.

I drove straight to Mendez's house. It was late. I knocked on his window. He let me in. He knew about the funeral. He knew about the fighting.

He handed me a drink. He held me.

And I cried—standing in yet another doorway, unsure of where I was going, but finally aware that staying had been costing me far more than leaving ever could.

Thoughts

For years, I carried the affair like a secret verdict against myself. I told the story in absolutes: wrong choice, moral failure, proof that I was untrustworthy with my own life. That version was tidy. It required no complexity, only shame.

But adulthood has given me a wider lens.

The affair was not a misunderstanding or a momentary lapse. It was a choice. I crossed a line I knew was there. I don't minimize that. I own it.

And still owning what I did does not mean I have to ignore everything that led me there.

I was living inside a marriage where my voice had been dismantled piece by piece, where leaving felt dangerous and staying felt unbearable. I had been trained to doubt my instincts, to accept confinement as virtue, to confuse endurance with love. When someone offered warmth without volatility, attention without threat, I mistook relief for safety.

The affair did not heal me. It did not free me. It postponed a reckoning I would eventually have to face anyway.

What it did was tell the truth my mouth could not yet form: that I wanted tenderness without fear, connection without punishment, a life where my nervous system could rest. The mistake was believing I could access those things through secrecy instead of courage.

I no longer tell this story to excuse myself. I tell it to be honest about how survival instincts can masquerade as desire—and how unhealed wounds will always look for exits.

The work came later. Naming harm without becoming it. Learning that wanting peace does not make you entitled to take it from the wrong place. Learning that integrity is not about perfection, but about alignment.

The affair was not the worst thing I ever did. Silence was. And I stopped choosing that.

Chapter 64

I think I deserve something beautiful.
Eat, Pray, Love by Elizabeth Gilbert

The New Year of 2010 found me alone in my car at the top of Scenic Drive in El Paso, Texas.

The road curved along the Franklin Mountains, a narrow ribbon of asphalt overlooking everything below—city lights scattered like constellations, the Rio Grande threading quietly through the dark, Ciudad Juárez glowing just across the border. Lovers came here. They parked along the edge, leaned against the low stone wall, and spoke softly into the night as if the view itself could hold their secrets.

That night, it held mine.

The air was cold enough to slip through the seams of the car. My breath faintly fogged the windshield. Below me, the city glittered—steady, faithful, indifferent. Above me, the sky stretched wide and silent. I sat curled into the driver's seat, the radio low, the countdown inching closer, my body folded inward like something bracing for impact.

Earlier that evening, Romero and I had gone with his family to a dance hall to celebrate New Year's Eve. Music pulsed through the walls, bass vibrating in my chest, laughter spilling across the room. It was supposed to be a celebration—a doorway into something better.

But somewhere between the car and the entrance, I crossed an invisible line.

I said something wrong.

Or maybe I didn't say anything at all.

With him, I was never sure.

By the time we sat down, he had already turned his back to me.

He didn't speak. Didn't look at me. The silence settled in, thick and familiar, pressing against my ribs. He laughed easily with his family, his voice open and warm in a way it rarely was with me. I sat beside him, invisible. Erased. I might as well have never been there.

The music grew louder, but it didn't reach me. The smell of alcohol and sweat hung heavy in the air. Around me, couples leaned into each other, bodies close, voices soft. I sat alone in plain sight.

I had learned, over time, the rules that were never spoken out loud—when to speak, when to stay quiet, how to anticipate the shift in his mood before it fully arrived. But that night, I had misstepped. Or maybe I had simply existed in the wrong way.

When I stood and walked across the dance floor to get myself a drink, it felt like something small but significant—a quiet reclaiming.

My feet moved without asking permission.

For a moment, I felt the ground beneath me again.

But when I returned, I saw it immediately.

The looks.

Disapproval. Judgment.

His mother's mouth tightened, her eyes narrowing just enough to make her meaning clear. Romero reached for my arm, his fingers closing firmly around it—not enough to leave a mark, but enough to remind me.

"You're not here alone," he said.

"How could you disrespect me like that?"

My arm ached where he held it.

I met his eyes and told him the truth.

"I felt alone. Your back was to me. No one was talking to me."

The words hung between us for a moment.

Then something in his face closed.

The truth didn't open anything.

It sealed the distance.

I grabbed my things and walked out. He followed, his footsteps sharp behind me. The argument started before we reached the car and filled it the moment the doors shut—voices ricocheting off the windows, sharp and practiced, worn into us from repetition.

I gripped the steering wheel, my hands tight, the leather warm beneath my palms.

By the time we reached home, it wasn't even midnight.

He got out of the car and went inside without looking back.

I sat there for a moment, the engine still running, the silence ringing louder than the fight had.

Then I shifted into reverse then drive and left.

The road up Scenic Drive curved beneath me, familiar and steady. As I climbed, the city fell away again, widening into view.

Chapter 64

I turned on the radio, just in time to hear the countdown begin—voices bright and celebratory, meant to be shared with someone who loved you.

I tightened my grip on the wheel.

Ten. Nine. Eight.

When the New Year arrived, I was alone. But I was still here.

The realization settled into me slowly, like warmth returning to cold hands. I leaned my head back and closed my eyes, just for a moment.

"God…" I whispered, barely audible in the quiet car.

"I don't know how to leave. But I know I can't stay like this."

The words felt small.

But they were the first honest ones I had spoken in a long time.

Sometime after midnight, exhaustion overtook me. I fell asleep in the driver's seat, my body finally surrendering. When I woke, it was 3:30 in the morning. The city had softened, its sharp edges dimmed by the hour.

For a moment, I just sat there, looking out.

From that height, everything made sense.

Distance had a way of telling the truth.

I drove home in the quiet.

When I walked through the door, he was waiting.

"Where were you?" he asked.

I set my keys down slowly.

"Wherever you go," I said, my voice steady,

"when you come home at four-thirty in the morning."

The words surprised even me. Something had shifted.

Not loudly. Not all at once. But deep inside, something had settled into place—a knowing that didn't need permission to exist.

My body understood before my mind could explain it.

I was strong enough to leave.

But life doesn't always open doors just because you're ready to walk through them.

His mother died in October 2010.

After the funeral, his nineteen-year-old son came to live with us. The house changed almost overnight—more noise, more tension, more bodies moving through already crowded space.

The walls felt closer. And I grew smaller inside them.

I saw it in my daughter, too.

The way her shoulders tightened when his voice rose. The way she withdrew into herself, her words becoming fewer, softer, as if she were learning to take up less space in a house that already felt too full.

Her body had already endured so much. Now it was learning silence.

In February 2011, her psychologist—who had been helping her navigate the lingering pain from her paralysis—said what I had not yet been able to name.

She told me the relationship I was in was ***emotionally abusive***.

And that it was affecting my daughter's health.

The word landed like light cutting through something dense.

Abusive.

I felt it move through me—first as relief, then as grief.

It was as if someone had pulled the car over and told me to step out, to look at the view clearly for the first time.

I could see it now.

The patterns. The control. The slow shrinking of myself.

And once you see, you cannot unsee.

Still, I stayed.

Timing. Fear. Responsibility.

All the doors I had convinced myself were locked.

In March, I traveled with my science fair students to the state competition. Before I left, I ended my affair with Mendez.

I didn't want escape anymore.

I wanted clarity.

At night in the hotel room, I read—books that felt like mirrors, reflecting my life back to me. Page by page, sentence by sentence, they named what I had been living inside. Silence. Control.

Love, distorted into something unrecognizable.

Each word felt like another step upward, like driving back toward that overlook where everything could finally be seen.

When Romero picked me up from the airport, the air in the car filled quickly—criticism spilling out before we even reached the highway. My daughter. My son. Everything they had done wrong while I was gone.

I didn't argue. I didn't defend. I watched. I listened. I saw it now.

Chapter 64

At home, I sat on the couch and turned on the television. Eat Pray Love had just begun. The timing felt almost too precise, as if something beyond me had aligned it there.

One line settled into me, anchoring itself deep:

The only thing more unthinkable than leaving… was staying.

That night, I slept.

The next day, I went to work. I spoke when necessary, but otherwise I stayed quiet—not the silence he imposed, but the silence I chose.

A listening silence.

A gathering silence.

A silence that was building something.

The following weekend, Romero stayed home instead of going to Ciudad Juárez to sell at his thrift stand. I got dressed for the gym, needing movement, space—air.

On the drive, my phone rang. His name lit up the screen.

"Why didn't you stay home with me?" he demanded.

I stared at the road ahead, then turned the car around.

As I drove back, my chest tightened—

not with fear this time, but with clarity.

"Lord," I said aloud, my voice trembling but sure,

"give me the strength to tell him the truth.

Give me the courage to ask him to leave."

When I pulled into the driveway, he was already waiting.

He opened the passenger door and got in.

"We need to talk," he said.

"I know."

"I feel like I'm losing you." I kept my eyes on the windshield.

"No," I said quietly. "You already lost me."

The words landed with a weight I could feel in my chest.

"I don't want to be with you anymore.

I need you to pack your things and leave."

He started talking—his son, logistics, time, reasons.

I shook my head, my voice steady now.

"You and your son need to pack your things and leave today."

The silence that followed was different.

It didn't belong to him anymore.

He opened the door and stepped out.

I sat there for a moment, my hands resting loosely on the steering wheel. Then I drove to the gym, tears streaming down my face, something inside me opening with every breath. Relief.

"Thank you, Jesus,"

I whispered, pressing my forehead briefly against the wheel.

When I returned, his son was gone. Romero was still there—pleading now, softer, promising change, offering counseling, another chance. But I had already stepped outside the car.

I had already seen the view.

I was finished.

In April, my son came home from the military, honorably discharged after four years. I told him everything.

Still, Romero refused to leave.

So I reached beyond myself.

A lawyer.

My pastor.

"Pack his things," my pastor told me.

"Put them outside. Change the locks."

At work, a friend helped me gather boxes. I brought them home and hid them behind the sofa, waiting for the night he would come home late—or not at all.

I moved quietly through my own life, preparing.

Back then, I didn't know exactly how it would end.

I only knew this:

The car had taught me how to leave.

Scenic Drive had shown me the truth from a distance.

Silence had stopped being a weapon and become a plan.

And somewhere—just beyond fear, just beyond the edge of everything I had known—a door was finally opening.

Thoughts

From this distance, I understand what that car gave me before I knew how to leave. It was the first place where my body felt like it belonged to me again. A place where I could hear my own thoughts, speak the truth out loud, and pray without being corrected or punished.

Scenic Drive was never about escape. It was about perspective. From up there, I could see the city continue without me, unchanged and steady.

That night taught me something simple and lasting: my life did not need to be held hostage by someone else's silence.

I once believed endurance was love. I believed staying proved strength. Now I know better. Strength was learning to listen to the quiet voice inside me that said, *This is not safety. This is not peace.*

I did not leave all at once. I left in increments—one drive, one prayer, one truth spoken softly but without apology. Freedom did not arrive with drama. It came with clarity.

And clarity, I have learned, is its own kind of mercy.

Chapter 65

... Every move you make
And every vow you break
Every smile you fake
Every claim you stake
I'll be watching you
Every move you make
Every step you take
I'll be watching you
Every Breath You Take by The Police

June 2011. My daughter was graduating from high school.

The day before the ceremony, I stood in the kitchen doorway and finally said the words I had rehearsed silently for years.

"Marie is graduating tomorrow," I told him. "I don't want you to go with me. You've ruined too many special occasions in my life, and I am not going to let you ruin this one. My ex-in-laws are coming over. We're having a cookout to celebrate her accomplishment, and I don't want you here for that either. So tomorrow, when you wake up, you need to leave. Go wherever it is you go when you don't come home."

That night, he didn't come home.

I woke at 4:30 a.m. The house was still, the kind of quiet that feels like a held breath. His side of the bed was empty. I stood there for a moment, listening to the silence on the other side of every door, and knew this was the morning I would not step back from. My pastor's words rang in my mind.

"Pack his things. Put them outside. Change the locks."

I began packing his belongings. Clothes, shoes, fragments of a life I no longer wanted crossing my thresholds. I changed the locks on the front door and the back door. For the first time, the doors answered to me.

I woke everyone up. We moved deliberately, quietly. I asked my son to lock the kitchen window. We loaded the car before the sun rose and drove to my ex-father-in-law's house, where the kids and I stayed all day—safe behind someone else's doors.

I knew he would call once he tried to come home.

Chapter 65

Sure enough, the phone rang. I didn't need to answer to know he had reached a door that would not open for him anymore and his things in boxes. We waited two more hours before returning.

When we walked inside, the violation was immediate. He had broken in through the kitchen window. One of the televisions was gone. A DVD player. The air mattress. Evidence of his leaving taken with force instead of acceptance.

My son Robert was devastated—the television he used for his PlayStation was missing. I looked at my children standing in a doorway that had already been crossed without permission and told them the only truth I could hold onto: it was a small price to pay for peace.

I thought the window had been locked.

I was wrong.

The stalking began quietly, then persistently, like someone testing handles in the dark.

I blocked every phone number I could think of, so he found other entrances. Flowers appeared at my workplace. I called him and told him I wanted nothing. They went straight into the school garbage bin.

He contacted my close friend Estela at her job, asking her to talk to me, to convince me to "come to my senses." Once, he even drove to her house and knocked on her door. She recognized him through the peephole and didn't answer. She called me immediately, fear sharp in her voice.

The scariest moment came three months after I packed his things.

My son Jimmy was living with me and working early mornings.

One day, running late, he forgot to lock the front door.

Romero had been waiting for a door like that.

I woke to a hand covering my mouth. He stood over me in my bedroom, whispering for me not to scream. My other two children slept behind closed doors down the hall. My body went rigid, my breath shallow. He told me he wasn't there to hurt me. He just wanted to talk. Before removing his hand, he made me promise not to scream. I nodded.

He spoke of love. Of regret. Of how sorry he was. He asked for another chance, and fear answered for me. I agreed to meet him for lunch later that day so we could talk calmly.

When he finally left, I sat up in bed and cried.

I waited until I heard the front door close. Then I ran and locked it, as if the lock could hear me, as if it could remember what had just passed through.

I called my son and yelled—not out of anger, but terror.

His carelessness could have cost me my life.

I did not meet Romero for lunch.

That Sunday, he showed up at church and sat beside me. I felt the walls close in even there. Trying to be polite, I told him my daughter wasn't feeling well and that I couldn't meet with him. We sat in the church lobby while he talked, his words pressing against me like hands on glass.

Then my pastor came and sat with us.

He didn't arrive by accident.

I had been in counseling with him since March of 2011. By then, Pastor Jorge knew I was being stalked. After three failed relationships— two of them marriages—I had finally asked for help. He supported my seeing a psychologist. The psychologist referred me to a psychiatrist. I went. I submitted to the work because I no longer trusted my own sense of which doors were safe to open.

Still, the stalking continued.

One afternoon, while I was coaching cross-country, I met my students behind a nearby athletic complex with sand dunes for endurance training. When practice ended, he was there—waiting for me.

I stayed polite, distant, my body angled toward escape. One of my students told their mother that I was in trouble. She asked me quietly if I wanted her to call the police. I nodded.

After the students were picked up, I was left alone with him. Across the street, the woman and her son waited with hazard lights on, keeping watch like an open door that refused to close.

Romero grabbed my arm and blocked my way to my car. He begged for another chance.

Two police cars arrived.

An officer asked what was happening. I told him we were separated, no longer living together, and that he refused to leave me alone. The officer asked if I planned to file for divorce.

When I said yes, he told me, "You need to file quickly and get a restraining order."

Close this door, he didn't say—but it was clear.

That night, I went home and researched how to file for divorce without a lawyer. It cost $183. Paperwork became another kind of boundary.

After that, the stalking slowed. Once a month instead of constantly. My divorce was finalized on November 14, 2011. He contacted me once before Thanksgiving. In December, he came by the house, but no one answered the door.

In January 2012, I traveled to Albuquerque to visit my cousin for New Year's Eve. While I was there, he called from a number I hadn't blocked. I answered.

When I realized it was him, I followed my pastor's guidance. I told him I had met someone at church.

"I knew you would eventually meet someone at church," he said. "I won't say I'm not hurt, but I wish you the best."

After that, I never heard his voice again. No knocks. No calls. No shadows at the threshold.

Obeying my pastor was not easy. Trusting his guidance felt like stepping into darkness and believing there would be ground beneath my feet. But I had already tried everything else.

Hebrews 13:17 KJV says *obey* means to be persuaded by—to trust and depend on your spiritual leader. If I said I trusted him, I had to prove it by walking through the doors he pointed me toward.

The word *submit* means to yield, to make room. It meant learning when to open myself to change and when to keep a door firmly shut.

My pastor asked me to volunteer at church. To be present every time the doors were open. To read my Bible daily. And when I met someone new, he said, that relationship had to be built on a foundation centered on Christ.

I didn't know then that obedience would become safety.

But it did.

<u>Thoughts</u>

For a long time, I believed faith meant leaving every door unlocked—being available, forgiving, accessible, endlessly open. I mistook endurance for holiness and silence for strength.

Age taught me otherwise.

I understand now that some doors are not meant to be reopened, no matter how softly someone knocks. Discernment is its own form of faith. Safety is not the absence of love; it is the presence of wisdom.

I no longer confuse obedience with disappearance. Trust does not require surrendering my body, my voice, or my instincts. God did not ask me to make myself smaller. He asked me to live.

The doors I closed that year did not harden my heart. They saved it. They taught me that peace has thresholds, and that crossing them—once, deliberately—is sometimes the bravest prayer a woman can offer.

Chapter 66

<u>Impressions</u>

**you're healing and that terrifies them. they've never met
a woman who can break several times and put herself
back together using nothing but self-love
Chameleon Aura by Billy Chapata**

I followed my psychologist's instructions. I followed my pastor's counsel. And slowly, deliberately, I stayed.

I stayed at church. I volunteered. I filled my days with work that asked something of me but did not wound me. I trained for a 5K, teaching my body how to move forward again—step by step, breath by breath.

That was when Eddie noticed me.

He sat in the same section of the sanctuary where I always sat. At first, we only exchanged greetings. Simple hellos. Familiar nods. Then one day, he asked for my phone number. We began talking regularly, our conversations steady and unforced. I told my pastor and my psychologist about him. Transparency had become a form of safety.

My pastor wanted to meet him.

When they sat together, Pastor Jorge questioned Eddie the way a father would—carefully, protectively. He learned that Eddie had been raised in a Christian home, that his parents and sister were active members of the church. When the conversation ended, Pastor Jorge gave his blessing with one condition: *Take it slow.*

I introduced Eddie to my two closest friends, Julie and Estela. He endured their interrogation with patience and humility. With my pastor's guidance and my friends' approval, we began seeing each other.

We were at church whenever the doors were open. We volunteered as greeters. We helped with toy drives and school supply giveaways. Eddie was patient. He was kind. His presence did not demand anything from me. It simply stayed.

Still, there came a moment when I wanted to walk away.

I confided in a friend named Gilbert.

"He's too nice," I told him. "I think I'm going to stop seeing him."

Gilbert didn't hesitate.

"Why would you return to vomit?" he asked. "He treats you with the respect and value you deserve. Don't stop seeing him. His love—and God's—will keep healing what's been broken."

Even as peace began to settle, life continued to test my breath.

My oldest son felt safe enough to leave home. He moved in with friends and prepared for a month-long training in Albuquerque for a new job. Before he left, I asked him to look up my cousin Mando and his son Vince—family nearby, just in case. I wanted him surrounded, even when I couldn't be.

I read books about adult children of alcoholics. I continued therapy. I met with my pastor. I volunteered. I cleaned the house—drawer by drawer, room by room—clearing space where chaos once lived.

And through it all, God stayed close.

On November 11, 2012, my sister called.

My brother's girlfriend couldn't reach him. Neither could I. That wasn't like my brother. Eddie and I drove to Las Cruces, where my brother had recently moved for work.

When we arrived, the front door was open. His car was gone. His phone and wallet sat untouched on the kitchen counter. The house was in disarray.

My breath caught.

I searched his mail, looking for clues. A bank statement. A list of places he frequented. Eddie and I drove—restaurants, gas stations, his workplace. Then hospitals. We called everyone in El Paso and Las Cruces. We even called morgues, asking about a John Doe. Nothing. Finally, I prayed.

Lord, I can't find my brother. My mom told me to look out for him, and I haven't done a good job. I'm sorry. Please—help me find him.

Eddie pointed ahead. "There's a hospital. Let's stop."

Inside, I approached the information desk.

"Do you have a patient by the name of Ramirez?"

The receptionist looked up.

"Yes. Room 224."

The elevator doors opened onto a quiet floor. When I walked into his room, relief overtook me. I wept—at the sight of him, at the mercy of God who had not let him disappear.

"How did you find me?" he asked.

"Don't ask," I said.

He told me he'd been in intense pain and rushed himself to the emergency room, leaving everything behind. When I called my dad during the search, he boarded a plane immediately.

More tests followed. On November 29, 2012, my brother was diagnosed with stage 3 Non-Hodgkin's Lymphoma. We didn't know then that my tío Richie had also been diagnosed. He kept his illness to himself.

My brother needed a bone marrow biopsy to see if the cancer had spread. I held his hand as they cleaned his skin and injected numbing medicine. Watching him suffer hurt almost as much as the pain itself.

"Breathe," I told him. "Deep breath. Now let it out slowly."

The needle passed through skin, muscle, then bone. My sister cried. I swallowed my own tears, fighting the instinct to stop it—to protect him from all pain.

Instead, I met his eyes.

Breathe. You've come so far.

Breathe. You have so much to live for.

Breathe. When the odds were stacked against us.

Breathe. When you joined the Navy to build a different life.

Breathe. When you took guardianship of our sister while working and studying.

Breathe. When you earned your degree in Criminal Justice

The results came back.

The cancer had not spread to his bone marrow.

Chemotherapy followed. My dad stayed with him. We surrounded him with love and presence—keeping him breathing when the road grew heavy.

Life continued, even in waiting rooms.

One day, while flipping through magazines in a doctor's office, Eddie asked me what kind of engagement ring I liked.

"God knows," I said. He pressed me, but my answer never changed.

"Ask Him. If you don't have that ring, then you're not the one."

Since childhood, I had imagined a white gold, princess-cut diamond ring. My mother used to sing *Mockingbird* to me. That ring lived quietly between God and me.

In December, Eddie asked Pastor Jorge for permission to marry me. He asked my children too. When he went ring shopping, he took my sons with him.

On December 7, 2012, he asked me to marry him with a white gold, princess-cut diamond ring. "I see you spoke to God," I said.

In **March 2013**, Eddie left for Marine training in Seal Beach, California. During my spring break, my dad and I traveled with him. While Eddie trained, we shopped for wedding details in the Los Angeles alleys—small, hopeful things. A flower girl basket. A ring pillow.

Later, we stopped at an In-N-Out Burger. I sat in the car with the passenger door open. My dad stood under a shade tree when his phone rang.

San Quentin Prison.

My Tío Richie.

He asked about my brother. About me. My dad told him we were in Los Angeles, preparing for my wedding. When he asked to speak to me, I shook my head no. I was still angry. It had been over ten years since we'd spoken. Three months later, he passed away.

Some conversations never happen.

Some truths remain unspoken. Healing does not erase complexity.

But by then, I had learned something sacred.

Even in uncertainty. Even in grief. Even in silence—

I knew how to breathe.

<u>Thoughts</u>

I understand that healing did not arrive all at once. It came quietly, disguised as ordinary days and faithful breaths. It came in rooms where nothing dramatic happened—only the steady work of staying present.

I once believed love would always announce itself with urgency or pain. That safety would feel unfamiliar, even boring. I mistook chaos for passion and endurance for devotion. Learning to breathe again required unlearning those lies.

Some relationships healed. Others did not. Some conversations were never spoken aloud. My Tío's voice remains unfinished in my memory—not because I lacked compassion, but because boundaries are sometimes the truest form of mercy we can offer ourselves.

Chapter 66

I no longer confuse forgiveness with access. I no longer believe that reconciliation is owed, or that silence is failure. There are losses that remain tender without being open. There are stories that do not close, only soften.

What I know now is this: God did not rescue me from suffering. He stayed with me inside it. He taught me how to breathe when fear tightened my chest, how to remain when everything in me wanted to disappear, how to choose gentleness over urgency.

Breath by breath, I learned that peace is not the absence of pain—it is the presence of steadiness. And steadiness, once learned, becomes a home no one can take from you.

Chapter 67

Con dinero y sin dinero
Yo hago siempre lo que quiero
Y mi palabra es la ley
No tengo trono ni reina
Ni nadie que me comprenda
Pero sigo siendo el rey
El Rey by Vicente Fernández

For my English readers: With money and without money I always do what I want and my word is the law I have no throne or queen nor anyone who understands me but I'm still the king. A famous Spanish song by Vicente Fernandez

Some dates arrive like doors you never meant to open. **April 10** was one of them.

April 10 was my grandmother's birthday, a date that once meant cake and candles, stories passed hand to hand. But that year 2013, the door opened onto something else entirely. April 10, 1984, was the day my Tío Richie murdered Mei Leung. And April 10, 2013, was also the day my son was arrested for possession of heroin—over four grams, less than two hundred. A legal phrase that would soon learn how to bruise my mouth.

I was out of town that week, away on a work trip, believing— foolishly—that distance could still protect me. My son called the house while I was gone. Back then, we still had a landline, a corded phone rooted to the wall like it belonged to a safer era. My father was in El Paso, staying close because my brother had just overcome cancer. He was finally in remission. We were standing at the threshold of relief, hands on the doorframe, daring to hope.

When the phone rang, my father happened to be at my house. He picked it up. First, the automated voice. *A collect call from the county jail.*

Then my son's.

The call came collect—its tone sharp, metallic, a sound that didn't belong in a quiet house. My father answered. Thank God he was there. He accepted the charges without hesitation, listened without interrupting, then carried the message to me like something fragile in his hands.

Jimmy was in jail.

Two days later— Friday April 12—my father called me on my cell phone. I was in Dallas at a teachers' union convention, surrounded by polished shoes, nametags, and voices talking about policy and progress. The world around me was orderly, fluorescent, intact.

"Jimmy's been arrested," he said.

That sentence knocked the air out of me.

My knees gave way. I fell—hard—right there in the hallway, as if my body understood before my mind could catch up. It felt like a trapdoor had opened beneath my feet, dropping me back into a life I thought I had locked behind me years ago.

Everything I had worked for cracked open in that moment. Every sacrifice. Every boundary. Every quiet decision I had made as a young mother to keep my son from inheriting my past. I had raised him deliberately, carefully, trying to teach him how to walk straight in a world that curves toward destruction.

And now he was walking the road I had spent my life running from.

In 1989, I left his father because I wanted a better life for my child. I wanted to close certain doors forever. I did not want my son to grow up thinking that chaos was normal or that survival counted as love.

But doors have a way of reopening when you aren't looking.

Wanting connection with his father he left Albuquerque and returned to El Paso, my son stepped through one door I had spent decades holding shut. Together, they decided to open a small corner store—a beer depot that had existed for years. They leased the building, resurrected its old name, reopened it as a convenience store. Simple. Groceries. Beer. A drive-thru window built for ease.

Because my son had good credit and no record, the store was placed in his name. On paper, everything looked clean. Legal. Harmless.

But that drive-thru window became something else entirely.

With his father's connections, heroin began passing through it— hand to hand, car to car. Transactions measured in seconds. A window designed for convenience became a mouth swallowing lives.

The store had already been under surveillance by the Texas Alcoholic Beverage Commission. On April 10, 2013, they approached my son. When they searched him, they found heroin in his pockets.

A door slammed shut.

That was the day everything divided into before and after. A grandmother's birthday turned into a marker of blood and loss. A phone call became a weapon. My knees learned the floor again. And a drive-thru window—once so ordinary—became the place where my worst fears proved they had been waiting patiently all along.

I had believed that love could barricade a child from certain outcomes. That if I closed enough doors, he would never find his way back to that world.

But love, I learned, does not control which doors our children choose to open.

And sometimes, it is the sound of a ringing phone that tells you the lock you trusted most has finally given way.

Thoughts

I understand that phone calls are doors. You do not see what waits on the other side until you answer, and once you do, there is no way to return to the moment before the ring.

I used to believe that if I closed enough doors, if I stood guard long enough, my child would never learn how easily they open. I believed love could act as a lock. I know better now.

What I did not fail to give my son was love. What I could never give him was control over his choices. That distinction took years to accept and even longer to forgive myself for misunderstanding.

I also know now that falling to my knees that day was not weakness. It was my body telling the truth before my mind could bear it. Some grief does not ask permission. It takes you to the floor and leaves you there until you learn how to stand again.

And the drive-thru window—so ordinary, so small—remains with me. A reminder that devastation does not always announce itself. Sometimes it arrives through the most familiar opening, quietly, efficiently, asking only that someone slide the window open and look away. I did not cause the door to open. But I lived with the sound it made when it did.

Chapter 68

Plexiglass Prayers

Arturo, his father was supposed to bail him out. When he didn't, the phone rang instead. The call came collect—Jimmy was in jail.

I drove back from Dallas that Saturday, the highway unspooling beneath me as if distance itself were trying to delay the truth. By Sunday April 14, I went to the store—the one my son and his father Arturo had been running together, half business, half mirage.

When I walked in, Arturo, his father, sat behind the counter. For a moment, he mistook me for a customer.

"Can I speak with you?" I asked.

When recognition crossed his face, we stepped outside.

"What's going on?" I asked. "How did my son end up arrested?"

Drugs, he said. He didn't know if Jimmy was using. Maybe a little. Maybe not. His words circled the truth, careful not to touch it.

"Come with me," I said.

"Let's go downtown. I need to see my son."

He agreed.

Eddie and I drove together. His father followed behind. At the county courthouse, we walked in side by side. The building felt too familiar—the same fluorescent hum, the same waiting air. I had stood in this place before, years earlier, a child clutching a phone, staring through glass at my own father.

History has a way of finding its echo.

I told the officer everything: that this was Jimmy's first arrest, that I'd been out of town, that I didn't know what I was walking into. He listened. He helped. He allowed me to see my son.

On the second floor, behind plexiglass, Jimmy appeared.

He sat on the stool. Picked up the phone. I did the same. His father stood beside me.

"What happened?" I asked.

"They found drugs in my pocket," he said.

"Whose were they?" I asked. "Tell me the truth."

Jimmy looked at his father. Looked again. Then back at me.

"They were his, Mom."

His father stepped away.

"I'll be back," he said. "I need to use the restroom."

He never returned.

Later I learned the truth—that drugs were being sold through the drive-through window of that store. That what Jimmy carried that day wasn't his, but the consequence still was.

I told my son I would try to get him out on the following Monday April 22. He told me there was money in his dresser—money he had saved. Use it for bail, he said.

When the visit ended, I found Eddie downstairs. We drove to the house where Jimmy had been living with friends. They let me in easily; they already knew why I was there.

I went straight to my son's room and opened the drawers he had described. Nothing. Not one dollar.

Gianni told me his father had come by on Friday April 12.

Had gone into Jimmy's room alone. I understood.

That's when I started to notice the other things. Foil—flat, crumpled sheets scattered everywhere. On the dresser. Under the bed. In the bathroom. Blackened lines stained their surfaces. Balloons lay deflated on the floor. A mirror held a fine dust I recognized without needing to name.

I took one sheet of foil with me.

I drove a few blocks and picked up my dad outside my grandmother's house.

He climbed into the car, quiet. I handed him the foil.

He looked once.

"He's either smoking heroin or meth," he said.

I nodded. Thanked him. Drove away.

The car was silent.

I drove home knowing something had crossed a line—but not yet knowing how far it would drag us.

Thoughts

I understand why that day felt like stepping into a room I had sworn I would never enter again.

It wasn't just the jail. It wasn't just the plexiglass, the phone, the fluorescent lights that made everyone look pale and guilty. It was the way time folded in on itself. The way my childhood stood up inside my adulthood and stared me down. I had once been the girl on the other side of that glass, searching my father's face for something safe. And now I was the mother, searching my son's.

I thought I had escaped that story.

I thought I had outrun it.

But pain has a way of traveling through bloodlines like an inheritance nobody asks for. It slips into family names, into holidays, into ordinary days. It waits. And then one day it calls collect.

That was the moment I realized I wasn't only fighting for Jimmy— I was fighting for the little girl I used to be, the one who learned too young what it meant to love someone who could disappear. And when I left that building,

I didn't just carry fear.

I carried a quiet vow.

Not again. Not without a fight.

Chapter 69

Mountains in the Courtroom

By Monday April 15 morning, I was back at work, moving through the day like someone underwater. I called a lawyer. On Tuesday, I sat across from him and told him everything—what I knew, what I suspected, what I feared.

"I don't think my son is telling me the whole truth," I said. "I want you to represent him. But I'm not bailing him out until he does."

I paid the retainer.

On Wednesday, April 17, the attorney met with Jimmy. He didn't like it. He didn't like staying in jail. He didn't like being cornered by truth.

Neither did I—but truth rarely arrives gently.

That weekend, Eddie and I packed every single thing my son owned. His TV. His bed. His dresser. His clothes. His cologne. His shoes into Eddie's truck. I worked quickly, methodically, as if speed might keep my heart from breaking.

The following weekend, April 27, I held a garage sale.

Everything must go.

Prices were slashed without mercy—not because

I needed the money, but because I needed the lie gone.

What didn't sell went to Goodwill.

The next day, April 28, I stood in the visitation line again.

Once, I had stood in this same kind of line as a little girl, waiting to see my father. Now I stood there as a mother, waiting to see my son. The glass hadn't changed. Neither had the phone.

Behind it, I asked him one question.

"Are you ready to tell me the truth?" He was.

He told me about heroin. About Albuquerque where it all started with trust - Vince. About how addiction slid in quietly and then took over everything. He told me how easy it had been to fall back into old patterns once his biological father re-entered his life.

I put twenty dollars on his commissary account—from the money I had made selling his things.

Then I asked him if he would go to rehab.

He said yes.

I didn't fully trust the answer, but I held onto it anyway.

Chapter 69

My dad came over later and asked what my plan was. I told him everything—the lawyer, the rehab, the bail.

"How are you going to pay for all that?" he asked.

"I'll refinance my house," I said.

He shook his head. Said I was doing too much.

"No," I told him. "I'm doing what no one did for you."

He didn't argue after that.

Jimmy's bond was set at $60,000. Six thousand to get him out.

Everyone told me to let him stay in jail. I prayed anyway.

"God," I said, "open doors and close doors. I'll do my part."

I found a ninety-day inpatient rehab facility in Weatherford, Texas—Stonegate. Eight hours away. I didn't know how I would afford it.

At the bond hearing on May 9, 2013, the judge allowed me to speak. I told him everything. He listened without interruption. Then he reduced the bond to $3,500 and ordered my son into the rehab program.

Even my brother—who had spent years in the court system—said he had never seen anything like it.

God moved a mountain.

The rehab facility was going to cost me $32,000. The good thing is that my son was still on my medical insurance this rehab facility was out of network, my portion was going to be $16,000. The rehab facility was a 90-day in patient rehab facility. I went ahead and contacted the facility and made arrangements for him to go there with a deposit of $5,000. That night, Eddie and I waited for Jimmy's release. Sitting in a restaurant booth, I prayed silently, asking how I would come up with the deposit.

My phone rang.

Stonegate.

The director told me to bring my son anyway.

To give him a postdated check.

To trust compassion over policy.

Another mountain moved. Matthew 14:13-21 KJV

Thoughts

There are choices you make as a mother that don't feel like choices at all. They feel like standing at the edge of a cliff with love in your hands, wondering if you are about to save someone—or lose yourself trying.

Back then, I didn't have the language for what I was doing. I only knew I could not watch my son drown and call it wisdom. I could not confuse punishment with healing. I could not stand in the doorway of his life and say, figure it out, when I remembered too clearly what it looked like when no one came.

People warned me. They said I was doing too much. They said jail would teach him. They said compassion would ruin him.

But compassion did not ruin my son.

Addiction was already doing that.

Compassion was the rope I threw anyway—knowing he might not grab it, knowing he might slip again, knowing I might be left holding nothing but my own trembling faith.

And still, I threw it.

Not because I was naïve.

Because I was a mother.

And because somewhere deep inside me, I believed God was not asking me to harden my heart—He was asking me to keep it open, even if it broke in the process.

That season taught me something I never forgot:

Love is not weak.

Love is costly.

And sometimes love looks like paperwork, court dates, empty savings, and prayers whispered through clenched teeth.

Sometimes love looks like standing in a courtroom and watching a door open that should have stayed shut.

And walking through it anyway.

Chapter 70

The Road to Stonegate

The wheels were rolling again, and all I could do was follow.

We went home and waited for the call that Jimmy—my son—had been released. The waiting felt like holding my breath underwater. The house was still, but my mind wasn't. Every sound outside made me flinch. Every minute that passed felt like a verdict.

When the call finally came, it wasn't from a police station or an official number. It was from a Wal-Mart.

Once he was released, Jimmy walked to a nearby Wal-Mart and used the phone there to tell me he was out. He could have run. He could have disappeared into the dark and become one more story I would have to tell myself with a broken voice. He could have called friends. He could have chosen anything.

But he didn't.

Instead, he called me.

It was the middle of the night when I got into my car. The streets were quiet, emptied out like the world had closed its eyes. Streetlights stretched across the windshield in pale stripes, and the road ahead looked endless, like it had no intention of ever letting me arrive.

When I pulled into the parking lot, Wal-Mart glowed in the distance—fluorescent and unforgiving. The light made everything look exposed. Too bright. Too honest. Jimmy stood there waiting, small beneath that artificial glare, his hands shoved into his pockets, his shoulders stiff like he was bracing for impact.

When he climbed into the car, the air changed. The silence settled between us like something physical. I wanted to touch his face, to make sure he was real, to make sure he was still mine. But I kept both hands on the steering wheel, gripping it like it was the only thing keeping me from falling apart.

I drove him home.

We didn't talk much. We didn't have to. The road said enough.

Back at the house, we moved quickly, like we were trying to outrun something that was gaining on us. We packed what we could, loaded the car, and prepared to leave. It felt less like a trip and more like an evacuation. Like we were fleeing a life that had become dangerous.

Eddie—my fiancé—came with us. He didn't complain. He didn't hesitate. He just got into the passenger seat and stayed steady, even when I wasn't.

We headed to Weatherford, Texas.

Jimmy sat quietly, his face blank, his body tense. He had little to say. There was almost no conversation. The only sound was the road beneath us, the tires humming against the pavement, the engine carrying us forward.

The miles felt heavy. Every exit sign looked like a warning. Every stretch of highway felt like a long confession neither of us knew how to make.

The farther we drove, the more I realized how powerless I was.

A mother is supposed to protect her child. A mother is supposed to know what to do. But I had reached a place where love wasn't enough, where rules weren't enough, where prayer and pleading couldn't pull him back.

I drove anyway.

I drove because driving was something I could do. It was movement. It was action. It was control—an illusion of control, but I clung to it like a lifeline.

When we arrived at Stonegate, the facility looked calm from the outside. Quiet. Controlled. Orderly. Like nothing bad could happen there. Like the chaos that had been devouring our family couldn't cross the threshold.

We got Jimmy settled in. We handed him over. We filled out paperwork. We listened. We nodded. We signed. We did everything they asked us to do because we wanted to believe in their certainty.

Then we left.

And the moment the doors closed behind him, something inside me cracked. I felt it like a physical break—like a bone snapping quietly beneath the skin. My son was in there, and I was out here, and no amount of motherhood could change that.

The drive back home was longer than the drive there. Not because the miles changed, but because the silence did. It deepened. It grew teeth. It swallowed every thought I tried to form.

I stared at the road and wondered how I had gotten here.

Part of the treatment plan was that we had to return every two weeks for family counseling. That became the rhythm of my life—work, worry, drive, return. Two weeks at a time. Two weeks of trying to pretend I was functioning. Two weeks of holding myself together with thread.

As the school year wrapped up, I packed my classroom and closed out grades. At the same time, I was planning a wedding. My mind stayed occupied, but my heart stayed in the same place: on that road to Weatherford, in that facility where my son was trying to become someone new.

Our first family counseling session was on Saturday, May 25th.

That day, the room was filled with the people who loved Jimmy, the people who had been orbiting his life, trying to keep him from falling completely into the dark. The session included me, my father, Eddie, and my two children, Marie and Robert—who were still living at home.

The psychologist spent most of that first session simply listening. He wanted to understand our family dynamics, how we interacted, how we spoke, how we avoided speaking. He asked questions that felt too direct, too sharp, like a finger pressing into a bruise.

How long had it been going on?

When did we first notice?

What had changed?

What had we ignored?

And as we answered, I felt the weight of my own voice. Every word sounded like an admission. Every explanation sounded like a failure.

Two weeks later, in early June, Eddie left for military training. He would be gone for most of the summer. The timing felt cruel, like life had decided I didn't deserve stability.

The next family counseling session was just my father and my two kids. And in that session, the ugly truth of addiction began to show itself more clearly—not just the drug use, but the criminal behavior that wrapped around it like a vine. The lies. The manipulation. The desperation. The way addiction doesn't simply take—it demands.

Over the next four sessions, it was only my father and me driving those ten hours back and forth from El Paso to Weatherford.

Just the two of us.

Two generations of love trying to understand something that made no sense.

We drove those highways like we were traveling into a storm. The car became a small, moving room of grief. Sometimes my father would speak, quietly, as if he didn't want to wake the pain. Sometimes he didn't speak at all. And sometimes I stared at the road so hard my eyes ached, because if I stopped looking forward, I was afraid I would fall apart completely.

Those sessions were enlightening.

And they were devastating.

I blamed myself on so many levels. I blamed his father on many others. I even blamed his stepfather. But I never once blamed Jimmy.

Not once.

Even as the truth unfolded, even as the stories came out, even as I began to understand the depth of the choices he had made—I still saw him as my child. My baby. The little boy I once tucked into bed. The boy whose hand used to reach for mine in parking lots.

And that is the strange cruelty of motherhood: even when your child becomes someone you don't recognize, your heart refuses to let go of who they used to be.

It was during those counseling sessions that I learned something that made my stomach turn.

Vince—the son of my second cousin—was the one who had introduced Jimmy to smoking heroin.

Someone close enough to be family.

Someone who had been around us, someone I would have never suspected, someone whose name should have meant safety and familiarity—not poison.

That revelation didn't just break my trust. It broke something deeper. It told me that danger could come from inside the circle, that the threat wasn't always a stranger on a street corner. Sometimes it was someone who sat at your table, someone who knew your family's names.

I wanted to scream. I wanted to rewind time. I wanted to grab my son by the shoulders and drag him backward through every moment that led to that first inhale.

But I couldn't.

All I could do was sit in that counseling room, swallow my rage, and pretend I was strong enough to hear the truth.

Addiction doesn't belong to one person. It spreads. It leaks into the walls of a home. It changes the air. It infects the people who love the addict until they begin to live the addiction too—waiting, worrying, checking, guessing, fearing. It steals sleep. It steals peace. It steals trust. And the cruelest part is that it makes you believe you could have stopped it, if only you had been smarter, stricter, more present, more something.

As a mother, I felt like I had done something wrong.

What did I do wrong?

Where did I go wrong?

I searched my memories like a woman digging through rubble, convinced that if I could find the exact moment—the pivot—the turning point—I could fix it. I replayed conversations. I replayed summers. I replayed friendships. I replayed the days I had been too tired, too busy, too distracted.

I couldn't understand it.

I couldn't accept it.

So I blamed myself.

And when I ran out of places to put the blame, I turned it outward.

That summer, while planning my wedding, I fell into a depression so deep it felt like sinking into a dark lake. I stayed underwater for days at a time, still breathing somehow, still showing up somehow, but not truly living.

And somewhere inside that depression, anger began to bloom.

I wanted revenge.

In my mind, Jimmy's father was responsible. I convinced myself he had ruined my son's life, and I began to fantasize about how I could make him pay. The thoughts came easily. They came like daydreams. They came like comfort, like rage was the only thing warm enough to keep me alive.

I had time on my hands. Too much time.

As a teacher, summers were supposed to be restful. But my fiancé was gone for training. My daughter Marie was working her first job at Fuddruckers. My son Robert was training for cross-country.

And I was alone with my thoughts.

Those students in my classroom at Rogelio Sanchez State Prison—when I taught "The Cycle of Addiction and Criminal Behavior"—they would have understood exactly what was happening to me. They would have recognized the pattern. Pain always demands somewhere to go. And if you can't put it where it belongs, you throw it like a weapon at whoever is closest.

That was when Jimmy's psychologist suggested I begin attending Al-Anon, in addition to seeing my own psychologist.

He spoke to my therapist and psychiatrist back in El Paso. They recommended medication for severe depression.

At the time, I didn't feel like a woman preparing for a wedding.

I felt like a mother losing her son.

And every time I got into my car, every time I drove another stretch of highway, every time I watched the miles pass beneath me, I felt the same terrifying truth pressing against my chest:

I could drive him to treatment.

But I could not drive him out of addiction.

Not with love.

Not with rage.

Not even with prayer.

All I could do was keep moving forward—mile by mile—through the silence.

And hope the road would eventually lead us somewhere that didn't hurt so much.

<u>Thoughts</u>

I understand why the road became my refuge.

Driving gave me something addiction refused to give me: direction. A destination. A sense that if I kept moving forward, I could outrun what was happening behind me. The car became my confession booth, the highway my prayer. Mile after mile, I tried to bargain with God and the universe—*If I do everything right, if I drive him to the right place, if I say the right words, then he will come back to me.*

But addiction doesn't respond to effort. It doesn't soften for a mother's devotion. It doesn't care how tightly you grip the steering wheel. I blamed everyone except the one person who could have broken my heart the most—my son. Because blaming him would have meant admitting he had choices. And admitting he had choices would have meant admitting I could not save him.

That was the first time I realized motherhood has limits.

Not in love—but in power.

Chapter 70

And it nearly broke me to learn the difference.

That summer, I learned the hardest truth of love: you can drive your child toward help, but you cannot drive them toward healing. Healing is a road only they can choose to walk.

And all a mother can do is sit in the silence, keep the engine running, and pray the child she raised finds his way home.

Chapter 71

Ashes, Nightmares, and the Day I Let Myself Dance

By early June 2013, my life had become a calendar of survival.

Two weeks at a time, I drove from El Paso to Weatherford for family counseling. Two weeks at a time, I tried to plan for the new school year like my mind wasn't elsewhere. Two weeks at a time, I tried to plan a wedding while my heart stayed tangled in fear.

Eddie was away at military training for the summer, leaving me with long days and longer nights. The house felt too quiet. Even when my children were home, the silence had a way of settling into the corners, lingering like a shadow that wouldn't leave.

I was doing everything at once—preparing activities for the new school year, answering emails, scheduling wedding details, driving highways, holding myself together with whatever strength I could borrow from God. But depression doesn't announce itself loudly.

It slips in. It takes a seat beside you.

And suddenly you realize you've been living with it for weeks.

June 7, 2013 arrived with the promise of something soft.

My sister—my maid of honor—had planned my bridal shower for that day. It was supposed to be a bright spot in the middle of a dark summer, a moment where I could remember that my life still held beauty.

Then the phone rang. And everything changed.

The news came like a cold wind through an open door: my Tío Richie had died.

My sister didn't know what to do. Her voice trembled when she asked if we should cancel the shower. She sounded like she was trying to protect me from one more blow.

I remember the pause before I answered. I remember how my throat tightened, how my body wanted to fold in on itself.

But something in me—something stubborn, something tired of being robbed—rose up.

"No," I told her. "Don't cancel it.

Death has already taken enough from me."

I wanted to believe that was true.

I wanted to believe I could hold the line.

But grief doesn't ask permission.

And it doesn't care what you've planned.

The bridal shower went on, but I wasn't truly there.

People laughed. People smiled. People handed me gifts wrapped in tissue paper and ribbon. Their voices floated around me, but inside my chest, something was unraveling.

Because the moment I heard my Tío Richie was gone, my nightmares returned.

Not slowly.

Not gently.

They came rushing back like a flood breaking through a dam.

In my mind, his death didn't mean peace. It meant freedom.

His spirit was free—no longer locked up in a cell, no longer restrained by California's correctional system. And instead of comfort, that thought filled me with dread, like a door had opened somewhere it shouldn't have.

That night, I slept—but not in the way a person rests.

I drifted into darkness and found him there.

In my nightmares, he chased me like he did when we were kids and I made him mad. I could hear his footsteps behind me, feel the panic rising in my throat, feel the helplessness that always came when I realized I couldn't outrun him.

I would wake up gasping, my heart pounding, the sheets damp with sweat. The room would be quiet, but my body wouldn't believe it. My body stayed trapped in the chase, trapped in the fear, trapped in the memory.

The nightmares continued for a year.

Grief did not soften the past.

It sharpened it.

My grandmother took his death hard.

She was surrounded by my father, her daughter, and her other son who lived in El Paso, but even with family near, grief has a lonely way of settling into the bones. It changes a person. It makes them do things that don't make sense to anyone else.

My father told me she began burning all the photographs of my Tío Richie.

One by one.

The flames took his face, his smile, the proof that he had once been young and alive. I imagined the smoke curled upward like a prayer, but it didn't feel holy. It felt like desperation. Like she was trying to erase the pain by destroying the evidence.

But pain doesn't burn away that easily.

His belongings—including his ashes—were given to Doreen Lioy because she was still legally married to him. She was supposed to give them to my Tía Ruth.

She never did.

Later, it was discovered that she had sold his belongings to a museum in Las Vegas, Nevada, where they were placed on display.

A man's life turned into an exhibit.

His possessions sold for profit.

Even his ashes treated like merchandise.

When I learned that, something in me went cold. There are betrayals that feel personal, and there are betrayals that feel like an insult to the dead. That was both.

It felt like even in death, my Tío Richie couldn't rest.

And neither could I.

By August, the summer had stretched thin.

My son finished rehab on **August 9, 2013.**

This time, instead of driving to pick him up, I flew him back to El Paso. I couldn't do that long road again—not with my wedding so close, not with my body already exhausted from months of grief and worry.

The next day **August 10** was my wedding.

I thought about postponing it.

I thought about the weight of everything happening—my son, my brother, my uncle's death, the nightmares that had returned with vengeance. I thought about how unfair it felt to celebrate while my family was breaking in pieces.

But then another thought rose up inside me, quiet but firm:

I deserve some happiness.

Not because life was perfect.

Not because things were healed.

But because I was still here.

Because I had survived.

Because joy had been delayed long enough.

So the wedding went on as planned.

My dad walked me down the aisle. His arm was steady, but I could feel the emotion in the way he held me close, like he was silently promising I would not fall.

My brother, my sister, and my children were part of the wedding party. Their faces looked like pieces of my life stitched together, imperfect but still whole enough to stand.

That day, I let myself breathe.

I let myself believe that maybe love could still be real, even after everything. Maybe happiness could still exist, even if it came carrying scars.

I let my hair down.

I danced.

I smiled.

I laughed.

And for once, I allowed myself to be happy without immediately waiting for punishment.

For once, I stopped scanning the room for disaster.

For once, I lived inside the moment instead of outside of it.

My son went to spend a few days with my ex-husband—whom he still calls Dad—while Eddie and I went on our honeymoon.

And as I stepped into that new chapter, I realized something that both comforted and frightened me:

Life doesn't pause for grief.

It doesn't pause for addiction.

It doesn't pause for trauma.

It keeps moving, like a road that doesn't care whether you're ready for the next mile.

But that summer taught me something I had never fully understood before:

Sometimes survival looks like holding on.

And sometimes survival looks like letting yourself dance anyway.

Even with tears still living inside you.

Even with nightmares waiting in the dark.

Even when the past rides quietly beside you,

invisible in the passenger seat.

Because happiness, I learned, is not the absence of pain.

Sometimes it is simply the decision to keep going.

<u>Thoughts</u>

For a long time, I carried guilt like a second skin.

Guilt for smiling while someone else was suffering. Guilt for celebrating while my family was unraveling. Guilt for wanting happiness as if joy was something I had to earn—something God only handed out to people whose lives were clean and calm.

But the truth is, joy is not betrayal.

Joy is survival.

That wedding day, I wasn't pretending the darkness wasn't there. It was there—addiction, grief, fear, and exhaustion sitting in the background like an uninvited guest. But I had reached a point where I couldn't keep postponing happiness until everything was fixed, because with addiction, nothing ever feels fully fixed. There is always another worry waiting around the corner.

When my Tío Richie died, I thought death would close the door.

Instead, it opened something.

The nightmares returned, violent and relentless, like my body remembered what my mind had tried to bury. It didn't matter that I was grown. It didn't matter that years had passed. Trauma doesn't care about time. Fear doesn't care about reason. It comes when it wants, and it takes what it wants.

That summer was full of cages—rehab walls, prison walls. Everyone was trapped or trying to break free, and I was somewhere in the middle, praying while still feeling chained.

I begged God to take the nightmares.

I begged Him to protect my son.

I begged Him to quiet my mind.

But some prayers are answered slowly, not because God isn't listening, but because healing is a process—one mile at a time, one night at a time, one breath at a time.

So I danced at my wedding because I needed one night where addiction didn't get to own the room.

Chapter 71

I laughed because I needed proof that the enemy had not stolen everything from me.

I smiled because I refused to believe grief had the final word over my life.

Even now, when I think of that summer, I see it as a long drive at night—headlights cutting through darkness, the road stretching forward, and the past riding silently beside me in the passenger seat.

It doesn't speak.

It doesn't need to.

Because God is with me.

And even when my hands are shaking on the steering wheel, even when the road feels endless, He keeps whispering the same thing into my spirit:

Keep going.

Chapter 72

The Picture on the Fridge

The picture on my refrigerator started to fade at the edges long before my hope did.

It was just a photograph—one ordinary snapshot taken in sunlight—but I treated it like a promise. It hung there among grocery lists and magnets, surrounded by the quiet evidence of everyday life. And every time I opened the door, cold air rushed out, the refrigerator light flickered on, and that photo stared back at me like it knew something I didn't.

Sanchez Middle School.

Some people collect souvenirs from vacations. I collected signs from God—small reminders that my life wasn't over, that the pain hadn't swallowed the whole story.

The picture stayed on the fridge like a promise. And every time I saw it, I whispered the same words as if I could speak them into existence.

"Lord, I thank You for my job at Sanchez."

Not *if.*

Not *maybe.*

But *thank You*—as if heaven had already signed the paperwork.

Before the picture, though, there was Phoenix.

When Eddie and I returned from our honeymoon, we drove my son to Phoenix, Arizona. He had made arrangements to stay with a friend he knew from the military. The desert opened around us like a wide, sun-scorched sea. Mountains rose in the distance, hazy and unmoving, and the highway stretched forward like it had no end.

I watched the landscape pass through the window and tried to keep my face calm, but my chest felt tight, like my heart was already mourning him even while he sat beside me.

A mother learns early that love comes with goodbyes.

The closer we got to Phoenix, the quieter the car became. Even the radio sounded too cheerful, too unaware of what it meant to drive your child toward a new life while your own soul begged him to stay.

When we finally arrived, I remember stepping out of the car and feeling the heat hit my skin like a hand. The air smelled like dust and asphalt. My son hugged me, and I held on longer than I should have, the way mothers do when they're trying to memorize the weight of their child in their arms.

I wanted to tell him a thousand things.

I wanted to warn him. Protect him.

Beg him to be careful with his life.

Instead, I swallowed my fear like a stone and whispered, "Call me."

Then I watched him walk away.

I watched his back get smaller as he crossed the parking lot, and when he disappeared inside, I stood there for a moment longer, staring at the door like I could will it open again.

On the drive home, the silence was unbearable. That kind of silence isn't peaceful. It's hollow. It's the sound of a house about to feel too big.

He stayed in Phoenix for nearly a year. During that time, I learned how to live with absence. Some days I was proud of him for trying to build a future. Other days I feared he was running from the weight of everything we had survived. I didn't always know the difference.

When he finally decided to return home in 2014, relief came first— hot and sudden, like rain after a drought. He enrolled in trade school and earned an associate degree in Cyber Security. Watching him move forward felt like watching light return to a room I thought would stay dim forever.

But even then, I couldn't shake the question that had been rising in me for years.

What was it all for?

There were nights I prayed until my throat ached. Not pretty prayers. Not polished prayers. The kind of prayers that sounded like grief.

"God, why did You have me go through so much? What was it worth? What did it produce besides scars?"

I had survived. I had endured. I had kept going. But I was tired of living like survival was the highest form of victory.

I wanted meaning. I wanted purpose.

I wanted to believe that my suffering wasn't wasted.

That's when I started thinking about applying to another school— one where many of the children came from low-income homes. Something in me felt drawn there. I didn't want to rescue anyone. I just wanted to serve children who carried burdens I understood. I knew what it meant to come to school with your body present but your mind somewhere else. I knew what it meant to smile through pain. I knew what it meant to crave stability like food.

I went to speak to the principal about a future position. My good friend Julie came with me because she knew her. I still remember walking through those halls—the smell of waxed floors and old paper, the faint trace of cafeteria food lingering in the air. The building felt familiar in the way all schools do: bulletin boards, faded posters, the quiet hum of fluorescent lights.

After the meeting, the principal told me that if a position became available, she would contact me. It wasn't a guarantee.

But it was a door cracked open.

As we walked outside, Julie stopped and lifted her phone.

"Stand right there," she said.

I stood in front of the school sign, the sun warm on my shoulders. Julie framed the picture, and then I heard it—the small click of the camera. A tiny sound.

But it felt like a seed being planted.

Sanchez Middle School.

When I got home, I printed the photo and placed it on my refrigerator. It wasn't just a picture. It was a declaration. It became my daily ritual—my stubborn, holy habit of believing God could still do something new with my life.

Every time I opened the refrigerator, I saw Sanchez.

Cold air. Bright light. And that photo staring back at me.

And I would speak it aloud:

"Lord, I thank You for my job at Sanchez."

Some people might call it foolishness.

I called it faith.

Around that time, I found myself reflecting on the three years Eddie had endured alongside me—my children, my past, my family, the chaos that seemed to follow us like a shadow.

There were moments I fully expected him to walk away.

Most people would have.

I expected Eddie to walk away—because life with me wasn't light.

It wasn't easy. It wasn't peaceful.

My son's addiction tested every boundary of hope. My daughter's illness tested every prayer I had ever whispered. Some days it felt like our home was built on shifting sand—like one phone call could collapse everything we had worked to build. But Eddie didn't run.

He stayed, not just as my husband, but as my covering—steady and unshaken. When I was tired, he reminded me not to surrender. When fear crept into my thoughts, he pointed me back to God, again and again, as if faith itself could be a lifeline. And maybe it was.

I remember one night in particular—one of those nights when the air felt heavy with worry and I could barely hold myself together. I was sitting at the kitchen table, staring at nothing, my hands wrapped around a cup of coffee that had gone cold. I didn't even realize I was crying until Eddie pulled out the chair beside me.

He didn't try to fix it with words.

He just reached across the table and took my hands.

And he prayed.

Quietly. Steadily. Like he believed God was listening even when I wasn't sure anymore.

Afterward he looked at me and said,

"Don't give up. God didn't bring you this far to leave you here."

That was Eddie. Not loud love. Not showy love.

Faithful love. The kind that stays.

And because he stayed, something shifted in me. I looked at him differently—not just as a husband, but as proof that God could still send goodness into the ruins of my past.

One day, I looked at Eddie and said,

"You know… about those kids you wanted…"

He looked up at me, his eyes searching my face.

"Let's do it," I finished.

In 2014, we began our journey of becoming parents of our own children. We traveled to Frisco, Texas and began the IVF process. My tubes had been tied when I was twenty-two, and IVF felt like the best route forward for our circumstances.

The process was clinical and exhausting—appointments, paperwork, injections, waiting rooms filled with quiet hope. But beneath all the medical details was something sacred.

It required faith.

It required believing in life before life could be seen.

In February of 2015, I conceived fraternal boy-girl twins.

When I found out, my body trembled—not just with joy, but with fear. I had prayed for this. I had longed for this. And now that it was real, I felt the weight of how fragile miracles could be.

At the first ultrasound, the room was dim and cold, the screen glowing like a small window into the unseen. When I heard the sound— two rapid heartbeats like tiny wings fluttering—I covered my mouth and cried.

I remember thinking, *God… You really did it.*

Not because I deserved it.

Not because life had been fair.

But because He was still God.

At the time, I was still working as an eighth-grade science teacher, balancing lesson plans with a life that felt both fragile and full. When my mother-in-law learned I was expecting, she didn't hesitate—she offered to care for the babies while I worked. Her willingness felt like a quiet blessing placed gently into my hands, a reminder that even in the heaviness, God was still providing.

In September 2015, my twins arrived—tiny, perfect miracles. The hospital room hummed softly with machines, and when their cries finally filled the air, they were gentle but determined, as if they already knew how to fight for their place in the world. My daughter, Izzie, weighed four pounds, nine ounces, and my son, Marty, five pounds, two ounces. When I first held them, they felt impossibly small against my chest, yet their presence filled every empty space inside me.

Teaching had always been a calling for me. It demanded service, dedication, and commitment without a time clock. It required the kind of love that kept giving, even when it wasn't appreciated.

As a child, math and science were my favorite subjects. I loved the way they explained the world. Science and math weren't just lessons— they were everywhere. They were proof that invisible things could still be true: gravity, atoms, electricity, the way the earth turned even when you couldn't feel it.

Maybe that's why I loved teaching.

Because I believed in unseen things.

Up to that point, I still enjoyed the work. The grading didn't bother me. The documentation didn't bother me. The endless emails didn't bother me. Even the meetings about meetings—the ones where administrators introduced a "new strategy" that was really an old idea with a fresh label—didn't surprise me anymore.

People who think teaching is a forty-hour work week with summers off are fooling themselves. Teaching follows you home. It lives in your evenings, your weekends, your sleep. It becomes part of your body.

But slowly, the joy began to thin out.

Not because of the children—but because of the system.

I remember sitting in a staff meeting under harsh fluorescent lights, surrounded by exhausted faces. The room smelled like burnt coffee and dry erase markers. An administrator stood at the front, smiling too brightly, talking about expectations and data and accountability. His voice was polished, confident, detached.

We were being lectured about performance while we were quietly drowning. When teachers voiced concerns—about behavior, safety, classroom disruptions—the responses were always the same.

"Build relationships."

"Be more engaging."

"Try a different strategy."

As if a strategy could replace support.

As if a relationship could replace consequences.

Then there were the parent conferences.

I remember one mother sitting across from me, arms folded tightly over her chest. Her child was failing—not because he didn't understand, but because he refused to try. He skipped assignments, disrupted class, laughed when corrected.

Yet she stared at me as if I was the one who had failed him.

"What are you doing to help him?" she demanded.

I explained missing work. I showed records. I offered solutions.

I spoke gently, professionally, carefully.

She didn't want solutions.

She wanted someone to blame.

And I walked away from that conference with the same familiar ache in my chest—the feeling of being alone inside a system that demanded everything from teachers and protected everyone except the ones doing the work.

Disruptions became normal. Cell phones were constant. Students fought in hallways like it was routine. Teachers were expected to keep control without real authority. When we asked for support, we were often met with silence.

And the silence was loud.

My breaking point came on an ordinary day.

The classroom smelled like pencil shavings and teenage cologne. The air held the faint sweetness of candy wrappers and the sharp sting of dry erased ink. Students were talking over one another, chairs scraping the floor, backpacks thudding down.

A student walked into my classroom late.

He didn't apologize.

He didn't slip into his seat quietly.

He entered like the rules didn't apply to him.

When I addressed him, he became rude and disrespectful. I did what teachers are trained to do: I began documenting his behavior, creating the paper trail that was supposed to protect me.

He turned to another student, smirked, and said loud enough for me to hear:

"When I come and shoot up the school, I wonder if she will document that?"

The room went still.

Not the quiet of obedience—the quiet of fear.

The kind of silence that makes your skin cold.

For a moment, time slowed. I could hear my own heartbeat. I could feel the blood rush through my body. I looked at my students and realized how young they were, how vulnerable they were. I realized how exposed we all were.

I called security immediately. He was removed from my class and placed in in-school suspension. Later, he was assigned to assist the assistant principal in the office for the remainder of the year—because I refused to have him back in my classroom.

After that day, something inside me changed.

I began to notice every sound in the hallway. Every slam of a locker made my shoulders tighten. Every unexpected shout made my heart jump. I started scanning doors. Counting exits. Calculating what I would do if the unthinkable happened.

And I hated that teaching had become a place where I felt unsafe.

When I decided to leave the public school system, it wasn't for a dramatic reason. There was no grand announcement. No applause. No celebration.

It was self-preservation.

The workload was enormous. The stress placed on teachers by administration and parents was relentless. The lack of safety for students and teachers became impossible to ignore. And I could not pretend anymore.

One evening after another long day, I came home exhausted. My feet ached. My mind buzzed. My spirit felt thin and worn, like fabric stretched too far.

I opened the refrigerator without thinking.

Cold air rushed out.

The light flickered on.

And there it was again—

Julie's photo of me standing in front of Sanchez Middle School.

The picture stayed on the fridge like a promise.

I stared at it, and for a moment I felt the strange collision of my life: teaching, praying, enduring, surviving, believing. I had spent years holding everything together—my children, my marriage, my faith, my career— trying to keep order in every room I walked into.

But that year, I finally learned the lesson myself:

Survival is not the same as living.

And as I stood there with the refrigerator door open, bathed in that small, bright light, I realized something simple and sacred.

I was allowed to choose peace.

I was allowed to choose safety.

I was allowed to step into the next chapter God had already been preparing—one quiet promise at a time.

Thoughts

Years later, I can see how God was answering me long before I understood the language of His response. I had asked Him what it was all worth—why I had endured so much, why my children had suffered, why life seemed to keep demanding more from me than I thought I could give.

But the answer didn't come like thunder.

It came like a photograph on a refrigerator.

It came in small mercies—steady love, unexpected provision, a husband who didn't leave, a door that cracked open when I thought every door was sealed shut. It came in the quiet courage of showing up again and again, even when my heart was tired. It came in the miracle of two heartbeats, forming in darkness, reminding me that life can still be created after loss.

I used to think faith had to feel strong to be real.

Now I know faith is often trembling hands and whispered prayers. Faith is speaking hope over your life when nothing in your circumstances agrees. Faith is standing in front of a school sign and believing God can rewrite your story. Faith is opening the fridge door after a hard day, staring at a picture, and choosing to believe anyway.

And teaching—teaching taught me something too.

It taught me that I could love deeply and still walk away. That leaving isn't always quitting. Sometimes leaving is wisdom. Sometimes leaving is obedience. Sometimes leaving is the only way to save the parts of you that the world keeps trying to grind down.

For years, I lived as if endurance was the same thing as purpose. I thought surviving meant I was doing what God required of me. But now I understand: God never asked me to stay in places that were killing my spirit.

That photo on my fridge wasn't just a picture.

It was proof that even in the middle of chaos, I was still allowed to dream. I was still allowed to hope. I was still allowed to want more than mere survival.

And maybe that was the lesson all along:

God wasn't only teaching me how to endure.

He was teaching me how to live.

Chapter 73

The Call at Six A.M.

April 2016

My phone rang, and I knew before I even reached for it that it wasn't good. Phones don't ring at six in the morning unless something is wrong. At that hour, a ringing phone isn't communication—it's a warning. It is the past demanding to be answered.

I blinked into the darkness, my hand trembling slightly as I picked it up. "Hello?"

My sister's voice came through the line, tight and careful, like she was trying to keep herself from breaking.

"Rosie… Grandma is really sick. She's in the hospital."

I sat up in bed, the weight of her words settling into the room before I could even respond. My heart thudded once—hard—like it had been struck.

"Okay," I said, my voice flat. "And?"

There was a pause. The kind of pause that holds years inside it.

"Well," she hesitated, "I feel like she's not going to make it. And you haven't spoken to her in eighteen years."

Eighteen years.

The number landed like a stone.

Eighteen years since I had heard my grandmother's voice. Eighteen years since her words had cut so deeply, I built my life on the other side of them. I had carried that silence like an inheritance—heavy, unseen, always there. I told myself I didn't need her. I told myself I was fine.

But the truth was, I had learned to live with a closed door and called it strength.

I swallowed hard and said what I had practiced saying in my mind for years—what I had promised myself I would say if this moment ever came.

"Okay. I'm not going over there if she doesn't want to see me. I'm not going to put myself through that rejection again. Talk to Tía. If Grandma wants to see me, I'll go. But I'm not going any other way, okay?"

I hated how steady my voice sounded, like I was negotiating a contract instead of the last chance at a goodbye.

My sister exhaled softly.

"Okay," she said. "Love you. Bye."

The call ended, but the ringing stayed inside me. It echoed through the rest of my morning, through my drive to work, through every moment I tried to pretend I was functioning. It was as if that phone call had reopened something I had spent years nailing shut.

After work, my sister called again.

"They're taking her into surgery this evening," she said. "Tía said Grandma wants to see you. Are you going?"

I didn't answer right away.

The truth was, my body didn't want to move. My heart didn't want to risk reopening a wound that had scarred over with bitterness and grief. I had lived nearly two decades without that side of my family, without my grandmother's approval, without her voice, without her love. I had learned to survive without it.

But survival isn't the same as peace.

Very reluctantly, I replied, "I guess. I'll see you there."

My husband came with me. There was no way I was going to walk into that place alone—not into that history, not into those faces, not into that old version of myself that still lived somewhere in their memory.

He didn't say much on the drive. He didn't need to. His presence was its own kind of prayer. His hand rested on my back as we walked through the hospital doors, steady and warm, like he was anchoring me to the present so I wouldn't drown in the past.

The hospital smelled like antiseptic and old sorrow. The fluorescent lights were too bright, unforgiving, as if they were designed to expose every fear you tried to hide. The air felt cold against my skin, and my palms grew damp. My throat tightened as if my body already knew it was walking toward grief.

We rode the elevator up in silence. Floor by floor. Each number lighting up like a countdown.

When the doors opened, time slowed.

They were wheeling my grandmother down the hallway toward surgery.

The sound of the gurney wheels against the floor was sharp and rhythmic, like a clock. Everyone stopped. Everyone turned. Faces I hadn't seen in eighteen years. Eyes that measured me, recognized me, judged me, remembered. I felt my stomach drop.

For a moment, I was no longer a grown woman with a husband beside her. I was the girl who had been dismissed. The girl who had been wounded. The girl who had walked away because staying hurt too much.

My Tía stepped forward and leaned close to my grandmother.

"Es Rosa," she said gently. "La de Julián."

The words struck me harder than they should have.

Rosa. The one who belonged to Julián. As if my name still had to be attached to a man to make sense.

I moved forward anyway, my knees weak, my breath caught somewhere between fear and longing. I stooped down until her face was close to mine.

Her skin looked thin, almost translucent. Her eyes were tired, but they held something familiar—something that reached past the years.

"Grandma," I whispered, my voice trembling. "Soy yo… Rosa. La de Julián."

Her eyes searched my face like she was trying to find the girl she once knew beneath the woman standing there now. She squinted slightly, as if the years between us were fogged glass.

Then she asked me if it was really me.

"Yes, Grandma," I said, my voice breaking. "It's me."

And then she began to cry.

Right there in the hallway, surrounded by nurses and family and strangers and machines, my grandmother cried. Her shoulders shook. Her frail hands trembled. Her mouth quivered like the apology had been trapped behind her teeth for years and had finally broken free.

She looked at me and said she was sorry.

Sorry for saying those awful things long ago.

"I take it back," she said through tears. "I want good things for your children."

Something inside me cracked open.

I had longed for those words for so long—longed for them in quiet moments, in angry moments, in moments when I told myself I didn't care anymore. I had buried the need for them deep, convinced I would never receive them. I had convinced myself I didn't want them.

But my heart betrayed me in an instant.

Tears came fast and hot, and I couldn't stop them. It felt like eighteen years of grief poured out all at once. Like my body had been holding it back, waiting for permission.

I began to cry too, because I didn't know what else to do with the miracle of being seen.

"I'm sorry too," I told her.

I wasn't even sure what I was apologizing for. For leaving. For staying gone. For pride. For silence. For all the years between us that neither of us knew how to cross. But in that moment, it felt like my apology belonged there too—like it was part of closing a door that had been left open too long.

Then the nurse interrupted, her voice gentle but firm.

"We need to take her now."

And just like that, they wheeled her away.

I stood there frozen, watching her disappear down the hall, and it felt like watching a part of my own history being taken somewhere I couldn't follow. I realized I had spent eighteen years believing rejection was the worst thing she could give me.

But regret was worse.

That night, I went home and stared at my phone as if it might ring again. As if another call could undo the years. As if sound could erase silence.

The next day, I returned to the hospital. The surgery had been successful, and she was recovering. I walked down the hallway slowly, my footsteps careful, like I might startle the fragile peace that had finally formed between us.

My cousin was there when I entered her room. She greeted me warmly and told my grandmother I had arrived.

When Grandma saw me, her face lit up with a huge smile—awake, alert, present. It was the kind of smile that made her look like herself again, like the grandmother I remembered before everything fell apart. Her eyes brightened, and for a moment she didn't look like someone who had almost slipped away.

She looked like someone who had returned.

I leaned down and kissed her cheek as I had done long ago. Her skin was warm. Human. Real. Then I sat beside her bed, close enough to hear her breathing.

Once again, she apologized for what had happened between us. Her voice was softer now, but her words were steady.

Then, as if she needed to cover the tenderness with humor, she shook her head and said, "I thought I was stubborn… but you outdid me."

I laughed—quietly, surprised at myself.

And I told myself it was a compliment.

But later, sitting there beside her, I understood something she didn't: it hadn't been stubbornness.

It had been survival.

I had stayed away because the pain of her rejection had been too sharp, too humiliating, too heavy to carry. I had chosen distance because it was the only way I knew how to protect myself. I had mistaken silence for strength, because silence was safer than hoping.

That evening, I stayed.

I talked with my cousins. I listened to their stories. I shared photos. My grandmother loved photos—she studied them like they were proof of life, proof that time had passed and something good had still managed to grow. She smiled at my children's faces like she was trying to memorize what she had missed.

It wasn't perfect.

Nothing was erased. Nothing was rewritten.

But something was softened.

For a little while, it was nice.

And in a strange way, that was the most heartbreaking part of all— realizing how easily we could have had this all along, if pride hadn't been stronger than love.

A couple of days later, she developed complications from the surgery.

And then she was gone.

Just like that.

The reconciliation came late, but it came. A small mercy at the end of a long silence. I didn't get her back for long. I didn't get years. I didn't get holidays, or Sunday visits, or the kind of grandmother-granddaughter relationship I had once imagined.

I got a hallway.

I got a smile.

I got an apology.

And then I got grief.

But grief felt different now, because she had seen me, and I had been seen. Because the last words between us were not cruel. Because her final gift wasn't money or heirlooms or recipes—it was release.

The phone rang at six in the morning, and by the end of that week the silence that had lasted eighteen years had been replaced by something else: sorrow, yes… but also mercy.

Some apologies come too late to change the past, but not too late to change what you carry.

I used to think forgiveness was loud—that it would arrive like a dramatic moment, like a movie scene where everything finally makes sense. But forgiveness came to me quietly, under fluorescent hospital lights, in the soft trembling voice of an old woman who finally let go of her pride. And when she died, I realized the door between us had not been locked forever.

It had only been closed.

It opened for a moment—just long enough for love to pass through.

Just long enough for God to do what I could not.

Just long enough.

And then it shut again.

But this time, it did not shut with rejection.

It shut with peace.

<u>Thoughts</u>

For many years, I believed rejection was the final word in my story with my grandmother. Her words had closed something inside me so completely that I learned to live as if the relationship had never existed. I told myself I was strong for walking away. I told myself I no longer needed her approval. I built a life far from that pain and called the distance healing.

But the truth is that rejection does not disappear just because we refuse to look at it. It settles quietly into the corners of our lives. It shows up in the way we guard our hearts, in the way we expect people to leave, in the way we prepare ourselves for disappointment before it ever arrives.

For eighteen years, I carried that rejection like a shield. It protected me, but it also isolated me. I thought staying away meant I had won something—that I had preserved my dignity by refusing to return to a place where I had once been wounded.

What I understand now is that both of us were trapped inside the same silence. She had her pride. I had my pain.

And between those two things stretched eighteen years of distance.

When my grandmother apologized in that hospital hallway, something shifted that I had believed was permanent. Her apology did not erase the past. It did not undo the years we lost or the hurt that had been spoken. Forgiveness does not work that way.

What it did was release me from carrying that moment forever.

Forgiveness, I have learned, is not the same as forgetting. It is not pretending that the harm never happened. It is the decision to stop allowing that harm to define the rest of your life.

For a long time, I believed forgiveness was something you gave to the other person.

Now I understand that forgiveness is something you give to yourself.

It is the moment when you decide that someone else's words—no matter how painful—will not be the final authority over your worth. It is the moment when you stop rehearsing the injury and start laying it down.

My grandmother and I did not get years to repair what had broken between us. We got a hallway, a hospital bed, a few conversations, and a handful of shared photographs. By most standards, it was far too little and far too late.

And yet, it was enough.

Enough for her to say she was sorry.

Enough for me to say I was sorry too.

Enough for the silence to break before the end.

Some people never receive that moment. Some people carry rejection all the way to the grave without hearing the words they needed most. I understand now that reconciliation is a gift not everyone is given.

What I carry today is not the memory of what she once said to me.

What I carry is the moment she took it back.

That moment did not change the past.

But it changed the weight of it.

And sometimes, that is what forgiveness does.

It does not rewrite the story.

It simply loosens the grip the past once had on your heart.

Chapter 74

The Crack in the Wall 2017

With the expansion of my growing family—expecting my sixth child—I knew something had to change.

For thirteen years, I had taught in the public school system. I had poured myself into lesson plans, parent conferences, science labs, and standardized tests. I had spent years building other people's children toward their futures while quietly holding my own life together behind the scenes. And I had done it the way I had always done everything:

By pushing forward.

By enduring.

By pretending that exhaustion was normal.

But pregnancy has a way of making you take inventory. It forces you to slow down and listen to your body, even when you don't want to. It forces you to admit what you've been ignoring.

After having my twins in 2015, my husband and I decided we wanted another set of boy/girl twins. It sounds almost unbelievable when I say it out loud—like a story someone else would tell—but it was our reality. Our home was already full of noise and laughter, of small hands and spilled milk, of bedtime stories and sleepless nights. And still, we wanted more.

So when February 2017 came, and I found myself pregnant again— pregnant with twins once more—I wasn't surprised. Just grateful.

There is a certain kind of hope that comes with expecting. A quiet, tender kind. It fills the corners of your life before anyone else can see it. It makes room in your heart without asking permission.

At first, everything felt normal. My body did what it always did— nausea, fatigue, cravings, the strange stretching sensation of life growing inside me. I was tired, but it was familiar tiredness, the kind that comes with motherhood and miracles.

And then, not long into the pregnancy, we found out something was wrong. We went in for an ultrasound. I remember the room clearly: dim lighting, cool air, the hum of machinery. The kind of quiet that feels too clean, too sterile. The walls were pale and blank, and the silence felt like a warning.

The technician spread the cold gel across my belly, and the wand moved slowly, methodically. Her face was calm, professional, but her eyes flickered in a way I couldn't ignore. She kept looking at the screen, then back at me, then back at the screen.

A small wall rose in my chest.

The kind of wall you build when your spirit senses something your mind hasn't caught up to yet. At first, I told myself not to panic. I tried to breathe. I tried to keep my voice steady.

But I could feel it—something wasn't right.

The technician's silence grew heavier, like a door slowly closing.

Then the doctor came in.

And in that moment, I understood that sometimes the worst news doesn't arrive like a storm. Sometimes it arrives softly, almost gently, wrapped in careful words and lowered voices.

The little girl didn't make it.

I stared at the screen as if staring harder could change the outcome. As if my eyes could bring life back. As if my love could force her heart to beat again. They said she had stopped growing at eight weeks.

There was no longer a heartbeat.

The words fell into the room like stones. Heavy. Final. Unmovable.

My body was still carrying her, but she was gone.

And grief—real grief—does not ask permission before it enters you. It moves in like a thief, stealing breath, stealing sound, stealing light. I remember feeling numb at first. My hands went cold. My throat tightened.

I wanted to scream, but nothing came out.

The ultrasound room suddenly felt smaller, like the walls were closing in. The air felt thick. I couldn't swallow. I couldn't speak.

I was looking at death on a screen while life continued inside me— her twin still growing, still alive.

It was a cruel kind of contrast. A cruel kind of mystery.

When we left the office, the sun was still shining. Cars still moved through traffic. People still walked into grocery stores, laughing and talking as if the world had not just cracked open.

That is one of the strangest things about loss: it isolates you.

The world keeps spinning while you stand still.

When I got home, I went into the bathroom and locked the door. I don't know why I locked it. There was no one chasing me. No one threatening me. But locking doors had always been a habit of mine—an instinct I developed long before adulthood.

Locking doors meant safety.

Locking doors meant control.

I sat on the edge of the bathtub and cried until my body shook. I cried until my face hurt and my chest burned. I cried the kind of cry that comes from somewhere deeper than tears—a cry that comes from the soul.

I thought about the little girl I had already imagined. I had already seen her in my mind. I had pictured tiny bows and soft blankets. I had pictured her curled against my chest, warm and breathing, her small fingers gripping mine.

I had already made room for her.

And now that space was empty.

I carried her absence like a weight inside my body. A silent grief tucked beneath my skin. No one could see it, but I felt it everywhere. In my stomach. In my throat. In the heaviness of my limbs.

Even the walls of my home felt different after that—like they knew something sacred had been lost.

Days passed, but I didn't feel like myself. I moved through life like someone walking through fog. I went to work. I smiled when I was supposed to. I answered questions. I graded papers. But inside, I was crumbling.

And then something else began to rise up inside me, quietly at first.

A question. How much longer can I keep living this way?

Teaching had been my identity for so long. The classroom was familiar, predictable. It was a place where I knew the rules, where I knew how to succeed. But I was tired. Not just physically. Spiritually.

I was tired of the constant demands, the endless pressure, the system that asked teachers to pour from cups that were already empty. I was tired of giving everything I had to everyone else and leaving nothing for my own children. I was tired of surviving.

And grief has a way of exposing truth. It cracks open the walls you've built and forces you to see what you've been avoiding. It shows you that life is fragile, that tomorrow is not promised, that comfort is not the same thing as calling.

My children were growing. My family was growing. And I could feel
God tugging at me, calling me toward something new.

I didn't know what that something was yet.

But I knew I could not stay the same.

Around that time, a friend told me about a school district based in
Huntsville, Texas. She said their campuses were located within prison
walls all across the state. They taught inmates—men who were
incarcerated—helping them earn diplomas, GEDs, and learn skills for life
beyond release. When she first said it, I felt something in me tighten.

Prison.

That word carried weight. It carried memory. It carried history.

Most people would be afraid of working in a prison because of the
inmates. But my fear wasn't rooted in them.

My fear was rooted in me.

I had grown up standing in lines to visit my father. I knew what it
felt like to be on the outside of those walls, waiting to be let in. I knew the
smell of concrete hallways and metal doors. I knew the sound of keys. I
knew the humiliation of being searched.

I knew what prison did to families.

I knew what it did to children.

And now someone was asking me to step into that world willingly.

To walk through those doors on purpose.

The thought of it made my stomach turn. It was like being asked to
step back into a childhood wound. Like being asked to reopen a scar that
had never fully healed. Still, I couldn't stop thinking about it.

The idea followed me like a shadow.

It showed up in my quiet moments. It lingered in my prayers.

It returned again and again, persistent as a heartbeat.

I told myself it was foolish.

I told myself I was pregnant, emotional, unstable in grief.

But the thought would not leave me alone.

And slowly, I began to wonder if maybe this was not foolishness.

Maybe it was purpose.

Maybe the loss of my baby girl had cracked something open in me—
not to destroy me, but to shift me.

Maybe that grief was the first crack in a wall I had been leaning
against my entire life.

A wall made of routine.

A wall made of fear.

A wall made of survival.

And maybe, just maybe, God was calling me to walk through a door I had never imagined I'd open.

As I pressed "submit" on that online application, my hands trembled—not because I didn't believe I could do it… but because I knew that if I walked into that place, my life would never be the same again.

By the time the interview process began,

I was five months pregnant.

And still carrying both life and loss inside me.

The months that followed were heavy, but they were also clarifying. Grief did not leave—but it changed shape. It softened at the edges. It made room for something else to grow alongside it.

Hope.

In October 2017, that hope arrived.

Milo came into the world weighing nine pounds, two ounces— strong, full, undeniable life. I remember the weight of him in my arms. The warmth of his body against mine. The sound of his cry—loud, insistent, alive. After everything, there he was.

Not a replacement.

Not a remedy.

But a reminder.

That life continues.

That love expands.

That even in the same body where grief once lived, joy can take up space again. Holding him, I understood something I hadn't been able to put into words before:

Loss had not hollowed me out.

It had made room.

Room for deeper love.

Room for clearer purpose.

Room for a different kind of courage.

Some doors do not open gently.

Some doors swing wide and change everything.

And I could already hear the echo of the hinges.

Thoughts

Years later, I understand that grief is not just sorrow—it is revelation. Losing my baby girl did not only break my heart; it cracked something open inside me that I had sealed shut for years. I had spent so much of my life building walls—walls of strength, walls of routine, walls of *I'm fine*, walls of survival. I thought those walls were protecting me. I thought they were necessary.

But in that ultrasound room, when the words *no heartbeat* entered the air, I learned that walls do not keep pain out. They only keep truth trapped in.

That loss became a fracture line in my life. A holy interruption. It forced me to see how fragile everything is, how quickly life can change, and how little control I truly had. It reminded me that tomorrow is never guaranteed—not for the living, and not for the unborn.

I had carried six children, but that day I carried something else too:

The realization that I could not keep living on autopilot.

I could not keep pouring from an empty cup and calling it faith. I could not keep sacrificing my peace and calling it normal. Something had to shift. Something had to move.

And even though I didn't understand it then, I see now that my baby girl's short life was not meaningless.

She was a turning point.

She was the crack in the wall that made room for a new door.

And through that opening, God began leading me somewhere I never imagined I would go—into the very place my childhood had taught me to fear.

Not to haunt me.

But to heal me.

Chapter 75

Inside the Walls

The first time I walked into a prison as an educator, the air felt different. It wasn't just the smell—though that was unforgettable. A mix of industrial cleaner, sweat, and something metallic that clung to the back of your throat. It wasn't just the sound—though the echoes were sharp, bouncing off concrete like a warning.

It was the feeling.

The weight.

The invisible pressure that settled on my shoulders the moment I stepped inside.

At the entrance, I passed through metal detectors. My clear bag was searched. My identification was examined. My body was scanned as if the world needed proof that I belonged there.

Then came the doors.

Heavy doors.

Steel doors.

Doors that didn't simply close—they *sealed.*

I heard the click of locks, the deep clank of metal meeting metal, and something inside me flinched.

Because I had heard that sound before.

As a child, I had heard it while standing in line to visit my father.

I had heard it while watching my mother's face tighten with worry.

I had heard it while feeling the strange mixture of love and shame that prison visits can carve into a child's heart. My fears were founded in my past.

And in that moment, I realized how thin the line was between then and now. The walls were the same. The coldness was the same. The echoing hallways were the same.

Only this time, I wasn't a little girl holding my mother's hand.

This time, I was the adult.

This time, I was walking in alone.

The guards carried keys that jingled as they walked—small sounds that held enormous power. Those keys-controlled doors, movement, time, freedom. The sound of them was constant, like a reminder:

Nothing in here belongs to you. Not even the air.

I walked down long corridors beneath fluorescent lights that buzzed overhead. The walls were plain and colorless, built for function, not comfort. Everything was designed to contain.

Contain bodies.

Contain violence.

Contain truth.

And yet, as I walked deeper into the prison, something unexpected happened.

I felt a strange calm settle over me.

Not because I felt safe.

But because I felt familiar.

The prison did not feel foreign to me. It felt like an old chapter I had never wanted to reread.

I was assigned a classroom and told what I could and could not bring in. The rules were strict. The boundaries were clear. Every movement mattered. Every decision carried weight.

Then the students began to arrive.

Men in uniform. Men with hard eyes. Men with long histories. Men who carried themselves like they had nothing left to lose.

The first time a student walked into my classroom, I understood something quickly:

Prison walls do not just hold people.

They shape them.

My biggest challenge is always the new student—the one who walks in and immediately begins building a wall between us.

He stands there like a tower.

Six feet tall.

Two hundred sixty pounds.

Muscles like armor. Tattoos like warnings. A stare so stoic it could freeze the air.

He doesn't say much at first.

He doesn't have to.

His silence speaks.

His posture speaks.

His eyes speak.

He looks at me, measuring me, judging me. He sees a woman who is five feet one, about one hundred twenty pounds, professionally dressed—an educated lady with calm hands and a controlled voice.

And I can almost hear his thoughts,

even if he never says them aloud:

What does she know about drugs?

What does she know about alcohol?

What does she know about selling drugs to make ends meet?

What does she know about this lifestyle?

I feel it in every glare.

I know it.

And for a moment, the room becomes a battlefield—not of fists, but of perception. A silent standoff between who he thinks I am and who I truly am.

He has built a wall around himself—

greater and older than the Great Wall of China.

But like the Berlin Wall, I know it will come down.

Not because I force it.

Not because I fight him.

But because walls always crack when truth enters the room.

And I have learned how to speak truth.

In public school, I built students up for the future. I planted seeds, watered potential, encouraged dreams.

But in the correctional system, I help men rebuild their futures for release. I help them pick up the pieces of their lives, not just academically, but emotionally.

Here, education is not simply learning.

It is unlearning.

It is undoing.

It is excavation.

In public school, I taught science. But now I teach life skills—tools they can use when they step beyond these gates. I teach positive self-talk. I teach conflict resolution. I teach them how to make amends in their relationships.

I teach them how to approach a job interview.

How to complete a job application.

How to build a resume.

And sometimes, without even planning it, I teach them how to face themselves.

What surprises people is that I am not intimidated.

Not because I am fearless.

But because I understand them.

My personal motivation for teaching has changed. It is no longer about self-preservation. It is no longer about simply paying bills or earning benefits. This work is different.

This work is sacred.

Because here is where I get to—yes, *get to*—because it is a privilege:

I get to use my past.

I get to take everything I survived and turn it into a bridge.

I grew up in instability.

I lived the life of a runaway.

I became a teenage mother.

I battled broken family relationships.

I lived through drug and alcohol abuse.

I survived domestic violence, addiction, sexual abuse, and child molestation.

And now I stand in front of men who have lived their own versions of darkness, and I offer them something many have never been offered before:

Understanding without judgment.

I tell them stories sometimes—not to shock them, not to center myself, but to dismantle the assumption that they are the only ones who have ever suffered. I often say,

"Well, let me tell you what happened to me…" or

"Let me tell you what I saw…"

And the room changes.

Because they realize something important.

He didn't know I had lived it.

He didn't know I had walked through hell and still found a way out.

That is when the wall cracks.

That is when the tattoos and muscles stop being armor.

That is when the fierce stare softens.

That is when a man begins to feel safe enough to become human again.

I reach that unreachable student—the one who grew up experiencing the worst things imaginable. The one who learned to numb himself because feeling was too dangerous. The one who was once a child with no protector.

And I teach him that he can make it to the other side.

I reach the unreachable student who is a son, a father, a husband carrying a burden of unforgiveness for the hurt he has inflicted on the ones he loves the most.

And I get to show him that grace is possible—real grace—if he is willing to do the work.

I am a living example that there is hope for the black sheep of their families who wear white. And in a world that has already labeled them, already dismissed them, already locked them away, I get to do something radical:

I get to see them.

I get to change the world—one black sheep at a time.

I get to break down walls within prison walls.

One of my proudest moments came from watching a student I'll call R.J. start in my Literacy 1–2 class. He entered with his head down, guarded, carrying the quiet shame of a man who had been told too many times that he wasn't smart enough.

He didn't speak much at first.

He didn't make eye contact.

He stayed behind his wall.

But day by day, I watched him push against it.

He began to participate. He began to read with confidence.

He began to believe.

He moved on to Literacy 2–3.

And eventually, he completed and received his GED.

When he told me he passed, his eyes shined with something I can only describe as freedom.

Not physical freedom.

But internal freedom.

Because even in prison, the mind can be released.

And then there are the moments that don't come with certificates.

The moments that come with silence.

The moments that come with shaking hands.

The moments that come with men learning, sometimes for the first time, what happened to them was not normal.

In my life skills class, I had a student who did not realize he was a victim of sexual abuse until he walked into my classroom.

He began sharing about a relationship he had when he was a young teenager with a woman ten years older than him. He spoke about it casually, almost proudly at first, as if he had been taught that boys should feel lucky for any attention from an older woman.

But as he kept talking, the details became darker.

The woman was married.

Her husband was involved.

The husband would pick him up and drop him off at the home he shared with his wife so the wife could have intercourse with this teenage boy.

The classroom grew still.

Even the air seemed to stop moving.

And for a moment, you could feel it—

the collective understanding rising like a wave.

This wasn't a relationship.

This was grooming.

This was abuse.

Between myself and his classmates, he slowly came to acceptance and realization that he was a victim.

I watched him sit with the truth as it settled into his chest like a stone. I watched a wall crumble.

I have heard countless stories of men who were molested or raped as children or as teenagers—men who have never told anyone until they walk into my classroom.

The numbers are staggering.

These men, not knowing how to deal with the guilt and shame, turn to drugs to numb their feelings. They turn to alcohol. They turn to violence. They turn to anything that will silence the screaming inside their heads. Because trauma does not disappear when ignored.

It only mutates.

One student told me he battled cancer as a child with his mother by his side. She sat with him through hospital visits and treatments, through

sickness and fear. But once he went into remission, she left him with a
father he did not know.

No warning.
No explanation.
She was just gone.
And the abandonment hollowed him out.
He turned to drugs to numb the pain of that emptiness—
the pain he still carries.
Another student told me his father injected him with
methamphetamine at the age of twelve.
Twelve years old. A child.
And now, as a grown man,
he battles addiction like a chain he never asked for.
When I listen to these stories, I don't hear excuses.
I hear origins.
I hear broken beginnings.
I hear childhood wounds that were never treated,
never spoken of, never healed.
And I see them—these grown men behind prison walls—
still carrying the same frightened child inside them.
Sometimes I look around my classroom and
I think about how many walls exist in that space.
The prison walls around us.
The emotional walls inside them.
The walls they built to survive.
The walls the world built to contain them.
And then I think about myself—
about how I once lived my own life behind walls, too.
Walls of silence.
Walls of shame.
Walls of survival.
And now, somehow, God has placed me here—not as a visitor,
not as a frightened little girl standing in line to see her father...
...but as a teacher.
As a voice.
As a witness.

As a woman who can stand in the middle of concrete and steel and still speak about hope. Every day I walk through those locked doors and hear those keys rattle, I am reminded that freedom is not only about leaving a place.

Freedom is about leaving a mindset.

Freedom is about tearing down the walls inside you.

And every time a man in my classroom begins to see himself differently—begins to believe he can change, begins to imagine a life beyond his past—I realize something:

Some of the strongest walls are not made of concrete.

They are made of pain.

And I have been called to do the holy work of breaking them down.

Thoughts

Years later, I understand something I couldn't fully name back then: God didn't bring me into prison to punish me with my past. He brought me there to redeem it.

The same walls that once separated me from my father became the walls where I found my calling. The same doors that once made me feel powerless became the doors I now walk through with purpose.

And I've learned that some men are not hardened—they are wounded. They are not unreachable—they are simply buried beneath years of shame.

In my classroom, I don't just teach life skills.

I teach men how to unlock the parts of themselves they were forced to hide.

I teach them how to rebuild.

How to confess.

How to forgive.

How to hope again.

Because walls can fall.

And when they do, what's left isn't weakness.

It's freedom

Chapter 76

A Room in the Backyard (2018–2019)

Toward the latter part of 2018, I finally said out loud what had been sitting heavy in my spirit for far too long.

I told Eddie the truth.

"My dad is living out of his van."

The words tasted bitter in my mouth, like shame. Like something I should have fixed a long time ago but didn't know how.

My father—my own father—was sleeping on the streets of San Francisco, curled up inside a van like an afterthought. Some nights he would stay in a shelter if he could find a bed, but most nights he parked wherever he could and disappeared into the city like so many others. The kind of people the world learns to step over without looking down.

And I couldn't stop thinking about it.

How could I call myself a child of God, a Christian woman who claimed she believed the Bible, who prayed, who worshipped, who tried to obey what God asked of her… while my father slept in a van?

The conviction didn't come gently. It came like a stone on my chest.

The verse kept circling in my mind, persistent as a heartbeat:

Honor thy father and thy mother.

Not *honor them if they were good parents.*

Not *honor them if they raised you right.*

Not *honor them if they didn't break you first.*

There was no "if" in that commandment. No loophole. No exception. Just a holy expectation.

And there I was, sleeping in a comfortable bed, under a roof, wrapped in warmth, while my father lay in the cold with a steering wheel in front of him and streetlights spilling through his windshield.

Some nights, I would lie in bed and stare at the ceiling, the blanket warm against my skin, and instead of comfort it felt like accusation. I imagined him out there, damp air creeping through cracked windows, the smell of old fast food and gasoline trapped in the upholstery. I imagined his body stiff from sleeping sitting up, his legs cramped, his pride folded in half like the seats he reclined.

And then I would whisper into the dark, *God, what am I doing?*

Chapter 76

Around that same time, Eddie and I had just purchased a Tuff Shed for our backyard. It was meant for storage—boxes, tools, holiday decorations, things we didn't need but couldn't seem to throw away.

But every time I stepped inside that shed, something in me shifted.

It was just wood and nails and empty space, but I couldn't stop seeing more. I would walk in carrying a box, the smell of fresh lumber rising in the heat, and I would pause and look around as if the walls were waiting for instructions.

This could be a room, I kept thinking.

Not a shed.

A room.

A refuge.

A small safe place where a man could sleep without fear.

A door that opened into dignity.

One afternoon, I finally said it out loud.

"What if we bought another Tuff Shed,"

I asked Eddie, "and converted it for my dad?"

I expected him to react. I expected him to hesitate.

I expected him to list reasons it wouldn't work.

But Eddie didn't say much. He just listened.

He sat there quiet, his face thoughtful, like he was turning my words over in his mind. Like he was weighing them, not against inconvenience, but against love. And I assumed that was the end of it. I assumed he was just being kind. But I was wrong.

In February of 2019, Eddie asked me to take the day off work because we needed to file our income taxes. He had already scheduled the appointment.

We drove there together, filled out the paperwork, signed our names, and listened as the tax preparer clicked away at the keyboard like our whole year could be summarized into numbers on a screen.

When it was over, Eddie smiled and said, "Let's go eat."

We went out for lunch, and for a moment the heaviness lifted. We ate, talked, and laughed a little, and I thought maybe the day would end like any other day—ordinary.

But when we got back into the car, Eddie turned the key and said casually, "Let's go for a ride. I've got one more place I want us to check out."

I didn't ask questions. I trusted him.

We drove for a while until we pulled into a parking lot, and when I looked up, I froze.

Tuff Shed. Not one shed.

An entire place that sold nothing but sheds. Row after row of them, lined up like little empty houses waiting to be claimed. I turned toward Eddie, confused, my heart starting to pound. And then he said the words that undid me.

"Go ahead," he told me. "Pick out the shed you want for your dad."

I couldn't speak. My throat tightened. My eyes filled before I could stop them. Because in that moment, I realized Eddie had heard me the first time. Not just with his ears—with his heart. He hadn't brushed off my guilt or my conviction. He hadn't treated it like an emotional moment that would pass. He had been carrying it quietly, the way he carried everything that mattered. I felt my heart melt into gratitude so deep it almost hurt. Eddie wasn't a man of long speeches, but he was a man of action. He didn't promise big things—he built them.

We walked through the lot together, looking at options, measuring sizes, discussing layouts. And as we stood there, surrounded by empty structures, it felt like God Himself was standing in that parking lot with us, whispering, *This is what obedience looks like.*

We chose one.

It was delivered soon after and installed in our backyard. At first, it looked like what it was: a plain shed, raw wood and unfinished corners, sitting quietly behind our home.

But Eddie didn't see a shed. Eddie saw a room.

Over the next few months, my husband poured himself into that space like he was building something holy.

He installed insulation. He added sheetrock. He put in flooring. He built a closet. He installed a toilet and a sink. He ran electricity, wired it carefully, and painted the walls. I watched him work, day after day, his hands dusty, his clothes streaked with paint, sweat gathering at his brow under the El Paso sun. And every time he stepped back to examine what he'd done, I thought, *This is love. This is mercy. This is a man building something with his hands that his mouth doesn't even know how to explain.*

That shed was no longer a shed.

It was becoming sanctuary.

Chapter 76

It's funny how God works—how He moves behind the scenes, arranging timing the way only He can. Because while Eddie was building that room, my father became ill.

In September of 2019, my sister and I found out that my dad had been hospitalized with gallbladder problems. As soon as we heard, we drove to San Francisco.

San Francisco has a beauty that can fool you. The city sparkles in certain places, but it also holds darkness in its cracks—people living unseen, suffering quietly, surviving day to day.

When we arrived, we discovered what my father had never admitted fully.

He wasn't just "staying" in his van.

He was living in it.

His life was stuffed into every inch of that vehicle—bags, blankets, clothes, old tools, paper clutter, plastic containers. The van smelled like survival: sweat, stale air, old food, and the metallic scent of a life that had been forced to shrink.

It hit me like a punch.

My father had been carrying his whole world inside that van. Everything he owned. Everything he had left. And he was too old to be living that way. Too vulnerable. Too exposed. Too tired.

My sister and I looked at each other and the decision was instant. This ends now.

I told her, "I'm preparing a room for him. A place for him to live."

Then I said, "You handle the car."

Because I knew my father.

I knew the excuses before he even spoke them.

He would say he didn't want to be a burden.

He would say he didn't want to inconvenience us.

He would say he didn't want to take up space.

But the truth was, my father's pride had been holding hands with his fear for years. He was afraid of being unwanted. Afraid of being too much. Afraid of being in the way.

So we decided to remove every reason he could hide behind.

I would give him the room.

My sister would provide a vehicle.

No excuses left.

When we approached him about coming back with us, we explained that we had prepared a room and were in the process of getting him transportation. We told him he wouldn't be trapped.

He would have independence.

He agreed.

But he was reluctant.

Even in his yes, there was hesitation. His shoulders carried the weight of a man who had spent too long surviving alone. He didn't know how to be cared for anymore.

Then came the van. As we prepared to sell it, we began to empty it out. What should have been a simple process turned into something emotional and exhausting. My father had accumulated so much stuff, and he didn't want to part with it.

Every item seemed to mean something. Every bag felt like a piece of his identity. Every old object was proof he had made it through another day.

Watching him cling to those belongings, I realized something painful: when people lose stability, they hold onto things because things don't abandon you. Things don't leave. Things don't disappoint.

But people do.

Still, we did what we had to do.

On a positive note, we couldn't get what he wanted for the van, so we had no choice but to leave with it for the time being. And soon we began the long drive back to El Paso—two cars traveling like a slow procession, a convoy of daughters escorting a father back into safety.

The highway stretched in front of us like a long ribbon of redemption. When we finally arrived, my father stepped into his new space. His own room. His own bed.

A dresser.

A television.

A refrigerator.

A microwave.

A restroom.

A closet.

It wasn't just a shed anymore.

Chapter 76

It was a tiny studio apartment tucked into my backyard, with its own entrance, its own privacy, its own dignity. A place where my father could shut the door at night and know no one would chase him away.

And something in me finally exhaled.

For the past few years, my father has lived with me.

And I thank God every time I look at that little building behind my house, because not long after, COVID-19 hit San Francisco like a wave.

My father has since learned that many of his friends passed away during the pandemic. People he used to see, people he used to talk to, people he used to share meals with—gone.

Sometimes he mentions them quietly, like he's still trying to accept it. Like his heart still doesn't know where to place the grief. And I can't help but think about what would have happened if he had stayed there.

If he had been sleeping in that van, exposed, vulnerable, alone.

I don't even want to imagine it.

But God.

God made a way.

He took my conviction and turned it into action. He used my husband's quiet listening and turned it into lumber and sheetrock. He took an ordinary shed and transformed it into mercy.

A shed meant for storage became a sanctuary.

And my father finally had a door that opened into safety.

<u>Thoughts</u>

Looking back now, I understand something I didn't fully grasp back then: honoring my father wasn't about pretending the past didn't hurt. It wasn't about rewriting history or denying what was broken.

It was about choosing compassion anyway.

It was about obedience that costs you something.

Because sometimes honoring your parents doesn't look like cards or phone calls or polite words. Sometimes it looks like building a room in your backyard with your own hands… so an aging man can sleep without fear. And sometimes, God answers prayers not through thunder or miracles in the sky—but through a quiet husband who listens, a shed that becomes a refuge, and a daughter finally making room.

Chapter 77

January 2021
Vindication on a Screen

When the Netflix docu-series *The Hunt for a Serial Killer* aired, my father and I sat down and watched the entire series together. We didn't space it out. We didn't pause to breathe. We watched it straight through, as if the truth—once it started spilling out—couldn't be stopped.

As the episodes unfolded, I realized how much of the case I had never known. I had lived inside the shadow of my Tío Richie's crimes for most of my life, but even I didn't know the full extent of what he had done.

And then the documentary revealed something that hit me like a blow to the chest: the molestation.

The number of children.

The scope of it.

The cold, horrifying reality that he hadn't just hurt me—
he had hurt *many*.

My father and I sat there stunned. I could feel the air shift in the room, like something invisible had stepped between us. The kind of silence that doesn't come from peace, but from grief. From shock. From a truth too heavy to carry politely.

That was when my father apologized to me.

Not casually. Not defensively. Not with the usual half-hearted tone people use when they're trying to move on quickly.

This time, it was sincere.

He looked at me and said he was sorry.

And I felt it in my bones—he believed me. Finally, after all these years, after all the quiet dismissal and avoidance, he truly believed that my Tío Richie had molested me.

That apology meant more to me than I can properly explain. It wasn't just about words. It was about what those words unlocked: validation, acknowledgement, and the lifting of a weight I had been dragging for decades.

For once, it didn't sound like an obligation.

It sounded like regret.

I was glad the documentary included that part of the crimes. Glad, because it didn't allow the truth to stay buried where families like mine had tried to keep it. Glad, because in a strange and painful way, I felt vindicated.

Gil Carrillo vindicated me.

The documentary proved what I had always said was true. It confirmed what my childhood had tried to scream out loud while the adults around me chose silence. God used that documentary—and God used Gil Carrillo—to prove to my family that I had been telling the truth all along.

It wasn't revenge I felt.

It was release.

For so long, the truth lived in my throat like a stone.

But now it was on a screen, spoken aloud, documented, undeniable.

I reached out to Gil Carrillo to thank him—not only for including those cases in the documentary, but also for making the decision not to include the children during the trial. I understood why he did it. I respected it. He was protecting them from being retraumatized, from being dragged into the public eye, from being turned into spectacle.

But there was still a part of me that wished those charges had been included. A part of me that wished the world had known everything while he was still alive to face it.

I carried that conflict quietly: gratitude and frustration tangled together like vines.

Not long after, I was approached about appearing on *The Tamron Hall Show*. When I discussed it with my husband and even with some of my students at the prison, they all agreed it could be a good opportunity. They encouraged me to use my voice for something bigger than myself— to make a plea to parents.

Because children don't always have the language to say what's happening to them.

Sometimes they show it through anger.

Through rebellion.

Through withdrawal.

Through failing grades.

Through emotional storms that adults label as "attitude" or "bad behavior."

I wanted to tell parents what I needed someone to see in me when I was young:

Pay attention. Look deeper. Ask better questions. Don't dismiss the signs.

But when the first take of the interview began, I was disappointed.

They insisted on asking me about my family—how they reacted, what they thought, how they processed everything.

And the truth is: I cannot speak for them.

I can only speak for myself.

My family has always wanted distance from the case and the crimes. They have always wanted to step away from the headlines, the whispers, the shame, the public association.

And I understand why.

One of the primary reasons for my family's silence has been trauma—deep, unresolved trauma. The emotional impact of my Tío Richie's crimes wasn't confined to his victims. It spilled outward like poison, seeping into everyone connected to him, including those who never committed a single act themselves.

The pain was generational.

The shame was inherited.

The grief was unspeakable.

For many of them, silence became a survival mechanism. Speaking his name aloud was like reopening a wound that never truly healed. A wound that still bled under the surface.

So they stayed quiet.

They tried to keep the door closed.

Another reason for the silence was the stigma. Being related to a notorious serial killer comes with a kind of judgment that doesn't care about innocence. The public rarely separates a criminal from the people who share his blood. The world doesn't ask whether you suffered too. It just assumes you're part of the darkness.

That association can lead to ostracization, harassment, and isolation. People look at you differently. They speak to you differently. Sometimes they don't speak at all.

To preserve privacy, to protect themselves, and to maintain even a fragile sense of normalcy, my family chose silence.

And that is why I was displeased with the first take of the interview.

Afterward, I expressed my anger about the questions. My family has always wanted their distance. They have always wanted their privacy, and I have tried my best to respect that.

That is why I can only speak on my experiences.

I can only speak from what I lived.

From what I saw.

From what I survived.

I will not be the voice for people who refused to use theirs when I needed it most.

Still, even with all that frustration, I knew one thing for sure: the truth was no longer mine alone to carry.

It was out.

And it had been spoken into the world.

One day, on my birthday, my children were preparing breakfast in bed for me. Their footsteps and whispers filled the house with a softness I once thought I would never have. I lay there smiling, listening, letting the warmth of the moment settle into me like sunlight.

I began thanking God for the years He had blessed me with. I thought about the prayers He had answered, the miracles I had lived through, the doors He had opened when I had nothing left but faith.

And then I remembered one prayer in particular.

I remembered praying to work at **Sanchez** Middle School.

I remembered asking God for it so many times,

almost like a child asking again and again, hoping persistence might make heaven move faster.

And as I lay there, I said quietly in my heart,

God, You never did answer that prayer about Sanchez Middle School.

And immediately, I felt it—clear as if He had spoken aloud.

Who said I didn't?

Where do you work?

I froze.

Because the answer was so obvious, I almost laughed.

Sanchez.

I worked at Rogelio *Sanchez* State Jail

I had been living inside the answered prayer without even realizing it.

And in that moment, I understood something I had forgotten in the noise of trauma and television interviews and painful conversations:

God doesn't always answer the way we expect.

Sometimes He answers so gently, so gradually, that we don't even recognize the miracle until we stop long enough to look around.

And there I was—alive, surrounded by love, in a home filled with laughter, and employed in the very place I once begged Him for.

Vindication on a screen.

Healing in a quiet bedroom.

And a God who had been answering me all along

Thoughts

Looking back now, I understand that the documentary didn't just expose my Tío Richie—it exposed the cost of silence.

For years, I carried the truth like a bruise no one could see. I carried it into adulthood, into motherhood, into classrooms full of children who reminded me of myself. And even when I tried to bury it, it stayed alive inside me, shaping how I trusted, how I loved, how certain memories could still make my body tighten before my mind even understood why.

But that night on the couch with my father, watching Netflix like any other family might, something sacred happened in the middle of something ugly. The truth finally had witnesses.

My father's apology didn't erase what happened, and it didn't give me back the girl I used to be before the abuse. But it gave me something I didn't know I still needed: confirmation. A moment where my pain was no longer questioned, minimized, or treated like an inconvenience.

It was the first time I felt like my childhood self could finally unclench her fists.

And I realize now how strange it is that God used a documentary—a television series, of all things—to break through what years of family denial could not. But that's how God has always worked in my life. He doesn't always come like thunder. Sometimes He comes through a screen, through a stranger's voice, through evidence that forces the truth to rise.

But the truth did not move everyone.

After the documentary aired and after I spoke publicly, not one family member called me to apologize for not believing me. Not one called to say they were sorry for the years I carried the truth alone.

Instead, many of them were angry with me for speaking on *The Tamron Hall Show.*

In their eyes, I had broken the silence they had worked so hard to maintain. Their anger told me something I had already begun to understand: for some people, protecting the family's reputation matters more than protecting the child who was harmed. Speaking the truth felt to them like betrayal, even though the betrayal had happened years before, when a little girl tried to tell what had been done to her and no one wanted to hear it.

That reality hurt, but it also clarified something for me.

I cannot wait for everyone to understand.

I cannot wait for everyone to agree.

Healing cannot depend on other people's apologies.

What I wanted from the Tamron Hall interview was to speak for the children who don't have words yet. The ones acting out, shutting down, or drowning quietly while adults label them as "bad." Children often show their pain through behavior long before they have the language to explain it. But the world is often more curious about the family of the monster than about the child who survived him. People want to know how we reacted, how we coped, how we lived with it—as if trauma is a story to be analyzed rather than a wound someone had to grow up carrying.

And maybe that is why my family stayed silent for so long.

Silence can feel safer than judgment.

Silence can feel like control.

Silence can feel like survival.

But silence can also become a prison.

And I have lived in too many prisons already.

Today, I have made peace with the fact that I cannot speak for my family. I can only speak for the little girl I once was—the one who tried to tell the truth and wasn't believed. I speak for her now because she deserves a voice. Because she deserved protection. Because she deserved someone to stand up beside her and say, *I believe you.*

And maybe that is what healing really is.

Not forgetting. Not pretending it didn't happen.

But finally living free enough to tell the truth without shaking.

And trusting that God—quietly, steadily, faithfully—has been answering prayers I didn't even realize had already been fulfilled.

What does it all mean now?
I Was Known Before I Was Born

For a long time, I thought my life was a punishment. Like I was marked by bad choices, bad men, bad timing—like pain was the only thing that ever knew my address. I lived through years where fear felt normal. Where silence felt safer than truth. Where love came with conditions, and survival came with a price.

I stayed too long in places that were killing me slowly. And I carried shame like it belonged to me. But it didn't. What happened to me is not who I am. I can't erase the past—the prison calls, the late-night panic, the broken promises, the moments I begged God to just let me breathe. But I can tell the truth about it.

I loved my children through chaos. I showed up when I was empty. I kept going when I didn't want to. And somehow, I'm still here. Not untouched. Not unscarred. But standing.

I used to think strength meant never breaking. Now I know strength is getting up anyway. **Proverb 24:16 KJV.** This is not a story about perfection. This is a story about survival. This is a story about a woman who finally stopped confusing pain with love. A woman who stopped apologizing for wanting peace. A woman who learned that freedom doesn't come all at once—It comes the moment you decide you've had enough. And once you walk out…You don't go back.

Jeremiah 1:5–12 KJV

Before I was born, God knew me. He created me. He saw me. He named me.

Before the physical and verbal abuse from my mother—God knew me.

Before the molestation I suffered at the hands of my Tío Richie—
God knew me.

Before the abandonment I felt when my parents left us behind in El Paso—God knew me.

Before the domestic violence I endured from my son's father at sixteen—God knew me.

Before I was raped—God knew me.

Before the promiscuity I used to fill the empty places—God knew me.

Before my abortion—God knew me.

Before the emotional abuse I suffered in my first two marriages—God knew me.

Before depression took up residence in my chest—God knew me.

Before anger and rage became my language—God knew me.

Before heartbreak cracked me open again and again—God knew me.

God knew me. Little old me. I am nothing but a speck of dust in this vast world, and yet…God knew me.

He knew my name. He knew my story before I ever lived it. And somehow, in a way I still cannot fully understand, He had plans for me.

Jeremiah 29:11–14 NLT

says *He has plans—not for disaster, but for good.*
Plans to give me a future and a hope. And

1 Corinthians 2:9 and **Isaiah 64:4 NLT** reminds me:

No eye has seen, no ear has heard, and no mind has imagined what
God has prepared for those who love Him.

But the devil comes for people like me.

He comes for the wounded.

He comes for the forgotten.

He comes for the ones who have been left unprotected.

John 10:10A NKJV says it plainly:

the thief comes to kill, steal, and destroy.

And I believe that's exactly what was happening.

Satan—Lucifer—the devil, whatever name you give that darkness—was working overtime to break me. To ruin me. To convince me I was too damaged to be loved, too dirty to be redeemed, too far gone to ever be restored. That is why those things happened to me.

Because the enemy wanted to destroy me before I ever realized I had a purpose.

But God…

God is love.

Even while Satan was trying to destroy me, God gave me something I didn't even know I had—tenacity. A stubborn will to survive. A fire that refused to die. The kind of strength you don't notice until you've been through the flames and somehow come out breathing.

I think of the salmon and what they represent.

They spend their early lives in freshwater, then eventually make their way to saltwater where they grow strong—enormous, even. And once they mature, they begin their impossible journey back upstream to spawn.

It is a do-or-die swim against the current.

And every time I think about the salmon fighting its way upstream,
I see myself.

Because I could have gone downstream in more ways than one.

I could have followed the current of my pain.

I could have surrendered to the statistics.

I could have become exactly what the world expects children from
broken homes to become.

They say children raised in dysfunction are more likely to be arrested
as juveniles. More likely to commit violent crimes. More likely to struggle
emotionally, socially, intellectually. More likely to become addicted, to
drown in substances, to repeat the cycles they were born into.

I had every reason to become a wreckage.

But God had a plan for me. He was waiting on me.

And I was corrupted by my experiences. The poison seeped into my
spirit and manifested in bitterness, rage, anger, harsh words, slander,
sexual immorality, lust, evil desires, malicious behavior… and so many
other ugly things I didn't want to admit were living inside of me.

When God created me, this is not who He created me to be.

The person He made—the woman He intended—was still there,
somewhere. But she was buried. Hidden deep beneath layers of trauma,
shame, survival, and self-hatred.

And it took work to unbury her.

I had to become like that lone salmon fish.

I had to go against the current.

Because healing doesn't flow with the world.

Healing fights upstream.

Isaiah 55:8–11 KJV says

God's Word will not return void. It will accomplish what it was sent out to do.

John 1:1 KJV says *Jesus is the Word.*

Which means if Jesus is given the opportunity,

He will accomplish what He was sent to do.

And what was He sent to do?

John 10:10B NKJV

To give life. A rich life. A satisfying life.

A life that looks nothing like the one the enemy tried to hand me.

God called me. He chased me. He searched for me.

All while I was unaware that I was only living as a broken version of what I was created to be.

He saw me—not as I was—but as I was meant to be.

He saw past the woman I had become.

He saw the girl buried at my core.

The one who still carried His fingerprint.

And I had to let go.

I had to trust Him.

That alone was terrifying.

Trust.

Talk about trust issues—I had them stacked like bricks inside my chest. How could I trust God when everyone I thought I could trust had failed me? How could I trust anyone after what had been done to me, after what had been taken from me?

But God wasn't asking me to pretend I wasn't wounded.

He was asking me to hand Him my wounds.

I had to trust Him to redeem me from my bad choices.

I had to trust Him to heal my mind, my body, and my spirit.

Trust is a scary thing when betrayal has been your teacher.

But I had to let go of my fear long enough to believe something different. And somewhere deep inside of me, a whisper rose up—quiet, steady, undeniable:

You were made for more than what you have experienced.

This is only the beginning.

So I surrendered.

Because it is the goodness of God that leads people to repentance. **Romans 2:4 NLT** says:

Don't you see how wonderfully kind, tolerant, and patient God is with you?

Can't you see that His kindness is intended to turn you from your sin?

I saw His kindness.

I saw His patience.

He was waiting for me.

Little old me.

And He did not force me to repent. He didn't shove me into change.

He didn't threaten me into obedience.

It was His goodness.

It was His mercy.

It was His gentleness that made me finally look around and realize that the only reason I was still standing was because God had been carrying me—even when I didn't know His name. Then I understood something that changed everything:

God had been comforting me long before I knew I needed comfort.

2 Corinthians 1:3–5 ESV says:

*Blessed be the God and Father of our Lord Jesus Christ, the Father of mercies and the God of all comfort… He comforts us **in all** our affliction, <u>so that we may be able to comfort those who are in any kind of affliction, through the comfort we ourselves receive from God</u>.*

And suddenly, my pain had meaning.

Not because it was good.

Not because it was fair.

Not because it should have happened.

But because God could take what was meant to destroy me and use it to heal someone else. If I was afflicted, it was not only for my survival—it was for someone else's comfort. If I was comforted, it was so that comfort could one day overflow from my life into another wounded soul.

And maybe that was always part of the plan.

That the girl who suffered would become the woman who speaks life. That the girl who almost drowned would become the woman who points others to shore. That the girl who was nearly destroyed would become living proof that the devil doesn't get the final word.

Because before any of it happened…

God knew me.

Epilogue
The Work That Remained

When the world shut down during the COVID-19 pandemic, my home became everything at once—shelter, classroom, church, refuge. Like so many families, we were forced to adapt overnight. I began homeschooling my three younger children using a Christian-based curriculum, never imagining that what started as a temporary solution would become part of our permanent life.

When we eventually returned to work, I assumed we would return to normal too. But normal had changed.

My work schedule still allowed me to homeschool, and somewhere along the way, I realized I didn't want to let it go. So I kept going. We kept going.

I still loved my job. I loved the rhythm of the prison school—the weight of the keys in my hand, the echo of the halls, the sharp buzz of the CO's radio breaking through the quiet. Most of all, I loved my students—the men who sat at those desks carrying years of regret, hope, pride, and pain. They were more than inmates to me. They were human beings. They were souls.

But during the 2022–2023 school year, everything shifted again.

The schedule changed from 4 a.m.–1 p.m. to 7 a.m.–4 p.m., and overnight, my life became a constant stretch of responsibilities with no place to rest. We still tried to hold on to homeschooling, but now it had to happen in the evenings. For two years, our home transformed into a classroom from 5 p.m. to 9 p.m. Night after night, we pushed through.

At first, I told myself we could handle it. I told myself it was worth it. I told myself this is what strong mothers do.

But over time, it became too much—not just for me, but for my husband and our children. The exhaustion settled into our bones. The days blurred together. We weren't just tired. We were running on fumes.

And then I had to make one of the hardest decisions of my life.

In August of 2024, I left the prison.

The last day I walked out, the gates closed behind me with the same heavy clang they always had. But this time, I wasn't coming back in the morning.

I stepped away from my teaching job and

became a stay-at-home mom.

It felt like grief.

It felt like surrender.

It felt like walking away from something sacred.

That prison had been a place of transformation—where I watched men rebuild themselves one lesson at a time. It was a place where I felt purpose. Where I felt called. But God was calling me somewhere else.

Even now, I still return.

Every Thursday night, I walk back through the gates of Rogelio Sanchez State Jail to teach a Bible-based class. Once a month, on Sundays, I attend the prison ministry church service. The doors still open. The walls still stand. The men are still there.

And somehow, a part of my heart will always be there too.

But my days look different now.

You will find me at the kitchen table teaching my three younger children—Marty, Izzie, and Milo—driving them to homeschool P.E., taking them to Boy Scouts and Girl Scouts meetings, piano lessons, and living a life that is loud, messy, ordinary—and holy. The kind of life that doesn't come with a paycheck, but comes with purpose.

And then God did something I never saw coming.

I was blessed with a four-year Bible college scholarship.

I couldn't have planned it if I tried. It came so unexpectedly, so impossibly, that I could only recognize it for what it was—

a gift. A reminder. A whisper from heaven.

Now I am working toward a second degree in Christian Ministry— still learning, still growing, still being shaped.

I may have stepped away from the prison classroom, but I did not step away from my calling.

Because God didn't just use me behind prison walls.

He uses me here too.

In my home. In my motherhood.

In the quiet work of pouring into my children.

In late-night prayers. In Sunday services behind razor wire.

In Thursday night lessons that still echo through those same halls.

And when the house finally quiets, when the lessons are put away and the day has softened into evening, I look at the life still unfolding before me—at Marty, at Izzie, at Milo—and I see the sacred work that remained. Not the work I once thought defined me, but the work that was always waiting for me here. In their laughter. In their questions. In the ordinary, holy rhythm of being present. This is where my calling lives now. Not behind gates, not within walls—but right here, in the lives entrusted to me.

And as I look around at the life that has unfolded, I see something else—something I once only prayed for.

My older children are grown, walking their own paths.

My son Jimmy now lives in Arizona with his wife and their two children. He owns his own business, building a life from the foundation of his cyber security associate's degree.

My daughter Marie went on to college, earning her associate's degree in translation and interpretation. She now lives in San Antonio with her husband and their two beloved fur babies, creating a life filled with language, love, and quiet joy.

My son Robert now lives in Kansas with his wife and their two children, making his way through the world—step by step, day by day.

And I look at them… and I know.

The chains I fought so long to break are no longer there.

They are broken.

They are burned.

They are covered by the blood of Jesus.

Looking back now, I can see that every road I walked—every mile, every scar, every unanswered prayer—was leading me here.

The gates still close behind me on Thursday nights with the same heavy sound they always have.

But now I understand something I didn't before.

God's work was never locked behind those walls.

I used to believe my purpose was tied to a job title, a classroom, a badge, and a schedule.

But now I know better.

My purpose was never confined to the prison.

And it was never confined to me.

God is still writing my story.

And for the first time in my life,

I am no longer afraid to turn the page.

Author's Note

For many years, I believed silence was safer than truth. Like so many survivors, I learned early that speaking about painful things often made people uncomfortable. It was easier for others to look away than to listen. But silence has a way of protecting the wrong people, and over time I realized that the only way to reclaim my voice was to use it.

This story was not written out of bitterness, but out of faith. It was written for the child I once was, for the women and men who carry wounds they were told to hide, and for anyone who has ever wondered if their story still matters. If there is one thing my life has taught me, it is this: God wastes nothing. Not the pain, not the broken roads, not even the years we thought were lost. Every chapter—both the ones we choose and the ones we survive—can be used for something greater.

If you've made it to the end of these pages, then you have walked with me—through the silence, the unraveling, the questions, and the moments that did not make sense until much later. You have seen what was broken, what endured, and what, by grace, was rebuilt.

Stories like this are not easy to tell. And they are not always easy to read. But they matter—because somewhere, someone is still sitting in the middle of their own untold story, wondering if their voice will ever return to them.

If something in these pages felt familiar—if it stirred something, named something, or gave language to what once felt unspoken—then this story has already done what it was meant to do.

But it doesn't have to end here. Stories continue in the lives they touch.

If you feel led, one of the most meaningful ways you can help this message reach someone else is by sharing a review.

Your words—simple, honest, your own—can become a bridge for another person searching for hope, clarity, or the courage to begin again.

And if your journey has intersected with mine in some way, I would truly love to hear from you.

Connect with the Author

Rosie Juarez is a survivor, advocate, educator, and writer dedicated to bringing awareness, healing, and hope to those who have experienced trauma. Through sharing her story, she hopes to encourage others to find their voice and reclaim their lives.

For speaking engagements, workshops, interviews, prayer, or to connect, please reach out at:

Email: redeemedinkpress@outlook.com
Website: www.rosierjuarez.com

You can also follow Rosie's work and advocacy online for updates, resources, and future projects on social media.

Instagram: @rosiejuarez1985
Facebook: Rosie Juarez Author

Thank you for reading.
Thank you for staying.
And most of all—thank you for carrying this story forward in whatever way you can.